'BORN TO CRIME,

Cesare Lombroso and the Origins of Biological Criminology

Mary Gibson

Italian and Italian American Studies
Spencer M. Di Scala, Series Adviser

PRAEGER

Westport, Connecticut
London

Library of Congress Cataloging-in-Publication Data

Gibson, Mary, 1950–
    Born to crime : Cesare Lombroso and the origins of biological criminology / Mary Gibson.
       p. cm.—(Italian and Italian American studies, ISSN 1530–7263)
    Includes bibliographical references and index.
    ISBN 0–275–97062–0 (alk. paper)
    1. Criminal behavior—Genetic aspects. 2. Lombroso, Cesare, 1835–1909. 3. Criminal anthropology. I. Title. II. Series.

    HV6047.G53 2002
    364.2'4—dc21   2001059152

British Library Cataloguing in Publication Data is available.

Library of Congress Catalog Card Number: 2001059152
ISBN: 0–275–97062–0
ISSN: 1530–7263

First published in 2002

Praeger Publishers, 88 Post Road West, Westport, CT 06881
An imprint of Greenwood Publishing Group, Inc.
www.praeger.com

Printed in the United States of America

∞

The paper used in this book complies with the
Permanent Paper Standard issued by the National
Information Standards Organization (Z39.48–1984).

10 9 8 7 6 5 4 3 2 1

To the memory of Annarita Buttafuoco

Contents

Series Foreword

Celebrated in his own day, Cesare Lombroso has fallen into neglect, yet he was a father of modern criminology and put it on a course independent of other disciplines. His thesis that crime had a biological basis brought him fame, stirred heated debate, and had important implications for the future.

Lombroso was a professor of medicine and psychiatry at the University of Turin. He wrote at a time when Italian unification had recently been completed, and many of his ideas had relevance for the problems of the new state. As Mary Gibson shows in her study, however, Lombroso's writings had a major international impact as well, and the debate about ideas associated with him is far from over. Even if, in the modern context, we associate notions of the kind Lombroso expressed with the Right, it is important to recall that the master and his disciples were socialists. Gibson skillfully traces how Lombroso influenced groups on different sides of the political spectrum and argues for a more subtle interpretation of his theories. In making this argument, she emphasizes how Lombroso acknowledged the multifaceted nature of criminal origins, refusing to call for harsh repression in all cases but accepting the idea of rehabilitation under certain circumstances.

Mary Gibson's book goes beyond a consideration of Lombroso's philosophy and has a wider significance. How do theories influence national debates on political action and reform—and how do they become "institutionalized"? By combing through an impressive number of archival, primary, and secondary sources, Gibson makes an important contribution to answering this question, in addition to broadening our knowledge about a fascinating era and a character whose sophistication and contradictions we had only been able to imagine before now.

Spencer M. Di Scala
Series Adviser
Italian and Italian American Studies

Preface

I conceived the idea for this book many years ago when I came across the startling fact that the founder of Italy's national police academy, Salvatore Ottolenghi, was an ardent follower of Cesare Lombroso. Although I had become immersed in Lombroso's theories of female crime while researching my earlier book on prostitution, I had never suspected that his conception of the "born criminal" had ever been incorporated into Italian legislation and administrative practice. Did Italian police choose their suspects based on facial types and physical malformations held by Lombroso to be signs of a biological propensity to crime? My initial focus on the incorporation of Lombrosian criminology into policing expanded over the years, because I discovered Lombroso and his students to be actively engaged in shaping Italian policy on related issues like female crime, race and deviancy, juvenile justice, morals legislation, and the fascist criminal code.

As the book grew in scope, my debts have multiplied to the many individuals and institutions that have supported the project. As always, I owe thanks to my mentor at Indiana University, William B. Cohen, for being a model of a passionate historian, dedicated to unearthing the secrets of the archives. John Cammett brought me to John Jay College, where I have profited from the interdisciplinary perspective on criminal justice of my colleagues and students. I am grateful to those historians and criminologists who have read parts of this manuscript and offered valuable comments including Nicole Hahn Rafter, Richard Jensen, Victoria de Grazia, Bernard Cohen, Patrizia Dogliani, Tamar Pitch, Peter Becker, and Richard Wetzell. Steven P. Hughes not only read an early draft, but also generously identified *Difesa Sociale* as an important source on policing and lent me his own photocopy of the journal.

Over the years, I have been fortunate enough to present my developing ideas to specialists in similar fields. My chapter on female crime benefited from the critiques of my fellow participants in the NEH seminar at Stanford University on the "woman question," directed by Karen Offen and Susan Groag Bell. Members of the Colum-bia University Seminar on Modern Italy sharpened my thinking about Lombroso's place in Italian culture and politics. Colleagues in both the International Associa-tion of Historians of Crime and Criminal Justice and the criminal justice network of the Social Science History Association (aka "the gang") have also heard shorter versions of many of these chapters and asked pertinent questions from an interna-tional perspective.

I am indebted to the Italian archivists and librarians who helped me locate perti-nent primary sources at the Central State Archives and the libraries of the Chamber of Deputies, Ministry of the Interior, Advanced School of Scientific Policing, and the Juvenile Reformatory in Rome. Funding for research trips to Italy came from the Fulbright Committee, National Endowment for the Humanities, American Philo-sophical Society, and the Professional Staff Congress of the City University of New York. I want to thank Jacob Marini, Director of Sponsored Research at John Jay College, for his tireless assistance in obtaining these grants.

Finally, I am grateful to Spencer di Scala for supporting the inclusion of this vol-ume in his series on "Italian and Italian American Studies," and Peter Kracht, Edi-tor at Praeger Publishers, for his support of the project. This book is dedicated to the memory of Annarita Buttafuoco, a pioneer of Italian women's history and a friend whom I miss dearly.

Portions of this book first appeared in "On the Insensitivity of Women: Science and the Woman Question in Liberal Italy, 1890–1910," *Journal of Women's History* 2 (Fall, 1990): 11–41, used here with the permission of Indiana University Press; and "Biology or Environment? Race and Southern 'Deviancy' in the Writings of Italian Criminologists," *Italy's "Southern Question": Orientalism in One Country*, ed-ited by Jane Schneider (1998) pp. 99–115, used here with the permission of Berg Press.

Introduction

In 1992, the National Institutes of Health withdrew its funding for a controversial conference on the relationship between genetics and crime. Scheduled to be held at the University of Maryland, the conference had elicited such a storm of protest that newspapers like the *New York Times* reported its cancellation. Critics charged that the conference, and the American government that was to fund it, were endorsing a theory that was inherently racist. They warned that genetics would be used to "prove" that blacks were innately violent and, therefore, deserved to be targets of surveillance and arrest by police. Such research would further the conservative agenda of building more prisons rather than diverting public resources to social programs that prevented crime. It would offer a "scientific" veneer for racial prejudice, so that right-wing politicians could claim that innate biological inferiority—rather than broader injustices in black communities like poor schools, bad housing, and unemployment—caused crime.

Only temporarily defeated, the organizers of the conference charged that the government had censured their views by withdrawing its financial support. Debate ensued within the field of criminal justice, with the newsletter of the American Society of Criminology running a full-page article in its bulletin defending genetic research.[1] The conference was held three years later, with funding restored after the organizers agreed to add panels on the social implications of their research.[2] That this conference was proposed and funded illustrates the resurgence of biological explanations of crime in the 1980s that has continued into the new millennium. The increasing popularity of research that purports to trace the etiology of crime to physical rather than social factors parallels the contemporaneous trend in psychiatry to treat patients with drugs rather than with psychotherapy. It is consonant with the thesis of *The Bell Curve*, the controversial book by Charles Murray and Richard Herrnstein, that intelligence is hereditary and correlated with race.[3] It also fits within the general framework of sociobiology, first proposed by Edmund O. Wilson in the 1970s, which holds that genes determine social life and that present inequalities are natural and not subject to change.[4]

Despite the popular perception that genetic explanations of the etiology of crime are new, biological determinism dates back to the birth of criminology and defined the thought of its founder, Cesare Lombroso. A professor of medicine and psychiatry at the University of Turin, Lombroso galvanized intellectual debate with the publication in 1876 of his seminal work, *Criminal Man*. In this book, he proposed that most lawbreakers were atavistic throwbacks on the evolutionary scale, resembling "primitive" peoples, animals, and even plants. Marked by physical anomalies like small heads, protruding cheekbones, flat noses, and large ears, these "born criminals" could not escape their biological destiny.

Although earlier European thinkers had pondered the causes of crime, Lombroso was the first to envision criminology as a new scientific discipline independent of law and public hygiene. As the authors of a new history of international criminology argue, only in the late nineteenth century did crime become the object of "a complex and specialized branch of knowledge."[5] The term "criminology" did not yet exist when *Criminal Man* was published; Lombroso himself used the phrase "criminal anthropology" to emphasize that human beings, rather than the law, were the objects of his study. Criminology appeared as an alternative—but not opposing—label less than ten years later, probably invented by his colleague and disciple, Raffaele Garofalo.[6] Although criminology did not triumph as the accepted international designation for the new field until the interwar period, it could trace its substance back to Lombroso and his conviction that crime constituted a natural phenomenon capable of being explicated through objective, empirical research.

It may seem surprising that Italy, a seemingly peripheral participant in the major political and economic innovations of nineteenth-century Europe, was the birthplace of a new academic discipline. But with the long-awaited achievement of unification in 1861, Italy experienced a ferment of intellectual debate about how to define and rule the fragile new nation. A veteran of the wars of unification and a firm supporter of the new liberal and secular state, Lombroso not surprisingly turned his medical gaze to groups who might threaten social stability. As Daniel Pick has pointed out, by identifying a minority of the population as born criminals, Lombroso could use them as a foil for defining the boundaries of nationhood and the shared characteristics of "normal" citizens.[7] Lombroso's genius lay in his intuition that not only the obvious political enemies of the new state like brigands and anarchists, but also common criminals like prostitutes and thieves, represented a challenge to nation building and the creation of a homogeneous population. In their atavism, born criminals threatened the project of modernization, of which unification was the crucial first step.

Criminal anthropology offered to the new ruling classes of Italy—the liberal aristocracy and the middle classes—a scientific way to understand the failures of unification and a blueprint for disciplining groups that resisted integration into the new national culture. Rejecting the moralism and authoritarianism of the royal and religious rulers of the old regime, they were attracted to a theory that promised to employ objectivity and empiricism for the purpose of social reform. Lombroso drew on the popularity and prestige of Charles Darwin to build an evolutionary scaffold that ranked certain groups as more successful in the struggle for existence than others: noncriminals over criminals, men over women, adults over children, and whites over blacks. In place of the social stratification of the old regime, criminal anthropology offered a biological hierarchy that guaranteed power and control to white, European adult men. In this way, the new criminological science replaced religion as a more modern rationale for opposing female suffrage and extending European imperialism.

For criminals who could not escape their biological destiny to threaten lives and property, Lombroso prescribed harsh penalties such as incarceration for life or death. Reform was impossible for individuals tainted by physical and psychological anomalies. But the appeal of criminal anthropology came not only from its promise to repress enemies of the new state but also its humanitarianism. While Lombroso was best known for the notion of the born criminal, he never doubted that the new Italy was riddled with social inequities that reduced the poor to lives of squalor and misery. Poverty, malnutrition, and disease could push even members of the "honest" poor, who exhibited no atavistic taint, to crime. Sympathetic to the plight of these "occasional criminals," Lombroso recommended that the law treat them leniently with alternatives to prison like parole, suspended sentences, and fines.

The tension within criminal anthropology between the "hard" approach to born criminals and the "soft" approach to occasional criminals constitutes a major theme of this book. Lombroso's ideas were much more complex and nuanced than his detractors have admitted, because he recognized the multicausal nature of crime. He was thus a champion of both repressive punishment, in the case of born criminals, and rehabilitation and alternatives to punishment, for occasional criminals. His rich and influential legacy stems from this mixture of conservative and liberal penology, the crux of which was proper classification.

Lombroso's eclectic theories immediately attracted a large following of students and disciples, who became known as the School of Positivist Criminology. The three pillars of this so-called Italian School were the physician Lombroso and the lawyers Enrico Ferri and Garofalo. While often used interchangeably with criminal anthropology, positivist criminology was preferred as a label by lawyers, legislators, and public administrators who did not themselves measure bodies. But all concurred that only positivism, or the empirical method, could discover the causes of crime and that the bodies of criminals represented the most important source of data. Although most admitted the importance of social factors in the etiology of crime, all viewed biological determinism as the key to understanding the most dangerous criminals. In this book, I will use the term "positivist criminology" as it was understood in late nineteenth-century Italy, as a bundle of ideas that grew directly out of criminal anthropology and Lombroso's notion of the born criminal. My narrow definition of the term "positivism" should not be confused with its more general philosophical usage to describe any type of modern research that tests hypotheses with empirical data.

Because of its complexity, positivist criminology was capable of offering answers to a variety of "social questions" that preoccupied the intellectual and political classes of post-unification Italy. The first half of this book explores how Lombroso and his followers extended the initial approach employed in *Criminal Man* to analyze the variable of gender and race in both the "normal" and "deviant" population. In both cases, the "hard" side of biological determinism dominated their conclusions, although a sociological strain undercut this rigidity. *The Female Offender*, published in 1893, set forth the standard argument of criminal anthropology that both "normal" and "criminal" women were less evolved than their male counterparts. Although such supposedly scientific proof of female inferiority directly contradicted the message of the nascent feminist movement in Italy, criminal anthropologists were not inalterably opposed to all changes in the status of women. Many supported legislation that would give women the right of divorce and limited suffrage, while others recommended light penalties for infanticide and abortion. In the case of race, Lombroso and his followers identified biological inferiority as the major cause of Italy's so-called southern problem, the perceived backwardness of the agricultural South in relation to the more industrialized North. Teaching that southerners had been tainted by mixture with less evolved African and Arab "races," criminal anthropology held them innately prone to violence, brigandage, and vendetta. Yet Lombroso also recognized that the widespread poverty in the South sprang not just from inherited weakness in the population but also the perpetuation of the "feudal" power of large landowners over the peasantry.

The second half of the book shows how criminal anthropology was institutionalized within Italy's system of penal justice. Rather than dying with Lombroso, his ideas were carried into Parliament, public administration, and the universities by his followers. The last three chapters trace various paths by which a criminological theory can be translated into practice. Focusing on the period between 1910 and 1940, this section analyzes how the followers of Lombroso influenced the political debate on police reform, juvenile justice, and the criminal law. In each case, criminal anthropologists could successfully turn their theory into legislation only if they exploited already existing "moral panics" about social breakdown and allied with other groups interested in the same issue. Because of the flexibility and even ambiguity of their theory, they could make common cause with a wide range of political groups, from feminists on the Left who shared their "soft" prescriptions for juvenile delinquents to right-wing advocates of "hard" measures to strengthen police prerogatives at the expense of civil rights.

Despite the national renown of Lombroso and his colleagues, their new theory was never universally adopted into the Italian system of criminal justice. Most success was gained under fascism, when Mussolini's government eagerly appropriated the positivist justification for surveillance over individuals or groups based on biological criteria. In their collaboration with the fascist regime, criminal anthropologists abandoned the humanitarian or "soft" aspects of their doctrine and emphasized the need to intern individuals exhibiting physical anomalies, in the name of protecting the "Italian race." By the late 1920s, positivist criminology lost much of its complexity and richness as its proponents increasingly championed "hard" biological determinism as a rationale for fascist policies discriminating against women, children, black Africans, and finally Jews.

The recent bibliography on Lombroso by both historians and criminologists is surprisingly thin, considering his international stature as the founder of a new discipline. Among historians, this can perhaps be attributed to the seemingly shallow nature of his thought and, in Italy, the disdain for positivism since World War II. Only a handful of biographies exist, all in Italian. By far the best is by Renzo Villa, who offers a superb analysis of Lombrosian discourse as a play of signs.[8] An older work by Luigi Bulferetti represents a more traditional biography.[9] Delfina Dolza has written a charming portrait of the Lombroso family, with an emphasis on the lives of his two daughters.[10] In English, only Pick has offered any extended discussion of Lombrosian thought as part of his volume entitled *Faces of Degeneration*.[11]

Criminologists have done little better, although Lombroso is dutifully cited as the father of criminology in standard textbooks. Likewise, general overviews of criminological theory invariably trace positivism back to Lombroso and often contain short excerpts of his writings.[12] Yet the best English-language account of Lombroso's life and work dates back to Marvin Wolfgang's chapter in *Pioneers of Criminology*, edited by Hermann Mannheim in 1960.[13] This same volume also contains useful contributions on Enrico Ferri and Raffaele Garofalo by Thorsten Sellin and Francis Allen, respectively. Piers Beirnes, the author of a more recent collection of thoughtful essays on major criminologists of the past, unfortunately devotes no chapter to Lombroso although his entire analysis presupposes a familiarity with criminal anthropology. In Italy, criminologists with a sociological bent similarly ignore Lombroso, although Pier Luigi Baima Bollone, a professor of legal medicine, has written a short book emphasizing Lombroso's place in the history of forensic science.[14]

This book intends not only to fill a historiographical gap, but to widen the focus of Lombroso studies in several ways. In contrast to the traditional biographical approach, I will demonstrate that the development of criminal anthropology in Italy was the work of a large group rather than the brainchild of one man. Although Lombroso was prolific and innovative in his thinking, he was often unmethodical in his writings. Many of his intuitions were picked up and more systematically explored by his students, the most famous of whom were Ferri and Garofalo. With missionary zeal, Lombroso trained or inspired two generations of followers, an interdisciplinary group of both doctors and lawyers. These disciples spread his doctrines not only as university professors, but also as administrators in the bureaucracies of the police, prisons, and courts. Several served in Parliament, lobbying actively to incorporate criminal anthropology into national legislation.

Second, this study seeks to place the birth of positivist criminology within a larger context, that of the political, economic, and social history of modern Italy. Anglo-American scholars have tended to discuss the theories of Lombroso without any knowledge of Italian society or ability to read the majority of his writings, or those of his followers, which remain untranslated. While this is not the case in Italy, traditional legal and intellectual histories have tended to trace the evolution and clash of ideas on a plane detached from everyday life. Instead, at the beginning of several chapters, I have briefly summarized how the rapid changes like population growth, urbanization, industrialization, and war affected in different ways the roles and status of men, women, and children in post-unification Italy. Although such changes did not necessarily lead to increases in actual crime, they fueled "moral panics" about "deviant" behaviors that seemed to threaten social stability. Positivist criminologists exploited these fears, putting themselves forth as the only experts who could scientifically identify and discipline the born criminals lurking among the honest citizenry.

Third, this book widens its lens from theory to practice and explores the various paths by which criminology may become institutionalized. Among legal historians, Lombroso has generally been dismissed as a thinker who failed to convince the Italian government to incorporate his ideas into penal law, specifically the Zanardelli Criminal Code of 1889. In contrast, I argue that it was outside of the criminal code that positivist theories made the most impact, usually under direct guidance of Lombroso and his followers, but sometimes not. In the bureaucracies of the police and prison systems, for example, Lombroso's students often held important posts from which they could oversee the implementation of key aspects of criminal anthropology. It was also the case that groups not directly tied to the Positivist School, like the short-lived police union formed after World War I, appropriated the prestigious philosophy of Lombroso to legitimize their own political struggle. As can happen with any new theory, criminal anthropology was also misinterpreted and used to justify specific penal policies—like *domicilio coatto* or internal exile—to which Lombroso was opposed. But because positivist criminologists had so successfully popularized the specter of the born criminal haunting respectable society, they ironically created a climate conducive to more repressive penal legislation than they wished.

Finally, this study widens the discussion of criminology to include politics. Current debates about crime assume that certain measures are inherently conservative, like the death penalty, or liberal, like sentencing drug offenders to rehabilitation rather than incarceration. Current criminologists who accept biology as an important explanation for the etiology of crime tend to identify themselves more to the right on the political spectrum than those who do not. But this study challenges any simple equation between criminology and politics by demonstrating that criminal anthropology was compatible with a variety of political philosophies including socialism, liberalism, and fascism. Lombroso and most of his colleagues in the first generation of the Positivist School belonged to the Italian Socialist Party (PSI). For them, positivism was eminently compatible with Marxism in its materialism, determinism, and humanitarianism. After World War I, however, most of Lombroso's successors collaborated with fascism, finding the dictatorship receptive to the positivist program of classifying and disciplining not only those convicted of crimes but also individuals—or even entire groups—suspected of a propensity to foment disorder or insubordination to the state. That Italian criminal anthropology appealed to both socialists and fascists demonstrates that complex criminological theories are not essentially of the Left or Right. The apparent compatibility of certain types of criminology with specific political positions can shift depending on historical context or which aspect of the argument is being emphasized. In Italy, criminal anthropology—and thus biological determinism—did not lead inevitably to fascist policies of criminal justice, but enjoyed widespread support among academics, politicians, and citizens of all political stripes.

Yet if Italian positivist criminology was not fundamentally fascist, it was nevertheless politicized and misused by both its creators and the Italian state. Its potential for harm was compounded by the mantle of science that covered its preconceptions and gaps in logic. Racism and sexism pervaded the research questions posed by Lombroso and his followers, leading them to conclusions that constituted scientific justifications for public policies of imperialism and sex discrimination. Unproven assumptions—for example, that physical features mirror psychological and mental life or that human beings can be neatly categorized as born or occasional criminals—made a mockery of positivism's claims to objectivity and logic. This passion for classification led to a penchant for surveillance of not only lawbreakers but any potentially suspicious individual; by devaluing civil rights in the name of social defense, the heirs of Lombroso created a climate conducive to the fascist assault on parliamentary democracy. The Italian case thus holds important historical lessons for the current proponents of biological criminology. Although contemporary theories, based on genes and hormones, seem scientifically sophisticated, they are not necessarily free of the flawed logic and repressive potential apparent in Lombroso's more simplistic notion of atavism. Criminology has yet to untangle the intellectual contradictions present at its birth.

NOTES

1. C. Ray Jeffrey, "Genetics, Crime and the Cancelled Conference," *The Criminologist: The Official Newsletter of the American Society of Criminology*, v. 18, n. 1 (Jan./Feb., 1993), p. 1. For a review of the various ways in which contemporary criminological theory employs biology, see Diana H. Fishbein, "Biological Perspectives in Criminology," *Criminology*, v. 28, n. 1 (Feb., 1990), pp. 27–72.

2. Natalie Angier reported on the conference in the "Science Times" section of the *New York Times* on September 19 and 25, 1995.

3. Charles A. Murray and Richard J. Herrnstein, *The Bell Curve: Intelligence and Class Structure in American Life* (New York: Free Press, 1994).

4. Edward O. Wilson, *Sociobiology* (Cambridge, Mass.: Harvard University Press, 1980).

5. Christian Debuyst, Françoise Digneffe, Jean-Michel Labadi, and Alvaro P. Pires, *Histoire des savoirs sur le crime et la peine* (Brussels: DeBoeck Université, 1995), vol. 1, p. 42.

6. For a discussion of the first use of the term "criminology," see Piers Beirne, *Inventing Criminology: Essays on the Rise of "Homo Criminalis"* (Albany: SUNY Press, 1993), pp. 233–37 and Christian Debuyst et al., *Histoire des savoirs sur le crime*, pp. 52–53.

7. Daniel Pick, *Faces of Degeneration* (Cambridge: Cambridge University Press, 1989) p. 109.

8. Renzo Villa, *Il deviante e i suoi segni: Lombroso e la nascita dell'antropologia criminale* (Milan: Franco Angeli, 1985).

9. Luigi Bulferetti, *Cesare Lombroso* (Turin: UTET, 1975).

10. Delfina Dolza, *Essere figlie di Lombroso: Due donne intellettuali tra '800 e '900* (Milan: Franco Angeli, 1990).

11. Daniel Pick, *Faces of Degeneration.*

12. For example, the writings of Lombroso are excerpted in two popular collections: *Classics of Criminology* edited by Joseph E. Jacoby, 2nd ed. (Prospect Heights, Ill.: Waveland, 1994) and *Criminological Theory: Past to Present. Essential Readings*, edited by Francis T. Cullen and Robert Agnew (Los Angeles: Roxbury, 1999). Lombroso is also discussed in leading textbooks of criminology like *Theoretical Criminology*, edited by George B. Vold, Thomas J. Bernard, and Jeffrey B. Snipes, 4th ed. (New York: Oxford University Press, 1998) and *Criminological Theories: Introduction and Evaluation*, edited by Ronald L. Akers, 2nd ed. (Los Angeles: Roxbury, 1997).

13. Marvin E. Wolfgang, "Cesare Lombroso, 1835–1909" in Hermann Mannheim, *Pioneers of Criminology* (Montclair, N.J.: Patterson Smith, 1972; orig. published 1960), 2nd ed, pp. 232–91.

14. Pier Luigi Baima Bollone, *Cesare Lombroso ovver il principio dell'irresponsabilità* (Turin: Società Editrice Internazionale, 1992).

Chapter 1

Criminal Man

In 1911, an inmate of the Mantellate jail in Rome was summoned from his cell and taken to another wing. Here he entered a classroom of police administrators who took notes while the professor, Salvatore Ottolenghi, submitted the prisoner to a physical and psychological examination. During the physical exam, Professor Ottolenghi measured the prisoner's body parts, concentrating on his facial features, and pointed out to his students any visible scars, calluses, or tattoos. The psychological exam followed, in which Professor Ottolenghi questioned the prisoner—in front of the class—about his childhood, family, health, moral habits, and criminal record.[1]

According to a transcript of this class, the inmate was a twenty-eight-year-old peasant who was serving two years in prison for beating the woman with whom he lived; Ottolenghi noted that she was not his legitimate wife since they had been married only in a church and lacked a civil marriage license.[2] Physically, the prisoner had an "antieurhythmic" face, marked by a receding forehead, overly developed cheeks, protruding bones, and a generally coarse form—in short, *un tipo inferiore* (an inferior type).[3] He had a scar from falling out of bed as a baby (so he said), a callus on his right arm from farmwork, and surprisingly no tattoos. He exhibited well-developed muscles, typical of a manual laborer.

When asked about his crime, the inmate admitted that he had assaulted his illegitimate wife, not with weapons but only with his hands; this, according to his conscience, was not "shameful." He claimed that although he did not frequent taverns, he had been drunk at the time, because the rural landlord had offered his peasant workers a bit of wine at the end of the day. Later in his testimony, however, he stated that he often returned home drunk, sometimes hardly able to stand up, and frequently mistreated his wife for gossiping with neighbors rather than preparing his dinner. It was these same neighbors who informed the police of the beatings suffered by his wife.

In his analysis of the case for the class, Professor Ottolenghi reminded his students that alcohol can activate the latent violence in some individuals. In his words, "Wine and liquor exaggerate individual impulsiveness and many times provoke a state of *morbid epileptic rage*, in which the conscience is not completely clouded, but a person is no longer in control of his behavior. . . . At other times a person becomes epileptic and violent and commits homicide."[4] Alcohol was most likely to provoke violence in those individuals who had inherited an inferior physique visible in an abnormal facial structure. The repentant inmate promised to marry his illegitimate wife and never abuse her again. But Ottolenghi concluded that the inmate would always be dangerous because of his "capacity for committing violent crimes," including homicide, when under the influence of alcohol.[5]

This case represented one of the many in which Ottolenghi sought to inculcate in his students the principles of criminal anthropology, a branch of the new school of positivist criminology. Following the lead of its founder, the renowned Cesare Lombroso, Ottolenghi claimed to have injected the scientific method into the search for the causes of crime and the tailoring of appropriate punishments. Positivist criminologists rejected the tenets of the so-called Classical School of penal philosophy, founded over a century earlier by another Italian, Cesare Beccaria. In his famous Enlightenment tract, *On Crimes and Punishments* published in 1764, Beccaria had argued that individuals should be held responsible for their actions and punished according to the severity of their crime. Since all citizens should be equal before the law, punishment would equal the crime, and judges would ignore all mitigating circumstances such as a person's wealth, rank, or even mental state. By the late nineteenth century, however, Italy again shook up the legal world when the new positivist criminologists, led by Lombroso and his circle of disciples like Ottolenghi, rejected classical penology as abstract, unscientific, and out of touch with the facts.

The facts, as illustrated by Ottolenghi's examination of the convicted wife-beater, were the criminals themselves, repositories of an infinite amount of physical and psychological data. Criminal anthropologists recommended that attention be switched from the crime to the criminal, and that the degree of punishment correspond not to the seriousness of the crime but the dangerousness (*pericolosità*) of the criminal. Dangerousness was legible on the defendant's body, because physical abnormalities, or "anomalies," constituted outward signs of inherited mental weakness and moral depravity. By measuring and counting these anomalies, positivist criminologists promised to identify "born criminals" (*delinquenti nati*), those individuals whose innate tendencies posed a special threat to society and who deserved a particularly harsh punishment.

Ottolenghi followed this line of reasoning when examining the convicted peasant. Once he classified the prisoners' facial features as inferior, he interpreted this anomaly as a sign that this wife-beater was capable of murder. Since Ottolenghi believed that the prisoner would probably commit further violence only when under the influence of alcohol, he did allow that environmental factors might interact with physiology to cause crime. Alcoholism, however, was considered by criminal anthropologists to be a hereditary condition and therefore in some ways an innate, rather than an external, influence on behavior. While Ottolenghi did not mention hereditary alcoholism in the case of the convicted peasant, he diagnosed him as caught in a "morbid epileptic rage" and therefore unable to control his behavior.

This belief that criminal behavior was determined—either by innate or by environmental factors—exemplified another hallmark of positivist thinking. It clearly rejected the Classical School's faith in free will and taught instead that criminals could not be held morally responsible for their deviant acts. Thus, punishment could no longer be based on the Enlightenment principle that those who chose to break the social compact deserved retribution; instead, criminal anthropologists cited social defense (*difesa sociale*) as the justification for punishment. The more dangerous the individual, no matter what crime he or she had committed, the more severe the punishment.

Ottolenghi's examination of the prisoner before a class of police officers illustrates one futher tenet of positivist criminology—that its principles should be institutionalized into the everyday workings of the criminal justice system, that is, the police, the prisons, and the courts. In the case of his students from the Public Security force (PS), the urban police of Italy, Ottolenghi preached that application of his new methods would make law enforcement a professional science. Armed with the proper physical and psychological instruments to categorize every suspect, the PS would finally bring order to Italian society and bask in respect from a populace that was notorious for its hatred of state authority, especially police. With missionary zeal, Ottolenghi also preached the adoption of criminal anthropology by prison administrators and the framers of the criminal codes.

That police officials were routinely schooled in positivist criminology attests to its ascendancy as the primary explanatory model for crime in early twentieth-century Italy. As early as 1876, Lombroso, the father of criminal anthropology, had gained national stature with the publication of his book *Criminal Man*, which labeled the majority of lawbreakers as atavistic, because they exhibited anomalies reminiscent of groups lower on the evolutionary scale like animals and non-European "savages." The instant success of this idea in Italian intellectual circles and its subsequent adoption as the center of debate in international congresses of lawyers, doctors, and police showed a hunger for a new approach to the "crime question." Before examing the theories of Lombroso and his wide circle of followers in more detail, it is necessary to explore the factors that made Italy—both its intellectual and ruling classes—so eager to adopt positivist criminology and champion it as the most recent example of the Italian tradition for legal genius stretching back to ancient Rome.

CONTEXT

The rush to embrace criminal anthropology reflected the widespread perception that crime was endangering the stability of the new state, whose unification, with the annexation of Rome as the capital, had been completed as recently as 1871.[6] Filippo Turati claimed that by 1882 Italy led Europe in rates of crime, giving it "a real primacy," but not the type "dreamed of by Gioberti," a patriot who had envisioned unification as moral renewal.[7] That Turati, a future leader of the Italian Socialist Party (PSI), could annunciate anxieties shared by his parliamentary opponents showed the multifaceted nature of the crime question. Liberal and conservative members of the ruling classes—whether on the floor of Parliament, as government administrators, or in the press—also complained that the new legal order seemed to command no more respect than the oppressive laws of the old regime.

It is difficult to assess the accuracy of the popular perception that crime was increasing in the young nation of Italy. The difficulty comes partially from the common weakness of criminal statistics, which measure only crimes reported to police. Those that remain undetected constitute an unquantifiable "dark figure," which varies according to type of offense.[8] Professional statisticians of late nineteenth-century Italy were sophisticated enough to recognize the existence of the dark figure of crime, which one of them labeled latent delinquency.[9] Yet they looked to criminal statistics as "the most vigorous symptom . . . that we have to define and measure the civil morality of a nation. . . . Thus, we can define and measure morality principally through immorality."[10] Despite their defects, criminal statistics would provide a "physiognomy of crime," reflecting patterns of morality and immorality in the new state.[11]

Despite the official preoccupation after unification with rampant "immorality" like banditry, murder, theft, and prostitution, the Italian state did not systematically collect criminal statistics until 1879.[12] In this year, all courts were required to compile "daily registers" (*registri giornalieri*) of trials completed. Based on these registers, the national state began to publish annually large volumes of judicial or "administrative" statistics.[13] These data concerned the number of cases, not criminals, proceeding through Italian courts at all levels. After 1890, the state began to issue a second series of volumes, which enumerated the number of individuals convicted of crimes. Entitled "statistics of criminality," these volumes added a social dimension to the Italian data, since they broke down the criminal population by sex, age, marital status, education, and profession.[14]

Because reliable criminal statistics do not exist for the period before 1880, it is difficult to generalize about trends in criminality during the first decades after unification. We must also throw out data compiled for the first volumes of judicial statistics, as the numbers are inordinately high and therefore suspect. But, by 1881, the courts were compiling the daily registers in a uniform enough fashion that trends begin to emerge. Contrary to popular wisdom, the period between 1881 and 1886 saw a decline in rates of crime from 9.1 to 8.4 per 1,000 population.[15] These figures included both what Italian law classified as *delitti*, serious crimes corresponding roughly to felonies and listed in the national criminal code, and *contravvenzioni*, misdemeanors that involved infringement of secondary regulations of matters such as health, alcohol, and vagrancy. The same downward trend appears if we look only at felonies, which fell from 7.8 to 7.2 per 1,000 population during the same six years.[16] More dramatically, felonies dropped from 86 percent to 68 percent of all crime, disproving the dire thesis that violence was on the rise. Instead, the number of misdemeanors was rising sharply, probably reflecting the tightened regulation of various aspects of social life by the myriad of laws passed by the new state.

A new cycle started in 1887, however, as crime rates began to rise until peaking in 1898. Crime in general increased to 25.9 per 1,000 in 1898, while felonies reached 15.8 per 1,000 the same year.[17] This was a decade of depression in Italy, and hunger, unemployment, and homelessness may explain increased lawbreaking. The 1890s were also a time of political upheaval, from the revolt of Sicilian peasants in 1893–94 to a socialist uprising in Milan in 1898, both of which were repressed by excessive government force. But the rise probably also reflected changes in the legal system. Most important, 1889 saw the passage of a new Criminal Code and a new PS law, both of which changed some definitions and classifications of crime. But even earlier, in the period between 1886 and 1887, criminal statistics showed such a huge leap in crime that they are not credible. Perhaps an improvement in the system of compiling the daily registers explains this anomaly.

After 1898, the crime rate began to decline slowly until 1908, when it turned slightly upward. But on the eve of World War I in 1913, the rate of felonies was 14.3 per 1,000, still below the peak in 1898.[18] Again, the rise in 1908 coincided with a dampening in the Italian economy. These general trends, however, mask distinct variations among different crimes. Homicide rates dropped consistently from 1881 until the outbreak of war, belying the characterization of Italy by many positivist criminologists as a backward nation of atavistic murderers.[19] Violent crime did continue in the form of assault, which increased in the 1880s and held steady until the war.[20] The most widespread crime was theft, and it increased steadily through both the 1880s and the 1890s, thereafter rising, albeit slowly, until the war.[21]

Over the long term, the picture painted by Italian criminal statistics was not bleak enough to fuel the hysteria of criminal anthropologists and government officials over immorality and disorder. Only the years between 1887 and 1898 showed a consistent rise in crime, while the periods before and after saw a general decrease. The two most common crimes, assault and theft, did increase until the turn of the century, but then remained steady. The murder rate dropped significantly throughout the entire period. As early as 1884, classical criminologists like Luigi Lucchini recognized the drop in crime since unification and tried to refute the "gloomy Cassandras" who predicted a "rising tide" of lawbreaking.[22] But he was vilified for such optimism, so inconvenient to the new positivist vision of atavism and decay.[23] For criminal anthropologists, hysteria about social disorder would make their advice indispensable, as they inserted themselves into various state bureaucracies. Their pessimistic interpretation of crime statistics helped to shape a public perception that would be receptive to new and "scientific" policies to combat deviancy.

If rates of crime were not actually rising, why was anxiety so acute in the last three decades of the nineteenth century? The black forebodings of criminal anthropologists could create a "moral panic" only in an era of fundamental social change, marked by an expanding and mobile population.[24] The visibility of increasing numbers of outsiders—especially on city streets—gave residents a sense of being engulfed by the unknown. This was especially true of the nineteenth-century middle class, whose culture rejected social life on doorsteps and in the piazza for more decorous family life within the home. It is not surprising that the growing and increasingly influential bourgeoisie of united Italy equated the contemporaneous explosion of population with an explosion in crime. The fact that the clothing, language, and manners of newcomers identified them as poor made them only more alien to members of the middle and upper classes.

Italy's population growth represented the first phase of the "demographic transition," a general European process in which a preindustrial pattern of high fertility and high mortality yielded to a modern model of low rates of birth and death. During the initial phase of this transition, better sanitation, diet, and medical care led to a drop in the death rate, so that the population as a whole soared. In Italy, the population increased 40 percent during the fifty years after the first census, from twenty-six million in 1861 to thirty-seven million in 1911.[25] The cities grew even faster, with Rome, Milan, and Turin more than doubling in size.[26] True to the general model of the demographic transition, this notable expansion of the Italian population resulted from a sharp decline in mortality rates from 30/1,000 in 1861 to less than 22/1,000 by 1911, while fertility rates stayed steady for several decades after unification.[27] Only in the 1890s did Italy show signs of the second phase of the demographic transition, a decline in the birth rate and the size of the average family. Despite lagging behind most other western European countries, Italy did finally reach the "modern" fertility rate of under 30/1,000 in 1920.[28]

Not only a decline in mortality, but also migration from the countryside explained the spectacular growth of Italian cities during the late nineteenth century. Since the Renaissance, Italy had remained a rather urbanized country, with Naples, for example, among the largest cities in Europe. Yet even these cities expanded rapidly during the first phase of the demographic transition, fueled by excess population from rural areas. Young men and women whose families could no longer support them were most likely to seek work in the cities, usually moving to a nearby provincial or regional capital. As early as 1871, Italians also began to seek a safety valve for demographic pressures in emigration. During the first few decades of unification, most emigrants were men from the northern provinces of Italy seeking seasonal work in the nearby European countries of Switzerland, France, and Austria-Hungary. By the 1890s, southern Italians surpassed northerners in supplying the ever larger yearly waves of emigration. These newer emigrants still tended to be men, but traveled further, usually to the Americas, often to become permanent settlers. That the Italian population expanded 40 percent between 1861 and 1911, despite emigration that relieved the nation annually of over 200,000 inhabitants by the turn of the century, demonstrates the severity of demographic pressures on the newly united state.[29]

The Italian economy remained stagnant during the first decades after unification, experienced only weak growth in the early 1880s, and plunged into depression after 1887. After the turn of the century, Italy experienced an "industrial take-off," but it was modest compared to that in England, France, Germany, and the United States. In 1871, most of the population worked in agriculture, with few owning land while the majority were day laborers, tenant farmers, or sharecroppers.[30] The failure of the state to redistribute land, confiscated mainly from the Church during the wars of unification, contributed to the misery of the peasants and intensified the swelling waves of migration and emigration. Yet the cities lagged behind the rest of western Europe in industrial growth, with large workshops or factories concentrated only in textiles and, after the 1880s, secondarily in iron and steel. Most manufacturing continued to be carried out on an artisanal scale. Lacking craft or even factory skills, most migrants to the cities were left with low-paying and often seasonal jobs in domestic service, garment making, construction, and on the docks. Many remained unemployed. Almost all fledgling industry was in the North; migrants to Rome, Naples, Palermo, and other expanding cities in south and central Italy were most likely to be underemployed.

From the political perspective of the early ministers of the newly united kingdom, governing would have been difficult even without demographic and economic problems. As Massimo d'Azeglio, a liberal proponent of the *risorgimento* or the movement for unification, remarked, "We have made Italy; now we must make Italians."[31] Serious breaches existed in Italian society between the North and South, Church and State, the educated and the illiterate, rich and poor. In order to hold the new, fragile state together, a series of prime ministers from both the Right and the Left created a centralized apparatus with power emanating from Rome through appointed prefects to the various provinces. Included in this national bureaucracy were the administrators of the police, prisons, and courts. Surprisingly little historical research has been done on these three major divisions of the criminal justice system, bureaucracies with coercive power that promised to be instrumental in homogenizing the Italian population. But in 1876, when Lombroso published *Criminal Man*, the criminal justice system was still in disarray; no new penal code or code of criminal procedure had yet been published for united Italy, while the police and prisons retained their reputations as hated and inefficient arms of repressive government.

Lombroso and his followers actively participated in debates about a new penal code, arguing that it be constructed on the foundation of the new criminal anthropology. They thus advocated a legal revolution, since the criminal code then in effect, handed down from the Kingdom of Piedmont, was classical in character. Its guiding philosophy derived from the famous Enlightenment tract, *On Crimes and Punishments*, written by Beccaria in 1764. Although other Enlightenment *philosophes*, most notably Montesquieu and Voltaire, had previously critiqued the criminal justice systems of the old regime, Beccaria was the first to systematically lay out

the principles of criminal law that would underpin the new, constitutional governments established during the late eighteenth and early nineteenth centuries
throughout Europe and the United States.[32] To the acclaim of the Parisian *philosophes*, Beccaria composed a short work that denounced the inequality, secrecy,
and arbitrariness that characterized both penal legislation and its enforcement by
the absolute monarchs of the old regime. In its place, he recommended the "useful
theorem" that "in order that any punishment should not be an act of violence committed by one person or many against a private citizen, it is essential that it should
be public, prompt, necessary, the minimum possible under the given circumstances,
proportionate to the crimes, and established by law."[33]

Beccaria's general theorem rested on his acceptance of the Enlightenment idea
of social compact, a compact that differentiated society from the state of nature. In
some distant past, according to Beccaria, makers of the social compact had given up
part of their freedom to a government in exchange for its promise to make and enforce laws protecting their lives and property. While the government thus had the
right of punishment, this punishment was to be public, that is, decided in an open
courtroom rather than devised secretly by an individual monarch as private revenge. To restrain the interference of the monarch in judicial proceedings, Beccaria
called for new criminal codes with what we would today call determinate sentencing. Through these codes, the "legislature" would prescribe punishments so clearly
that the judge's only duty, once guilt had been proven, would be to mechanically
apply the appropriate article.[34] In this way, judges—who in the eighteenth century
were usually aristocrats and often appointees of the king—would not have the discretion to tailor sentences according to their whims, social class, or directives from
the sovereign.

Instead, punishment would be "proportioned to the crime" or the amount of
damage inflicted on society by a specific type of illegal behavior. Beccaria recommended using "geometry" to draw up a scale of crimes and their respective punishments in order to exclude the intrusion of private interest.[35] His frequent use of
mathematical metaphors showed his interest in logic and in the procedure of de-
ducing specific laws as corollaries of general maxims. Fundamental to this equation
of crimes and punishments was the principle of equality before the law for all social
classes. Under the old regime, it was understood—and sometimes written into
law—that members of the upper classes would receive exceedingly light penalties,
especially if their victims had come from a class below them. To Beccaria, this system was not only unjust but also a source of the judicial arbitrariness that so vexed
him.

Beccaria also insisted that judges take into account only the outward behavior,
and not the motivation or mental state, of the defendant. Axiomatic in his argument was a belief that human beings exercised free will when committing crimes.
They were thus responsible for their actions, no matter what their intentions. Attempts to judge motivation would needlessly muddy the mathematical precision of
his equation between crimes and punishments because, as mental states varied
widely among individuals and even within the same person over time, "it would be

necessary to frame not only a separate law code for each citizen, but a new law for each crime."[36] And he clinched his argument by observing that "sometimes men with the best intention inflict the worst evil on society, and, at other times, they do the greatest good for it with the most wicked will."[37]

Rejecting most of the traditional justifications for punishment like vengeance against criminals or indemnification of victims, Beccaria argued that the only purposes of punishment should be deterrence—prevention of further crime by both the defendant and other members of society.[38] To accomplish this, punishment needed to be certain, quick, and "the least possible in the case given." Beccaria was typical of his age in showing a modern distaste for bodily mutilation and torture, distinctive characteristics of the "dark ages" from which Europeans hoped to escape. Using a utilitarian calculus of pleasure and pain, he reasoned that punishment need only exceed the expected pleasure or proceeds from a certain crime by the smallest possible margin. Excessive punishment would not increase deterrence because "to the degree that punishments become more cruel, men's souls become hardened, just as fluids always seek the level of surrounding objects."[39] This distaste for corporal punishment led Beccaria to prefer fines and the rather new institution of the penitentiary over more traditional corporal retribution such as whipping, branding, and the galleys.

Of all the physical punishments typical of the old regime, Beccaria argued most eloquently and forcefully against torture and the death sentence. Torture, used routinely and legally as a way to extract confessions in both ecclesiastical and civil courts, was intolerable to Beccaria for violating the Enlightenment principle that a defendant should be considered innocent until proven guilty. Furthermore, confessions extracted under torture correlated not with truth but with physical weakness, since only the strong could resist the pain of the rack or the wheel. Beccaria ridiculed the legal tradition that considered "pain the crucible of truth, as though the criterion of truth lay in the muscles and fibers of a poor wretch. This is a sure way to acquit robust scoundrels and to condemn weak but innocent people."[40] In the case of capital punishment, Beccaria not only abhorred it as physical barbarity, but also as a violation of the social contract. Human beings had given only a small part of their liberty to the sovereign state, not so much that the law could require cruel and excessive punishment, much less death. Capital punishment was also hypocritical, since it was "absurd . . . that the laws, which are the expression of the public will and which detest and punish homicide, commit murder themselves."[41] Instead, he recommended for the worst criminals life sentences, which have "everything needed to deter the most determined spirit."[42]

As a man of the Enlightenment, Beccaria preached the efficacy of reason rather than fear as the best deterrent of crime. Once discretion in sentencing was taken away from judges, the certainty of punishment would impress itself on the minds of those contemplating breaking the law, convincing the majority of the irrationality of their act. For those who went ahead with their illegal schemes, a trial should follow quickly so that neither the convict nor the public would have time to forget the inexorable connection between crime and punishment. To further the transparency of the law and dispel "the dark spirit of cabal and intrigue" typical of criminal procedures under the old regime, Beccaria also insisted that laws be written in the vernacular rather than Latin and made available to the populace through the printing press.[43] This trust in the strength of the intellect to overcome base passions, typical of the philosophes, is also evident in Beccaria's firm and optimistic recommendation that education was "the most certain way . . . to prevent crimes."[44] And in his view, preventing crimes—through the deterrent effects of a clear, certain, humane and just law—was more important than merely punishing them.

This overview of Beccaria's treatise smoothes out its many contradictions, and indeed several criminologists have recently challenged the coherency of Beccaria's ideas.[45] I too find many inconsistencies in Beccaria, partially attributable both to philosophical immaturity and the desire to avoid censorship by Church and state of his writings. As Beirnes has pointed out, Beccaria did not set out to establish a "Classical School" of penology with a sacred text, uniform philosophy, and disciplined disciples. Beccaria never returned to law in his later writings and had little contact with his intellectual heirs, who often modified his ideas. The notion of a "school" of criminology was that of the positivists, who retroactively cast their predecessors in the same organizational mold. But if the term "Classical School" oversimplifies a complex reality, it is crucial for understanding the mentality of the positivist criminologists who coined the term and made it a staple of legal debates in late nineteenth-century Italy.

CRIMINAL MAN

Criminal anthropology developed in an intellectual atmosphere radically different from that which had inspired Beccaria. By the 1860s in Italy, positivism was gaining ascendancy not only in the scientific disciplines but also in philosophy, history, sociology, and psychology. Such a broad movement escapes precise definition, but most fundamentally its adherents championed the methodology of empiricism as opposed to deduction. In other words, researchers believed in collecting data as the basis for general laws rather than devising abstract metaphysical systems that lacked connection with the facts of natural and human life. In proposing that the human sciences pattern themselves on the natural sciences, leading Italian positivists like the historian Pasquale Villari and the philosopher Roberto Ardigò directed their criticism at both the idealism of the Hegelians and the spiritualism of Catholic thinkers. In addition to a commitment to the experimental method, positivists also shared, as Eugenio Garin has argued, a moral purpose. Positivism itself became a "lay faith" of Italian academia, serving an important "ethical-political function" in the first decades after unification.[46] This function was to provide the new Italian state with a modern and progressive philosophical foundation as a replacement for a religion that resisted change and opposed the *risorgimento*.

Beyond a commitment to empiricism, Italian positivists shared no rigid doctrine. The eclecticism within the positivist camp sprang partially from its roots in a variety of foreign philosophies. First, the word "positivism" itself was coined by Auguste

Comte, an early French sociologist.[47] He taught that knowledge had evolved historically through three stages: from the theological stage, inspired by divine revelation; through an intermediate metaphysical stage, based on abstract philosophy; to the final and highest stage, that of positivism or empirical reasoning. Because the physical sciences, most recently biology, had already entered the positivist stage, he predicted that the sciences of man were soon to follow. Second, English evolutionism was introduced into Italy with the translation of *Origin of the Species* in 1864, five yours after its initial publication. Despite the lag, this work incited widespread enthusiasm and, by 1870, almost all postivisits were converted to Darwinism.[48] Third, Italian positivists imbibed German materialism, especially Ernst Haeckel's theory of monism.[49] According to monists, human intelligence and morality were rooted in physiology, with the unitary cell determining all aspects of life. Haeckel also formulated the "biogenetic law" that each individual repeats the history of the species during his or her own development from conception to adulthood, both physically and emotionally.

Within this climate of enthusiasm for science, it is not surprising that Lombroso and his colleagues labeled themselves as positivists. They also gladly adopted the neologism of criminology, a word popularized in the 1880s and signaling the establishment of a new discipline independent of traditional study of law. Broad enough to encompass the medical, psychiatric, and legal aspects of Lombroso's school, positivist criminology connoted in Italy a modern approach to analyzing crime quite at variance with the old-fashioned penologists of the Classical School. Yet divergences existed among the pioneers of positivist criminology, and the following section will examine the similarities and differences among the famous "triad" of criminologists that established the school's international reputation: Cesare Lombroso, Enrico Ferri, and Raffaele Garofalo.

Cesare Lombroso

Recognized as the "master" of positivist criminology, Lombroso was a generation older than Ferri and Garofalo and first enunciated most of the theories that were later tested, and sometimes revised, by his colleagues. Lombroso's radically new approach to the issue of crime came primarily from his training in medicine rather than law. Born in 1835 into a Jewish family of northern Italy, Lombroso pursued his medical studies at the Universities of Padua, Vienna, and Pavia, graduating from the last in 1858. With the outbreak of the wars of Italian unification in 1859, he volunteered as a doctor in the revolutionary forces and was stationed in Calabria until 1863. Like many young doctors of that period, Lombroso identified science with the *risorgimento*, believing that empirical research was crucial for destroying the obscurantism of the old regimes of the peninsula and building a foundation of knowledge for a new, united, and liberal Italy. In an early positivist enterprise, he measured and studied 3,000 soldiers in Calabria in addition to his routine duties as a physician.[50] From 1863 to 1872 as the director of a succession of insane asylums in Pavia, Pesaro, and Reggio Emilia, Lombroso continued to focus on human subjects as the source of knowledge, in this case conducting research on the insane. Once appointed to the Chair of Legal Medicine and Public Hygiene at the University of Turin in 1876, he turned his attention to a third group, inmates of the Turinese penitentiary. Although he changed professorships several times—to that of psychiatry and clinical psychology in 1896 and criminal anthropology in 1906—Lombroso continued to serve as a prison physician in Turin, examining 200 prisoners each year.[51]

According to Lombroso, the central idea for his life work in criminology came to him in 1871 in a literal flash of light while doing an autopsy on the body of Giuseppe Villella, a notorious brigand. While contemplating the skull of Villella, as Lombroso often reminisced, "I seemed to see all at once, standing out clearly illumined as in a vast plain under a flaming sky, the problem of the nature of the criminal, who reproduces in civilised times characteristics, not only of primitive savages, but of still lower types as far back as the carnivores."[52] The discoveries that prompted this epiphany were a small hollow at the base of the skull and, underneath it, an enlarged segment of the spinal cord. The latter reminded Lombroso of an anatomical feature typical of some "inferior races" in Bolivia and Peru as well as "the lower types of apes, rodents, and birds."[53]

Even late in life, Lombroso referred to the skull of Villella—which he preserved until his death—as the "totem, the fetish of criminal anthropology" because the crucial notion of atavism—or the reversion of criminals to a lower state of physical and psychological evolution—had sprung from it.[54] Yet Villa, in his excellent intellectual biography of Lombroso, has shown that Lombroso's earliest reports of this autopsy were contradictory in terms of dates, the specific features of the skull, and even the crimes committed by Villella.[55] It thus appears that Lombroso fabricated, or at least embellished, the story of Villella's skull in order to fashion a dramatic founding event for his new discipline of criminal anthropology. This episode also showed him bending his data to fit preconceived theories, a practice that would become all too common in the writings of positivist criminologists.

Despite Lombroso's perpetuation of the myth that criminal anthropology sprang fully formed from the skull of Villella, he owed debts to both earlier and contemporary thinkers. As an indefatigable reader of several languages and a doctor trained partially in Vienna, Lombroso drew on a large and international body of literature not only in medicine and penology but also history and linguistics in formulating his theory of crime.[56] He was influenced by Comte and Haeckel, as well as the phrenology of Franz Joseph Gall and the degeneration theory of B. A. Morel. From phrenologists he copied the practice of examining the head for unusual physical features, based on the assumption that external anatomical features constituted signs of interior psychological developments. He did not, however, adopt their map of the skull, which correlated bumps and depressions with specific emotions. Nor did he accept their optimistic view that unhealthy physical—and therefore mental—features were particularly susceptible to improvement under positive environmental conditions. Lombroso absorbed from Morel the general notion that pathology, especially "social diseases" like alcoholism, syphilis, and tuberculosis, could cause both physical and moral degeneration in an otherwise "normal" person. Like atavism, degeneration presumed that all individuals could be ranked on an evolutionary scale teleologically leading toward the apex of civilization, marked by the virtues of the white, European middle classes.

Villa has minimized the influence of Darwin on Lombroso, arguing that the latter—although familiar with the *Origin of the Species* before its translation into Italian—was more deeply affected by other sources. Villa identifies comparative linguistics, especially the work of Paolo Marzolo, as decisive in Lombroso's early conception of evolution and the possibility of reversion to earlier stages of civilization. Himself a doctor, Marzolo tried to reconstruct the linguistic evolution of humanity through the empirical collection of phrases and modes of communication thought to be typical of earlier stages of civilization.[57] And indeed Lombroso's lifelong interest in the jargon and art of criminals attests to his youthful linguistic studies. Like physical deformities, "primitive" cultural artifacts constituted signs of evolutionary failure. Yet even if Lombroso's earliest research was not directly informed by Darwinism, he was eclectic enough to draw on Darwin's name by the 1880s, if only to enhance the prestige of his school. And the influence of Darwinism on his younger colleagues, like Ferri, is undeniable.

A prolific writer, Lombroso produced over thirty books and 1,000 articles during his lifetime. His most famous work, *Criminal Man* (*L'uomo delinquente*), went through five editions between 1876 and 1897.[58] With Guglielmo Ferrero, he issued a companion book, *The Female Offender* (*La donna delinquente*) in 1893 with a second edition ten years later.[59] Topics of other monographs included insanity, genius, race, legal medicine, and political crime.[60] Many of Lombroso's articles, as well as innumerable book reviews and short commentaries, appeared in the *Archives of Psychiatry, Criminal Anthropology, and Penal Sciences* (hereafter *Archives*), a journal founded by Lombroso and his burgeoning group of disciples in 1880.[61] As one of the most prominent intellectuals in late nineteenth-century Italy, Lombroso was also invited to write for more general publications like *Nuova antologia*, geared toward middle-class readers. It was a measure of his prestige and authority as a public intellectual that his opinion was sought not only on issues of criminal justice but on quite separate topics like foreign policy.

As a scientist, Lombroso rejected the armchair theorizing of the Classical School for empirical research. As he repeated throughout his life, the focus of study should not be the crime but the criminal.[62] Unlike classical criminologists who drew up scales of crime and punishment based on moral principles, Lombroso espoused observation of the bodies of criminals to find the facts. Experimental science, therefore, became the model for positivists, replacing the deductive mathematical analogies of Beccaria. To his credit, Lombroso spent vast amounts of time collecting data by examining inmates in Italian prisons. For him, the prison was a laboratory in which he used a variety of odd machines to measure and experiment on the physical body. He also performed autopsies on dead criminals and examined bones of ancient peoples preserved in archeological museums. Lombroso's books are filled with the results of his observations and experiments: lengthy tables illustrate the data and pages of photographs train readers in the detection of abnormality.

That Lombroso's theory changed significantly throughout his professional career is clear from a comparison of the five editions of *Criminal Man*. Issued as a short volume of under 250 pages when it first appeared in 1876, it grew to three volumes of text totaling 2,000 pages by the fifth edition. This final edition also included a fourth volume or *Atlante*, which constituted a curious appendix filled with a variety of illustrative evidence including maps of criminal geography; graphs of the distribution of crimes; photographs of offenders; and representations of the tattoos, handwriting, and art of prison inmates. Lombroso's daughter, Gina, issued a short synopsis of her father's work in 1911, two years after his death, also under the title *Criminal Man*. Because this posthumous volume is the only one to have been translated into English, many readers do not have access to the original formulation of Lombroso's theory or to the evolution of his ideas during the height of his popularity in the last three decades of the nineteenth century. Gina's synopsis, as well as a compendium produced by Lombroso for foreign audiences, *Crime: Its Causes and Remedies*, lack the wealth of detail and broad scope of the last editions of *Criminal Man*. They also synthesize a rambling and often contradictory set of observations into a falsely compact and coherent theory.

As a comparison of the five editions of *Criminal Man* reveals, Lombroso revised, or at least expanded, his theory in three main areas: the classification of criminals; the identity of the born criminal; and punishment. Although positivist criminology later became known for its careful system of classification, the first edition of *Criminal Man* lumped all lawbreakers together in a single group that was then compared to the insane and, sporadically, control groups of "normal" men. The phrase "born criminal" did not yet appear, as it was coined four years later by Ferri.[63] In 1876, Lombroso simply referred to "criminals in general," and systematically listed their physical characteristics; compared to "healthy" individuals they exhibited small and deformed skulls, greater height and weight, light beards, crooked noses, sloped foreheads, dark skin, eyes, and hair, large ears, protruding jaws, less muscular strength, and little sensitivity to pain. This last, according to Lombroso, constituted the exterior sign of inward moral obtuseness because criminals rarely exhibited remorse for their crimes. Unable to control their passions, they indulged in wine and gambling. Lacking intelligence, they were adept at crime because they needed only to repeat the same behavior. Lombroso also included chapters on tattoos among prisoners, as well as their slang, their writing, and their art, although these characteristics would seem social rather than biological in derivation. But from Lombroso's eclectic point of view, the scientist had to be alert to any and all external clues to a fundamental internal atavistic nature. The criminal was an ill person, and the criminologist had to be creative in locating and reading the symptoms.

In the second edition of *Criminal Man*, Lombroso used the term "habitual criminal" to name the carrier of the physical, moral, and intellectual anomalies already defined for "criminals in general." He also began to build a system of classification, establishing two new categories of the "insane criminal" and the "criminal by passion." The first edition had already argued that criminals and the insane shared many abnormal anatomical and biological traits. By the second edition, he argued that some criminals were themselves insane and deserved specific treatment different from either the sane criminal or the noncriminal insane. Completely new was the chapter on criminals by passion, included in response to critics. Criminals by passion were unlike habitual criminals in many ways: they tended to have high reputations before committing their crime; they repented immediately; and their motives were "generally generous and often sublime."[64] These might include anger against an adulterous spouse or commitment to a banned political ideal. In both cases, the jealous husband or political rebel would uncharacteristically lose control of his emotions momentarily, but did not exhibit the physical or moral anomalies of a common murderer.

In the final three editions of *Criminal Man*, Lombroso continued to elaborate new categories of deviants. Some were borrowed from Ferri, who had urged his teacher to extend his analysis beyond atavism. While never as clear and systematic as Ferri in his classification, Lombroso nevertheless introduced a series of criminal types that became stock figures in the popular imagination. Most obviously, he adopted Ferri's label of the "born criminal," a tag that quickly gained international recognition. It also drew instant criticism, as opponents ridiculed his inability to identify any single anomaly that disfigured all born criminals. In response, Lombroso proposed that any individual exhibiting a cluster of anomalies be labeled atavistic, although he was always vague about the minimal number of malformations necessary for being so categorized. He also maintained that even "isolated" anomalies marked a criminal as constitutionally flawed and therefore potentially dangerous. Such fuzziness in definition became alarming in light of his theory of punishment, which depended on the precise categorization of offenders.

Lombroso also expanded the category of the insane criminal to distinguish three further variations: the "alcoholic criminal," the "hysteric criminal," and the *mattoide*. In the first case, drunkenness could turn even an individual possessing few anomalies to a path of crime, because "by itself, it gives courage, incites the passions, dims the mind and conscience, and disarms any reserve so that one commits crimes as an automaton, almost a somnambulist."[65] Thus, while not necessarily atavistic, alcoholics exhibited the same character traits as born criminals: impulsiveness, cruelty, lack of remorse, and laziness. Often inheriting a weak constitution from alcoholic parents, they were predisposed to violent acts like murder, rape, and homicide.

The category of the hysteric criminal was also elastic since some of its members had few signs of mental illness like convulsions or low intelligence. But all possessed "an egoism, a preoccupation with themselves that makes them eager for scandal and public attention as well as an excessive impressionability so that any little thing makes them bilious, cruel . . . and irrational."[66] Although most hysterics were female, *mattoides* were invariably male and represented one of Lombroso's most innovative classifications. Meaning "half crazy" in lay terms, *mattoide* entered positivist terminology to designate unstable but heroic individuals who combined the vulgar with the sublime. Self-fashioned prophets and revolutionaries, they rose from humble origins to harangue the masses with utopian ideas. Combining "unusual and well-expressed ideas" with those that were "mediocre and base," their voluminous writings marked them as truly mad.[67] In adding three categories that relied little on physical anomalies, Lombroso began to "psychologize deviance," a trend that was amplified by his successors.[68] He also widened the net of criminality to include persons labeled dangerous not because of past crimes but because they possessed neurotic traits reminiscent of born criminals.

Finally, the last editions of *Criminal Man* included an entirely new category, that of Ferri's "occasional criminal." Lombroso was always uncomfortable with the category of the occasional criminal, complaining that it "does not offer a homogeneous type like the born criminal and the criminal by passion: but it is constituted of many disparate groups."[69] In his schema, these groups included the pseudocriminal, marked by few if any anomalies; the criminaloid who exhibited enough anomalies to be predisposed to crime; and the habitual criminal, now a label for recidivists who began their careers as pseudocriminals, but had reached the depravity of born criminals. In all cases, these individuals broke the law because environmental pressures or temptations overcame their natural goodness.

By the final edition of *Criminal Man*, Lombroso had recognized a spectrum of deviant types outside of the born criminal. Some were composed of individuals with few anomalies, like the three subcategories of the occasional criminal, while others were intermediary between the occasional and born criminal, like the insane criminal and the criminal by passion. This proliferation of categories increased the weight of sociological factors in Lombroso's explanation of the causes of crime. Because of the notoriety of the concept of the born criminal, Lombroso is rarely credited with including environmental factors in his discussion of the etiology of deviance. Yet as early as the first edition of *Criminal Man*, he argued that "there is no crime which is not rooted in multiple causes" including education, hunger, and urbanization.[70] In the later editions he devoted increasing space to the sociological causes of crime and lowered the percent of criminals in the category of the biologically perverse from over 50 percent to 33 percent.[71] Even with this drastic reduction of his original category, Lombroso could retain a general theory that denied free will, because he conceptualized environmental and biological forces as equally deterministic.

Despite his increasing willingness to acknowledge the role of external forces on the individual, Lombroso remained throughout his life most enthusiastic about analyzing the identity of the born criminal. While he relied on the research of others to paint a portrait of the occasional criminal, he indefatigably continued to collect primary data on the innate factors that pushed certain individuals to a life of crime. The identity of the born criminal, however, did not remain static throughout the revisions of *Criminal Man*. In the first edition, he identified all born criminals as atavistic. After describing the anomalies in the size and shape of a series of skulls, he remarked on "the singular coincidence between the abnormalities found in criminal men and those observed in the normal skulls of the colored or inferior races."[72] Not surprisingly, since exterior physical defects signaled interior moral depravity, such similarities extended to the emotions. The ferocity of criminals, for example, was "common to ancient and savage peoples but rare and monstrous today."[73] Atavism even explained the popularity of tattoos among lawbreakers, since "tattoos are one of the special characters of primitive man and of those in the wild."[74] In short, criminals were "savages living in the middle of flourishing European civilization," identifiable by their physical and moral anomalies.[75] They represented throwbacks on the evolutionary scale, a freakish reappearance in modern European civilization of its brutish past.

By the third edition of *Criminal Man*, Lombroso admitted that the concept of atavism was inadequate to explain the presence of multiple anomalies in all born criminals. Such a radical reconsideration resulted partially from the widespread criticism of his key concept, including that of Ferri and other followers. Rather than abandoning his beloved notion of atavism, Lombroso simply added that of degeneration to explain physical and psychological malformations that had resulted from fetal disease rather than inherited weakness. Such a disease might prevent a normal fetus from, in Haeckelian terms, recapitulating all the stages of human evolution. Their development blocked in the womb, babies could thus be "born" with predisposition to crime, legible in anomalies left by the disease. The theory of degeneracy allowed the interplay of biology and environment, since social factors like alcoholism, venereal disease, or malnutrition might cripple the health of a mother and therefore her fetus. But even if caused by external forces, degeneracy was thought to become a hereditary condition that progressively weakened future generations.

Although the adoption of degeneracy theory, of French origin, might seen to signal a defeat for criminal anthropology, instead it broadened its scope and applicability. Lombroso could now count any malformation, even if not attributable to atavism, as one of the cluster of anomalies needed to identify a born criminal. Furthermore, it widened the psychological dimension of his theory, because he held that many symptoms of degeneracy were mental rather than physical. As part of this tendency to psychologize deviancy, he developed two new categories of the born criminal: the morally insane and the epileptic. Introduced in the third edition of *Criminal Man*, moral insanity designated individuals who appeared normal in physique and intelligence, but were unable to distinguish between good and evil behavior. Generally classed as borderline cases between normality and madness, the morally insane were pronounced by Lombroso as identical to atavistic criminals in their compulsion to harm others and their lack of remorse. Once tested for physical sensitivity, they exhibited, as expected by Lombroso, a dullness of touch compatible with their moral vacuity. To support his thesis of "the analogy and complete identity between the morally insane and the born criminal," he enumerated studies that had found largespread moral insanity among the prison population.[76]

In the fourth edition of *Criminal Man*, Lombroso finally enunciated his last subcategory of the born criminal, the epileptic. While subscribing to the common notion of the time that epileptics might commit crimes during convulsions, he also proposed the category of "hidden epilepsy" (*epilessia larvata*) that might promote deviant acts even in the absence of physical trauma. Thus, for Lombroso, epilepsy became a universal substructure of all criminal behavior, enveloping both moral insanity and atavism. In the final edition of *Criminal Man*, Lombroso declared the difference between the three catgories to be primarily that of scale: "as the morally insane criminal merges with the congenital criminal, only differing in an exaggeration of its characteristics, so the epileptic delinquent . . . offers an exaggeration of the morally insane criminal . . . and as when two things resemble a third, then all three are equal, so it is certain that born criminality and criminal insanity are nothing but special, if variant, forms of epilepsy."[77] From this perspective, Lombroso began to find a combination of atavism, moral insanity, and epilepsy in many of his subjects of research. He thus gained flexibility in classifying them as born criminals, because even "isolated" physical atavisms became significant when combined with the innate moral depravity of moral insanity or epilepsy. As the definition of the born criminal became increasingly elastic, criminal anthropologists gained ever widening discretion to label a variety of deviants as born criminals.

A third theme undergoing significant modification over the five editions of *Criminal Man* was that of punishment. In the first edition, Lombroso made only scattered references to the penal implications of his theory of atavistic criminals, suggesting, for example, that they were not likely to be deterred by the death penalty because of their extreme insensitivity to pain.[78] By the second edition, however, he had inserted a special section on "therapy for crime," in order to make his new science of practical use to lawyers and magistrates. Again, his decision to devote increasingly large sections of each edition to punishment came largely at the behest of Ferri, who—as a lawyer—realized that his colleagues had little interest in theory unless it had explicit prescriptions for sentencing. Thus, by the final edition of *Criminal Man*, Lombroso devoted 300 pages to a detailed discussion of the appropriate punishments for various categories of lawbreakers.

Although his practical advice became increasingly specialized over the years, Lombroso's basic philosophy of punishment never changed. In opposition to the Enlightenment principles of Beccaria, he counseled that punishment be tailored to individual criminals rather than to their crimes. He explicitly rejected the principle of moral responsibility, arguing that criminals acted out of compulsion, whether from their innate physical and psychological degeneracy or from the social environment. Yet, even if criminals did not freely choose to break the law, society still had the right to punish them in its own defense. This principle of social defense was itself not so different from Beccaria's belief that the major purpose of punishment was to prevent those guilty of crime from further threatening society. Lombroso directly broke with Beccaria, however, over the mode of determining appropriate punishments. To Lombroso, a mathematical scale of crimes and punishments was too abstract, since both born and occasional criminals might steal or even murder. Therefore the law should allow wide discretion to judges to assess the degree of "dangerousness" of each defendant as a basis for issuing the appropriate sentence. In short, the positivists rejected the classical penchant for determinate sentences for flexible, conditional penalties.

In place of the classical scale of crimes and punishments, Lombroso argued for the correlation of types of criminals with punishments. Thus, mistakes in the classification of offenders could bring undeserved consequences. Despite his early rejection of the death penalty, Lombroso gradually came to advocate it in the case of born criminals convicted of a series of bloody crimes or members of organized gangs, like *mafiosi* and brigands, who threatened the security of the state. In so doing, he betrayed the liberal principles of his youth as well as defied a public consensus that had abolished capital punishment in the Zanardelli Criminal Code of 1889. To his adversaries he responded that "to say that this punishment goes against the laws of nature is to pretend not to know that it is written in very clear letters in [nature's] book and that the entire progress of the animal world, and thus our own, is based on the struggle for existence, involving immense slaughter."[79] Society need have no pity for such born criminals, because they were "constituted for evil" and "do not resemble us, but instead ferocious beasts."[80] Capital punishment would simply accelerate natural selection, ridding society of the unfit.

For born criminals who had committed less heinous crimes and for habitual criminals, Lombroso recommended perpetual incarceration, preferably on islands or in the remote countryside. Work would be mandatory, because "we must worry less about their well-being than about putting them to use."[81] In this way, they would defray the costs of their incarceration while being prevented from further menacing society or corrupting occasional criminals. Like capital punishment, life imprisonment emulated "the process of natural selection, to which we owe not only the existence of the race but possibly also of justice, which depends on the elimination of those who are most violent."[82] Insane criminals would also be separated from society for life, but in special criminal insane asylums (*manicomi criminali*) where they would receive treatment. A crusader for these special institutions as a humane alternative to incarceration, Lombroso also envisioned the establishment of specialized mental institutions for groups like alcoholic or epileptic criminals.

For criminals by passion and occasional criminals, Lombroso sought alternatives to penitentiaries. Unlike the Classical School, which had vaunted prisons as a humane and enlightened alternative to corporal punishment, positivists derided them as "schools of vice." They would only ruin reformable criminals by mixing them with congenital deviants. When unavoidable, prisons should be modeled on the "Pennsylvania," or cellular system where inmates lived and worked in separate cells to prevent communication and moral contamination. Preferable to prison were fines or, if the defendant were poor, community service. For nondangerous criminals, he counseled the courts to recommend house arrest, police surveillance, or simply judicial reprimands. He was also enthusiastic about suspended sentences and parole, two modern alternatives to incarceration pioneered in France and the United States that he crusaded to have introduced into the Italian criminal code.

The variety of punishments proposed by Lombroso raises the question of his political allegiance. Today, support for the death penalty or incarcerating criminals for life based on biological traits characterizes conservative criminology concerned above all with retribution and the maintenance of order. On the other hand, liberals prefer indeterminate sentences supplemented by parole as humane tools to encourage reform of lawbreakers. That positivism was the font of both conservative and liberal approaches to criminality shows that it was more multifaceted than usually conceded. It has been best known for its conservative or "hard" approach to born criminals rather than its liberal or "soft" prescriptions for occasional criminals. This illustrates the difficulty of automatically identifying certain intellectual theories with a specific political position. Positivist criminology was not innately of the Right or the Left, but could be compatible with both positions depending on historical circumstances and which part of its doctrine was being emphasized.

A fervent supporter of the liberal *risorgimento* in his youth, Lombroso came gradually to embrace a humanitarian socialism. Although he never theorized the compatibility of socialism and positivism as clearly as Ferri would, he joined the PSI in 1893, wrote for its newspapers and periodicals, and served as a socialist representative on the city council of Turin from 1899 to 1905. His socialism has been described by one biographer, Bulferetti, as "sentimental," since Lombroso was not particularly orthodox and did not believe, for example, in economic determinism.[83] He was, however, extremely sympathetic to the poor, and worked, while on the city council, for better hospitals, schools, and daycare for the working class.[84] Dolza, the author of a recent biography of Lombroso's two daughters, evaluates his political position more positively. She sees Lombroso as emblematic of "positivist" intellectuals who, wishing to educate the public, felt "a moral duty to put their own research at the service of the collectivity."[85] This conviction, that scientific research could discover truth and improve society, was similar to the Progressive spirit in the United States at the turn of the century. Thus, Lombroso's life shows a continuity between his championing of science as necessary to the new, secular society being born in the *risorgimento* and his later adhesion to socialism. In the year of his death in 1909, he still described himself as a "convinced follower of socialist thought."[86]

Lombroso's personal and intellectual contacts were not, however, limited to socialists. Perhaps the best-known professor in Turin during the 1880s, his house became the center of cultural interchange for both locals and visitors.[87] Guests included a wide spectrum of intellectuals including Gaetano Mosca, Robert Michels, Achille Loria, Max Nordau, Max Weber, and Ellen Key. According to Michels, "all of these people, although differing in age, temperament, language and mentality, felt themselves drawn together into one bundle by the boundless esteem and sincere affection which each of them, taken separately, felt in his or her own heart for Lombroso."[88] Such statements testify to the many attractive qualities of Lombroso: his restless energy, curiosity about all subjects, imaginative if not always careful opinions, and enthusiasm for popularizing his doctrine beyond academic circles.

Finally, an analysis of Lombroso's research must point out its methodological flaws, many of which were recognized by his early opponents.[89] He cannot be faulted for some of these problems, which simply reflected an early and unsophisticated stage in the development of the social sciences. But his books were characterized by haste, slipshod logic, and a tendency to ignore data that did not support his theories. Despite his claims to emulate science, Lombroso's methods of collecting and counting his data were anything but rigorous. He made no attempt to sample systematically the populations under study, although it is perhaps understandable that he eagerly measured any available criminal body in the early years simply to accumulate data. More damaging to the credibility of Lombroso's research was that most of his studies lacked control groups against which to compare his data on criminals. In the successive editions of *Criminal Man*, for example, his tables enumerating rates of various anomalies in the prison population only occasionally offer comparative data on "normal" men. That control groups were common in social science research by the late nineteenth century is clear from the severe criticism of some contemporaries.

Lombroso's statistical expertise never went beyond the computation of the frequencies of certain traits in each group of subjects. Although this simple level of computation was typical of statistics at the beginning of his career, he ignored the subsequent development in his lifetime of more sophisticated techniques like the analysis of regression and standard deviation. Even his tables of frequencies were inadequate to support his conclusions, since he never clarified how many atavisms were necessary to label an individual deviant. More fundamentally, Lombroso never distinguished between correlation and causation, claiming that a high frequency of atavisms in an individual caused criminal behavior. He thus ignored two other more plausible explanations: that both atavisms and criminal behavior stemmed from a third independent variable or that the correlation was entirely random.

It is also strange that Lombroso, as a self-proclaimed positivist, mixed various types of "soft" qualitative evidence with his statistical data. As is clear from the story of Villella, Lombroso was drawn to sensational examples that buttressed his case, substituting these for more rigorous research on homogeneous groups. He cited uncritically the results of his colleagues, even those who did not fully agree with his theories, as if the density of references would substitute for consistent data. Most surprisingly, *Criminal Man* and other writings of Lombroso are packed with quotations from literature and folklore, a characteristic that displayed his wide reading in a number of fields but casts further doubt on his claim to be scientific. For example, in support of his view that epileptics were born criminals, he pointed to the works of a number of great authors: "Shakespeare surmised epilepsy in the mind of Macbeth, who suffered from Hallucinations. Goncourt saw epilepsy in the murderer of the girl Eliza. Dostoiewski described all his criminals as epileptic in his 'Crime et Châtiments.' Zola, without knowing it, gave us a complete type of psychic epilepsy in the murderer of 'La Bête Humaine.' "[90] Thus, fictional examples came to carry the same explanatory weight as data drawn from his own experiments and interviews.

That Lombroso could continually cite works of literature and proverbs to document his theories undercuts the claim of positivist criminology to scientific objectivity. Instead of breaking traditional stereotypes of criminals, criminal anthropology tended simply to give supposedly scientific support for popular prejudices, as expressed in adages. Lombroso admitted as much when he boasted that "the knowledge of a criminal physiognomic type . . . is often instinctive among the common people," giving rise to epithets like "a thief's face" and "the look of an assassin."[91] Villa has tellingly labeled Lombroso's work as "simply an encyclopedia of images," an iconography of evil that drew on traditions as old as the medieval bestiary and representations of Hell.[92]

While sounding a trumpet call for a focus on the criminal rather than on crime, Lombroso never clearly defined the category of "criminal," a serious omission for any scientist. Since his subjects came from Italy's penitentiaries, he seemed to have accepted the state's official categories of crime. This was a curious stance, considering Lombroso's bitter criticisms of the Italian penal codes of 1859 and 1889, both based on the principles of the Classical School. Even if he believed Italian inmates to have been properly convicted, the value of this group as a scientific sample would have been limited, since many criminals are never arrested and many others improperly acquitted during the court procedures. Without a precise definition of crime, Lombroso's myriad pages of statistical tables lose any pretence of objective validity. Although many criminologists after Lombroso have been similarly sloppy in delimiting the subject of their research, it is particularly surprising in someone so critical of the traditional categories enshrined in classical criminal law.

Of Lombroso's many legacies, the one that captures both the fascinating and repulsive aspects of his thought was the Museum of Criminal Anthropology, still located in Turin. Housed in the museum was a macabre collection of hundreds of objects amassed by Lombroso over a lifetime beginning in his student days in 1859. Considered by Lombroso as "data" relevant to criminal identification, these objects included skulls, skeletons, pickled brains, photographs, wax effigies of "deviant" faces, patches of dried skin bearing tattoos, weapons of lawbreaking, and art created by inmates.[93] In building his collection, Lombroso accepted gifts from anthropologists, wheedled artifacts left behind in Italian prisons, and—with the help of his students—robbed graves. He proudly organized public expositions of this material in connection with the National Exposition of 1884 in Turin, the first Congress of Criminal Anthropology of 1885 in Rome, and the Universal Exposition of 1889 in Paris. Put under the direction of his son-in-law, Mario Carrara, in 1904, the Museum remained after Lombroso's death as a school in the positivist science of reading the body for signs of immorality, insanity, and criminality.

Enrico Ferri

Born in 1856, twenty-one years after Lombroso, Ferri was to become his most visible and indefatigable disciple. Even before meeting Lombroso, he wrote a law thesis, defended in 1877, critiquing the notion of free will and arguing that individuals were not morally responsible for their behavior.[94] He believed that the free choice of all members of society, whether mentally competent or not, was constrained in some degree, and it was useless for judges to try to measure such an abstract concept. But if criminals did not have a moral responsibility (*imputabilità morale*) for their criminal acts, they did have a legal responsibility (*imputabilità legale*) to repay society for damage to persons or property. Thus, he did not throw out the notion of punishment, but shifted its foundations from moral retribution to social defense.

Such an interpretation clashed radically with that of the Classical School, and thus most of Ferri's professors at both the Universities of Bologna and Pisa, where he did postdoctoral work under the guidance, respectively, of Pietro Ellero and Francesco Carrara. Despite his unorthodoxy, he was offered the chairs of both Ellero and Carrara after their retirements. While writing his thesis, Ferri was not yet convinced that lawyers should become involved in measuring heads and the other nitty-gritty work of criminal anthropology. But, by 1879, he was visiting Lombroso in Turin and learning to examine prisoners. In 1880, he helped Lombroso launch the *Archives* and contributed to the first volume.

Perhaps because of his legal training, Ferri's writings were much more systematic than Lombroso's. It was Ferri who kept pushing Lombroso to develop a definitive classification of criminals, a task that was never completed in the latter's writings because he kept inventing new categories or revising old ones. Perhaps in exasperation, Ferri created his own system of classification, one that changed little over his lifetime and seems to have inspired Lombroso's multiple attempts. Ferri arranged his categories along a scale of dangerousness, beginning with the occasional criminal, who had few abnormal physical and psychological traits and was therefore fairly innocuous. More of a threat to society in increasing order were criminals by passion, who were normal except for exceptional outbreaks of emotional violence; habitual criminals who were occasional criminals pushed to recidivism by life in an evil environment; insane criminals with maladies familiar to psychiatrists; and, finally, born criminals. While responsible for coining the term "born criminal," Ferri's determinism was somewhat "softer" than Lombroso's; for example, in response to French critics of criminal anthropology, he allowed that born criminals were merely predisposed to crime and could lead normal lives if raised in the proper environment.[95] He was even more optimistic about the reformability of the other four categories, thus becoming a proponent of innovative measures to prevent crime and rehabilitate offenders. This strain of social reform has often been ignored in analyses of positivist criminology.

His classification of offenders formed part of what Ferri came to call criminal sociology (*sociologia criminale*), which he differentiated from both classical jurisprudence and, to a lesser extent, criminal anthropology. As a lawyer, he criticized the Classical School, which considered crime only a "juridical problem" to be properly named and defined.[96] While the majority of humanity immediately asks why a heinous crime has been committed, the classical jurist limits himself to questions like: "What is the name of the crime committed by that man under such circumstances? Must it be classed as murder or patricide, attempted or incompleted manslaughter, and, if directed against property, is it theft, or illegal appropriation, or fraud?"[97] From Ferri's point of view, "rivers of ink have been spilled" over defining the difference between legal notions such as incompleted and attempted crime, while classical legal education ignored the social dimension of crime.[98] Criminal sociology would repair this imbalance, by directing its attention to the social phenomenon— the criminal—rather than the juridical fact of the crime.

To answer the question of the causes of crime, Ferri developed a model of multiple causation. Showing great respect throughout his life for the "genius" of Lombroso and even labeling himself at times a criminal anthropologist, Ferri softened his master's emphasis on inherited stigmata and pathological epilepsy.[99] Although these physical and psychological defects were significant, they constituted only one of three categories of criminal causation. The second category was telluric, or forces in the physical environment such as climate, the fertility of the soil, or the time of day. Finally, social factors—including poverty, illiteracy, and bad families—constituted the last category. Yet, although an ardent and active socialist, Ferri denied that poverty alone leads to crime since most of the poor led honest lives. The etiology of every crime lay in a combination of the three categories—anthropological, telluric, and social—so that even the occasional criminal acted under some type of mental imbalance brought out under certain environmental conditions.

That all crime was determined—either by instinct or the environment—was to Ferri a source of optimism rather than pessimism. At least it offered a way to measure criminality and understand its causes. The principle of free will, subscribed to by the Classical School, could not be measured and thus contradicted "the law of causality, which is at the very foundation of modern scientific thought." As Giuseppe Galileo had destroyed the misperception that the earth, and therefore humanity, was the center of the universe and Darwin had destroyed the "anthropocentric illusion" that humans are essentially different from plant and animal life, now positivists were using the same scientific reasoning to overthrow the myth of free will.[100] Instead, criminal sociology offered the prospect of a bright future in which positivists could isolate all the material causes of crime and identify which combination of factors had motivated each delinquent.

Positivist criminology also promised more justice, since punishment would no longer be based on moral retribution, dear to many nineteenth-century classicists. Ferri went back to Beccaria's original emphasis on prevention, although giving it a new interpretative twist. For Ferri, "penalties have the same relation to crime that medicine has to disease," and therefore criminology had to follow the recent evolution of medicine toward isolating the microbes causing illness.[101] Once the etiology of crime had been analyzed, legislators needed to "apply the rules of social hygiene" in order to provide a telluric and social environment that discouraged deviancy.[102] Social hygiene would rely essentially on what Ferri labeled penal substitutes (sostitutivi penali) like the elimination of poverty, protection for orphans, improved education, and good housing. Those who still defied the law, especially if classified as occasional criminals, would be given suspended sentences, fined, or at most sent to humane reformatories to be educated and trained to work. The most incorrigible—insane and born criminals—would be sentenced to mental asylums and penitentiaries respectively, but always under an indeterminate sentence so that even the most vicious would have hope of release. Each institution, whether orphanage, reformatory, mental hospital, or prison, would be run by experts trained in positivist criminology who would scientifically individualize the treatment of inmates and accurately recognize the signs of recovery necessary for release or parole.

Of all the positivist criminologists, Ferri was the most active in the PSI. Yet his conversion to socialism came late, after a much publicized sparring with Turati in the early 1880s over the role of biological determinism in crime.[103] During that period Ferri, like Lombroso, was still drawn to republicanism and resented the attacks of some socialists on the pioneering work of positivist criminologists. But Ferri became radicalized in the next ten years and joined the PSI in 1893, a year after its founding. The next year he published an impassioned defense of the compatibility of Darwinism—seen as the essence of criminal anthropology—and Marxism. Entitled *Socialism and Modern Science*, this book helped to establish positivism as an important philosophical strain in Italian socialism.

According to Ferri, the compatibility between Darwinism and Marxism rested first on their agreement that society is not static but will evolve and progress. Because Darwinism had established change as fundamental to society, he argued that the present capitalist system was not the economic embodiment of the struggle for existence, as many bourgeois writers claimed, but was bound to be superceded. According to Ferri, it would be "ridiculous" for a Darwinist to believe in the immutability of property relations since the economy—like the political structure, the family, and culture—was subject to continual evolution.[104]

Second, both Darwinism and Marxism were compatible in their materialism, with the former privileging biological facts and the second economic conditions. As opposed to religion or idealist philosophies that appealed to God or some kind of universal spirit to explain the world, positivist criminology and socialism were both scientific and empirical. Ferri saw no contradiction between biology and economics, arguing that economic conditions "are the resultant of the *ethnical* energies and aptitudes acting in a given *physical* environment," phrases that echoed his anthropological and telluric categories.[105] Criminal sociology needed to meld with socialism and its emphasis on the dynamic development of the proletariat to avoid "sterility," while socialism could assure its maturation from utopianism to science by becoming positivist. Based on such an understanding, "the two currents of evolutionist naturalism and scientific socialism will increasingly come to resemble each other and finally become identical by drawing their energies from the eternal ocean of life and of empirical truth."[106]

Finally, Ferri denied that the Darwinist principle of the struggle for existence was antithetical to a future peaceful socialist society free from class conflict. He predicted that competition would become more benign and increasingly intellectual rather than economic as society progressed to a higher stage. Thus, each individual who worked for the collectivity could be guaranteed economic support without contradicting Darwinian principles. Yet he insisted that some individuals would always fail in the struggle for existence and continue to commit crime even in a socialist society. Although the social determinants of crime could be eliminated, human anthropology and the physical environment would always remain in some ways outside human control. As a natural fact, inborn criminality like physical disease would always exist, since "crime . . . is a department of human pathology."[107]

Ferri had a public platform for his political ideas, as a left-wing member of the Chamber of Deputies after 1886, first as a republican and then as a socialist. He used his position to oppose the increasingly repressive policies of the Liberal governments of the 1890s against the peasants and urban working class. When the Pelloux government in 1899 tried to push a series of decrees through Parliament undercutting civil rights, Ferri—a brilliant orator—participated in the successful filibuster, talking "for hours and hours without ever saying . . . things that were not useful or pertinent to the discussion."[108] By 1903, he had risen high enough in the PSI to be given the editorship of *Avanti!* the party newspaper, a position he held for five years. One biographer has labeled him "the most powerful man in the party" during this period.[109] His name also appeared frequently in *Critica sociale*, the highly respected intellectual weekly of the PSI. Despite his differences with the editors, Turati and Anna Kuliscioff, he was honored with a salute to the first issue of his journal, *The Positivist School* (*Scuola Positiva*), in 1891; respectful and sometimes enthusiastic reviews of his books; and the opportunity to air his views on the compatibility of positivism and socialism.[110]

Despite Ferri's prominence in the party, however, his views represented only one current of Italian socialism. His analysis of criminality was frequently labeled conservative by his socialist colleagues, since he insisted that an equal distribution of wealth could not rid society of born criminals. On the other hand, Ferri led a band of "revolutionary intransigents" in Parliament, who opposed the efforts of revisionist socialists to make alliances with other parties of the Left. This contradiction between Ferri's advocacy of evolution in his academic writings and revolution in everyday politics attests to his failure, like many others in the fledgling socialist party, to construct a coherent ideology.

In addition to politics, Ferri turned to several other arenas to spread his positivist faith. His best known book, *Criminal Sociology*, went through five editions between 1881 and 1929, the year of his death.[111] After helping Lombroso found the *Archives* in 1880, he established his own journal, *The Positivist School*, which was slanted more toward law than medicine. This magazine gave positivists a voice in a field that was still dominated by organs of the Classical School such as the *Rivista penale* of Luigi Lucchini. More than any other criminologist, Ferri was known as a great and stirring orator, and he lectured on positivist criminology throughout Europe and Latin America.[112] He was also a brilliant criminal lawyer, gaining a national reputation as early as 1885 for his successful defense of a group of peasants from his native province of Mantova who had been arrested for insurrection. Ferri published several collections of his speeches as a defense lawyer, with the explicit aim of illustrating to the public how positivism worked in practice in the courtroom.[113]

Equally concerned to convey positivist principles to his students, Ferri founded in 1912 a special postgraduate institute within the law school at the University of Rome called the School of Applied Law and Criminal Justice (*Scuola d'applicazione giuridico-criminale*). Ferri had received a professorship at the University of Rome in

1906, thirteen years after being fired from the University of Pisa for his membership in the PSI. The institute had two purposes, the first to integrate criminal anthropology, criminal psychology, and legal medicine into the traditional law curriculum.[114] He recruited noted positivist criminologists like Sergio Sergi (son of the famous Giuseppe Sergi), Benigno di Tullio, Sante De Sanctis, Alfredo Niceforo, and Ottolenghi as his teaching staff for such subjects. Second, he sought to turn the school into a laboratory, where students would learn to examine criminals, dissect the corpses of victims of criminal homicide, and use instruments of criminal identification. Replicating procedures learned many decades earlier from Lombroso, he took students to prisons, criminal insane asylums, and juvenile reformatories to become familiar with the human "data" processed by the courts. He delighted his students and gained fame for his ability to walk into a prison and identify murderers based solely on physical features.[115] Ferri's specialty was a course entitled "The theoretical and practical examination of real trials," in which he replaced the abstract discussion of legal principles with a close reading of famous criminal cases, including those he had won. Although it has changed its name, the institute of criminal law in Rome still proudly displays Ferri's bust in its library.

Raffaele Garofalo

Born in 1852, Garofalo was of the same generation as Ferri and almost equally well known as a disciple of Lombroso.[116] In fact, the three were constantly invoked as the "glorious triad of the founders of that great movement for the reform of penal law known by the name of the Italian Positivist School."[117] Although Garofalo had some differences with Lombroso and Ferri, he accepted the label of criminal anthropologist and collaborated on both the *Archives* and *The Positivist School*.[118] He routinely visited prisons and insane asylums to familiarize himself with the physical and psychological traits of inmates. Like his positivist colleagues, he explicitly and vehemently criticized the Classical School of penology, referring to it as the "juridical school." He ridiculed traditional legal education for emphasizing abstract formulas like the maxims from the medieval Digest of Roman Law, knowledge that might be relevant to civil disputes, but useless for criminal trials.[119]

Garofalo's difference with Lombroso was more of emphasis than substance. He accepted Lombroso's contention that criminals exhibited higher rates of certain physical anomalies and that "all who deal with the physical study of the criminal are forced to the conclusion that he is a being apart."[120] Yet, since no single anomaly characterized all criminals, Garofalo was cautious in accepting the existence of one atavistic type, preferring instead to posit three "physiognomic types": the murderer, the violent criminal, and the thief.[121] As he recounted in his major work, *Criminology* (*Criminologia*): "In visiting prisons and penitentiaries and observing the inmates, I have frequently been able to distinguish those under sentence for homicide from others whose offense was theft or obtaining money by false pretenses, although I knew nothing of their previous history. On these occasions, as appears from my notes, I came to the wrong conclusion not more than seven or eight times out of a hundred."[122] Such a boast was similar to that of Ferri and reinforced the Lombrosian notion that physical anomalies were the key to criminality and that they could be easily "read" by any well-trained expert.

Unlike Lombroso, however, Garofalo was careful about defining crime, and his definition rested more on psychology than physiology. Garofalo faulted the Classical School for simply equating crime with any behavior that violated the law and instead substituted the idea of "natural crime." Beginning with the axiom that the two basic human sentiments are pity and probity, he defined natural crime as a violation of either of these sentiments. Pity condemned crimes against persons while probity condemned crimes against property. In other words, crime was any behavior that public opinion as a whole would censure, although this consensus would vary depending on the level of civilization obtained by each society. If criminals acted in a way consistent with the moral standards of savage society, their behavior would be considered reprehensible in nations with a higher stage of evolution.

Moral or psychological anomaly characterized all criminals and made them "deficient person[s] incompatible with society."[123] Garofalo rejected the category of occasional criminal and found Ferri's system of classifying criminals to be "without a scientific basis and [lacking] homogeneity and exactness."[124] Instead, he suggested a system based on a uniform criterion, that is, the degree to which each criminal is predisposed to crime. For Garofalo, authors of crimes against property (probity) were less dangerous than authors of crime against persons (pity), but no natural crime could be explained by environmental factors alone. Garofalo has been credited with making the measurement of "dangerousness" central to the positivist program of penal reform.

Like Ferri, Garofalo gave much of his attention to translating his positivist theory into practical reforms in criminal law. Punishment must be based on the recognition that "absence or weakness of the moral sense always carries with it the possibility of new crimes."[125] In the case of horrific offenses like murder, such behavior itself proved an individual's "capacity for crime"; in less extreme cases, a physical and psychological examination could measure this capacity. To protect itself, society must eliminate the socially unfit just as nature eliminates the biologically unfit through natural selection. Recidivism was the clearest sign that an individual was unable to adapt to society. In contrast to Ferri, who believed that many recidivists had learned their criminal trades in prison and were reformable rather than innately vicious, Garofalo pronounced recidivism to be overwhelmingly hereditary, warning that "recidivism is the rule, reform of the criminal is the exception."[126] He continued: "Without doubt, external causes such as tradition, prejudices, bad examples, climate, alcoholic liquors, and the like are not without an important influence. But in our opinion, there is always present in the instincts of the true criminal, a specific element which is congenital or inherited, or else acquired in early infancy and becomes inseparable from his psychic organism. There is no such thing as the 'casual' offender."[127] Prison reform, therefore, would never reduce rates of crime.

This rigid logic led Garofalo to a spirited defense of the death penalty. In a polemic with Ferri and most other socialists who applauded the Zanardelli Criminal

Code of 1889 for abolishing capital punishment, Garofalo found it indispensable for eliminating the most dangerous elements of society. He admitted that the "infliction of the death penalty would wear the aspect of intolerable cruelty" if criminality were a disease and criminals "suffering beings."[128] But Garofalo refused to adopt wholesale the "medical model" dear to Ferri and made a distinction between temporary periods of disease, like insanity, and the permanent character of moral anomaly. Disease disabled both the savage and the civilized, while behavior that was morally reprehensible in modern Europe was atavistic, that is, normal in lower stages of social evolution. The most heinous criminals deserved no pity and therefore no reprieve from the punishment of death.

For those with a lesser degree of psychic anomaly, Garofalo prescribed three other appropriate social reactions. "Complete elimination" through internment in isolated agricultural colonies, whether at home or abroad in imperial lands, was appropriate for dangerous criminals. Garofalo professed no illusions that this type of imprisonment would bring reform for,

if it be true that the moral instincts of mankind are the result of countless experiences of utility undergone by our ancestors throughout thousands of centuries, how can we suppose it possible for these experiences to be artificially reproduced in as short a space of time as the life of a human being? How, then are we to believe that the man whose instinct has not inherited the product of these experiences of past generations, can be artificially raised to the moral level of other men? And for that matter how can such experiences be possibly undergone by a prisoner deprived of all contact with the outside world?[129]

He did recommend indeterminate sentences in order that release could follow rare cases of rehabilitation, but in general he believed that "experimental pedagogy" could reform only children. Second, for the insane, alcoholics, and other individuals whose condition might be temporary, Garofalo recommended "partial elimination" in specialized hospitals until recovery. Finally, reparation through fines or community labor was sufficient punishment for those criminals with only mild psychic abnormality; in this manner the victim would be compensated, but the offender would not risk more serious depravation in the evil environment of the prison.

Garofalo's support for the death penalty symbolized a broader political rift with the dominant socialist sympathies of his colleagues in criminal anthropology. Unlike Lombroso and Ferri, Garofalo denied the compatibility of socialism and positivism, even denying that positivism was materialist. Instead, he turned the tables and charged proponents of the Classical School with materialism since "it is they who have made a tariff of crimes, and are responsible for a system of laws in which the objective fact is alone considered and the nature of the crime counts for nothing. It is they who have materialized criminal law. The positivism that we advocate, on the contrary, is purely a question of means. It signifies no philosophic system but simply the experimental method."[130] While Garofalo was not convincing in his denial that the scientific method is materialist, he was clearly trying to combat the identification of criminal anthropology with the political Left. He characterized his own positivism as spiritual rather than materialist in its focus on moral anomaly as the determining factor in crime. And in contrast to the general anti-clericalism of Lombroso and Ferri, Garofalo pronounced religion to be "a moralizing force which an enlightened government would do well to encourage and in no event can afford to impede."[131]

Garofalo denied capitalism caused crime, even writing a polemical pamphlet entitled *The Socialist Superstition* in 1895 to refute Ferri. His purpose was "to show how erroneous is the recent assertion that natural evolution leads to collectivism and ... to prove that the theory of collectivism is neither scientific nor logical."[132] Claiming that socialists "have no right to speak in the name of positivism," he defined positivism sparely as the application of the experimental method and Darwin's theory to society.[133] According to Garofalo, the "facts" of history demonstrated that social evolution was leading to increased individual liberty, based on the ownership of private property, rather than to socialism. Admitting that truely defenseless groups in society—like abandoned babies and the elderly—should be protected by the state from the rigors of capitalism, Garofalo nevertheless labeled this view as Christian rather than socialist. Finally, while granting Ferri's point that the struggle for existence was becoming increasingly less physical and more intellectual, he denied that men would ever stop competing for property and women to satisfy their basic economic and sexual needs. By proposing a future socialist society where "miraculously" all material needs would be met, socialists were "depriving Darwin's law of its character as a general principle and destroying precisely that part of it which is fundamental."[134] By such arguments, Garofalo hoped "to tear the *mask of science* brusquely off the socialists."[135] Lacking the humanitarian strain apparent in Lombroso and Ferri, Garofalo denigrated the lower classes as an "uneducated and howling crowd" not fit to take over power from the bourgeoisie, whose virtues included "moderation, gentleness, constancy, prudence, good manners, respect for ability, esteem for intelligence, [and] love of art and literature."[136]

Because of his conservatism, Garofalo's relations with Lombroso and Ferri became strained and his collaboration on the *Archives* and *The Positivist School* became increasingly rare. Rather than weakening the Positivist School, however, Garofalo's conservatism widened its appeal to lawyers and politicians outside of the PSI. His influence reached into high social circles, as he came from a noble family and was a member of aristocratic bodies such as the Royal Order of the Crown of Italy, the Heraldic Council, and the Order of Saint Maurice. Despite his political differences with Lombroso and Ferri, he remained a committed positivist throughout his long life and dedicated himself to applying his scientific insights to the Italian criminal justice system. He had an opportunity to do so in his various positions as lawyer, prosecutor, and judge. As a law professor at the University of Naples, he influenced several generations of students. Finally, he also pursued a political career, serving as a noble appointee to the Senate from 1909 to his death in 1934. Unlike many senators who treated their honorific seats in the upper chamber with little seriousness, Garofalo used his as a platform for promoting legal changes consistent with his positivist philosophy.

CRITICS

The hegemony of Lombroso and his circle over the new field of criminology did not go uncontested. Although detractors were not well organized, they fell into two general camps: first, those who advanced a sociological explanation for crime and, second, those who continued to defend the doctrine of free will and trace the etiology of crime to immorality. The first group defined its method as broadly positivist, that is, using experimental methods to measure the material causes of crime. In common with most criminal anthropologists, its members also tended to identify with the political Left. In contrast, the second group remained idealist, using philosophy or religion as the basis for its legal prescriptions. Under this broad rubric fell both the liberal heirs of Beccaria and conservative defenders of Catholicism.

The groundwork for the sociological critique was laid by Turati in a long essay entitled "Crime and the Social Question." First serialized in 1882 in the journal *La Plebe*, it was reissued three times as a short pamphlet.[137] This essay represented the thinking of a youthful Turati who considered himself a member of the positivist camp. Like many socialists of his generation, Turati valued positivism as "the only intellectual refuge today" for those trying to combat traditional idealism and nostalgia for absolutes.[138] He praised Ardigò, the teacher of Ferri and an early and important apostle of positivism, as "the greatest philosophical genius of contemporary Italy."[139] Like Ferri, he pronounced the doctrine of free will to be merely "the fable of silly women" and ridiculed the attempts of the Classical School to weigh the moral responsibility of each criminal.[140] To Beccaria he preferred Lombroso, Garofalo, and especially Ferri, a group seeking to isolate the material factors that pushed certain individuals to break the law. He agreed that criminals were not morally responsible for their acts and should receive penal substitutes, rather than prison, when appropriate.

Despite these areas of broad agreement, Turati treated the positivist triumverate to a sharp critique. While concurring fully with the experimental method, he differed with their emphasis on the atavistic nature of crime. Instead, he classified a large majority of criminals as either habitual or occasional. In this way, he downgraded biology while elevating social conditions as the overwhelming cause of lawbreaking. The crucial factor in the equation was class, since "the rich man has a hundred legal means to satisfy his most pressing needs; for the poor, crime often offers the only open and easy way."[141] Never a vulgar materialist, Turati admitted that "the social question is not all related to the stomach."[142] Instead, "*poverty* means lack of *education* in the widest sense of the word. It means ignorance of the rules of social intercourse, ineptness in conforming to individual interests, bad examples, honesty betrayed, weak nerves, excitability of base passions, inability to reflect, [and] permanent deficiency in satisfying vital needs."[143] The inequity of the class system denied the poor both "their physical bread and their moral bread."[144]

Turati's analysis led him to conclude that "bourgeois Society is the biggest criminal and is the unpunished accomplice to the misdeeds that it coldly punishes."[145] Already repressed by poverty and ignorance, the poor were not morally responsible for their acts and did not deserve further punishment except in extreme cases. Referring to Ferri's phrase, Turati concluded that "the real penal substitute" was "the egalitarian diffusion . . . of wealth and education, of the joys of love and of thought."[146] Such a social transformation would reduce crime by two-thirds and open the way for a gradual elimination of all crime in a future socialist society.

These conclusions marked Turati as more optimistic than Ferri, who foresaw the perpetual continuation of atavistic crime even in a future socialist society. Yet both worked within a positivist framework, accepting Darwin's struggle for existence as applicable to both individuals and classes in human society. Like Ferri, Turati compared crime to a disease whose causes, like those of other natural phenomena, could be measured and would become predictable as criminology refined its methods. For Turati, those causes were overwhelmingly environmental, leading him to conclude that "the Socialist ideal in criminal matters is clear: establish a social order where crime is no longer necessary nor useful."[147]

With "Crime and the Social Question," Turati initiated an interchange with criminal anthropologists, and especially Ferri, that would continue for several decades. Initially, their quarrel remained within the positivist family, as Turati continued to be listed as a contributor on the masthead of the Archives until 1892. After that, Turati's criticism of Ferri—expressed in the pages of Critica sociale, the intellectual socialist weekly that he founded in 1891 with Anna Kuliscioff—became more acidic. He and Ferri found themselves in rival factions of the PSI, as Turati supported reformism within a democratic framework against Ferri's increasing fervor for revolution. Yet after his pamphlet of 1882, Turati never wrote another major piece on crime and passed the mantle of sociological criminology to a political colleague, Napoleone Colajanni.

Colajanni's initial task was to reply to Ferri's Socialism and Crime, published as a response to Turati's series of articles in La Plebe. That Ferri replied so quickly demonstrates the importance of Turati's opinion within the intellectual community even as early as the 1880s. At the request of Turati, Colajanni agreed to take up the fight, resulting in a book called Socialism that appeared in 1884.[148] In this work, he reviewed the positions of Turati and Ferri, beginning with their common preference for positivist over classical criminology and their enthusiasm for the theory of evolution. Admitting that Ferri had not been given a fair reading by the socialist Left, Colajanni nevertheless endorsed Turati's emphasis on the sociological causes of crime. In fact, he downgraded the role of biology even further by surmising that the struggle for existence itself would gradually wither away as altruism replaced egoism as the motor of evolution. If individual competition characterized the animal world, collectivism represented the more advanced instinct of human society. Even Turati judged this conclusion a bit rash, arguing that the tension between egoism and altruism was the essence of social life. He counseled in a letter to Colajanni "that the issue is not to *suppress* competition but to render it *legal, just, beneficial, contractual, [and] on equal grounds.*"[149]

Unlike Turati, Colajanni retained an interest in criminology, perhaps because of its relation to his training as a physician and career as professor of statistics at the Universities of Catania, Palermo, and Naples. Thus, in 1889, he published a more detailed and scientific critique of criminal anthropology in his two-volume *Criminal Sociology*. As in his earlier work, he opened with praise for his adversaries, pointing to their fame outside Italy. But he then systematically picked apart the methodology and premises of their research. From a scientific point of view, he found their data meager and criticized the absence of any series of statistics tracing the same behavior over time. Even when colleagues in Lombroso's circle studied the same phenomena, they collected their data in such different ways that the resulting tables were not comparable. Control groups were eschewed or so small as to be useless. And data were not classified by class, a variable that was probably more useful than biology in explaining uniformities among criminals.

Worse than these methodological flaws, however, were the flaws in positivist theory. Most fundamentally, Colajanni pointed out that "the greatest uncertainty" still existed about the relation between "the physical and the moral; organs and their function; [and] the brain, psyche and moral character."[150] Research, for example, had established no correlation between brain size and intelligence, a fundamental premise of criminal anthropology. For Colajanni, a scientific criminology based on such flimsy presuppositions "recalled strongly the Biblical parable about the blind leading the blind."[151] Criminal anthropologists had failed to find "even *one* trait that is absolutely *exclusive* . . . to delinquents."[152] Instead, all atavisms appeared in "normal" as well as "deviant" individuals, so that no one physical trait constituted a marker of criminality.

Furthermore, Colajanni pointed out that correlation did not equal causation: "Such is the case of the coexistence of *crime* and of *pathological characteristics* in an indigent person: the former and the latter probably both derive from one unique cause, *poverty*."[153] Like Turati, he chided criminal anthropologists for displaying "a supreme disdain" for the importance of social factors leading to delinquency.[154] Economic deprivation explained the preponderance of criminality among members of the lower classes, all of whom tended to exhibit supposedly atavistic characteristics like insensitivity. Such physical traits, however, were not the cause of crime but rather the result of lives filled with misery and hardships. Even after Colajanni distanced himself from socialism in the 1890s, he continued to champion the rights of the poor as a Republican member of parliament, representing his native Sicily.

The second group of opponents of criminal anthropology differed from the sociological approach in championing the doctrine of free will. Most active and effective in this category were the heirs of Beccaria, prominent jurists like Enrico Pessina and Lucchini who carried on the eighteenth-century tradition of fitting punishment to the crime rather than the criminal. Like proponents of the Classical School throughout Europe, Pessina and Lucchini had modified the extreme character of the Enlightenment doctrine of free will, admitting that certain conditions, like insanity, prevented individuals from exercising moral choice. But in a spirited defense led by Lucchini's journal, the *Rivista penale*, they countered the positivist attempts to redefine all crime as biologically or environmentally determined.[155] As liberals, they were also troubled by the positivist doctrine of "social defense," which seemed to define the purpose of law as the defense of the state. Instead, they insisted on the

Beccarian tradition of the law as a tool to defend individual rights from authoritarianism of the sovereign, be it monarchy or parliament.[156]

A quite different defense of free will came from the Catholic Church, a firm opponent of criminal anthropology. For the most part, Catholic critics did not engage the details of the positivist argument, but issued blanket condemnations of materialism and determinism as incompatible with religious spiritualism. An exception was Agostino Gemelli, a Franciscan trained in medicine, professor of psychology, and founder of the Catholic University of Milan. In a series of books beginning in 1907, Gemelli urged his co-religionists to answer specifically the claims of criminal anthropology that had gained such popular acclaim. He warned that the school of Lombroso had "a large number of followers scattered throughout the courts, the universities, the high schools, the insane asylums, the prisons and that the criteria proposed by them for judging the cause of crime are becoming in Italy the practical criteria for evaluating moral responsibility, for educating youth, for guiding society toward civil progress."[157] Instead of condemning all science, Catholics must distinguish between good and bad science and use the former to disprove positivism.

In his own effort to do so, Gemelli conceded that criminal anthropology had several merits, such as focusing attention on the psychology of criminals and advocating that the criminally insane be sent to asylums rather than prisons. Yet its methods had been faulty and its claims confusing and overblown. Much of his criticism echoed Colajanni, although he explicitly distinguished himself from the sociological school because of its environmental determinism. He faulted Lombroso and his colleagues for relying on small samples; limiting control groups to soldiers, who were not necessarily "morally normal"; and failing to differentiate among criminals according to sex, age, and profession. Their use of statistics was simplistic, ignoring the new biometrics pioneered by Francis Galton and Karl Pearson. Also outmoded were their theories, since he claimed that Haeckel's biogenetic theory of recapitulation had been disproved, and Mendel had shown that acquired characteristics cannot be inherited.

Having blamed at different times atavism, degeneration, epilepsy, and moral insanity for crime, Lombroso, according to Gemelli, had brought confusion rather than clarity to the criminological debate. Agreeing that each of these factors might motivate the criminal behavior of a small number of individuals, Gemelli promoted a more complex investigation of the etiology of crime, including sociological and especially psychological factors. But he warned against substituting psychological for biological determinism, arguing that "character is formed through the exercise of individual will" rather than mechanically inherited.[158] He claimed that his own psychological studies had shown that heredity was not "fatal," since "its influence can be paralyzed or at least attenuated by a broad education and a resolute will."[159] He thus asserted that science had validated the existence of free will and that Catholics could happily continue to preach individual responsibility without being labeled "backward and ignorant souls."[160]

CONCLUSION

The criminal anthropology of Lombroso, Ferri, and Garofalo was attacked not only within Italy, but also by some foreign criminologists, most particularly the French. The most important debates occurred at the International Congresses of Criminal Anthropology, initiated by the Italians in Rome in 1885. At this first meeting, Lombroso's theory of atavism reigned virtually uncontested as the European consensus on the etiology of crime. By the second congress of 1889 in Paris, however, the French counterattacked with an alternative explanation for crime based on environmental factors. The offensive was led by the physician Alexandre Lacassagne, anthropologists Léonce Manouvrier and Paul Topinard, and the sociologist Gabriel Tarde. After pointing out many methodological weaknesses in the research of Italian positivists, they proposed a general approach that blamed crime on poverty, vicious parents, and alcoholism more than heredity. Although this "sociological" approach somewhat resembled that of Turati and Colajanni, the "French School" was not uniformly socialist or even positivist. As Robert Nye has convincingly argued, it sought to construct a theory that was flexible enough to meld with the continuing emphasis of the French legal community on free will.[161] In this way, the French cleverly avoided the kind of irreparable split with the Classical School that had occurred in Italy and was hindering the campaign of criminal anthropologists to insert their theories into legal reforms.

In response to this aggressive French maneuver, the Italians forgot their theoretical differences and closed ranks at the Paris meeting. They demanded that a special commission compare one hundred criminals to a control group of equal size and count the number of atavisms possessed by each. The Italians trusted that the results, to be reported at the next international congress scheduled for Brussels in 1892, would vindicate through empirical data their belief in biological determinism. In the intervening years between the second and third congresses, however, the commission dropped the study and, in response, the Italians refused to appear in Brussels. But they rejoined future congresses, where jockeying continued between France and Italy, clearly fueled by nationalist sentiment.

Thus, the tripartite split among the positivist, classical, and sociological schools was replicated within Europe. In all countries, most lawyers, prosecutors, and judges remained faithful to the classical doctrines of free will and moral retribution. Through the leadership of the French, the sociological approach won more adherents in Europe as a whole than in Italy. It offered an important alternative to criminal anthropology for legal doctors, anthropologists, and sociologists who found classical doctrines old-fashioned and ineffective. Postivist criminology, while defeated in France, had champions in other European nations such as Hans Kurella in Germany, and Pauline Tarnowski in Russia.[162] Through his compendium *The Criminal*, Havelock Ellis was most responsible for introducing Lombroso to the English-speaking world.[163] His work seems to have had less impact on England than the United States, where criminal anthropology found followers like Arthur Mac-

Donald, August Drahms, and W. Duncan McKim.[164] Italian positivists also found receptive audiences in Spain, Portugal, and Latin America.

Despite some setbacks in the international arena, positivist criminology developed steadily as a well-respected and popular discipline in Italy through the 1880s and 1890s. One mark of its health was the growing number of disciples who collaborated with Lombroso. With the exception of the anthropologist Giuseppe Sergi, who was born in 1841, these disciples were decidedly younger than Lombroso, attesting to the continuing attraction of his personality and ideas on students in a variety of fields. The second generation of positivist criminologists, born between 1852 and 1869, included not only Ferri and Garofalo, but also Ottolenghi and Mario Carrara trained in legal medicine, Eugenio Florian, Scipio Sighele, and Adolfo Zerboglio trained in law, and De Sanctis trained in psychiatry. The fascination of criminal anthropology stretched even into a third generation of men like the sociologists Niceforo and Ferrero and professors of clinical medicine, Giacinto Viola and Nicola Pende. Along with Lombroso, this large group of disciples not only trained other students but also carried their positivist convictions into their careers in the courts, prisons, insane asylums, reformatories, and other public institutions. Criminal anthropology was not confined to the ivory tower.

Thus, it would be wrong to identify positivist criminology with only one figure, Lombroso, or even with the triad Lombroso–Ferri–Garofalo, since it constituted a much broader intellectual and professional movement. The emphasis of many historians and criminologists solely on Lombroso has minimized the impact of a movement that held the allegiance of doctors, lawyers, psychiatrists, anthropologists, and sociologists spread throughout Italy. The *Archives* tied together this disparate group, who were dedicated to, in the words of the first issue, pursuing that "mirage in the desert, of a complete reform of the penal system and psychiatry."[165] Published in 1880, this initial issue listed sixty-eight regular contributors on the title page, half specializing in law and half in psychiatry. Over a fifth were from other European countries, including Germany, Austria, Hungary, and even France. Ten years later, the list of contributors had risen to 107, with Russia now included. And these names were only the most prestigious, for many articles and book reviews were penned by additional collaborators. As might be expected, the *Archives* constituted a forum not only for new empirical research but also for the practical application of this research through proposed legislation.

In accordance with their increasing stature within the intellectual elite, positivist criminologists became frequent contributors to journals outside the specialized field of criminal justice. They reached a middle-class audience through articles in *Nuova antologia,* the leading digest of literary, political, and social analysis. During the period 1899 through 1901, the *Nuova antologia* featured up to three articles yearly by Lombroso as well as contributions by Ferri, Garofalo, Sergi, and De Sanctis. Criminal anthropologists also found a welcome outlet for their views in the leading socialist publications like *Critica sociale* and *Avanti!*. Despite the editorship by Turati and Kuliscioff, neither sympathetic to theories of biological determinism, *Critica sociale* welcomed articles by many socialist positivists like Lombroso, Ferri,

Zerboglio, Ferrero, and Niceforo. Their books received prompt, respectful, and often enthusiastic reviews. The socialist daily, *Avanti!*, not only hosted articles by positivists, but made their major works available in special series aimed at workers. For example, the series in "Philosophy, biology, and criminology" included five books authored by Lombroso as late as 1914, five years after his death.[166]

By 1890, the "triad" of Lombroso, Ferri, and Garofalo had published the key texts for the study of criminal man. Despite attacks by the French at international congresses, criminal anthropology continued to exhibit "exuberant vitality," according to an enthusiastic commentator in *Critica sociale*.[167] The crime rate appeared to be rising, and public opinion demanded remedies. Positivist criminologists were only too eager to comply. Using their studies of men as a yardstick, they now turned their attention to other seemingly troublesome groups in society: women, children, and dark-skinned Southerners.

NOTES

1. This was one of several cases described by Salvatore Maggiulli, a student of Salvatore Ottolenghi's, in "Clinica Criminale: Lezioni fatta dal Prof. Ottolenghi agli Alunni Delegati di P.S. nel 9 corso di Polizia Scientifica," *Bolletino della Scuola di Polizia Scientifica* (hereafter *Boll. SPS*), v. 2 (1911), pp. 74–76.

2. With unification, the Italian state reversed the policy of the old regime and recognized only civil marriages. Many Italians followed the traditional pattern and married only in Church, causing a temporary but steep rise in "concubinage" and "illegitimacy." Under the Concordat of 1929 between Mussolini and the Catholic Church, religious marriage gained equal legal footing with civil marriage.

3. *Boll. SPS*, v. 2 (1911), p. 75.

4. Ibid.

5. Ibid., p. 76.

6. The Kingdom of Italy was proclaimed in 1861, but Venice was not annexed until 1866 and Rome until 1871.

7. Filippo Turati, "Il delitto e la questione sociale," reprinted in Luigi Cortesi, ed., *Turati giovane: Scapigliatura, positivismo, marxismo* (Milan: Ed. *Avanti!*, 1962), p. 141. Vicenzo Gioberti's famous tract promoting the *risorgimento* was titled *On the Moral and Civil Primacy of the Italians*.

8. Different types of official statistics can only approximate the "dark figure" of real crime, and each has its flaws. Most scholars prefer to rely on the numbers of complaints to police or the number of arrests, because they precede the intervention of the courts. On the other hand, these numbers at the "front end" of the process also include many unverifiable crimes and innocent defendants. Homicide statistics tend to be more accurate than those for minor crimes, because bodies are difficult to hide. Many thefts go unreported while statistics for "victimless" crimes like prostitution and drug use are almost worthless.

9. Augusto Bosco, *La delinquenza in vari stati d'Europa* (Rome: R. Accademia dei Lincei, 1903), p. 216.

10. The original quote comes from Angelo Messedaglia in 1865 and is repeated approvingly in Filippo Virgili, "La criminalità italiana secondo le ultime statistiche penali e carcerarie" Pt. 1, *Scuola positiva*, v. 21 (1911), p. 433.

11. The phrase is from Bosco, *La delinquenza*, p. 8. For the general development of governmental statistics in Italy, see Silvana Patriarca, *Numbers and Nationhood: Writing Statistics in Nineteenth-Century Italy* (New York: Cambridge University Press, 1996).

12. Earlier volumes of criminal statistics do exist, but they are chronologically discontinuous and employed no standard method of data collection.

13. These volumes were entitled *Statistica giudiziaria penale* (Statistics of the Criminal Courts) and compiled by the *Direzione Generale della Statistica* (Division of Statistics) in the Ministry of Agriculture, Industry and Commerce from 1880 until 1908 and by the *Ufficio per la Statistica Giudiziaria* (Office of Judicial Statistics) of the Ministry of Justice beginning in 1909. For the history of criminal statistics in Italy, see Virgili, "La criminalità," Pt. 1 (1911), pp. 435–446; and Gaetano Zingali, *La statistica della criminalità: Studio teorico* (Bologna: Il Seminario Giuridico, 1916), pp. 37–38. Virgili uses the term "administrative" to refer to statistics of the courts.

14. During the 1890s, these volumes were entitled *Notizie complementari alle statistiche giudiziarie penali* (Appendices to the Statistics of the Criminal Courts). After a gap in publication between 1901 and 1905, they resumed under the title *Statistica della criminalità* (*Criminal Statistics*).

15. Rates are computed based on the raw numbers in ISTAT, *Sommario di statistiche storiche italiane, 1861–1955* (Rome: Istituto Poligrafico dello Stato, 1958), p. 91. These are rates of crimes adjudicated by all levels of Italian courts; I have interpolated between censuses to get yearly totals for population.

16. Rates tabulated from data in ISTAT, *Somm. stat. storiche* (1958), pp. 90–91.

17. Ibid., pp. 90–91.

18. Ibid. Sociologists and historians are just beginning to study this decline in homicide. See Dario Melossi, "Andamento economico, incarcerazione, omicidi e allarme sociale in Italia: 1863–1994" in *Storia D'Italia*, Annali n. 12 [*La criminalità*, ed. Luciano Violante] (Turin: Einaudi, 1997), pp. 35–62, and "Omicidi, economia, e tassi di incarcerazione in Italia dall'Unità ad oggi," *Polis*, v. 12, n. 3 (Dec., 1998), pp. 415–35; and Daniele Boschi, "Homicide and Knife Fighting in Rome, 1845–1914," in Pieter Spierenburg, ed., *Men and Violence* (Columbus: Ohio State University Press, 1998), pp. 128–58.

19. Homicide rates (including infanticide) dropped from 1.7 per 10,000 population in 1881 to .9 in 1913; they dropped even below .8 in 1906 and 1907, according to ISTAT, *Somm. stat. storiche*, p. 92. For a detailed analysis of the drop in homicide, see Alfredo Spallanzi, *Sull'omidico in Italia dal 1881 al 1911* (Rome: Ludovico Cecchini, 1916).

20. Assault increased from 14.9/10,000 in 1881 to 30.2 in 1888; after that it oscillated between 25 and 30 until 1914. Based on ISTAT, *Somm. stat. storiche*, p. 92.

21. From 26.5 per 10,000 in 1881, rates of theft passed 30/10,000 by 1888 and 40/10,000 by 1897. They remained in the high thirties and low forties until a sharp rise during the war. Based on ISTAT, *Somm. stat. storiche*, p. 92.

22. Luigi Lucchini, *La criminalità in Italia* (Venice: M. Fontana, 1884), p. 11.

23. See, for example, Virgili's rabid attack on Lucchini in "La criminalità," Pt. 2, v. 22 (1912) pp. 565–575.

24. Historians of crime have adopted the phrase "moral panic" to indicate a wave of social anxiety not accompanied by a real rise in crime.

25. Agopik Manoukian, "La rappresentazione statistica dei vincoli familiari," in Manoukian, *I vincoli familiari in Italia: Dal secolo XI al secolo XX* (Bologna: Il Mulino, 1983), p. 440.

26. Ufficio del Censimento, *Censimento della popolazione del Regno d'Italia al 10 giugno 1911*, vol. 1, pp. 55, 143, 154, 187, 194, 218, 264, 305, 320.

27. Manoukian, "La rappresentazione statistica," p. 447.

28. Ibid., p. 446.

29. Spencer Di Scala, *Italy: From Revolution to Republic, 1700 to the Present* (Boulder, Colo.: Westview, 1995), p. 141.

30. At the completion of unification in 1871, 60 percent of the population worked in agriculture. See Martin Clark, *Modern Italy, 1871–1982* (New York: Longman, 1984), p. 12.

31. Quoted in Clark, *Modern Italy*, p. 30.

32. For the biography of Beccaria, see Marcello Maestro, *Cesare Beccaria and the Origins of Penal Reform* (Philadelphia: Temple University Press, 1973) and Elio Monachesi, "Cesare Beccaria and the Origins of Penal Reform," in *Pioneers in Criminology*, ed. Mannheim, pp. 36–49.

33. Cesare Beccaria, *On Crimes and Punishments* (Indianapolis: Hackett, 1986), p. 81. The original title in Italian is *Dei delitti e delle pene*.

34. Beccaria is vague as to the constitution of this legislature.

35. Beccaria, *On Crimes*, p. 15.

36. Ibid., p. 16.

37. Ibid.

38. Contemporary criminologists call these primary and secondary deterrence, respectively.

39. Beccaria, *On Crimes*, p. 46.

40. Ibid., p. 29.

41. Ibid., p. 51.

42. Ibid., p. 50.

43. Ibid., p. 13.

44. Ibid., p. 79.

45. Piers Beirnes has documented the influence on Beccaria of the Scottish school of eighteenth-century philosophy, a school whose determinism is at odds with the general image of *On Crimes and Punishments* as a testament to free will in *Inventing Criminology*. Graeme Newman and Pietro Marongiu question the "myth" that Beccaria's ideas were new, coherent, or particularly influential on subsequent legal reforms in "Penological Reform and the Myth of Beccaria," *Criminology*, v. 28, n. 2 (May, 1990), pp. 325–46. While I find their discussion of why Beccaria has been mythologized to be persuasive, many of their other targets are straw men. It has long been known, for example, that the Verri brothers had a strong influence on Beccaria and no serious historian believes that books alone, like *On Crimes and Punishments*, bring about radical social change.

46. Eugenio Garin, "Il positivismo italiano alla fine del secolo XIX fra metodo e concezione del mondo," *Giornale critica della filosofia italiana*, Series 5, vol. 1 (Jan.–Dec., 1980), p. 4. A similar point is made by Giovanni Landucci, *Darwinismo a Firenze: Tra scienza e ideologia (1860–1900)* (Florence: Leo S. Olschki, 1977), p. 21, and Giuseppe Montalenti, "Comment a été accueillie en Italie la révolution darwinienne," in Yvette Conroy, ed., *De darwin au darwinisme: Science et idéologie* (Paris: J. Vrin, 1983), p. 20.

47. Comte's major works were *Positive Philosophy* (1830–1842) and *Positive Polity* (1851–1854).

48. Landucci, *Darwinismo*, p. 12; *Descent of Man*, published in 1871, was translated into Italian in 1882. For the reception of Darwin in Italy, see also Montalenti, "Comment a été

accueillie en Italie," and Pietro Corsi and Paul J. Weindling, "Darwinism in Germany, France and Italy," in David Kohn, ed., *The Darwinian Heritage* (Princeton: Princeton University Press, 1985), pp. 683–729.

49. Haeckel's major work is *Generelle Morphologie der Organismen* (Berlin, 1866).

50. Wolfgang, "Lombroso," p. 170.

51. Ibid., p. 171.

52. Cesare Lombroso, *Criminal Man summarised by* G. *Lombroso Ferrero* (New York: Putnam's, 1911), pp. 6–7.

53. Ibid., p. 6.

54. Cited in Villa, *Il deviante*, p. 176.

55. Villa, *Il deviante*, pp. 148–49.

56. For an early review of writers who inspired Lombroso, see Giuseppe Antonini, *I precursori di C. Lombroso* (Turin: Bocca, 1900); Villa also carefully traces Lombroso's precursors in *Il deviante*. In English, see the polemic against the "myth" that Lombroso founded scientific criminology by Alfred Lindesmith and Yale Levin, "The Lombrosian Myth in Criminology," *American Journal of Sociology*, v. 42, n. 5 (March, 1937), pp. 653–71.

57. Villa, *Il deviante*, pp. 92–102; in honor of Paolo Marzolo, Lombroso named his firstborn child Paola Marzola Lombroso.

58. The five editions of *L'uomo delinquente* appeared in 1876 (256 pages); 1878 (746 pages); 1884 (610 pages); 1889 (1241 pages in two volumes); and 1896 (1903 pages in three volumes plus a volume of tables). None of these editions was ever translated into English; the truncated version of *Criminal Man* available in English was compiled by Lombroso's daughter, Gina, and published in 1911 after his death. *Crime, Its Causes and Remedies*, was a compendium of his ideas written late in life for foreign readers (published first in French in 1899 and later in English in 1911). It is therefore not possible for English-language readers to follow the development of Lombroso's ideas through the various editions of his major work, *Criminal Man*.

59. *The Female Offender* was translated into English as early as 1895, but in a severe abridgement of the Italian original.

60. A good bibliography of books by Lombroso can be found in Villa, *Il deviante*, pp. 283–88. Excerpts from some of his less well-known writings are now available in Cesare Lombroso, *Delitto, genio, follia: Scritti scelti*, eds. Delia Frigessi, Ferruccio Giacanelli, and Luisa Mangoni (Turin: Bollati Boringhieri, 1995).

61. Founded as the *Archivio di psichiatria, antropologia criminale e scienze penali* (hereafter *Archivio*) the journal revised its name several times, significantly replacing "penal sciences" with "legal medicine" after 1904.

62. For example, see C. Lombroso, "Criminal Anthropology: Its Origin and Application," *Forum*, v. 20 (1895–96), p. 34. This article is one of only a few writings directed by Lombroso to an American audience.

63. Villa identifies its first use in an article by Ferri in the *Archivio*, v. 1 (1880), p. 369.

64. C. Lombroso, *L'uomo delinquente*, 2nd ed. (Turin: Bocca, 1878), p. 133.

65. C. Lombroso, *L'uomo delinquente*, 5th ed. (Turin: Bocca, 1896–97), v. 2, p. 415.

66. Ibid., p. 445.

67. Ibid., p. 470.

68. The phrase is Villa's; see *Il deviante*, p. 200.

69. C. Lombroso, *L'uomo delinquente*, 5th ed., v. 2, p. 491.

70. C. Lombroso, *L'uomo delinquente*, 1st ed (Milan: Hoepli, 1876), p. 120.

71. In the fifth edition of *Criminal Man*, Lombroso holds that 40 percent of all criminals are "born criminals" (v. 1, p. vi); two years later, *Crime: Its Causes and Remedies* includes the lower figure of 33 percent.

72. C. Lombroso, *L'uomo delinquente*, 1st ed., p. 13.

73. Ibid., p. 67.

74. Ibid., p. 54.

75. Ibid., p. 108.

76. C. Lombroso, *L'uomo delinquente*, 5th ed., v. 2, p. 55.

77. Ibid., p. 189.

78. C. Lombroso, *L'uomo delinquente*, 1st ed., p. 60.

79. C. Lombroso, *L'uomo delinquente*, 5th ed., v. 3, p. 587.

80. Ibid.

81. C. Lombroso, *L'uomo delinquente*, 5th ed., v. 3, pp. 582–83.

82. Ibid., p. 583.

83. Bulferetti, *Cesare Lombroso*, pp. 361, 385.

84. Ibid., p. 426.

85. Delfina Dolza, *Essere figlie*, p. 52.

86. Quoted in Dolza, *Essere figlie*, p. 65.

87. Villa, *Il deviante*, p. 206.

88. Quoted in Dolza, *Essere figlie*, pp. 53–54.

89. Stephen Jay Gould has a useful discussion of these flaws in his book, *The Mismeasure of Man* (New York: Norton, 1981), pp. 123–42.

90. C. Lombroso, "Criminal Anthropology," pp. 40–41.

91. Ibid., p. 38.

92. Villa, *Il deviante*, pp. 161, 168–69.

93. Baima Bollone devotes a chapter to the Museum in *Cesare Lombroso*, pp. 143–63. For photographs of selected objects in the museum, see Giorgio Colombo, *La scienza infelice: Il museo di antropologia criminale di Cesare Lombroso* (Turin: Boringhieri, 1975) and the final section of Umberto Levra, ed., *La scienza e la colpa. Crimini, criminali, criminologi: Un volto dell'Ottocento* (Milan: Electa, 1985).

94. The thesis, entitled "L'imputabilità e la negazione del libero arbitrio," was published in 1881 by Zanichelli of Bologna. For Ferri's biography, see entries in the *Enciclopedia italiana di scienze, lettere ed arti* (Rome: Istituto Giovanni Treccani), 1936, vol. 15, p. 64; Engenio Florian, Alfredo Niceforo and Nicola Pende, eds., *Dizionario di criminologia* (Milan: Francesco Vallardi, 1943), v. 1, pp. 361–65; and Franco Andreucci and Tommaso Detti, eds., *Il movimento operaio italiano: Dizionario biografico, 1853–1943* (Rome: Riuniti, 1978), v. 2, pp. 342–48. In English, see Thorsten's Sellin's chapter on Ferri in Mannheim, *Pioneers of Criminology*, pp. 277–300. A bibliography of his principle writings can be found in the appendix of *Enrico Ferri: Maestro della scienza criminologica* (Milan: Bocca, 1941), pp. 261–70.

95. Ferri, *The Positivist School of Criminology: Three Lectures* (Chicago: Charles H. Kerr, 1913), pp. 91–92.

96. Ibid., p. 71.

97. Ibid.

98. Ibid., p. 75.

99. Ibid., p. 77.

100. Ibid., p. 64.

101. Ibid., p. 98.

102. Ibid., p. 99.

103. Ferri, *Socialismo e criminalità: Appunti* (Turin: Bocca, 1883).

104. Ferri, *Socialism and Modern Science (Darwin–Spencer–Marx)* (New York: International Library, 1900), pp. 96–97. This was a translation of *Socialismo e scienza positiva (Darwin, Spencer, Marx)*, published six years earlier.

105. Ferri, *Socialism*, p. 164.

106. Ferri, *Positivismo*, p. 327.

107. Ferri, *Socialism*, p. 43.

108. Andreucci and Detti, *Dizionario biografico*, v. 2, p. 346, quoting a contemporary of Ferri, A. Angiolini.

109. Ibid.

110. See *Critica sociale* for the "Saluto" to *Scuola positiva* in vol. 1 (1891), p. 138; reviews of *Sociologia Criminale* in vol. 2 (1892), pp. 206–207 and *L'omicidio nell antropologia criminale*, vol. 4 (1894), pp. 191–92; and Ferri's article entitled "La scienza e la vita nel secolo XIX," vol. 7 (1897), pp. 327; 347–49.

111. The first two editions were entitled *I nuovi orizzonti del diritto e della procedura penale* and appeared in 1881 and 1884; the third edition, entitled *Sociologia criminale* appeared in 1892 followed by the fourth in 1900 and the fifth in 1929–30. It was translated into Spanish in 1887, Russian in 1889, French in 1893, German in 1896, English in 1917, and Japanese in 1923. See "Dati bio-bibliografici" in *Enrico Ferri: Maestro*, pp. 261–70.

112. On Ferri as an orator, see Scipio Sighele, "Ferri Oratore" in *Enrico Ferri: Maestro*, pp. 161–71. Ferri was invited twice to give a tour of lectures in Latin America, in 1908 and 1910; he also gave courses at the University of Brussels (1885–1903) and the *École des hautes études* in Paris (1889–1901).

113. Ferri, *Difese penali, studi di giurisprudenza, arringhe civili*, 2nd ed. (Turin: UTET, 1923), vol. 1, pp. 1–2.

114. On Ferri's school, see Giulio Andrea Belloni, "La Scuola d'applicazione," in *Enrico Ferri: Maestro*, pp. 207–19.

115. An example is cited in the "Rievocazione" in *Enrico Ferri, Maestro*, p. 11. He boasted about this ability as early as 1889 in a letter to Napoleone Colajanni; see *Democrazia e socialismo in Italia: Carteggi di Napoleone Colajanni*, ed. Salvatore Massimo Ganci (Milan: Feltrinelli, 1959), pp. 278–81.

116. For Garofalo's biography, see the *Enciclopedia Italiana* (1932), vol. 16, p. 402; and Florian et al., *Dizionario*, v. 1, pp. 398–99. One of the few analyses of Garofalo in English is Francis A. Allen's chapter in Mannheim, *Pioneers*, pp. 254–75.

117. The phrase is that of Filippo Grispigni from his entry on Garofalo in Florian, *Dizionario*, v. 1, p. 398.

118. Raffaele Garofalo, *Criminology* (Montclair N.J., Patterson Smith, 1968; orig. published in English, 1914), p. xxx. Published in 1885 as *Criminologia*, this work appeared in a second edition in 1891. It was translated into French, Spanish, and Portuguese.

119. Garofalo, *Criminology*, p. 364.

120. Ibid., pp. 67–68; he was quoting another positivist, Antonio Marro.

121. Ibid., p. 72.

122. Ibid.

123. Ibid., p. 61.

124. Ibid., p. 132.

125. Ibid., p. 239.

126. Ibid., p. 95.

127. Ibid.

128. Ibid., pp. 104–105.
129. Ibid., pp. 263–64.
130. Ibid., p. xxxii.
131. Ibid., p. 142.
132. Garofalo, *La superstizione socialista* (Turin-Rome: Roux Frassati, 1895), p. 5.
133. Ibid., p. 91.
134. Ibid., p. 90.
135. Ibid., p. 8.
136. Ibid., p. 17.
137. Cortesi, *Turati*, p. 138. On Turati and positivism, see also Ganci, "La formazione positivistica di Filippo Turati," *Rivista storica del socialismo* (Jan.–June, 1958), pp. 56–68; and Franco Catalano, *Filippo Turati* (Milan-Rome: Edizioni *Avanti!*, 1957), pp. 39–46.
138. Quote is from Turati's "L'Ardigo," originally published in *La Farfalla* in 1882 and reprinted in Cortesi, *Turati*, p. 135.
139. Turati, "L'Ardigò," in Cortesi, *Turati*, 124.
140. Turati, "Il delitto e la questione sociale," reprinted in Cortesi, *Turati*, p. 159.
141. Ibid., p. 172.
142. Ibid., p. 193.
143. Ibid.
144. Ibid., p. 172.
145. Ibid., p. 149.
146. Ibid., p. 212.
147. Ibid., p. 171.
148. Napoleone Colajanni, *Socialismo* (Catania: Tropea, 1884). For biographical information on Colajanni see Andreucci and Detti, *Il movimento*, v. 2, pp. 63–65, and his entry in the *Enciclopedia Italiana* (1931), vol. 10, pp. 713–14.
149. Quoted in Ganci, "La formazione," p. 66.
150. Colajanni, *La sociologia criminale* (Catania: Tropea, 1889), vol. 1, p. 150.
151. Ibid.
152. Ibid., p. 198.
153. Ibid., p. 197.
154. Ibid., p. 178.
155. See for example, Enrico Pessina, "Il diritto penale in Italia da Cesare Beccaria sino alla promulgazione del codice penale vigente" in Pessina, ed., *Enciclopedia del diritto penale italiano* (Milan: Società Editrice Libraria, 1906) v. 2, pp. 539–768; and Luigi Lucchini, *I semplicisti del diritto penale* (Turin: UTET, 1886).
156. On the liberalism of Pessina and Lucchini, see Floriana Colao, *Il delitto politico tra Ottocento e Novecento* (Milan: A. Giuffrè, 1986), pp. 81–83; 86–87.
157. Agostino Gemelli, *Le dottrine moderne della delinquenza: Critica delle dottrine criminali positiviste* (Florence: Lib. Ed. Fiorentina, 1908), p. 23.
158. Ibid., p. 128.
159. Ibid., pp. 131–32.
160. Ibid., p. 154.
161. Robert A. Nye gives an excellent analysis of the French/Italian rivalry in "Heredity or Milieu: The Foundations of Modern European Criminological Theory," *ISIS*, v. 67, n. 238 (Sept., 1976), pp. 335–55.
162. Hans Kurella wrote a biography of Lombroso that appeared in English in 1911 called *Cesare Lombroso: A Modern Man of Science* (London: Rebman).

163. Havelock Ellis, *The Criminal* (New York: Scribner and Welford, 1890).

164. For a pioneering analysis of this group, see Nicole Hahn Rafter, *Creating Born Criminals* (Urbana: University of Illinois Press, 1997). Both MacDonald's *Criminology* (1893) and Drahms's *The Criminal* (1900) had prefaces by Lombroso. McKim's work is *Heredity and Human Progress* (1900). For the influence of Lombroso in the United States, see also Arthur E. Fink, *Causes of Crime: Biological Theories in the United States, 1800–1915* (Philadelphia: University of Pennsylvania Press, 1938). According to David Garland, the English eschewed theory in general—whether positivist, classical, or sociological; writings on crime tended to focus on the practical workings of criminal justice institutions. See his article, "British Criminology Before 1935," *The British Journal of Criminology*, v. 28, n. 2 (Spring, 1988), pp. 1–17.

165. *Archivio*, v. 1 (1880), p. 2.

166. One of these works was co-authored with Mario Carrara and another with R. Laschi. See Società Anonima Editrice, *Avanti!*, *Catalogo della Libreria* (Milan: *Avanti!*, 1914).

167. Olindo Malagodi, review of books by Sighele and Lombroso, *Critica sociale*, vol. 3 (1893), p. 127. On criminal anthropology in the pages of *Critica sociale*, see Morris L. Ghezzi, "La questione penale nella *Critica Sociale*" in Emilio R. Papa, ed., *Positivismo e cultura italiana* (Milan: Franco Angeli, 1985), pp. 405–13.

Chapter 2

The Female Offender

In 1893, three leading criminal anthropologists—Guglielmo Ferrero, Augusto Bianchi, and Scipio Sighele—began publication of a series of volumes meant to popularize positivist theories of crime. Entitled *The World of Crime* and later *Chronicles of Crime*, these volumes summarized the proceedings of famous criminal trials, and included "scientific" analysis. In their first volume, Ferrero criticized the reasoning of the court in the case of Ernesta Bordoni, who was accused of murdering Gaetano Zannini. He recommended an alternative perspective based on biological determinism, which was not surprising considering Ferrero was co-author with Lombroso of *The Female Offender* (*La donna delinquente, la donna normale, e la prostituta*).

Ferrero described Bordoni as a kind of elite prostitute who was fortunate enough to work outside the system of legalized brothels. Stating that she came from an impoverished neighborhood of Bologna "crowded with hovels that seemed almost to be mud huts of savages," Ferrero hinted at her atavistic origins.[1] While admitting that Bordoni was "one of the most admired seamstresses of the quarter of Porta San Vitale," he predicted that she would have ended up in a squalid brothel if she had escaped criminal indictment.[2] Accused of killing her ex-boyfriend with a kitchen knife on March 1, 1891, Bordoni claimed that she had acted in self-defense. Zannino, the boyfriend, had insisted that she resume their relationship and, when she refused, hit her several times. Some witnesses to the incident threw doubt on Bordoni's version, claiming that she was initially quite friendly to Zannino, but later initiated the violence after shouting, "You villain, I'll kill you."[3] Her actions seemed premeditated, since she had borrowed an especially sharp knife from a neighbor before going to meet Zannino. Furthermore, the prosecution argued that she had been instigated by her half-brother, Rodolfo Ferri, because of an incestuous love he harbored for her. Found guilty of murder but without premeditation, Bordoni received a relatively light sentence of four years imprisonment. Her half-brother Ferri got a much heavier punishment of fifteen years, since he was held to be the instigator of the episode.

Ferrero found this verdict "very strange"; it seemed illogical to pronounce Bordoni's action spontaneous and unpremeditated if it had been instigated by her half-brother.[4] But Ferrero mentioned this inconsistency only in passing, reserving the bulk of his article for analyzing the physical and psychological deficiencies of Bordoni. From her photograph, he identified two anomalies: "a low forehead and small head in relation to her body; and an elongated face, which I would call almost horsy, without any expression whatsoever."[5] Psychologically, Bordoni was morally insane, since she lacked modesty, the second most important virtue for women after motherhood. Her act of homicide could not be excused as a defense of her honor, since she lacked the innocence of a renaissance Juliet. Neither could it be explained as a "crime of love" since Bordoni had testified that she had never loved anyone. Identifying these last words as "the confession of a real moral idiot," Ferrero labeled her violence as "a crime of hate" motivated by "one of those intense, blind, and irrational hatreds" typical of born criminals, epileptics, and hysterics.[6] This type of hatred needed no external stimulus, but could arise automatically from a "morbid incitement of the psychic centers" and expand to such exaggerated intensity that it exploded into violence.[7] According to Ferrero, normal people had the mental power to block or redirect this nervous energy, but Bordoni's lack of emotional restraint recalled the behavior of children, primitives, and even wild animals.

The influence of Lombroso on this analysis would be clear even without Ferrero's explicit acknowledgment of "the profundity of the theory of Lombroso."[8] Ferrero used Lombrosian terms to describe Bordoni and, more important, replicated his theoretical confusion. Although Ferrero first diagnosed Bordoni as morally insane, he later cited atavism, disease, insanity, epilepsy, and hysteria as possible roots of her perversity. Lombroso had cited all of these factors, in successive editions of *Criminal Man*, for the diagnosis of the male born criminal. What distinguished Ferrero's analysis of Bordoni from positivist case studies of men was its emphasis on her sexuality. Because Bordoni had "a string of romantic intrigues, and not all of them platonic" by the age of eighteen, Ferrero pronounced her morally insane.[9] On the other hand, her lover, Zannini, was "basically an honest worker" despite his affair with Bordoni.[10] Although Bordoni was known in her neighborhood as an excellent seamstress, Ferrero asserted that she was also a *grisette*, a part-time prostitute. And he concluded that if she had been instigated by her half-brother, only a sexual relation like that of incest could explain such submission. Although murder was rarely traced to sexuality when committed by men, Ferrero typified the general impulse of positivist criminology to link women's crimes to gender.

Ferrero's detailed analysis of the Bordoni case represented a general shift in interest for positivists. Criminal anthropologists focused their early research and theorizing, including the notion of the "born criminal," on men. Like almost all other criminologists, they had initially studied only male experience when defining both normality and deviancy. Unlike many later schools of criminology, however, Lombroso and his colleagues recognized that their findings on male crime could not be automatically universalized to include women. Consistent with their tendency to subdivide and categorize different classes of deviants, positivists began to visit female prisons in the late 1880s and 1890s to measure, test, and interview women.

CONTEXT

Although criminal anthropologists suggested that an alarming escalation in female crime had inspired their research on women, criminal statistics in fact exhibited little change from 1890 until 1914. It is true that absolute numbers of women convicted for crime climbed from about 24,000 per year in 1890 to almost 33,000 in 1898, an increase of almost 38 percent.[11] When adjusted for the growing population, however, rates of female crime rose only modestly from 7.8/10,000 to 10.2/10,000 during the same period. After the turn of the century, these rates dropped consistently to a low of 5.2/10,000 in 1915, the year of Italy's entrance into World War I. As we saw in Chapter 1, this pattern—of rising crime during the 1890s followed by a decrease after 1900—was not unique to women.

The similarity between male and female trends in offending is confirmed by another statistic, the percentage of all criminals who were women. In 1890, women composed 18.3 percent of all offenders, a number that dropped to 17.75 by 1898. Thus, during the 1890s, male lawbreaking increased slightly faster that of women, contradicting the myth of an explosion of female crime. After 1900, women's share of all crime rose modestly, always remaining under 20 percent of total crime.

Rather than rising crime rates, what is instead most striking about the national statistics is the high number of women convicted for violent crimes. Between 1890 and World War I, the percent of female criminals convicted for theft dropped steadily while that for violent crime rose. Thus, by 1909, over 50 percent of all women sentenced for punishment by Italian courts had committed a crime against persons rather than property. This statistic must be viewed with caution, since it does not include women indicted but acquitted for crime. Probably the courts were more lenient with thieves than murderesses, tending to acquit the former and convict the latter. But only further research can explain this astonishingly high percentage of violence among female criminals in Italy.

If female crime rates remained largely stable during the 1890s, why did criminal anthropologists perceive rising deviancy among women? Their anxiety arose not from specific criminal behavior but more generally from the demographic, economic, and political developments of late nineteenth-century Italy. These changes affected all women, often shaping their experiences differently from those of men. This is partially because women and men entered unified Italy with different roles and statuses and partially because women—despite changes brought on by the demographic revolution, industrialization, and political unity—remained subordinate to men throughout the nineteenth century. Fear of women, as reflected in the numerous studies of female delinquents by positivist criminologists, sprang largely from anxiety over the "modernization" of women's roles as they entered the industrial workforce or demanded legal and political equality. In a contradictory way, it also arose from a fear that women were not as successful as men in the modernization process and had become anachronistic symbols of Italy's failure to transcend its pre-capitalist economy.

The first phase of the demographic transition, in which mortality rates fell but fertility rates remained high, put particular stress on women. Married women were saddled with exceptionally large families in contrast to both preindustrial times and the later "modern" era after the adoption of birth control. In contrast to the small families of early modern Italy, married women during the first decade of unification after 1861 raised nearly five children on the average. This number fell slowly to 4.5 by the turn of the century and 4.0 during World War I. By the 1920s and 1930s, the average number of children per family had finally returned to the preindustrial average of slightly over three.[12] Women had even more pregnancies than these figures would indicate, since the rate of stillbirths was high, reaching a peak of 4.4 percent of all births during the decade 1900–1910, dropping to 4.0 percent only in 1921–30 and under 3.0 percent after World War II.[13] Thus, the first six decades after unification, from 1861–1921, constituted a unique demographic period in Italian history, one in which married women bore, cared for, and helped to support extraordinary numbers of children. The burden was especially heavy for poor and working-class women because they had the most offspring.

Single women were not exempt from the cares of childbearing as illegitimacy rates peaked in the late nineteenth century. The two decades between 1871 and 1891 saw the highest rates of illegitimacy, with over 7 percent of all babies being born outside of marriage.[14] This figure dropped to about 6 percent by the turn of the century and remained between 4 and 6 percent until the end of World War II. The rise in single motherhood was not new, dating from legal, social, and economic changes of the late eighteenth century. Most historians agree that the rising illegitimacy rates of late eighteenth- and early nineteenth-century Europe did not result from changing attitudes among women toward a celebration of either immorality or sexual liberation. Rather, women continued their traditional behavior—that is, premarital intercourse—with the traditional expectation that it would lead to marriage. In Italy, several factors explained the collapse of this assumption.

First, women were no longer protected by the Church, state, or their families from abandonment by suitors. Although the Church had accepted even a secret vow between a man and woman to constitute marriage during medieval and renaissance times, it required a Church ceremony after the sixteenth-century decrees of the Council of Trent. Before these decrees, single women could appeal, often successfully and with the support of their families, to ecclesiastical courts for a sentence that would require their suitors to marry them, provide them with a dowry to attract future proposals of marriage, or to support any illegitimate offspring. By the late eighteenth century, the Church was reluctant to hear such cases and increasingly denounced all women who engaged in premarital sex. While recent studies have shown that popular opinion toward seduced and abandoned women changed only slowly, by the end of the eighteenth century most relatives and friends had been persuaded by the new Church doctrine to denounce and even desert single women who had lost their virginity.[15] This increasing rigidity in moral attitudes was incorporated by the state in the new civil codes, passed during the Napoleonic invasions, that legally forbade paternity suits by women.

Second, more men were in a position to take advantage of their new freedom to escape marriage without legal penalties. The beginnings of demographic growth forced many men to leave their villages—and thus family and community pressures to legalize their betrothals—since the land could no longer absorb more workers. Their new urban jobs, like construction, hauling, or dock working, were often temporary and underpaid. This economic instability often made marriage impossible even for those men who wished to legitimize their children. Frequent migration from town to town or even emigration to northern Europe and the Americas also prevented men from establishing the type of long-term relationships that would have led to marriage. Why women engaged in premarital sex, despite the risk of unwanted pregnancy, is not entirely clear and probably varied from region to region. Some areas resembled other parts of Europe where premarital sex was expected and even encouraged, since very little "slippage" occurred between betrothal and marriage, and any children conceived before marriage would be legitimated at birth. Some women may have also hoped that a sexual relationship and even pregnancy might bind their suitor to them and increase the likelihood of marriage, a quite frequent scenario in preindustrial times. Finally, as women increasingly migrated alone to find work, they may have hoped that men would now supply the emotional and financial support formerly derived from their families. Yet no matter what their strategy, many women found themselves poor and alone with the prospect of a child to support.

The desperation faced by both single and married mothers unable to care for their children is reflected in the sharp increase of admissions to foundling homes. Italy had pioneered the idea of building institutions for abandoned children with the establishment of the Milanese foundling home in 898, and they became refuges for a growing number of children during the renaissance. The late eighteenth century saw the beginning of a second surge of abandonment, involving mostly single mothers. In order to discourage infanticide, most foundling homes had installed the *ruota*, or a revolving compartment in the door, so that babies could be left anonymously. While the *ruota* has traditionally been explained as a means of protecting women's honor, David Kertzer has recently suggested that it really shielded men from public censure as did the Napoleonic prohibition of paternity suits.[16] During the nineteenth century, married women as well as men increasingly took advantage of the *ruota* so that in some places like Milan up to 75 percent of foundlings were legitimate. In all of Italy, over 35,000 babies per year were admitted to institutions by the middle of the century. That this practice resulted from hard economic conditions and not inhumanity is clear from the high rate of babies who arrived with identifying papers or symbols so that they could later be retrieved. In fact some families did return to claim their babies, showing that abandonment was often used as a temporary measure by families with too many mouths to feed.

The ruling classes were directly confronted with the problems of poor women as large numbers of migrants from the countryside congregated in both northern and southern cities. While men began to look at emigration to the Americas as an economic solution, women tended to move lesser distances from home. Yet, like men, they faced the prospect of living and working alone after being raised in a society where they were always part of a family—their own, their husband's, or their rural employer's. For the middle and upper classes, women were also categorized by their relationship to men; the sight of large numbers of unattached women on city streets, therefore, provoked anxiety. Women, unlike men, were not feared for their physical violence, yet they symbolized the sexual disorder associated with female autonomy.

Women migrated, of course, to search for work and find a niche in the slowly industrializing economy of late nineteenth-century Italy. As in the rest of Europe, the percent of women counted as "active" laborers by the census decreased, from a high of 40 percent in 1861 to 37 percent in 1901, 29 percent in 1911, and 20 percent in 1931.[17] This trend was reversed only after World War II, creating a "U" curve of women's employment in the late nineteenth and twentieth centuries. Several factors explain the steady withdrawal of women from the active workforce, not least the demographic pressure of larger families. Louise Tilly has shown for Milan, for example, that between 1881 and 1901 the decline involved only women over twenty-one, while the number of younger working women remained steady. Women over twenty-one were more likely to be married and forced to leave jobs that could not be combined with child care. After 1901, this return to the home was sometimes facilitated by the gradually rising salaries of their husbands.[18]

Changes in the structures and types of labor itself also made the workplace less hospitable to women, especially women with children. In urban areas, women were concentrated in domestic service, garment making, and textile production, all of which became feminized during the nineteenth century. Most unskilled, migrant workers had little choice but to go into domestic service, an occupation that paid little but promised room, board, and protection for naive newcomers to the city. Women tended to be dismissed at marriage or pregnancy, however, and after the turn of the twentieth century demand for servants fell as a new middle-class ethic counseled mothers to take the upbringing of their children into their own hands. A second large occupation of women, garment making, was seasonal and poorly paid, but in the nineteenth century offered women the possibility of working in their own homes. By the twentieth century, however, this trade was being concentrated in large workshops, forcing women to quit after marriage and the assumption of household duties.

Factory work offered the most elite and well-paid employment for lower-class women predominantly in textiles but also in smaller industries such as cigar making. In the late nineteenth century, almost 80 percent of all textile jobs were held by women, although their pay lagged one-third to one-half behind that of men. But

Italian textile production, and thus the sector in which women had been most successful, had reached its peak. Decline first hit the female workers in the Sicilian silk industry, which lost its tariff protection from foreign competition after unification. Spinners and weavers were reduced to a preindustrial level of home production for their families once the factories closed. While production in the North, based on wool and cotton cloth, never experienced such a drastic contraction, the industrial take-off beginning in the 1890s was built on newer industries such as steel and machine tools. This spurt in heavy industry created mostly male jobs, while the female preserve of textiles shrank in output and number of employed.

One final characteristic of the female workforce was its youth. Although married women withdrew from the workforce in large numbers after the turn of the twentieth century, they had never been as fully represented as single women. By the age of fourteen or fifteen, urban girls had to begin to earn their keep while rural teenagers were sent to the city to find work. Fewer girls attended high school than boys because the state did not yet provide anything beyond elementary education for girls in many areas, and most poor families did not see the need for female education. Since the average age of marriage for women remained steady at twenty-four to twenty-five throughout the late nineteenth and early twentieth centuries, the bulk of the female workforce was aged fifteen to twenty-five.[19] As David Kertzer and Dennis Hogan have shown for Casalecchio outside of Bologna, this rather late age of marriage for women did not vary by occupation or change during industrialization but characterized artisans/merchants, sharecroppers, agricultural wage laborers, and factory workers.[20] Thus, both rural and urban lower-class women needed work during the long interval between childhood and marriage and sometimes beyond. In addition, 11 to 13 percent of women in late nineteenth-century Italy experienced "definitive celibacy," that is, had never married by the age of sixty.[21] These women tended to stay in the workforce throughout their lives.

Not only demographic and economic forces but also changes in women's legal and political status directed the attention of positivists to female crime. Despite the valiant participation of many women in the struggle for Italian unification, the first civil code of united Italy, the Pisanelli Code of 1865, denied legal equality to women. Modeled after the Napoleonic Code of 1804, the Pisanelli Code subordinated women to their husbands. At marriage, a woman had to adopt her husbands' name and reside where he chose. Although women did have the right to own property, they had to get the permission of their husbands, according to the doctrine of *autorizzazione maritale*, to carry out financial transactions such as opening bank accounts, taking out mortgages, or bequeathing gifts. Another traditional doctrine, that of *patria podestà*, gave men the exclusive right to make decisions about minor children, while a woman became the legal head of the household only in the absence of the father through separation, desertion, emigration, or prolonged imprisonment. Divorce was not legal, and the grounds for separation favored husbands. A man could petition the courts for separation after the simple adultery of his wife, while women had to prove what might be called "aggravated adultery" on the part of their husbands, that is, the flagrant and public maintenance of a mistress for an extended time.

As in other European nations, Italian women began to organize in the late nineteenth century to rectify these legal inequalities. Until 1880, proponents of female emancipation gathered informally around journals like *La Cornelia* and *La Donna* that called for the legalization of paternity suits, equality in family law, and access of girls to education. In 1881, the leading female emancipationist, Anna Maria Mozzoni, founded the League to Promote Female Interests in Milan, one of the first formal feminist organizations in Italy and one that spawned local imitators in other cities. Interclass in membership, these leagues called for better working conditions for women, especially in the new textile factories, in addition to the older demands for civil rights. After 1890, the trend toward organization accelerated, with bourgeois women increasingly emphasizing the vote, while socialist feminists initiated a campaign for protective legislation for working mothers. By such a concerted challenge to their subordination, women defied traditional categories of "normal" and "deviant." In response, positivist criminologists devised their own supposedly scientific and neutral standards of body and mind for the "normal" woman. Such a challenge promised to take the power of defining the future of women away from organized feminism and restore it safely to male experts.

THE NATURE OF "NORMAL" WOMEN

The defining event in the shift in criminal anthropological research from a focus on men to women was the publication in 1893 of *The Female Offender*, co-authored by Lombroso and Ferrero. Modern criminologists recognize this book as positing the first theory of female crime in the Western world.[22] Lombroso's interest in women was not entirely new in 1893, however, as even the first brief edition of *Criminal Man* contained scattered comparisons between male and female criminals. Having as yet done little empirical research on women, Lombroso based his earliest comments mostly on the work of others, notably Alexandre Parent-Duchatelet, the French author of a well-known study of prostitution published in 1857. Although not a proponent of biological determinism, Parent-Duchatelet had included measurements of height and weight and other physical features in his detailed description of the familial background, habits, and psychology of prostitutes. Based on these statistics as well as a handful of his own observations, Lombroso pronounced prostitutes to be anthropologically similar to female criminals. Thus, as early as 1876, Lombroso had formulated the central tenet of his future book on the female offender, that prostitution is equivalent to criminality. Each succeeding edition of *Criminal Man* repeated this equation in its section on the variable of "sex" (*sesso*) in the identification of the born criminal.

Not until 1893, however, did Lombroso, with the help of Ferrero, expand his discussion of female criminality into a volume independent of *Criminal Man*. *The Female Offender* became an instant classic in the field of criminology and a touchstone for future works on female crime. Like *Criminal Man*, this companion volume on women was translated almost immediately into German and French.[23] But unlike *Criminal Man*, which had as yet not been translated into English, editions of *The Female Offender* appeared in both London and New York in 1895.[24] The American edition was reissued twice in the 1890s, reflecting a strong interest in female crime.[25] Thus, positivist theories on women became more accessible than those on men for researchers in Great Britain and the United States.

The Female Offender constituted only one work in the outpouring of Italian research on gender, biology, and crime in the 1890s. Contributions to the *Archives of Criminal Anthropology*, the central journal of positivist criminology, offer a good indicator of the increasing interest in the subject of female crime. Until 1889, the overwhelming majority of articles continued to take men as their subjects. With the issue of 1889, however, articles on women begin to dominate the pages of the *Archives*. From five articles in 1889, the contributions on women climbed to nine in 1892 (more than half the issue) and remained frequent through 1898. In total, during the decade after 1889 the *Archives* published thirty-three articles and six book reviews on female crime. That interest in gender was widespread is confirmed by the large number of authors who presented results of their research on women. The thirty-three articles and six book reviews represented the work of twenty-four authors, many of whom wrote on women more than once. Those who penned at least two entries on women were Lombroso, Ottolenghi, Raffaele Guerrieri, Luigi Roncoroni, Mario Carrara, G. B. Moraglia, G. Salsotto, and Pio Viazzi.

Why criminal anthropologists' research on women converged on the decade of the 1890s is not entirely clear. It might be supposed that any thorough program of scientific research would consider the variable of gender. Yet most schools of criminology, until the development of a feminist perspective in the 1970s, have constructed their theories on solely male data without apology. The evolution of the Italian positivists from a focus on men to women constitutes, therefore, the exception rather than the rule in criminological research. A more likely explanation for the shift in focus lies in the centrality of the debate about the woman question in late nineteenth-century Italy. It is no coincidence that the same decade that saw an outpouring of research on female crime also witnessed the first strong organizations of both socialist and bourgeois feminists.

Criminal anthropologists understood that their research on women was not being initiated in a scientific vacuum but rather within the context of feminist demands for change in female status and roles. In his preface to *The Female Offender*, Lombroso claimed that "not one line of this work . . . justifies the many tyrannies of which women have been and still are victims, from the Taboo that forbids them to eat meat and to touch coconuts to that which prevents them from studying, and worse, from practicing a profession once they have learned it."[26]

In his review of *The Female Offender* for the *Archives*, Ferri also denied that the findings of positivist criminology justified discrimination on the basis on sex.[27] Several years later in 1896, Salvatore Ottolenghi, a student of Lombroso, returned to the relation between the findings of scientific criminology and the status of women. In his book *The Sensitivity of Women*, he explained why he and his colleagues conducted experiments to answer such questions as "Do women feel more or less than men?" He responded, "It is not simply out of curiosity that renowned authorities are addressing themselves to this question; it is intimately related to the difficult problem of the position of women in society and anthropology."[28]

Positivist research had a broad impact on current debates about the woman question, in part because criminal anthropologists had to define female normalcy before they could measure female deviancy. In response to past criticism of their methodology, they set up control groups in many of their studies of female delinquency and the data from these control groups initially undergirded their generalizations about normal women. This empirical evidence promised to provide a modern and objective evaluation of women's nature, one that, as Ferri touted, would differ from "the usual rhapsodies and more or less romantic ramblings that, for a long time, many have written about women."[29] Ferrero also emphasized the innovative nature of the positivist approach, pointing out that "if woman has been the subject of the highest aspirations, desires, and thoughtful care, she has also been up to the present day scientifically ignored."[30] As in their research on men, however, these data were often mixed with personal experience, historical anecdotes, and, above all, traditional proverbs to round out a supposedly scientific portrait of typical womanhood. To the disappointment of feminists, the revolutionary methodology of criminal anthropology did not result in an analysis that sharply challenged nineteenth-century conventions but instead confirmed most of them. Science proved that normal women were decidedly inferior in biology, intelligence, and morality to their male counterparts.

Scores of measurements documented the physical inferiority of women. Perhaps most notorious were the studies of brain weight and skull size, a standard method of scientific investigation stretching back to the heyday of phrenology in the early nineteenth century. Criminal anthropologists, like their predecessors, interpreted smallness to mean inferiority. Other examples of women's inadequacy compared to men were their short limbs and skeletons, thin facial hair, smaller internal organs, and paucity of red corpuscles.[31] When faced with certain female measurements that exceeded those of men, positivist criminologists simply redefined big to mean immature and undeveloped. Finding, for example, that women had higher pulse rates, more body fat, and longer trunks than men, they pointed out that these qualities also characterized children and therefore signaled physical infantilism rather than superiority. This equation of women with children ran throughout their works, with Lombroso labeling both groups as "innocuous semi-criminals" and calling women "big children."[32]

One of the most widespread methods used to measure gender differences was the sensitivity test, performed by administering electric shocks to various parts of the body. That sensitivity testing was considered crucial to defining female nature is clear not only from the many publications on the subject but also the almost fetishistic interest criminologists took in the machines used for the tests. Roncoroni and Giovanni Albertotti even provided readers of the *Archives* with an article comparing the merits of various electrical measuring devices, called algometers.[33] Attached most often to the hands—but sometimes also to the tongue, nose, forehead, thighs, stomach, breasts, and even clitoris—the electrodes recorded "general sensi-tivity," the first perception of the current, and "sensitivity to pain."

After testing both sexes, criminal anthropologists pronounced women to be less sensitive than men, one of their only findings that contradicted nineteenth-century sexual stereotypes. Although this conclusion became an article of faith among posi-tivist criminologists for years to come, even their own data did not entirely support such a generalization. Lombroso began the flurry of research into female sensitivity with a short article in 1890, in which he pronounced—on the basis of readings from seventy-six "normal" women—that "touch is more obtuse in women than in men."[34] In his extended treatment three years later in *The Female Offender*, he admitted that this finding "seems to openly contrast with traditional views," but "the contradiction is explained by [women's] greater excitability and lesser degree of inhibition."[35] In other words, while women may appear more emotional than men, scientific testing had gotten below the surface to expose basic female insensitivity. According to Lombroso, his algometric readings established that twice as many men as women pos-sessed "fine" touch, roughly equal rates had moderate touch, and four times as many women as men had "obtuse" touch.[36]

Other researchers had different problems with their data. Ottolenghi, for exam-ple, found a very high sensitivity to pain among a significant minority of normal women. He explained away these results by saying that women, being highly im-pressionable, thought they felt pain before the electric current actually hurt their hand and lied to testers. Thus, these readings denoted excitability, a label borrowed from Lombroso, rather than real sensitivity. Ottolenghi was also disappointed with his results on general sensitivity, which showed men to be more obtuse than women. Again, he reclassified these data so they would not contradict the positivist dogma of women's inferiority. He demoted the importance of general sensitivity, saying that it measured only the superficial sensitivity of the skin and that even ba-bies and blacks could outscore white men on this test. Much more significant were the tests for sensitivity to pain, in which men outscored the majority of women. Sen-sitivity to pain was fundamental to human nature, being linked "essentially to the psychic center" of the individual and indicative of "cerebral evolution."[37]

Criminal anthropologists eschewed mathematical data altogether to evaluate one area of female sensitivity, that of sexual sensitivity. Giuseppe Sergi opened the discussion of sexual sensitivity in a letter "to the illustrious Professor C. Lombroso" published in 1891 in the *Archives*.[38] Saluting Lombroso as his friend, he congratu-lated him on his "bold initiative" to study female sensitivity, the results of which had been published a year earlier in the *Archives*. Agreeing with Lombroso that women were generally insensitive, he offered his own "empirical" evidence, most of which related to female sexuality. First, he pointed out that Darwin had found weaker sex-ual desire in female than in male animals and argued that the same must be true of humans. He also asserted that "we know that women even in the lower stages of civ-ilization show little sexual sensitivity" since "men in many lower races have to use methods that would seem painful to excite women."[39] Based on his experience with "a few women whom I have known,' Sergi argued that this sexual frigidity also characterized modern women since "it is known that many more caresses and much more solicitude is necessary to induce a woman to give in willingly and to make her feel sexual pleasure."[40] Even women who loved their husbands often felt "coldness and annoyance" at marital advances and, when they gave in, did it "passively without enthusiasm or predilection."[41] Sergi did not bemoan this natural frigidity in women but found it socially useful since "the lesser acuity of sexual desire in women is a natural brake on the greater desire in men."[42]

Two years later in *The Female Offender*, Lombroso substantially reinforced Sergi's findings. His only dispute was with the nature of "savage" women, whom Lombroso characterized as sexually lascivious. He agreed that "civilized" women, who had evolved toward ever greater sexual modesty, experienced little physical sensation during sexual intercourse. How else, he asked, could women "fall back so easily into pregnancy despite the pain of childbirth?"[43] The answer lay in the insensitivity of the female sexual and reproductive organs. Further proof for the dullness of female sexual desire lay in the preference for platonic love, the rarity of female sexual psychopathy, and the "obligation of chastity" required of women in most societies.[44] It is notable that neither Sergi nor Lombroso pursued even the semblance of experimental research to obtain these results. Unlike the data on general sensitivity and sensitivity to pain based on algometric readings, the "empirical" data on sexual sensitivity came down to analogies with animals and savages, observations of a few personal friends, and social practices like the "obligation of chastity."

The importance of the sensitivity tests, as well as the measurements of other parts of the body, lay in their ability to reveal the interior intellectual and moral nature of women. Drawing on his medical experience of studying symptoms in order to diagnose disease, Lombroso insisted that physical characteristics were the signs of the hidden, immaterial, and therefore immeasurable attributes of the character of an individual or a group. Herein lay the nexus between criminal anthropology and the woman question, since positivists held as an article of faith that exterior, physical inferiority reflected an equally real interior mental and psychological inferiority. In terms of intelligence, criminal anthropologists built on the long-held belief that smaller skulls or less weighty brains translated into mental weakness. They added their data on sensitivity, arguing, as Lombroso did, that "women . . . feel less as they think less."[45] Ottolenghi made this insight the linchpin of his book, *The Sensitivity of Women*. In introducing his text full of algometric tables, he explained that "all our actions are strictly linked to thought, and one who does not feel cannot think. How women behave in individual and collective life and their reaction to the most varied organic and psychological stimuli depends essentially on how they feel."[46] As we saw earlier, he concluded that women were deficient in cerebral development.

Even the few women widely recognized in nineteenth-century Europe as successful writers did not constitute empirical proof for positivist criminologists that women should seek intellectual distinction. After all, history provided few examples of female geniuses, and the handful of women who did succeed in the intellectual arena were considered degenerate. Most often this degeneracy displayed itself in a virile physical appearance. For example, Lombroso pointed out that Madame de Staël, the famous novelist and essayist from the early years of the nineteenth century, "had a man's face."[47] The French novelist George Sand "had a low voice and willingly dressed like a man."[48] He was especially malicious in his portrait of the British writer George Elliot, whom he described as having a "masculine look, enormous ugly head, unkempt hair, big nose, thick lips, huge mustache and jaw, [and] long horse's face."[49] Unable to identify masculine qualities in Mary Wollstonecraft's physiognomy, he nevertheless managed to label "the first proponent of women's emancipation" as degenerate because she was "the daughter of a moral idiot and a maniac," "the sister of lunatics," and herself "suicidal and unlucky."[50] To avoid degeneracy and retain femininity, normal women should not attempt to develop their powers of thought beyond a moderate and modest level.

In terms of moral qualities, criminal anthropology also confirmed rather than challenged most nineteenth-century platitudes about women. Niceforo, for example, pronounced that scientific tests established the following traits as typical of the female sex: "impulsiveness, fickleness, puerile vanity, love for exterior appearance, and triviality, all the noted psychological attributes, in a word, that are common to children and savages."[51] The only major challenge to common stereotypes was the subtraction of sensitivity from the female sphere. Women's emotionality, once valued as signaling the unique moral strength of women, was now exposed as the superficial expression of nervous irritation.

Modern women were credited with piety, a kind of backhanded compliment from a group of anti-clerical if not atheistic men. Ferrero made a special study of this female trait in response to what he considered an obvious and "spontaneous" conundrum: "Is woman pious or cruel?"[52] He concluded that "piety and cruelty coexist in women. Their weakness makes them cruel and pious at the same time."[53] In other words, from their lack of physical strength, women had resorted to cruelty and piety in the struggle for existence. Cruelty sprang from women's insensitivity to pain, assuring that "painful images are more pallid in the brains of women than men and therefore sensitivity is less of an obstacle in vendettas that can satisfy hatreds only through inflicting the sharpest pains." Happily for men, since the founding of Christianity women had begun to use piety rather than cruelty to protect themselves and other weak beings like children. Although women were now in "a condition of unstable equilibrium" between these two contradictory impulses, future evolution would assure that increasing piety suffused true femininity.[54]

Like piety, sexual modesty was also evolving in normal women as civilization progressed. According to Viazzi, a leading socialist intellectual and firm believer in criminal anthropology, the sense of shame about their sexuality that was now a hereditary trait among European women was a blessing to society. Women would assume the role of restraining or at least hiding the bestiality of sexual intercourse and spiritualizing it into love. He shuddered to think of the social consequences "if women put aside their modesty and emulated men in the search for sexual unions, while adolescents would do the same; with all probability, this would lead quickly to the extinction of the race from exhaustion."[55] In his book *The Modern Eve*, Sighele repeated this positivist truism, that the male sex drive was essentially different from and much stronger than the female: "That instinct which is active in men translates into passive *coquetry* in women. A man who attempts and succeeds in satisfying an ardent but transitory desire for a woman whom he has met on a street or in a drawing-room has not committed any more serious crime than a woman who encourages and accepts the verbal expression of love by an admirer."[56]

Sighele counseled that women realize themselves not through the unnatural search for sexual satisfaction but "in their mission as mothers." For him, the following words of Friedrich Nietzsche were "the gospel truth: woman is an enigma whose solution is maternity."[57] This echoed Lombroso's declaration that "female love is basically nothing but a secondary aspect of maternity."[58] For positivist criminologists, maternity not only encapsulated the sexuality of normal women but provided the key for understanding how they could exceed men in moral qualities such as piety and modesty. According to Ferrero, maternity explained why women naturally strove through piety to protect the weak—especially children—in contrast to men who destroyed the weak in the Darwinian struggle for existence. And modesty assured that women would channel their sexual energies into reproduction rather than seeking sexual satisfaction. It is noteworthy that when positivists conceded female moral virtues like piety and modesty, they tied them to the biological function of maternity and thus denied women the type of autonomous spirituality typical of men.

The physicality of maternity, as envisioned by criminal anthropologists, derived from women's necessary role in the struggle for existence. According to Lombroso, women evolved more slowly than men because of their biological conservatism, "a conservatism whose primary cause is to be sought in the immobility of the ovule compared to the zoosperm."[59] Expending most of their "vital force" in pregnancy, childbirth, and nursing, women were biologically incapable of summoning up the energies necessary to rival men intellectually or assume political roles in the public arena.[60] Because of her sedentary and passive life, Lombroso declared it an "undoubted fact" that "atavistically [the female] is nearer to her origin than the male."[61] Putting more energy into the active struggle for existence, normal men had far surpassed normal women in biological, and therefore intellectual and moral, evolution. Sergi put it more bluntly when he declared that "women are men who are arrested in their development."[62]

The future promised further sexual differentiation since, as Ferri put it, "darwinistically" women had to perpetuate the species through "the great miraculous function of maternity."[63] While men struggled in the public sphere of economics and politics to assert their strength and intelligence, women would withdraw into the home to nurture children and other weak family members. Again, women's apparent altruism in tending the sick, for example, arose not from superior moral qualities but from biology. As Sergi observed, "Men who nurse the sick in their families deteriorate rapidly, while I have seen women, even mothers, assist tranquilly, conserving good humor and appetite. This greater resistance to, and tolerance of, the pain and suffering of others is not due to the will or heroic strength of women but to their relative insensitivity."[64] In fact, women's preoccupation with the restricted sphere of the family made them unfit for public life since it "impeded them, unlike men, from approaching in their conduct that equilibrium between rights and duties, egotism and altruism, which is the goal of moral evolution."[65] Always putting the family first, they could not grasp universal principles like equal rights and justice before the law that applied to all members of society. According to Ferrero, evolution would only increase women's handicap in public affairs since natural selection was continually widening the divergence between the sexes so that women were becoming weaker, more sedentary, more maternal, and more pious—that is, more feminine.

By asserting that the sublimity of maternity should make up for the inferiority of women, positivist criminologists protested too much. Ferri, who had promised that science would replace the tradition of "romantic ramblings" about women, gushed about the joys of motherhood. He paternalistically argued that positivist research offered women not despair but "a comforting conclusion . . . in securing for them, through strict scientific induction, as well as by romantic fantasy, all our enthusiastic devotion, in the name of holy motherhood."[66] By proclaiming maternity as the essence of normal womanhood, positivist science had simply reinforced traditional stereotypes of the period. The new scientific definition of the female sphere seemed even more restrictive by stripping women's nature down to the biological. Sensitivity, once thought typical of women, was now linked to evolutionary success and assigned to men. Characteristics such as piety and sexual restraint were reduced to automatic reflexes of biological motherhood. Morality was no longer identified with the female reserve of religiosity, but redefined as the male ability to grasp universal and public laws.

Positivist criminologists thus endorsed a nineteenth-century bourgeois model of womanhood stripped of political activism. Poor women who had migrated to the cities in search of work were considered atavistic in their refusal to retreat into the passivity of the domestic sphere. Visible and active on public streets, they risked falling back into sexual promiscuity typical of the lower rungs of the female evolutionary ladder. Instead, middle-class women who eschewed work and had withdrawn into the home represented the future of womanhood, according to criminal anthropologists. But such a future would be fatally compromised by feminist organizations that sought to diminish rather than increase the differences between the sexes. Intelligence and activism would drag bourgeois women, like female geniuses, down to the level of the lower or even criminal classes. For the most part, positivist criminologists taught women to accept their subordination in law and society, holding up the degeneracy of the female offender as a warning against violating the Darwinian laws of the struggle for existence.

THE FEMALE OFFENDER

In 1891, Ferrero wrote that the new focus of criminal anthropology—the female offender—constituted "a subject that could be said to be almost completely new."[67] This new research, however, was faced with a problematic and incontrovertible fact: women in Italy, and Europe in general, made up only 10 to 20 percent of all criminals. Theoretical confusion ensued immediately from the contradiction between this remarkably low rate of female crime and the general inferiority of women assumed by positivistic criminologists. If women as a group were less evolved than men and closer to their atavistic origin, should they not provoke higher incidence of crime than men? Should not a group so far behind men on the evolutionary ladder exhibit a larger number of anomalies in both their normal and criminal members? Yet Lombroso's own figures attested that only 14 percent of all female offenders were born criminals, that is, marked by at least four physical anomalies.[68]

Criminal anthropologists offered several explanations for this inconsistency. First, because of women's evolutionary conservatism and lack of differentiation, they were incapable of the spectacular biological throwbacks typical of men. Instead, "because the cerebral cortex is less active in women—as in the inferior animals and especially in the least civilized and barbarian women—the irritation that causes degeneration established itself there with less constancy and tenacity."[69] Or, as Roncoroni put it, women's "cortical centers" were less prone to variation since they were "less numerous, less complex, and less coordination existed among them."[70] In other words, the passivity of women deprived them of reaching either the intellectual and moral heights of normal men or the extreme atavistic depths of the male born criminal. Only those who had the energy and potential to strive for the top ran the risk of falling to the bottom. The flip side of few female geniuses was the relative paucity of "born" female offenders.

Positivist criminologists also made use of Darwin's notion of sexual selection to explain the physical normality of many female criminals. Because men over the millennia had chosen the most attractive women for marriage and reproduction, those with disfiguring anomalies had not been able to pass down their defects. In fact, according to Lombroso, the end for such women in primitive tribes might have been even more grisly since "men not only refused to marry a deformed female, but ate her."[71] L. Rinieri di Rocchi, who was unable to accept his own finding that Sienese women exhibited fewer anomalies than their male counterparts, insisted that women somehow hid those ugly deformities that were embarrassing to them. He also argued that the ordered and regulated domestic life of women allowed many innate "morbigenic germs" of degeneration to remain latent, the same germs that were triggered by the typical male life of activity and work.[72]

Lombroso further argued that criminal statistics underestimated the frequency of female crime. Police were less likely to detect those offenses that he considered most typical of women, like abortion, receiving stolen goods, poisoning, and thefts by servants.[73] On the other hand, women were less likely to commit the more visible crimes favored by men. "Male crimes" like homicide and assault, according to Lombroso, required "in a great number of cases not only physical force but also a certain strength and complexity of the intellect" that were "as a rule deficient in women in comparison to men."[74] Therefore, the "dark figure" was proportionately larger for female than male crimes, because "female crimes" were more easily hidden. This notion of the undercounting of crime among women fit neatly with the positivist conviction in the innate duplicity and secretiveness of female nature.

While few in number compared to men, female offenders exhibited striking anomalies not found in their normal sisters. In the work of Lombroso and Ferrero, these included smaller cranial size, signs of degeneration in the brain, and reduced sensitivity of touch, sight, smell, taste, and hearing. A variety of studies confirmed female insensitivity when measured on the hand, tongue, arm, and clitoris.[75] As with the comparisons between "normal" women and men, researchers sometimes had to explain away contradictory results. Antonio Marro, for example, in his book *The Characteristics of Criminals*, admitted finding the hands of "normal" women in his control group to be less sensitive than those of female offenders. He noted, however, that he had drawn his control group from former peasants who now worked as nurses in an insane asylum. Both the farmwork of their youth and the frequent washing of their hands in carbolic acid as nurses had coarsened their sense of touch.[76] Criminal anthropologists generally bemoaned the necessity of relying on lower-class women for their control groups. According to the class bias built into their theory, upper- and middle-class women were more highly evolved—and thus more "normal"—than working-class women. But few elite women would voluntarily participate in positivist experiments, so that criminal anthropologists had to rely on employees and inmates of state institutions, like hospitals and orphanages, who did not have the liberty to refuse.

Marro also noted that criminal women exhibited "thick hair," a sign of atavism because it recalled the fur of animals.[77] Yet it was not unattractive and was useful for hiding ugly anomalies of the face and head.[78] In a study of forty criminal women, Salsotto found an anomalous distribution of hair in their anal-genital areas. Although "everyone knows" that normal women have hair on the "monte di Venere" and only men have hair stretching back to the anus, Salsotto found seven female offenders with thick hair around the anus. To further confirm his hypothesis that criminal women resembled men, he noted that several of those with abnormal anal hair also exhibited "a virile physiognomy" accentuated by so much hair on the upper lip that they appeared to have "real mustaches."[79] In another study of eighty female offenders, Ottolenghi found a high rate of another anomaly—premature gray hair—compared to both male criminals and normal women. While he was surprised to find female criminals surpassing males in this defect, he concluded that "this, however, does not conflict with our earlier conclusion that premature gray hair relates directly to psychic activity. Criminal women react more emotionally than criminal men to their agitated life while, vice versa, the normal woman turns gray much later than the normal man since she leads a much more tranquil life and is so much less intelligent and active than he."[80]

Criminal anthropologists fell into additional confusion when trying to explain the implication of these physical anomalies for the interior psychological life of female criminals. While the female offender was less physically deformed than the criminal man, Lombroso and Ferrero insisted that the former was far more cruel than the latter. In support of this contention, they cited the Italian proverb that

"Rarely is a woman wicked but when she is she surpasses the man."[81] The number of born criminals among women might be small, but they were doubly monstrous since criminality was not only deviant but primarily a male activity. In a separate article, Ferrero linked the special cruelty of the female offender to "the tendency of women to not so much destroy their enemy as to inflict the maximum pain, to put him through an ordeal, to torment him and to paralyze him with suffering."[82] A product of women's weakness, this innate cruelty was "one of the first sentiments produced by evolution and organized by heredity."[83] As mentioned earlier, Ferrero believed that piety was slowly replacing cruelty in the character of civilized women. But the born criminal would continue to exhibit "the worst characteristics of the female psychology"; besides cruelty these included deceit, dishonesty, a tendency to vendetta, and a passion for clothes.[84]

Yet criminal anthropologists saw more in the psychology of the female offender than simply an exaggeration of the worst characteristics of all women. Perhaps paradoxically, they also saw in her "a very strong resemblance to the masculine type."[85] As Salsotto had found "masculine" hair on the anus of many born criminals, Lombroso and Ferrero recognized psychological traits typical of normal men: "excessive eroticism, a weak maternal instinct, pleasure in a dissipated life, intelligence, audacity, subordination of weaker and more impressionable persons sometimes using muscular strength, a taste for violent exercise [and] vices."[86] In short, atavism or degeneration returned women to a savage past when little differentiation had existed between the sexes. At a more advanced state of evolution, what was normal for men was criminal in women. Science decreed even further divergence between the psychology of the two sexes in the future.

To balance this repulsive portrait of the female born criminal, positive criminologists pointed out that the majority of women who broke the law were only occasional criminals. Anomalies being relatively rare in women, environmental influences accounted for most female deviancy. Since women were by nature so impressionable and weak, conditions such as poverty, overcrowded housing, abandonment by parents, or the instigation of husbands and lovers could easily push them into crime. Sighele's famous work, *The Criminal Couple*, illustrated how atavistic men could turn weak but "normal" women into their accomplices in crime. Such female collaborators were not innately corrupt, most often committing minor property crimes that they did not consider wrong.

The positivist analysis of the female offender failed to convince some critics who still saw a basic contradiction between the insistence by criminal anthropologists that women as a group were generally inferior and their low rates of crime. Such criticism came most often from the French school and rallied the Italians to add a further dimension to their theory of female crime. The key to solving this contradiction, they argued, lay in broadening the definition of female crime to include prostitution. Only by adding rates of prostitution to crime could criminologists measure the authentic quantity of female deviancy. As Ferri wrote, quoting Sergi, "If woman in society supplies only an insignificant quota in the figures of crime, she does indeed fully manifest in prostitution the degeneracy peculiar to her sex."[87] That the criminal code did not condemn prostitution was discounted by Lombroso in the first edition of *Criminal Man*, when he declared that nevertheless "public opinion counts prostitutes among the criminal population."[88] He concluded that, with the inclusion of prostitutes, "the quantity [of crime] between the two sexes is equal, and perhaps greater among the weaker sex."[89]

According to Lombroso, prostitutes were even more atavistic than criminal women. He answered his critics by arguing that: "Sergi has observed that even among savage women murder is infrequent while prostitution is the general rule; and to a certain point this would explain and confirm what I have said that prostitutes rather than female born delinquents are the real criminals."[90] Lombroso did not hesitate to identify prostitution as the typical form of female crime, pointing out that "the primitive woman was rarely a murderess, but she was always a prostitute."[91] As proof of the atavistic nature of prostitution, Lombroso and Ferrero claimed to have found enough physical anomalies in 38 percent of all prostitutes to pronounce them "born" to their fate as opposed to only 14 percent of female criminals.[92] The assumption that displays of sexuality among women represented reversion to primitive or animal origins bolstered positivist arguments that chastity, passionlessness, and monogamy were natural to normal, European women and would become more so as evolution proceeded.

The prominence of prostitution in Lombroso's conception of female crime is evident from the full Italian title of *The Female Offender*—"The female offender, the prostitute and the normal woman." In this work, he and Ferrero cited a plethora of physical measurements and observations to support their theory that prostitutes were less evolved than other women, including female born criminals. They found in prostitutes small cranial capacity, narrow or receding foreheads, prominent cheekbones, short stature, short arms (because they work less), excessive weight, left-handedness and prehensile feet (like monkeys). They shared with delinquent women the tendency toward especially dark hair and eyes. Conducting his famous sensitivity tests, Lombroso found touch, taste, and smell to be duller in prostitutes than in any other group of women, a conclusion seconded by a positivist colleague, Guerrieri.[93] Typically, Lombroso added stories to document more colorfully this extreme insensitivity, recalling, for example, a prostitute with a wounded hand who had rejected medication and amputation for fifteen days even after gangrene had set in. For Lombroso, the only possible explanation for such irrational conduct was that she simply did not feel any pain.

Insensitivity extended even to the clitoris of prostitutes, a finding seemingly at odds with theory that they, like savage women, were sexually unrestrained. As Umberto Mantegazza and Giuseppe Ciuffo concluded after comparing Tuscan and Sardinian prostitutes, "It is not at all true that prostitutes in general are more sensitive than normal women during the sexual act; a good half of our women were frigid, feeling little attraction or in fact indifference to men or being revolted and disgusted at carnal coupling. The other half is divided between those with a medium sensitivity to coitus and those with a genital hypersensitivity."[94] In other words, most prostitutes were either nymphomaniacs or frigid. Interestingly, the latter seemed more repugnant to criminal anthropologists, because frigidity was thought to lead to abnormal sexual practices more typical of men such as masturbation and homosexuality. Thus, both the nymphomania and the frigidity of prostitutes confirmed their reversion to a lower stage of evolution and contrasted markedly with the more advanced tendency of normal women to sublimate their sexuality into childbearing.

Other positivist criminologists came up with measurements to confirm Lombroso's theories. In studying the skulls of twenty-five prostitutes, Gaspare Bergonzoli found only one free of anomalies while 20 percent exhibited three abnormal characteristics.[95] Giulio Masini compared the larynxes of fifty prostitutes and twenty normal women, finding physical abnormalities in almost all of the former group and hardly any in the latter. Furthermore, the prostitutes with the most acute anomalies had "deep, I would say almost masculine, voices."[96] A. Ascarelli reported to the sixth Congress of Criminal Anthropology held in Rome in 1906, that "even an examination of fingerprints confirms that the professional prostitute is anthropologically inferior to the normal woman."[97]

Any inconsistencies in results were reinterpreted to support the intuitions of the master. Moraglia was initially troubled when he found that the mouths of prostitutes more closely resembled those of normal women than the abnormal mouths of female criminals. Fearing that this discovery might contradict the positivist maxim that "prostitution is a psychological equivalent to crime in women," he resolved the conundrum by insisting that prostitutes had to be relatively beautiful in order to attract customers and "the mouth is not an unimportant part of the appearance."[98] Nature had hidden their interior anomalies by a pleasing exterior. This line of argument echoed Lombroso's hypotheses that the exterior abnormalities of prostitutes were hidden by their youth; were not particularly ugly (like wide jaws and dark hair); and were quantitatively fewer than the malformations within.[99] Moraglia clinched his argument by noting that atavistic expressions broke through this false exterior beauty during sexual intercourse. After conducting "all those experiments which time and circumstances allowed," Moraglia proved that prostitutes exhibited "a fierce or ferocious physiognomy with a more or less marked gnashing of teeth during masturbation and even more during sexual intercourse at the climax of orgasm."[100] For Moraglia, the atavistic facial expressions of prostitutes clearly had their antecedents in very ancient times when women tried to stave off the routine but violent sexual advances by men. Thus, in the sexual act, the true but hidden savagery of prostitutes was revealed.

Several other characteristics, seemingly social in nature, confirmed the label of atavism for prostitutes. The first were tattoos, although criminal anthropologists had to admit that these physical signs of a savage nature appeared on fewer female than male bodies. In a study of 531 Neapolitan prostitutes, Abele De Blasio found only 47 with tattoos, most of them ornamental rather than symbolic.[101] According to Orazio Albertis, 7 percent of Ligurian prostitutes exhibited tattoos, mostly initials of lovers or successions of lovers.[102]Lombroso identified tattoos on only 2.5 percent of his sample of prostitutes, but his theories remained confirmed by the even greater paucity of tattooing among female criminals and normal women.[103] Prostitutes also used strange jargon, interpreted by positivist criminologists as holdovers of primitive speech. Emilio Grasselli, for example, found that prostitutes used different types of slang for pimps (*pucio*) and disinterested lovers (*ninin, piceur*) while they tagged genital intercourse as *fric frac* and anal intercourse as "pulling the cart" or slave labor.[104] Neapolitan prostitutes were especially fond of dancing the fast-paced tarantella, which, according to De Blasio, was "an erotic dance which is reminiscent of the orgies of some savage peoples."[105]

That prostitutes represented the nadir of female atavism illustrates the central role of sexuality in the positivist analysis of the female offender. A variety of social phenomena prompted such extreme anxiety about the proper channeling of female sexuality into marriage and motherhood. In the case of lower-class women, criminologists interpreted the increase in illegitimacy and overcrowding of foundling homes as signs of spreading sexual license threatening evolutionary progress. New demands by feminists—for paternity suits, equality in family law, equal wages, and the vote—also threatened the traditional hierarchy of the sexes. For Italian criminal anthropologists, who tended to be socialist and even sympathetic to limited political rights for women, the sexual sphere remained the last bastion of dominance. Even the PSI did not envision equality in the "private" domains of sexuality and the family, where criminal anthropologists could continue, without conflict between personal and political values, to maintain their privileges. If sexuality was the root of female behavior, then nature dictated women's eternally subordinate status.

PUNISHMENT

In developing a theory of punishment for women, criminal anthropologists had to take into account not only the arguments of the Classical School, but also the nineteenth-century debate over female legal capacities. Should women and men have equal accountability (*imputabilità*) in the criminal courts? Inequality was already enshrined in the Pisanelli Civil Code of 1865 during the years when a new penal code was being debated. It would seem only logical that if civil law viewed women as too immature to control their own families and property, criminal law would similarly absolve women—like children—from full responsibility for illegal behavior.

Yet when the new state finally enacted its first criminal code in 1889, the so-called Zanardelli Code contained no general principle differentiating between the legal accountability of men and women. Making little reference to gender, it implicitly affirmed that the two sexes were equally able to distinguish right from wrong and to choose whether to break the law. In the best tradition of the Classical School, the criminal code held both men and women to possess free will, prescribing for them identical standards of evidence and degrees of punishment in the great majority of cases.

The Zanardelli Code, however, did contain a few exceptions to this principle of equal accountability before the law. These exceptions did not uniformly treat women more harshly or more leniently than men. In the case of adultery, the punishment was equivalent for the two sexes, but husbands enjoyed much broader legal grounds for bringing charges. Men could have their wives arrested for even short or clandestine affairs, while wives had to prove that their husbands "maintained a concubine in the family house or elsewhere in a notorious manner."[106] Although these measures pertaining to adultery discriminated against women, the sections of the penal code on infanticide and abortion offered the possibility of reduced sentences if the crimes had been committed to save a woman's "honor."[107] A defendant could invoke the attenuating circumstance of "honor" if the child was illegitimate in the case of a single woman, or the offspring of an adulterous affair, in the case of a married woman. Not only women benefited from this possibility of reduced punishment, however, but also any male accomplice who sought to protect the honor of his "wife, mother, offspring, adopted daughter, or sister."[108] Thus, light penalties for infanticide and abortion did not proceed from a recognition of women's diminished legal responsibility but from the traditional right of men to seek legal protection for their families' "honor."[109]

The other exceptions to the principle of sexual equality before the criminal law concerned punishment. In the case of *contravvenzioni*, or misdemeanors, women convicted of less than a month of jail and who were not recidivists might be allowed by the judge to serve their sentence at home.[110] House arrest for minor crimes was also extended to children, again showing the propensity of lawmakers to classify women as children or immature versions of adult men. In all other cases of incarceration, the law simply stated that women would be sent to "special institutions."[111] According to a detailed commentary on the Zanardelli Code by Pessina, a respected leader of the Classical School, this article was purposely worded in a vague manner in order "to avoid special measures for women in the list of punishments."[112] The state would thus retain the right to punish women as severely as men and postponed any mitigating measures to less important and less binding prison regulations.

The Zanardelli Code represented, to Lombroso's chagrin, a triumph of the Classical School, in its assumption that all adults possess free will and the ability to discern right from wrong. Punishment, therefore, was calibrated to fit the severity of the crime, not the characteristics of the offender. But opinions about women's accountability in criminal matters did not divide neatly along the lines of the two major schools of legal thought. Many disciples of the Classical School, like Ellero, pointed out the irrationality of subordinating women to men in the civil code but holding them equally culpable in criminal matters. Like a good student of the Enlightenment, Ellero held that "men and women share the same origin and essence and are therefore intrinsically equal, as their souls are identical."[113] Yet he contradicted himself by then comparing women to "children and idiots who cannot take care of their own needs."[114] Women's problem lay in their uterus, which "dominates the entire organism," making bones and tissues weak and emotions "changeable and impetuous."[115] Because the body was a "slave" to the uterus, women became especially impressionable and melancholy during puberty, menstruation, pregnancy and menopause. These were separated only by short periods of time, comparable to "the lucid intervals during insanity, during which the freedom and consciousness of the will is in doubt."[116] Because of such innate physical and mental inferiority, women quite rightly enjoyed fewer civil and political rights than men and in "recompense" they should be subject to lesser punishments.[117] The law should not hold a woman morally responsible for behavior not fully under her control.

Ellero's analysis highlights the long tradition of explaining women's nature in biological terms even among the Enlightenment proponents of universal rights. It also sounded surprisingly close to the expected reasoning of the Positivist School proceeding from its dogma of women's biological and mental weakness. It is not surprising, therefore, that Vito Antonio Berardi came to quite similar conclusions as Ellero based on "the new Positivist outlook."[118] In words strikingly similar to Ellero's, Berardi declared that the uterus holds "a tyrannical sway over the organism," so that it is called "the second brain of a woman."[119] It caused women "to become excited for the most trifling reason," especially during the "pathological" states of puberty, menstruation, pregnancy, and menopause.[120] He concluded, like Ellero, that the law should hold women less accountable than men before the criminal law, since biological constraints hampered their freedom to make moral choices.

Despite the apparent logic of Berardi's argument, it did not represent the mainstream opinion of the Positivist School. As F. Puglia explained in the *Archives*, criminal anthropology had of course established the biological inferiority of women and approved the inequalities in the civil code according to the following rationale: "the lesser psychic energy of women, which is a consequence of their biological inferiority, legitimizes the limitation of their *civil* rights, because management of one's affairs requires experience in life, sometimes cunning . . . and firmness of purpose."[121] But women's emotional and volatile nature did not make them any less accountable in criminal law, since they needed only to "be aware of the law, the nature of the action which they commit and the consequence of that action."[122] Puglia admitted that the law should hold women less responsible for crimes committed during periods of emotional instability like pregnancy, but not because they lacked the ability to make moral choices. According to positivist precepts, what was crucial was not free will but social defense, and he argued that "a woman is less dangerous when she commits a crime in these circumstances."[123] In other words, pregnant women were not necessarily born criminals and thus future recidivists, but only temporarily abnormal while controlled by their uterus. In such cases, lawmakers should provide leniency through provisions in auxiliary prison statutes.

Thus, in the end, most criminal anthropologists agreed with the provisions on female criminal responsibility in the Zanardelli Code, although they decried its general embodiment of classical principles. That the two legal schools converged only on women shows that traditional paternalism overrode consistency of argument in both cases. Unwilling to set married women free from their husband's control in matters of property and family, they agreed that gender subordination be written into civil law. On the other hand, the classical authors of the Zanardelli Code, with the approval of their positivist colleagues, became champions of gender equality when discussing criminal responsibility. Considered too weak and childlike to control their own property, decide how to educate their children, or vote, women miraculously matured into perspicacious and even cunning adults when indicted before penal tribunals. Yet the possible mitigation of prison conditions, suggested both in the Zanardelli Code and by criminal anthropologists, was at the discretion of the male judges and prison administrators, not a right that women could claim on the basis of their supposed physical and mental inferiority. Both the civil and penal codes thus followed an identical logic, that of maintaining control over women in the hands of men.

As long as sentencing was at the discretion of judges, advised by expert witnesses trained in criminal anthropology, positivists generally recommended leniency for women. Women's punishment, like men's, should theoretically correspond not to the severity of their crime but to their anthropological status. For female born criminals, those "double monsters" who were deviant both in their sex and their behavior, only incarceration would prevent further danger to society. Even for the "poisoners, swindlers, [and] murderesses," however, a convent might be more appropriate than the penitentiary. According to Lombroso, "because of the great susceptibility to suggestion of women, it is likely that under the influence of the nuns, religiosity would replace love, which is the most frequent cause of crime, and thus honesty and religious fanaticism would be substituted for criminal tendencies."[124] This advice was particularly suspect coming from an anti-clerical, nonpracticing Jew, who saw no value in religion except to keep women under control. Positivists never linked religion with the reformation of boys or men, who presumably harbored too highly evolved an intelligence to be influenced by religious superstition. Interestingly, the positivist recipe for female internment again dovetailed with that of the state, which not only relied on religious reformatories to take care of female juvenile delinquents, but staffed public prisons for women with nuns.

Criminal anthropologists also agreed with the articles of the Zanardelli Code that mitigated punishment for infanticide, if performed to protect the honor of a single mother. As Sighele reminded readers of the *Archives*, "The positivist school . . . does not classify crimes but criminals," thus shifting the focus to the character and motives of the defendant.[125] To him, a discussion of whether infanticide was identical to homicide was irrelevant, since social defense had to be calibrated to the probability of recidivism. Women with a history of arrest or prostitution should not be eligible to plead for mercy, since they were considered already without honor and most likely born criminals. Yet most defendants were criminals by passion, who killed their infants simply to preserve their reputations and those of their families. According to Sighele, in them "the sentiment of cruelty . . . has predominated only for an instant, it has been a flash of lightening that has disastrously interrupted the normality of their life."[126] The "victim of a fatal moment of aberration," a single woman accused of infanticide was not likely to harm other members of society and rather than imprisonment, which would corrupt her and make rehabilitation impossible, deserved simply exile from her home town.[127]

The alternative to infanticide, according to criminal anthropologists, was an increase in the already high numbers of children deposited at foundling homes. Because of the high mortality rates in foundling homes, Lombroso called them "the real assassin[s] who kill [their charges] legally."[128] Furthermore, those children who did survive live in the orphanage, or with foster families, tended nevertheless to become criminals or prostitutes in higher proportions than legitimate children. As Carlo Lessona asked readers of the *Archives*, "Who, if caught between disgrace and the death of a being incapable of feeling pain, would not prefer the latter to certain poverty for [the mother] and her unhappy offspring?"[129] For positivists, the balance clearly lay in favor of preserving the honor of single mothers, so that rather than thoughts of suicide they might entertain hopes of future marriage. Social defense would best be served by preserving legal families and minimizing the production of illegitimate children.

Criminal anthropologists supported the mitigation of punishment for abortion on similar grounds. Single women who committed abortion to preserve their honor were not likely recidivists in crime and otherwise would burden foundling homes with additional abandoned children. In the debate as to whether the fetus was a person and abortion equaled homicide, they relied on the arguments of Raffaele Balestrini. In an article entitled "Darwinism and criminal law," published in the *Archives* in 1885, Balestrini cited Haeckel's biogenetic law to reject the equation of fetuses with human beings. According to Haeckel, each human embryo retraced the Darwinian evolution of the species, from the cell, to the invertebrate, the fish, and finally the mammal. Balestrini concluded that "for the whole period of its life in the uterus, the fetus successively takes on various forms of animal organisms and that only at the moment of birth does it definitively possess the physical and psychological characteristics of humanity."[130] The law granted rights only to "individuals in society," and fetuses were neither persons nor living in society.[131] Since the law did not consider even children as fully formed human beings and thus limited their rights, it was absurd to award them to a fetus. Thus, abortion for the sake of honor deserved the same light punishment accorded to infanticide.

Despite the attention given by jurists to infanticide and abortion, most women were arrested not for these crimes of passion but for more petty occasional crimes. By nature weak and impressionable, according to criminal anthropologists, women were easily led by the instigation of others or bad environmental influences to break the law. Poverty pushed women into high rates of petty theft. Prison was unsuitable for these occasional criminals, since positivist criminologists believed that such a life would harden these victims of society into habitual deviants. They instead recommended penal substitutes such as fines and suspended sentences. Lombroso also suggested a few novel punishments tailored to the supposed inherent vanity in all women, like cutting their hair or sequestering their household furniture. Rather than weakening the penal principles of female responsibility, judges should be given the discretion to order such penal substitutes.

To reduce occasional criminality in women, positivists recommended preventive measures, usually addressed to female sexuality. Lombroso stressed the importance for women of control and guidance by their families. Claiming that a higher percentage of female than male foundlings and orphans became delinquent, he explained that "this is, however, quite natural, for a woman being weaker and more passionate than a man, has more need of the support and restraint of the family to keep her in the right way, from which she is more easily turned than a man, on account of the slippery path of prostitution that is always open to her."[132] For many female orphans, he counseled that prostitution "is checked only by the intervention of an early marriage."[133] He also advanced maternity as a "moral antidote" to crime and prostitution, while admitting that its beneficial effects were usually only temporary.[134] While positivist writings sometimes mentioned the need to teach female offenders some type of work, the emphasis was never on making women self-sufficient but providing their supposedly weak natures with appropriate discipline. Once separated from the evil influence of male instigators, female offenders needed to be passed into the protection of families or nuns.

In the case of prostitutes, the state would provide a system of surveillance through its "regulation system." Requiring all prostitutes to register with police and undergo frequent medical examinations, the regulation system had been ensconced in Italian law since unification and received the approval of positivists. If prostitution was the equivalent of crime, why was it to be legalized and tolerated rather than repressed? Part of the positivist answer lay in the impossibility of reforming women born with an atavistic tendency to sexual deviance. As Roncoroni pointed out, "The born prostitute has always existed, exists now, and will always exist and seems to be everywhere the same in her fundamental traits and undergoes only a few modifications in external appearance."[135] Sighele agreed, warning that "the phenomenon of prostitution has roots that are too ancient and too deep for some short-sighted persons to deceive themselves into thinking that it could be eradicated by inaugurating free love among young ladies!"[136]

Furthermore, prostitutes satisfied a social need, that of fulfilling the strong and often uncontrollable male sex drive, "that current which if left to itself would bring social harm and scandal."[137] Instead of prisons, born prostitutes should be confined to legal, state-licensed brothels where they would be kept under surveillance of madams, police, and physicians yet available to male customers. Lombroso decried illegal or "clandestine prostitutes" as "the most harmful sort" since they escaped government surveillance. He recommended the extension of the system of state-regulated brothels from the cities to the countryside since "it is especially necessary to make sexual intercourse accessible to all dissolute-minded young men."[138] Without such a sexual safety valve, such men might threaten respectable women through rape and adultery, young men through pederasty, and themselves through masturbation.

Was there not a contradiction between the positivist equation of prostitution with crime and its insistence that prostitutes remain unpunished? Of course prostitutes enjoyed a life of only semifreedom in tolerated brothels, being under the control of often domineering and exploitative madams. Registered with police, legal prostitutes were constantly under surveillance as well as subject to inspections by public doctors twice a week. That the regulation system was onerous is clear from the frequent attempts to escape its control. But prostitutes could flee from brothels and thus retained a degree of liberty absent from inmates in prison. This favored treatment stemmed from pleasure that they provided men. Unwilling to give up access to brothels that the state guaranteed to be legal, orderly, and free of disease, male positivists accepted the notion, long-rooted in Catholic theology and Italian political wisdom, that prostitution was unfortunate but necessary. Thus, they broke the logic of their analysis, which would have relegated born prostitutes to prison, to uphold male sexual prerogative over women.

CRITICS

The strongest outcry against the positivist theory of the female offender came not from other criminologists but from the emerging movement for female emancipation in Italy. From the birth of Italy in 1861, women like Anna Maria Mozzoni and Jesse White Mario had called for the equality of the sexes in education, the professions, and civil law. Journals like *La Donna* [*Women*] tried to spread the notion that the new "citizen mother" needed and deserved equal rights with men if she was to train properly the children of the new nation. By the 1890s, the proponents of sexual equality had begun to coalesce into a series of organizations like the Leagues to Protect Female Interests, the Female Union, the National Council of Women, and the women's section of the Italian Socialist Party. They were ready to answer the positivist claim to have established scientific proof of the inferiority of women but less interested in the analysis of female crime, except in their opposition to the regulation of prostitution by the state. Feminists, as they began to call themselves after the turn of the century, realized that the criminal anthropological thesis of the natural inequality of the sexes had quickly gained notoriety far outside of specialized legal circles and threatened their slow but steady campaign to improve women's position in society.

The opposition between positivist criminologists and feminists was not, however, as clear-cut as might appear from their views of the nature of women. On this score, the two positions were irreconcilable: the former insisted that women were more atavistic than men and that evolution would bring further differentiation between the sexes, while the latter held human nature to be universal and foresaw a convergence of roles for men and women. Yet criminal anthropologists did not condemn all legal changes pursued by feminists. Such positions did not always follow logically from positivists' scientific findings on female nature, leading to inconsistencies and contradictions in their public utterances on the civil and political position of women.

It is thus difficult to define a unified positivist stance on the "woman question," the nineteenth-century label for the debate over the relation of the sexes in society, economy, and politics. A survey about the woman question, conducted in 1899 by the socialist Guglielmo Gambarotta, provides a useful map of the variations in political opinions on this subject among criminal anthropologists. Of the 200 "illustrious, very well-known men" to whom Gambarotta sent the survey, ten were positivist criminologists, a choice illustrating their prominence as intellectuals outside academic circles.[139] Published under the title *Inquiry about Women*, the survey began with a general question: Should women's rights be identical, equivalent, or inferior to those of men? He then listed several specific categories, including the right to vote. At the turn of the century, female suffrage was still considered a more radical demand than equality in education, work, and family law, partly because only a minority of men were as yet eligible to vote. But at the time of Gambarotta's survey, feminists were becoming emboldened to make female suffrage the centerpiece of their platforms, taking their cue from international organizations like the International Council of Women and the International Suffrage Alliance. Thus, the response of criminal anthropologists to Gambarotta's question about suffrage provided an important gauge to their positions on the woman question.

Of the ten positivists surveyed, only two favored inequality between the sexes. One of these, Ferrero, confined his remarks to the vote, arguing that granting suffrage to Italian women "would constitute a coup di grace to the nation." Already incapable of governing effectively, the ruling class would only be weakened by the addition of women, whose most serious defects included: "a narrow-minded spirit of conservatism, a very mean social egoism, a stolid veneration for everything that emanates from the government, an absolute incapacity to rise above the consideration of family good to that of the state, [and] an unhealthy passion for all political vanities."[140] Although Ferrero left the door open for female voting in nations with a more progressive political culture, he elsewhere discounted female suffrage as "entirely profitless to a [woman]; it is a weapon for which she has not the least need."[141] From Ferrero's evolutionary perspective, men labored while women were increasingly able to withdraw into the home to pursue their natural maternal function. Shielded from the struggle for existence, women had no need of the "weapon" of suffrage, which was already wielded for their protection by their husbands.

The second proponent of inequality, Niceforo, universally condemned the female sex drawing explicitly on positivist research:

Women are inferior to men: *physically*, physiologists have found the signs of inferiority in their tissues, in the corpuscles of their blood, in the evolutionary development of their brain; *intellectually*, analysts of their intelligence have found an absolute lack of genius, an unimaginative mold to their conceptions, the almost subconscious assimilation of ideas, the pettiness, poverty, monotony, and one-sidedness of their thoughts.[142]

He added that emotionally women lacked "sensitivity" and instead exhibited "impulsiveness, fickleness, puerile vanity, love for exterior appearance, and triviality, all the noted psychological attributes, in a word, that are common to children and savages."[143] Niceforo ridiculed the idea of legal equality and affirmed the natural role of women to be motherhood.

Despite the consonance of their scientific findings on women with those of Niceforo, the other eight respondents avoided his misogynist tone. While none favored complete equality, all granted that women deserved "equivalent" rights to men. As Mario Pilo put it, "I wish that women might be legally equal to men, with different rights in relation to their different physiological nature, but equivalent."[144]

For Sighele, equivalency offered a compromise between political and professional exigencies. On the one hand, this position recognized "justice, which can no longer suffer legal inequality in the civil world between the sexes, which almost evokes a distant memory of slavery."[145] On the other hand, equivalency gave credit to "science, which has demonstrated the intellectual inferiority of women in relation to men—corollary of their physiological and psychological difference—and cannot suffer that unlike beings have identical rights."[146] Less agreement existed on whether women's "different physiological nature" made them qualified to vote. For Marro, "women must take part in administrative and political councils that deal with matters directly related to the family and upbringing of children" but had no place in discussing other issues such as war.[147] Sighele suggested using the experimental method appropriate to positivism: give women local, administrative suffrage first and weigh the effects before advancing to national, political suffrage. Others, like Lombroso, Pilo, and Zerboglio, affirmed women's right to vote without qualification, and Viazzi expressed impatience with the question itself, recommending "the same for women as for men."[148]

More unanimity reigned on the question of divorce, although even feminists hesitated to raise an issue that would elicit such fierce opposition from the Catholic Church. Only a few criminal anthropologists, like Enrico Morselli, opposed divorce; from his evolutionary point of view, "Divorce is an inferior institution, historically and ethnografically."[149] Having "a direct connection to all the degenerate states of the mind," divorce was naturally typical of the "primitive" races.[150] Such an argument was consonant with the generally expressed positivist belief that monogamous marriage represented the highest state of sexual relationship, especially for women. Yet in his rebuttal of Morselli, Ferri represented the views of most of his colleagues. He defended divorce as a "penal substitute," that is, a measure that would prevent crime, in this case adultery and domestic homicide. Lombroso agreed, writing more graphically that the indissolubility of marriage caused "dislike to grow into nausea and crime" and sometimes "loathing for the entire [opposite] sex."[151] An unhappy man often turned to "unnatural passions" like the rape of young girls or homosexuality, while a woman sometimes responded with poison to "tortures by her spouse."[152] For Lombroso, divorce offered "a safety valve" for pent-up unhappiness and fit into the general positivist legal scheme to replace repressive criminal penalties with preventive civil measures.[153]

It is difficult to reconcile the advanced positions of many criminal anthropologists on reforms in women's civil status, like suffrage and divorce, with their unremittingly uniform pronouncements on women's physical and psychological inferiority to men. Of course they dressed up some of their positions in positivist garb, like the argument that divorce was a "penal substitute" needed to prevent murder between spouses. But the disjunction between their political and scientific views on women was striking. The close relationships between many positivists and educated, sometimes feminist women, may partially explain their sympathy for certain improvements in female civil status. Lombroso, for example, had two well-educated daughters who as adults became well-known contributors to important publications like the *Nuova antologia*. He was especially close to Gina, who in her youth pleaded to be allowed to attend medical school and later became her father's assistant. In the preface to *The Female Offender*, Lombroso praised "my dearest Gina" as "the last and only thread that links me to life and the most steadfast collaborator whose inspiration is more productive than any of my work."[154] In the same preface he thanked Kuliscioff, a prominent socialist feminist, who was frequently at his house and a favorite of his daughters. While often in disagreement with Kuliscioff, Lombroso was clearly familiar with her views and even cited her famous lecture, "The Monopoly of Men," in the pages of *The Female Offender*.[155]

In addition to personal relationships, the political allegiance of criminal anthropologists—largely to the socialist party—shaped their views on the woman question. While hesitant to make feminist demands a legislative priority, the PSI nevertheless was the only party to support sexual equality in principle. Over the years, its members had supported unsuccessful bills on divorce and suffrage, and they provided the bulwark of the campaign for protective legislation for women and children, passed in 1902. Many positivist criminologists were caught in an uncomfortable contradiction between their scientific findings on the inferiority of women and the more progressive stance of the PSI. A few, like Niceforo and Ferrero, unabashedly translated their professional stance into a political one and opposed increased rights for women. The majority, however, ignored the implications of their research and publicly declared an enlightened stance toward the woman question. Lombroso most obviously exemplified this bluff by prefacing a book unremittingly denigrating to women with the innocent disclaimer that "not one line" of it justified the oppression of women. Gambarotta's formula of "equivalency" between the sexes offered Lombroso and his colleagues a comfortable position of compromise from which they could support specific popular legal changes yet continue to preach the fundamental physical, intellectual, and psychological inequality of the sexes.

On the other hand, as friends and political allies of criminal anthropologists, supporters of women's emancipation were loathe to criticize positivist findings. It was especially difficult for them to attack the new science of criminology when their hopes had been pinned on reason as the weapon to undermine reactionary and religious prejudices against women. From its inception, the movement for female emancipation had expanded the eighteenth-century Enlightenment principle of the inalienable rights of man to include women. Nineteenth-century socialism added the promise that history was progressing toward the economic and social equality of humanity. Both philosophies rested on a reverence for reason and science, which therefore became the obvious weapons for feminists to wield when arguing that the restrictions on their sex were irrational and unnatural. What a delusion for them to find that the modern discipline of criminal anthropology claimed to have incontrovertible scientific proof of the inequality of the sexes! They were faced with the delicate task of critiquing specific positivist pronouncements without attacking science itself.

In some ways, supporters of female emancipation had to combat the notorious findings of criminal anthropologists from a position of weakness. As women, they neither possessed the vote nor positions in parliament from which to influence legislation affecting the legal position of women, whether in civil or criminal law. Furthermore, the movement was sharply divided, after the establishment in 1892 of the PSI, between bourgeois and socialist wings. The former pursued legal, educational, and political equality, while the latter denigrated this emphasis on civil rights as superficial and elitist, focusing instead on economic reforms for working women. Perhaps more problematic was the organizational division between the two wings, as liberal, middle-class women refused to join the PSI and its women's sections, while the male socialist leadership encouraged the withdrawal of its female members from bourgeois organizations. Yet over the years bourgeois and socialist women did collaborate in support of certain issues, like the vote, and organized feminism presented an acknowledged pressure group on parliament. Members of both wings were deeply troubled and often offended by the new scientific dogma on women and responded publicly in books, political articles, and speeches. The attack on criminal anthropology was more forthright among bourgeois feminists, who had fewer personal ties to criminal anthropology, than among socialists, political allies of its leading lights.

Proponents of bourgeois feminism employed several approaches to refute "scientific" claims of female inferiority. First, some writers offered opposing "scientific" evidence to contradict positivist tests, especially those concerning the size and weight of the brain. Irene de Bonis de Nobili, active in the suffrage campaign, criticized the evidence of "some false scientists who believe they can demonstrate the inferiority of women."[156] She cited alternative scientific opinion that correlated intelligence not with the size of the brain but with the ratio of the weight of the brain to that of the body. Since women weighed much less than men, "from this point of view *women's brains are heavier than men's*."[157] In her book *Women and Feminism,* Maria Marselli-Valli recounted a favorite feminist anecdote that made a mockery of the positivist correlation between intelligence and brain weight. After the death of Ernst Bischoff, a strong proponent of this correlation, an autopsy revealed that his brain weighed "less than that which he himself had established as the average for women."[158] Furthermore, F. P. Diana pointed out in a public lecture that the reasoning of "the anatomical-physiologists" had no "scientific value" since no one yet knew precisely how the brain functioned.[159] Several writers simply expressed irritation at the debate over women's intelligence. Even Ernesta Michelangeli, in her rather moderate book, *The True Mission of Women,* dismissed those who opposed medical education for women with the exasperated words: "Go away! This little story of [women's] intellectual weakness is now discredited forever."[160]

Diana introduced another common theme of bourgeois feminism when she wrote: "I am not a philosopher nor a physiologist nor a forensic doctor, and I bow reverently to those illustrious scientists but . . . I say that certain questions are better resolved by practical observation and by reference to history than by the reasoning and theories of scientists."[161] For example, she argued that women's lack of educational opportunities, not their sex, accounted for the paucity of female geniuses. Bonis de Nobili, while paying tribute to "objective science, real science," also advised positivists to consult history and "everyday observation" when theorizing about the nature of women.[162] She offered examples of famous and patriotic women like the heroines of the *risorgimento* and the recently deceased Queen Victoria to counter scientific claims of female inferiority. Other writers, like the lawyer Teresa Labriola, pointed out the social value of lower-class women: they were not just reproducers like animals but "worker[s], an economic force, producer[s]."[163] In the future, an increasing number of women would enter the workforce, making it absurd to deny them the rights possessed by male workers.

While most bourgeois feminists accepted physical differences between the sexes, they denied that these differences vitiated women's right to legal equality. Bonis de Nobili argued that "to be a voter . . . one is not required to have a certain strength measured by a dynamo-meter. From this point of view, porters would make the best voters."[164] Similarly, "physical and psychological sensitivity" should not determine the right to suffrage.[165] She concluded that nature had created a different "natural function" for the sexes, but had not determined their "social functions," which were open to change.[166] Just as nature had been appealed to wrongly in the past to justify the rule of a few men over the rest, it now was being unjustly used to perpetuate the disenfranchisement of women.

Other feminists agreed that rights could not be denied on the basis of physiological difference. Using the vocabulary of the natural rights philosophy of the Enlightenment, Diana argued eloquently for women's equality in work, education, and politics:

Reason and good sense affirm that the natural differences that exist between the sexes do not authorize a difference in treatment in exercising rights, because one cannot fix limits on human nature. Women in their human essence, in front of law and justice, are equal to men; they are capable of understanding truth and desiring good, of improving themselves through education, and of reaching high human ideals.[167]

Alluding to criminal anthropologists, she proclaimed it an insult for an adult woman to be treated "like a little girl or an idiot."[168] Labriola argued along similar lines for female suffrage, stipulating that the right to vote should not be based on "special characteristics" of a particular group but on "the universal human personality."[169]

Socialist feminism, like the PSI itself, was divided in its assessment of the value of positivist research. The leading socialist feminist and female socialist within the PSI, Kuliscioff, clearly rejected scientific arguments for the inferiority of women and received active support for her rebuttals from some socialist men like her collaborator and companion Turati.[170] As early as 1890, in her well-known lecture "The Monopoly of Men," Kuliscioff questioned the attempt by "modern physiologists and psychologists" to measure intelligence by measuring the size of the brain. "Who does not know," she continued, "that the size of the brain also shows significant variation among men of great ability!"[171] Like bourgeois feminists, she gave an example of one such man—in this case eminent urban planner of Paris, Baron von Haussmann—who was found to have a brain equal to the average size of that found in women. She pointed out that other factors, such as the molecular and chemical composition of the brain, were probably also related to intelligence, but could not be measured under a microscope. Instead of physical inferiority, Kuliscioff argued that environmental restraints like lack of education accounted for the lower intelligence and small number of geniuses among women. When put to use, women's brains would grow and develop as they had already begun to do in more advanced countries like England and France. She concluded that no more needed to be said, since the debate about brain size was "exhausted and not very serious."[172]

As the co-editor of *Critica sociale* with Turati, Kuliscioff subsequently took the opportunity to respond to articles by criminal anthropologists and positive reviews of their books by other socialists. Although these responses were often unsigned or signed only by Turati, they are clearly informed by Kuliscioff's reasoning. Lombroso and Ferrero's *The Female Offender*, for example, was allotted space in three successive issues for an extended review by Zerboglio, which drew frequent critical comments from the editors. In several long footnotes, they mocked both Lombroso's findings and Zerboglio's enthusiastic acceptance of them. Alluding to the full Italian title of the book—*Criminal Women, Normal Women, and Prostitutes*—they prophesied that "when a female genius writes about the physiology of normal, criminal, and 'kept' men (and the last category is much vaster than it would seem at first glance), she will easily be able to turn the tables" on positivism's hierarchy of the sexes.[173] More specifically, they questioned Lombroso's assertion, accepted by Zerboglio, that dissimulation, credulity, vanity, tendency to gossip, and a stunted sense of justice characterized the female sex. As to the last, they asked: "How many times, when faced with the endless lying and cowardice of *male* justice based on class, have we not asked ourselves if *female* justice might not at least mitigate its brutality!"[174]

More generally, Kuliscioff and Turati accused Lombroso and the entire school of criminal anthropology of confusing biological and social categories in defining the traits of each sex. The first were innate, but the second were eminently artificial and subject to change. The inferiority of women was not inborn and immutable but caused by environmental injustices. In "The Monopoly of Men," Kuliscioff had identified these injustices as mainly economic ones that prevented women from equal access to work and pay. This tendency to confuse biological and social determinants constituted "the eternal Achilles heel of the anthropological school, which has never ceased to be a masculine school, saturated with masculine prejudices."[175]

Socialist feminist journals registered mixed reactions to positivism. *Vita femminile*, the organ of the League for the Protection of Female Interests, commanded an eclectic group of writers, but was dominated by socialist women. According to Rosanna DeLongis' study of this periodical, the feminist editors urgently sought "*scientific* articles that discuss and possibly combat certain arguments of certain scientists who treat women with little favor."[176] Because it was impossible to reject or ignore experimental science, which was at the height of its prestige, *Vita femminile* was searching for, as DeLongis writes, "a friendly science against an enemy science or, better, *real* science against its distorted use by those who opposed the progress of women."[177] Yet the journal published articles by the positivists Giuseppe D'Aguanno and Sergi, both of whom repeated the Lombrosian dogma about women's physical, intellectual, and psychological inferiority. D'Aguanno tried to balance his negative analysis by praising motherhood, while Sergi supported complete freedom for women only because he was certain that few would go against their nature and choose to compete with men for education and jobs. *The Female Offender* received both positive and negative reviews in the periodical, showing the extreme confusion and division among socialist feminists in the face of criminal anthropology. Despite its pronouncements on women, positivism proved attractive to some socialist women, and they appropriated its materialist and evolutionary language to forecast female progress in the future. In her analysis of *Eva*, another socialist feminist journal, Maria Pia Bigaran found the same tendency to use positivism in order to convince readers that change toward a just and egalitarian society was inevitable. "Harmonic" and "healthy" natural laws, according to this comforting view, guaranteed the improvement of women's status.[178]

Preoccupied with defending "normal" women from the charges of inferiority, feminists for the most part ignored the positivist analysis of the female born criminal. Unlike the women's movements in the United States and England, which were successfully promoting the establishment of separate female reformatories, the Italian was largely silent on the treatment of women by the criminal justice system. The exception was the regulation of prostitution, which feminists vigorously denounced as "white slavery." Since their profession was legal, prostitutes had little contact with courts and prisons. Instead, they were subject to constant surveillance by the "morals police," special squads entrusted with keeping prostitutes off the streets and enclosed in their brothels. For feminists like Mozzoni, such surveillance reduced prostitutes to second-class citizens, because they could be arrested and registered by police without court review. Once arrested, prostitutes were like "prisoners of the Holy Inquisition, who are sentenced secretly without being charged, indicted, defended, or sentenced by a jury."[179] Such denial of due process to prostitutes constituted a "legal monstrosity" in a nation with a proud and liberal legal tradition.[180]

For feminists, poverty and male sexual irresponsibility—not biological atavism—caused prostitution. Underpaid and segregated in unskilled jobs, many women could not support themselves and their families without engaging in at least part-time prostitution. Others were forced into prostitution after male employers or lovers had abandoned them at pregnancy. According to female emancipationists, the system of legalized brothels only encouraged such "libertinage" and enshrined the "moral double standard."[181] Instead the state should reinstate paternity suits, so that abandoned women could recover enough financial support to keep themselves out of prostitution. It should also tighten legislation against child abuse and incest, alarmingly frequent in the lives of underage streetwalkers. To protect poor and homeless girls, feminists established shelters in several cities, the most famous of which was the *Asilo Mariuccia* in Milan. Unlike Catholic conservatories for girls, the feminist shelters sought to train their charges for self-supporting factory jobs in the industrializing economy.[182]

In short, the organized women's movement demanded the abolition of special laws that legalized brothels and placed them under police surveillance.[183] On the other hand, they opposed draconian laws outlawing prostitution. While deploring prostitution as degrading, feminists preferred to attack the inequalities between the sexes in the family, workplace, education, and civil law that gave rise to it. They believed that prostitutes, as they gained control over their lives, would voluntarily leave the profession. Meanwhile, legal and moral attacks on male licentiousness and irresponsibility would decrease demand. By closing the tolerated brothels, the state would show that it no longer endorsed the double standard in morality.

In their efforts to debunk the positivist conception that the etiology of female deviancy lay in sexual atavism, feminists received support from neither the classical nor sociological schools. Despite the ferocity of the attacks by proponents of both schools on the criminal anthropological theory of male crime, the publication of *The Female Offender* brooked little opposition. Male criminologists of all stripes continued to view women as fundamentally weak creatures controlled by their emotions and sexuality. For them, Lombroso's analysis rang true and deserved quibbling only at the edges. Colajanni, for example, made the expected point that the etiology of female crime lay in social, not biological, causes. Yet he agreed with Lombroso that prostitution was the equivalent of crime and joined him in ridiculing feminists, whom he called vulgar and sentimental. In both the condescension of his tone and the brevity of his analysis, Colajanni showed little interest in devoting the same rigorous and humane analysis to women as he had to men.[184]

CONCLUSION

Because of the poverty of critique from either the classical or sociological schools, the positivist analysis of female crime enjoyed a robust and relatively unrivaled primacy for decades, not only in Italy but also in Europe and the Americas. In contrast, Lombroso's *Criminal Man* drew immediate and vituperative attacks, prompting a proliferation of alternative explanations for the etiology of male crime. But after the spurt of research by criminal anthropologists in the 1890s, few criminologists of any school bothered to collect fresh data on the female offender until the feminist challenge of the 1970s.[185] In the few new studies that did appear, Lombrosian assumptions continued to prevail. Consequently, the impact of positivism has varied according to the gender of the criminal studied and has been more long-lasting in the case of women. What was the intellectual legacy of criminal anthropology to the understanding of female crime?

The answer is not entirely clear, as might be expected when supposedly neutral, "scientific" research is guided by an a priori assumption, in this case the inferiority of women. As we have seen, individual researchers juggled their data when they failed to support their theories, and criminal anthropologists as a group failed to agree on

the social and political implications of their research. In general, however, they recommended "chivalry" toward the female offender. Most often an occasional criminal, she was weak, impressionable, and in need of protection. Forms of punishment
should conform to female nature, training her to regain the virtues of her sex—such
as piety, domesticity, and maternity—that would form a bulwark against her innate
vices. The paternalism of this approach was reinforced by the procedures for mitigating punishment, which rested on the discretion of male judges and prison administrators, who were advised in turn by male criminal anthropologists. Yet, on
balance, male defendants might envy such a prescription for mild retribution.

Other parts of the legacy were more onerous. Criminal anthropology gave new
vigor to the ancient image of the hysterical and murderous woman, twice as cruel
and vengeful as her male counterpart. While careful readers of positivist writings realized that the school considered only a small percentage of female offenders to
have been "born" to their fate, public perception fixed on the more lurid stories.
Never reluctant to tout sensational findings, Lombroso and his followers publicized
scandalous cases of female poisoners and arsonists, perpetuating a stereotype that
could be resurrected conveniently during moral panics.

Perhaps most damagingly, the Positivist School placed sexuality at the center of
the analysis of female crime. The imperious reign of their reproductive systems
caused women to commit not only "female" crimes like prostitution, abortion, and
infanticide, but also "male" crimes like homicide, assault, and theft (in the form of
kleptomania). Sexual desire lured women into the role of criminal accomplices to
men who robbed or embezzled. Atavistic sexuality—like lesbianism or nymphomania—marked the born criminal or prostitute and justified lifelong surveillance. But
sexuality also ruled the occasional prostitute, so that positivism tainted this benign
classification in the case of women. Ruled by an innate and eternal sexual force,
even "normal" women fell easily into occasional crime or prostitution. Thus, the
positivist insistence on the primacy of biological determinism in the motivation of
all women led to the collapsing of those categories so important for categorizing
men: the born criminal, insane criminal, criminal by passion, and the occasional
criminal. Analyses of female criminals in all categories became monotonously fix-
ated on sexuality, a tendency that became the most significant and disturbing legacy of positivism to criminology.

Although the theories of criminal anthropology had little impact on the understanding of "normal men," at lease those in the "white race," they became integral
to the entire debate about the proper role and status of women in Italian society. As
the standard against which all other groups were defined, men needed no definition
as indicated by the lack of control groups in *Criminal Man*. The apex of evolution
was known even without empirical tests. The future of women, however, was contested, not only by feminists but also by the growing numbers of lower-class women
leaving their families to seek jobs in the cities. For positivists, women's participation
in political life and economic modernization constituted an unhealthy challenge to
the laws of evolution and threatened the future of European civilization. Unnatural
attempts to modernize their status simply led to degeneracy, as illustrated by the

masculinity of female intellectuals and the increase in prostitution among the poor. Only the willingness of women in all classes to obey the laws of evolution, as interpreted by criminal anthropologists, would assure the continued ascendancy of Italy within Europe and Europe over its colonies.

In prescribing maternity as women's natural role in the struggle of the fittest, criminal anthropologists accepted reforms that perpetuated that role. Suffrage, at least on the local level, would allow women a voice in issues tied to the family. Happy to defy the Church, positivists even promoted divorce as a measure that would solidify, rather than destroy, the institution of marriage. But within marriage, wives were to remain subordinate to their husbands and sexual liberty for women was roundly condemned. Educated women should either turn their talents to buttressing the family, like Lombroso's daughter Paola, who organized a series of children's books, or assist the work of male relatives, like Gina, who became her father's secretary. That most criminal anthropologists subscribed to the moderate view of the equivalency of the sexes, however, did little to cushion the daunting impact of their scientific theories on the debate about the woman question at the turn of the century. Reduced to biological machines in positivist writings, women were said to pursue their role of motherhood through instinct rather than moral and intellectual choice. Destined never to reach the male peak of evolutionary success, they would remain eternally in need of male guidance, even about family affairs. Such a view, enunciated by a group of well-respected scientists, not only crippled the Italian feminist movement, but created an atmosphere conducive to the further restriction of women's rights under fascism.

NOTES

1. Guglielmo Ferrero, Augusto G. Bianchi, and Scipio Sighele, *Il mondo criminale italiano*, vol. 1 (Milan: Omodei Zorini, 1893), p. 86.

2. Ibid., p. 87.

3. Ibid., p. 89.

4. Ibid., p. 104.

5. Ibid., p. xi.

6. Ibid., pp. 95, 97.

7. Ibid., p. 98.

8. Ibid., p. 101.

9. Ibid., p. 92.

10. Ibid., p. 91.

11. ISAT, *Somm. stat. italiano*, p. 97.

12. Manoukian, "La rappresentazione statistica," p. 444.

13. Ibid., p. 447.

14. Ibid.

15. For the classic formulation of this argument, see Sandra Cavallo and Simona Cerutti, "Female Honor and the Social Control of Reproduction in Piedmont between 1600 and 1800," in Edward Muir and Guido Ruggiero, eds., *Sex and Gender in Historical Perspective* (Baltimore: Johns Hopkins University Press, 1990), pp. 73–109. Gene Brucker presents a microhistory of one such case in *Giovanni and Lusanna: Love and Marriage in Re-*

naissance Florence (Berkeley: University of California, 1986). Margherita Pelaja has recently challenged this interpretation, showing that even in the early nineteenth century Roman women successfully used the Papal Court of the Vicariate to pressure their lovers into marriage. See her book, Matrimonio e sessualità a Roma nell'Ottocento (Roma-Bari: Laterza, 1994).

16. David Kertzer, Sacrificed for Honor: Italian Infant Abandonment and the Politics of Reproductive Control (Boston: Beacon, 1993).

17. Mary Gibson, Prostitution and the State in Italy, 1860–1915 (New Brunswick, N.J.: Rutgers University Press, 1986), p. 177.

18. Louise Tilly, "Urban Growth, Industrialization, and Women's Employment in Milan, Italy, 1881–1911," Journal of Urban History, v. 3 (1977): 467–84.

19. Manoukian, "La rappresentazione statistica," p. 444.

20. Kertzer and Dennis Hogan, "Reflections on the European Marriage Pattern: Sharecropping and Proletarianization in Casalecchio, Italy, 1861–1921," Journal of Family History, v. 16 (1991), pp. 34–36.

21. Ibid., p. 42.

22. See, for example, Dorie Klein, "The Etiology of Female Crime: A Review of the Literature," Issues in Criminology," v. 8, n. 2 (1973), pp. 3–30, and Carol Smart, Women, Crime and Criminology: A Feminist Critique (Boston: Routledge and Kegan Paul, 1976).

23. The German edition appeared in 1894 and the French in 1896; a second French edition came out ten years after the first.

24. The first Italian edition of 1893, entitled La donna delinquente, la prostituta e la donna normale was published in English, in an abridged version, as The Female Offender in 1895.

25. Appleton, the original publisher of The Female Offender in 1895, reissued the volume in 1898 and 1899.

26. C. Lombroso and Ferrero, La donna delinquente, la prostituta e la donna normale (Turin: Roux, 1893), p. x.

27. Archivio, v. 14 (1893), p. 477 [Ferri].

28. Salvatore Ottolenghi, La sensibilità della donna (Turin: Bocca, 1896), p. 3.

29. Archivio, v. 14 (1893), p. 483 [Ferri].

30. Ferrero, "The Problem of Woman. From a Bio-sociological Point of View," The Monist, v. 4 (1894), p. 261.

31. Archivio, 14 (1893), p. 476 [Ferri]; v. 13 (1892), pp. 2–3 [G. Sergi].

32. Lombroso and Ferrero, The Female Offender (Littleton, Colo.: Fred B. Rothman, 1980; orig. published in English, 1895), pp. 148, 151.

33. Archivio, v. 14 (1893), pp. 423–29 [L. Roncoroni and G. Albertotti].

34. Archivio, v. 11 (1890), p. 558 [C. Lombroso].

35. Lombroso and Ferrero, Donna delinquente, p. vii.

36. Ibid., p. 50.

37. Ottolenghi, Sensibilità, p. 26; Mario Carrara also ignored or downgraded data not supporting the insensitivity thesis; see Archivio, v. 19 (1897), p. 641 [M. Carrara].

38. Archivio, v. 13 (1892), p. 1, 8 [G. Sergi].

39. Ibid., p. 5.

40. Ibid.

41. Ibid.

42. Ibid., p. 6.

43. Lombroso and Ferrero, Donna delinquente, p. 66.

44. Ibid., p. 56.

45. Ibid., p. 66.
46. Ottolenghi, *Sensibilità*, p. 3.
47. *Archivio*, v. 12 (1891), p. 483 [C. Lombroso].
48. Ibid.
49. Ibid., p. 484.
50. Ibid.
51. Alfredo Niceforo in Guglielmo Gambarotta, *Inchiesta sulla donna* (Turin: Bocca, 1899), p. 58.
52. *Archivio*, v. 12 (1891), p. 431 [Ferrero].
53. Ibid., p. 406.
54. Ibid., p. 432.
55. *Archivio*, v. 16 (1895), p. 43 [P. Viazzi].
56. Scipio Sighele, *Eva moderna* (Milan: Treves, 1910), p. 14.
57. Ibid., p. viii.
58. Lombroso and Ferrero, *Donna delinquente*, p. 132.
59. Lombroso and Ferrero, *The Female Offender*, p. 109.
60. *Archivio*, v. 14 (1893), p. 485 [Ferri].
61. Lombroso and Ferrero, *The Female Offender*, p. 109.
62. *Archivio*, v. 13 (1892), p. 2 [G. Sergi].
63. Ferri in Gambarotta, *Inchiesta*, p. 191.
64. *Archivio*, v. 13 (1892), pp. 7–8 [G. Sergi]
65. Lombroso and Ferrero, *Donna delinquente*, p. 157.
66. *Archivio*, v. 14 (1893), p. 485 [Ferri}.
67. *Archivio*, v. 12 (1891), p. 566 [Ferrero].
68. Lombroso and Ferrero, *The Female Offender*, p. 104.
69. *Archivio*, v. 10 (1889), p. 382 [C. Lombroso]
70. *Archivio*, v. 14 (1893), p. 14 [Roncoroni].
71. Lombroso and Ferrero, *The Female Offender*, p. 109.
72. *Archivio*, v. 13 (1892), p. 574 [L. Rinieri di Rochi].
73. C. Lombroso, *L'uomo delinquente*, 5th ed., v. 3, p. 229. The *Archives* published statistics certifying the propensity of women to commit such crimes; see, for example, Virgilio Rossi's article on convictions for poisoning in v. 12 (1891), pp. 523–24.
74. C. Lombroso, *L'uomo delinquente*, 5th ed., v. 3, p. 226.
75. Lombroso and Ferrero, *Donna delinquente*, pp. 385–88.
76. Antonio Marro, *I caratteri dei delinquenti: Studio antropologico-sociologico* (Turin: Bocca, 1887), p. 410.
77. Ibid., p. 407.
78. *Archivio*, v. 4 (1883), p. 374 [Marro and Lombroso].
79. *Archivio*, v. 6 (1885), p. 292 [G. Salsotto].
80. *Archivio*, v. 10 (1889), p. 194 [Ottolenghij].
81. Lombroso and Ferrero, *The Female Offender*, p. 147.
82. *Archivio*, v. 12 (1891), p. 404 [Ferrero].
83. Ibid., p. 405.
84. Lombroso and Ferrero, *Donna delinquente*, p. 467.
85. Ibid.
86. Ibid.
87. Enrico Ferri, *Criminal Sociology*, p. 65.

88. C. Lombroso, *L'uomo delinquente*, 1st ed., p. 142; these words were still repeated in the 5th ed., v. 3, p. 227.

89. Ibid., 5th ed., v. 3, p. 227.

90. *Archivio*, v. 10 (1889), p. 381 [C. Lombroso].

91. Lombroso and Ferrero, *The Female Offender*, p. 111.

92. Ibid., p. 106.

93. *Archivio*, v. 14 (1893), p. 190 (R. Guerrieri).

94. Umberto Mantegazza and Giuseppe Ciuffo, *La prostituzione studiata specialmente in Toscana e Sardegna* (Cagliari-Sassari: G. Dessi, 1904), p. 79.

95. *Archivio*, v. 14 (1893), p. 330 [Bergonzoli].

96. *Archivio*, v. 14 (1893), p. 145 [Masini].

97. *Archivio*, v. 27 (1906), p. 821 [Ascarelli]; this article was reprinted in the proceedings of the Sixth International Congress of Criminal Anthropology; see *Comtes-Rendus du VI Congrès international d'antropologie criminelle (Turin, 28 Avril–3 Mai 1906)* (Turin: Bocca, 1908), p. 422.

98. *Archivio*, v. 16 (1895), pp. 322–23 [G.B. Moraglia].

99. Lombroso and Ferrero, *The Female Offender*, p. 101.

100. *Archivio*, v. 16 (1895), p. 323 [Moraglia].

101. *Archivio*, v. 5 (1884), p. 199 [A. De Blasio].

102. *Archivio*, v. 9 (1888), p. 572 [O. Albertis].

103. Lombroso and Ferrero, *The Female Offender*, pp. 115–16.

104. *Archivio*, v. 12 (1891), p. 521 [E. Grasselli].

105. Abele De Blasio, *Nel paese della Camorra* (Naples: Luigi Perro, 1901), p. 159.

106. Criminal Code of 1889, Art. 354.

107. Criminal Code of 1889, Art. 369 (infanticide), and Art. 385 (abortion).

108. Ibid.

109. For example, see Guido Ruggiero's essay, "'More Dear to Me Than Life Itself,'" in his volume, *Binding Passions: Tales of Magic, Marriage, and Power at the End of the Renaissance* (New York: Oxford University Press, 1993), especially pp. 62–64.

110. Criminal Code of 1889, Art. 21.

111. Ibid., Art.

112. Enrico Pessina, *Il nuovo Codice Penale Italiano con brevi note dilucidative* (Milan: Hoepli, 1890), p. 70.

113. Pietro Ellero, "Della minore responsabilità penale delle donne," *Opuscoli criminali* (Bologna: Fava e Garegnani, 1874), p. 90.

114. Ibid.

115. Ibid., p. 93.

116. Ibid., pp. 93, 95.

117. Ibid., p. 96.

118. Vito Antonio Berardi, *La donna e la imputabilità giuridica* (Bari: Gissi, 1881), p. 5.

119. Ibid., p. 9.

120. Ibid., p. 10.

121. *Archivio*, v. 7 (1886), p. 80 [F. Puglia].

122. Ibid.

123. Ibid. A similar argument is made by A. Loiy, who explicitly critiques Berardi's position in *Archivio*, v. 8 (1887), pp. 548–49.

124. C. Lombroso, *L'uomo delinquente*, 5th ed., v. 3, pp. 558–59.

125. *Archivio*, v. 10 (1889), p. 316 [Sighele].

126. Ibid., p. 317.

127. Ibid., pp. 318–19; for a similar position, see Ferri, "I delitti della donna," *Difese penali* (Turin: UTET, 1923), 2nd ed., v. 2, p. 685, orig. published in 1910.

128. Lombroso, *L'uomo delinquente*, 5th ed., v. 3, p. 561.

129. *Archivio*, v. 7 (1886), p. 640 [C. Lessona].

130. *Archivio*, v. 6 (1885), p. 494 [R. Balestrini]. Balestrini recapitulated his arguments in more length in his later book, *Aborto, infanticidio ed esposizione d'infante* (Turin: Bocca, 1888).

131. Ibid., p. 491.

132. Ibid., pp. 147–48.

133. Ibid., p. 165.

134. Lombroso and Ferrero, *The Female Offender*, p. 154.

135. *Archivio*, v. 14 (1893), p. 171 (Roncoroni).

136. Sighele, *Eva moderna*, p. 34.

137. Lombroso, *L'uomo delinquente*, 5th ed., v. 3, p. 558.

138. Lombroso, *Crime*, pp. 406–407; 259.

139. Gambarotta, *Inchiesta*, p. 9.

140. Ibid., pp. 65–66.

141. Ferrero, "The Problem of Woman," p. 272.

142. Gambarotta, *Inchiesta*, p. 57.

143. Ibid., p. 58.

144. Ibid., p. 159.

145. Ibid., p. 63.

146. Ibid, p. 64.

147. Ibid., pp. 173–74.

148. Ibid., p. 62.

149. Ferri, "Divorzio e sociologia," *Scuola positiva*, v. 3, n. 16 (1893), p. 744.

150. Ibid.

151. *Archivio* v. 2 (1883), p. 89 [Crivellari, Lombroso, Ferri] For other defenses of divorce, see Sighele, *Eva moderna*, pp. 41–44 and E. Masé-Darl, *Archivio*, v. 11 (1892), pp. 60–61, and v. 12 (1893), p. 268.

152. Ibid.

153. C. Lombroso, *L'uomo delinquente*, 5th ed., v. 3, p. 337.

154. Lombroso and Ferrero, *Donna delinquente*, pp. x–xi.

155. Ibid., p. 177. On her relationship with Lombroso's daughters, see Dolza, *Essere figlie*, pp. 60–63.

156. Irene de Bonis de Nobili, *Per il voto alle donne* (Rome: Righetti, 1909), 23. Bonis de Nobili based this book on several lectures that she delivered to the Comitato Nazionale ProSuffragio Femminile (National Committee for Female Suffrage).

157. Ibid., p. 24.

158. Maria Marselli-Valli, *Donne e femminismo* (Florence: Rassegna Nazionale, 1908), p. 7.

159. F.P. Diana, *Femminismo e anti-femminismo: Conferenza tenuta nel Circolo degli Impiegati il 6 Maggio 1904* (Agrigento: Montes, 1905), pp. 31, 32.

160. Ernesta Michelangeli, *La vera missione della donna* (Bologna: Zanichelli, 1901), pp. 106–107.

161. Diana, *Femminismo e anti-femminismo*, pp. 32–33.

162. Bonis de Nobili, *Per il voto alle donne*, p. 24.

163. Teresa Labriola, *Per voto alla donna: Conferenza (24 marzo 1906)* (Rome: E. Loescher, 1906), p. 16. Labriola was one of the earliest women to receive a law degree in Italy. She published widely and taught philosophy of law at the University of Rome. She personally experienced the limitations on women's professional lives, since women were prohibited from the bar in Italy until 1919. Although a member of the directorate of the Comitato Pro-Suffragio Femminile before World War I, Labriola became increasingly conservative during the war and finally adhered to fascism in the 1920s.

164. Bonis de Nobili, *Per il voto alle donne*, p. 251. Marselli-Valli echoed this argument when she pointed out that the smartest men would be "giants" if intelligence were correlated with strength. See *Donne e femminismo*, p. 9.

165. Ibid., p. 118.

166. Ibid., p. 120.

167. Diana, *Femminismo e anti-femminismo*, p. 39.

168. Ibid., p. 42.

169. Labriola, *Per voto alla donna*, pp. 20, 14.

170. Kuliscioff's writings on the woman question have been edited and appended to a play about her life: *Anna Kuliscioff. Con gli scritti di Anna Kuliscioff "Sulla condizione della donna,"* eds. Marcla Boggio and Annabella Cerliani (Venice: Marsilio, 1977). Analyses of Kuliscioff's role in the women's movement can be found in Claire La Vigna, "The Marxist Ambivalence Toward Women: Between Socialism and Feminism in the Italian Socialist Party," in Marilyn J. Boxer and Jean H. Quataert, eds., *Socialist Women: European Socialist Feminism in the Nineteenth and Early Twentieth Centuries* (New York: Elsevier, 1978), 146–81 and Beverly Tanner Springer, "Anna Kuliscioff: Russian Revolutionist, Italian Feminist," in Jane Slaughter and Robert Kern, eds., *European Women on the Left* (Westport, Conn.: Greenwood, 1981), 13–27. A recent biography is Maria Casalini, *La signora del socialismo italiano: Vita di Anna Kuliscioff* (Rome: Riuniti, 1987).

171. Boggio and Cerliani, *Anna Kuliscioff*, p. 141. "Il monopolio dell'uomo" was Kuliscioff's best-known statement on the woman question aside from her articles in *Critica sociale*.

172. Ibid., p. 142.

173. *Critica sociale*, v. 3, n. 13 (1893), p. 207. Zerboglio's three-part review of *La donna delinquente* appeared in *Critica sociale*, v. 3 (1893), n. 13, pp. 205–207; n. 14, pp. 222–23; and n. 15, pp. 236–39.

174. *Critica sociale*, v. 3, n. 15 (1893), p. 238.

175. *Critica sociale*, v. 3, n. 13, p. 207.

176. Quoted in Rosanna DeLongis, "Scienza come politica: *Vita femminile* (1895–1897)," *Nuova DonnaWomanFemme* 21 (1982), p. 37.

177. Ibid.

178. Maria Pia Bigaran, "Per una donna nuova: Tre giornali di propaganda socialista tra le donne," *Nuova DonnaWomanFemme* 21 (1982), p. 60.

179. Rina Macrelli, *L'indegna schiavitù: Anna Maria Mozzoni e la lotta contro la prostituzione di Stato* (Rome: Riuniti, 1981), p. 178.

180. Ibid.

181. Ibid., p. 179.

182. For an excellent history of the shelter in Milan, see Annarita Buttafuoco, *Le Mariuccine: Storia di un'istituzione laica l'Asilo Mariuccia* (Milan: Franco Angeli, 1985).

183. These laws were the Cavour Law of 1860, the Crispi Law of 1888, and the Nicotera Law of 1891. Prostitution was not mentioned in the criminal codes before fascism.

184. See Colajanni, *Sociologia criminale*, v. 2, pp. 83–96, for his brief analysis of gender and crime.

185. Both Klein and Smart survey the few exceptions.

Chapter 3

Race and Crime

In 1902, Lombroso published an article entitled "The Last Brigand" in *Nuova antologia*, the magazine most widely read by the educated classes.[1] The article marked the arrest of Musolino, a "celebrated brigand" from Calabria who had for years evaded capture.[2] The study of bandits had been a specialty of Lombroso, beginning with the famous episode in which a flash of light around the skull of the brigand, Villella, inspired his original theory of atavism. But as an archaic type of crime associated with premodern, rural society, brigandage had practically disappeared in northern Italy and was waning in the South. Obviously delighted at the opportunity to analyze one of the last figures of that dying breed, which had constituted the human data for his early work, Lombroso described Musolino for his popular audience in his own well-known positivist terms.

Not surprisingly, Lombroso pronounced Musolino to be a born criminal, based on physical and psychological evidence. As was often the case, Lombroso had not collected this evidence himself, but relied on photographs and the observations of other criminal anthropologists. Nevertheless, he authoritatively listed the signs of anatomical degeneration in the brigand: a receding forehead, protruding eyebrows, and an asymmetrical face. Even more damning were his psychological anomalies including "an instinct for killing and revenge."[3] After attempting homicide twenty-four times, often successfully, Musolino felt no remorse. Instead, he exhibited a "diseased sense of vanity," eagerly awaited publicity in the press, claimed to be protected by a special saint, compared himself to the Count of Montecristo, and predicted that he would be elected to Parliament.[4]

At the root of such impulsive and egocentric behavior was epilepsy, which was "the basis of born criminality" according to the latest edition of *Criminal Man*.[5] That Musolino had purportedly suffered episodes of epilepsy since the age of twelve was consonant with his family history. His uncle and three cousins were criminals, another cousin and three sisters epileptic, his grandfather and uncle "apoplectic," and his father suffered "dizziness, which constitutes the embryonic form of epilepsy."[6] In short, the brigand was "a born delinquent by heredity" marked by the "contradictory character" typical of epileptics: "now excessively agitated and verbose, later silent and stupid like an idiot . . . now suspicious [and] diffident, later childishly trustful; and intermittently alternating a beastly blood-thirsty ferocity with a certain affability."[7] Lombroso explained Musolino's strange behavior by biological determinism, which had distributed a germ of degeneracy throughout his entire family.

The second part of Lombroso's analysis apparently took a sympathetic turn, declaring Musolino to have "extraordinary intelligence."[8] Only in this way could he explain the bandit's rapid promotion to the position of *capo* (head) of the local mafia, his genius for evading capture for so many years, and even his ability to compose verses that were "not worse than those of many little poets in Italy."[9] He noted that Musolino enjoyed widespread sympathy among the rural poor, who "considered vendetta to be a right and even a duty," especially against the rich and powerful.[10] Lombroso also admired his sense of proportion in meeting out "barbarous justice" and his refusal to stoop to petty crimes like theft.[11] Such reservations led Lombroso to admit at one point in the article that perhaps Musolino did not represent "the complete criminal type," but fell halfway between a criminaloid and a born criminal.[12]

Lombroso suggested two other factors that had shaped Musolino's criminal nature—social environment and race. Typically, neither was integrated into the discussion of epilepsy. Consonant with his socialist sympathies, Lombroso outlined the extreme poverty and illiteracy of Calabria, partly the fault of the state, which led to high rates of crime and sympathy for outlaws. Of more importance for explaining Musolino himself was race, and Lombroso assumed that his readers understood the racial peculiarities of the South. For example, Musolino was long-headed with a protruding jaw, normal for "this regional type," but inferior to northern physique.[13] He easily committed homicide because it "is not considered so serious a crime as in other parts of the country."[14] Yet, despite "the really inferior stage of moral development" exhibited by Calabrians, they displayed a lively intelligence.[15] Lombroso attributed this mental acuity to their racial origins, which included the blood of ancient Romans, Greeks, and Phoenicians who were superior to the Arabs, Africans, and other lowly ancestors of most other southerners. Such an analysis illustrates how criminal anthropologists made race central to their biological categorization of criminals.

EVOLUTION AND RACE

Race was embedded in positivist criminology, as it was in most other types of social Darwinism of the late nineteenth century. Criminal anthropologists collaborated in the construction of the notion of "scientific racism," which defined race as an inherited and measurable trait that determined the biological, psychological,

and intellectual profiles of discrete human groups. That race was integral to positivist theory from its origins is attested by Lombroso's publication of a small book on
the subject in 1871, five years before the publication of the first edition of *Criminal
Man*. Entitled *White Man and Colored Man: Lectures on the Origin and Variety of the
Human Races*, this volume owed much to both Darwin and Marzolo. In a footnote,
Lombroso remarked that Darwin's new book—the *Descent of Man*—had just appeared, and that compared to such a grand work his own "poor lines seem the attempt of a Pigmy."[16] We thus have proof that Lombroso read Darwin's books
immediately upon publication, even before their translation into Italian. But the
pride of inspiration went to his late teacher, "my Marzolo," who had died "without
having been able to complete and disseminate his great work, to which he was tied
more closely than to life."[17] Such a dedication shows that despite his close appropriation of much of Darwin's terminology and reasoning, Lombroso's interest in race
had originally been nurtured by Marzolo. Happy to "vulgarize a few of [Marzolo's]
favorite ideas," Lombroso enthusiastically chose race as a topic for "a few lectures
on popular science for ladies."[18] These lectures, promptly published as a book, constituted another example of the positivists' urge to spread their ideas beyond an academic audience, or even the male political class, to the general public.

White Man and Colored Man contained two main arguments, the first closely tied to
Darwin and the second to Marzolo. First, to identify himself as squarely within the
Darwinian camp, Lombroso set out to disprove "the hypothesis of several contemporaneous Adams" at the origins of humanity.[19] Labeled polygenism, the hypothesis
that the white, yellow, and black races were different species, with independent origins, was widespread among biologists throughout Europe. Lombroso admitted that
he had formerly adhered to polygenism, which was "seductive" because it apparently
explained the enormous inequalities among the races.[20] Yet, if evolution explained
the development of animal life from the most simple forms to the complex, "How can
only man escape this law applicable to all other beings?"[21]

In response, Lombroso set out to convince his audience of the truth of
monogenism, or the single ancestry of all humans. He clearly pronounced himself in
favor of the Darwinian theory of the descent of man from animals, noting that "the
brains of monkeys differ from those of humans only in volume."[22] From monkeys descended the Negro, "the only really cosmopolitan race," vestiges of which were
found all over the world.[23] As it migrated, the black race evolved into the yellow
and, finally, white races. Lombroso cited the Darwinian mechanisms of the "struggle for existence" and "natural selection" as explanations for "this tendency of our
races to vary in form and to retain these sudden transformations under the influence of climate, food, the use and disuse of organs, sexual selection, [and] the ag-
gression of enemies."[24]

In his enthusiasm to prove the variability of the races, Lombroso even offered examples of change too recent to be attributed to natural selection. He claimed, for
example, that European Americans represented "a transformation of the white
race, a really new race" in relation to their English ancestors.[25] Faced with a new climate, extreme solitude, and hostile Indian tribes, the weak among the English set-

tlers had perished in the struggle for existence, leaving a stronger and more independent white race. In short, the environment of the New World had aroused "some qualities that had possibly remained latent in the brain of the pacific English-man when he remained tranquilly at the family hearth."[26] Through such examples, Lombroso criticized those biologists and anthropologists who ignored the role of environment in racial evolution. With his emphasis on monogenism and variability, he never endorsed the extreme racist ideology of the late nineteenth century that held that races were independent, immutable, and contaminated by mixing.

On the other hand, Lombroso's second major argument in *White Man and Colored Man* emphasized the centrality of racial difference to the study of biology, psychology, and culture. Drawing inspiration from Marzolo's work in comparative linguistics, Lombroso returned to the opening theme of his book, the extreme disparities among races. He repeated approvingly his teacher's belief that languages offered a significant clue to the developmental level of a civilization, claiming that "the phonetic alphabet and inflected language were the forces that elevated the white race from the stone age to the steam age."[27] His own research on the brain, "that sublime organ which allows us to call ourselves the kings of nature," supported Marzolo's linguistic evidence that whites represented the pinnacle of evolution.[28] According to Lombroso, "the European skull is distinguished by a splendid harmony of form: it is not too long nor too round nor too pointed or pyramidal."[29] Furthermore, the expert could "read" the structure of the forehead—which was large, smooth and high—as a clear sign of "the strength and predominance of thought" among Europeans.[30] In short, "only we Whites have reached the most perfect symmetry in the features of our bodies."[31]

How then could such an elevated creature as the European be descended from monkeys? Only by positing that whites occupied the highest position on a ladder of races extending down through the Mongols, Semites, and Bushman, to the lowly Negroes.[32] According to Lombroso, while the link between monkeys and whites might seem far-fetched, the kinship between monkeys and blacks was obvious. Negroes resembled animals not only in the small size of their skulls, but also the dark color of their skin, their "particular odor," the membranes on their eyes, shape of their throats, and the curliness of their hair, "which transforms the most beautiful ornament of man into a veritable wig of wool perched on the skull of the poor African and his not very gentle wife."[33] Such atavistic physical features were outward manifestations of a similarly animalistic emotional life characterized by the hegemony of strong but often short bursts of passions like anger over rational thinking. Morality was similarly stunted, "force being the only law, the only virtue among the colored races."[34]

Attempting to summarize his argument "in one sentence," Lombroso asserted that "we must say that there are two general races: the White and the Colored."[35] By concluding his book with these words, Lombroso seemed to contradict the spirit of his first argument for monogenism and the common ancestry of all races. Rather than emphasizing the bonds among the members of the human species, his final declaration reintroduced an enormous differentiation between whites and all other races. In the end, he left audiences at his lectures and readers of his book with the impression that scientists were more interested in studying human differences than uniformity. And indeed, positivist criminologists integrated an elaborate racial typology into their analyses of geographical variations in lawbreaking both within and outside of Italy.

CONTEXT

Lombroso's emphasis on racial difference was neither original nor exceptional in late nineteenth-century Europe, where many biologists, anthropologists, and statisticians were trying to turn racism into a science.[36] Nations involved in imperialist ventures like the "scramble for Africa" justified their wars as civilizing missions of whites over inferior black, brown, and yellow populations. Within Europe, Jews were increasing defined as a race rather than a religious group and denounced as foreign enemies bent on undermining the nation-state, whether France or Germany. At the same time northern Europeans began to classify themselves as "Aryans," racially superior and more pure than their shorter and darker neighbors to the south and east. And the new theorists of degeneration warned that even homogeneous "races" such as the French were threatened with biological and mental weakening from alcoholism, syphilis, tuberculosis, and other "social diseases."

In Italy, the context for the discussion of race was slightly different. In the writings of criminal anthropologists as well as in more general public debates, race was most often linked to the "Southern Question," or the perceived problem of the underdevelopment of southern Italy in relation to the North. Race did not constitute a unifying factor and foundation for Italian nationalism as it had in England, France, and Germany. Instead, the belief that two different races inhabited the North and South provided a barrier to the government's ambition to homogenize the peninsula and make "new Italians" out of the subjects of the patchwork of old regime states. This preoccupation with the "two Italies" focused attention on southerners, rather than two other groups more familiar to European racial theorists, the Jews and black Africans. But all three groups—southerners, Jews, and blacks—found a place in criminological discourse, although they provoked different levels of anxiety depending on their position in Italian society.

It was not until unification that the label of backwardness became affixed to the South. During the previous century, Naples—the most populous city in Italy and one of the largest in Europe—was the center of a lively artistic and cultural life.[37] Only in the 1870s and 1880s did writers like Villari, Leopoldo Franchetti, and Sidney Sonnino begin to create the image of a feudal and immobile South, inhabited by a politically passive but irrationally violent population. Yet, as Silvana Patriarca has shown, geographers and statisticians shared no consensus on where to draw the boundary between northern and southern Italy.[38] Despite the absence of any official definition of North and South, the latter nevertheless became reified as a problem or "question." Positivist criminologists participated in the creation of the Southern Question by minimizing variation among regions in the South and exaggerating divergences with the North. They thus contributed to a new discourse that, by the end of the nineteenth century, began to characterize differences between the two geographical areas as not merely ones of degree but of opposition.

Many areas south of Rome did in fact suffer a variety of economic and social problems, but these did not have biological origins.[39] Most of the population worked in agriculture, either as tenant farmers on the *latifondi*, or large estates, of wealthy absentee landlords or as peasant proprietors of minuscule plots too small to support a family. Although large tracts of common lands and Church property were sold off by the new Italian state, most ended up in the hands of noble or bourgeois landowners rather than the peasantry. Under the free trade philosophy of the governments of the 1860s and 1870s, export of wheat—a mainstay of the *latifondi*—suffered; by the reimposition of protective tariffs in 1887, the market for all agricultural products was in a slump that would last until the end of the 1890s. In such a climate, landowners failed to invest in improvements that might have increased productivity.

Even more bleak was the situation of industry. Contrary to the stereotype of backwardness, the South did not lack industry before 1860 in areas like silk production. But unification caused the deindustrialization of the South as it swept away protective tariffs within the country and lowered them significantly on foreign imports. Unable to compete with the more efficient production in northern Italy and other nations, southern industry collapsed. The protective tariffs of 1878 and 1887 came too late to revive native industries. Only after the turn of the twentieth century did the state develop initiatives to reintroduce industry to the South, most of which were of limited success.

Such a weak economy was especially disastrous in a period of strong demographic growth, like the years after 1880. While Italy's annual increase in population was about 10 percent in both the North and the South, the former region could more easily absorb workers into its growing economy.[40] In the South, on the other hand, few cities were industrializing so that Naples and Palermo, for example, were bulging with the unemployed poor. Thus, emigration, which had previously been directed toward Europe and involved peasants from the entire peninsula, began to take on a new pattern after 1885. Southerners now dominated the growing wave of migrants destined mostly for the Americas. By 1900, over 600,000 people left Italy each year, of which 70 percent were southerners.[41]

Although extreme poverty and unemployment also characterized certain areas of the North, like the Veneto, after unification, the South was increasingly labeled as economically backwards by writers, social scientists, and policy makers.[42] In addition to poverty, these experts identified a cluster of abnormal characteristics supposedly unique to the South: low levels of literacy, high rates of disease, widespread superstition, and a preference for violence to settle disputes. This last not only alarmed state officials but encouraged positivist criminologists to apply their new evolutionary theories to the South. In 1876, the year of the publication of the first edition of *Criminal Man*, Franchetti was already warning that Sicilians considered acts of violence to constitute "the normal state of things . . . necessary and normal although harmful, like the heavy rains that make the year's harvest rot in their fields."[43] Government statisticians were also warning that homicide rates in the South were strikingly higher than in the North, although they were inconsistent over the years in their location of the boundary between the two regions.[44]

That the South was identified with two types of organized crime, brigandage and the mafia, reinforced its image as a violent and homicidal backwater.[45] Although brigandage still characterized certain regions in the North in the nineteenth century, it caused a national emergency in the South during the years immediately following unification. Illegal activities by brigands traditionally included smuggling and the theft of livestock, whether sheep or cattle. In 1861, after the disbanding of Giuseppe Garibaldi's army, such activities escalated into a series of violent insurrections in the peninsular South and Sicily. The new central government, still dominated by the Piedmontese, sent the army to crush the uprisings, claiming that brigands were in league with the nobility to restore the rule of the Bourbons and extend the power of the Pope. Historians have painted a more complex picture, arguing that banditry enjoyed widespread support from the lower classes, who were impoverished by the collapse of the southern economy and resentful of the taxes and conscription imposed by the new Italian state. By 1864, the major insurrections were quelled, but the bandit had become irrevocably a southern figure in the minds of government officials and criminal anthropologists.

More clearly a southern phenomenon, the Sicilian mafia resembled brigandage in being decentralized and making illegal profits from smuggling and cattle rustling. In the late nineteenth century, it extended its activities from the rural hinterlands to cities like Palermo, illicitly monopolizing trade between rural producers and urban distributors. *Mafiosi* also acted as labor brokers both in the countryside on the large *latifondi* and in the cities, extorting payment from peasants and urban poor alike. The camorra, a parallel organization in Naples, similarly developed an extensive system of patronage, in which its members extorted money for "protecting" the property of store owners or finding jobs for the unemployed. Able to deliver votes to friendly politicians, the mafia and camorra became enmeshed in the political system. Such interdependencies between organized crime and parliamentarians shielded the former from the type of governmental repression directed against brigands, but deepened the stereotype of a corrupt and undemocratic South.

Preoccupied with the Southern Question, public opinion in Italy showed less anxiety over Jews, increasingly labeled as a separate race in other European nations. Jews had not always enjoyed such acceptance, having been confined in ghettos until 1848 in most cities and until 1870 in Rome. Only with unification were a myriad of restrictions on Jewish life removed, like the prohibition on owning property, attending public schools, engaging in any jobs less menial than peddling rags and clothes, and wearing a special badge. Even after the abolition of the ghettos, anti-Semitism continued in popular literature and attitudes.[46]

Yet Jews were integrated into all walks of Italian life more quickly than in other European countries. Many Jews fought in the *risorgimento* and afterwards retained a strong patriotic attachment to the new state, which had guaranteed their liberation. By the turn of the twentieth century, Jews even held high posts in state administration and the military that were still reserved elsewhere in Europe for the old Christian nobility. Examples of prominent Jews in Italian government before World War I included Ernesto Nathan, Mayor of Rome; General Giuseppe Ottolenghi, Minister of War; Sonnino, Prime Minister and Secretary of State; and Luigi Luzzatti, Prime Minister. Such Jewish mobility signaled a society that was not amenable to the virulent anti-Semitism that was already plaguing many of Italy's neighbors in the last decades of the nineteenth century. Furthermore, the leading intellectuals of scientific racism in Italy, unlike their foreign colleagues, did little to fan the flames of anti-Semitic passion. Their leader, Lombroso, was himself a Jew, and his disciples followed his cue in excluding Jews from the biological analysis deemed appropriate for southerners.

Such tolerance did not extend to the third group, black Africans, who constituted a certain preoccupation in Italian foreign policy. Italy had little direct contact with Africa in the nineteenth century, as it failed in the "scramble for Africa" to acquire any major colonies. The Italian army tried to conquer Ethiopia in 1896, but was soundly defeated at Adowa. Following this humiliating defeat, many groups turned against colonial ventures, while others became consumed with plans for revenge. In 1911, under increasing pressure from the newly formed Nationalist Party, Italy declared a successful war to take over Libya, which became a colony in 1912. Although Ethiopia was not finally conquered until the 1930s, Italian resentment fueled racial stereotypes of Arabs and black Africans. Lombroso, like socialists in general, was opposed to colonialism, but books like *White Man and Colored Man* offered scientific underpinnings for Italian feelings of racial superiority over Africans.

RACE AND CRIME

Although Lombroso and many of his fellow positivist criminologists made race central to their analysis of southern "deviancy," the term itself posed special problems for Italian thinkers. First, archeological research had revealed such a variety of peoples migrating to the Italian peninsula throughout its long history that every writer rejected the idea of one "Italian" race as ridiculous. How could one identify the races in Italy? The distinction between white and black, employed in colonial ventures, was not useful, nor was the northern European tendency to trace the origin of a nation to a pure "Aryan" stock. Were the labels that turned up in archeological research, such as Umbrians, Ligurians, Latins, and Etruscans, applicable to different races? What about the more recent migrations of Greeks, north Africans, and Albanians to the South? Could different groups be lumped together as an Italic or Mediterranean race? Having admitted the existence of more than one race in Italy, criminologists were logically forced to criticize the German passion for pure races. Could race mixing be invigorating rather than enervating and a sign of decline? If so, was race mixing useful only among "whites"? Both their generally positive evaluation of race mixing and their anti-German sentiment assured that Italian criminal anthropologists would never blindly follow the most extreme northern racial theorists.

A second set of complications in the application of race to behavior arose from the personal biographies of positivist criminologists. Most notably, Lombroso himself was Jewish and was sensitive to the new racial anti-Semitism in northern and eastern Europe that questioned the patriotism and threatened the civil and political rights of Jews. In criticizing anti-Semitism, Lombroso deemphasized the hereditary nature of race in a manner that contradicted many of his writings on southern Italy. Ambiguities also arose from the adherence of Lombroso and most of his positivist colleagues to socialism and their humanitarian impulse to improve the living conditions of the poor, whether in the North or South. Thus, their writings often exhibited a tension between the biological determinism of racial analysis and a naive but often sincere desire for social reform and progress.

The following analysis of the writings of Lombroso, Ferri, and Niceforo will outline the contours of the Italian racial theory at the turn of the twentieth century. While our focus will be on the differences between northern and southern Italy, we must include criminologists' views of Africans, Jews, and Aryans to better comprehend their reasoning on matters of race. Each section will begin with the author's definition of race before proceeding to its role in the etiology of crime

Lombroso

Although Lombroso took race for granted as an important determinant of behavior, he was slipshod in his definition of the term. In *Criminal Man*, he sometimes divided Europe into two large groups designated the "Germans" and the "Latins" or, alternately, the "blondes" and the "dark-haired."[47] In other instances he multiplied the number of races, dividing Italy into three parts: the Semitic South; the Latin Center; and the Germanic, Ligurian, Celtic, and Slavic North.[48] Yet on the same page he might add even more categories: Umbrians, Etruscans, Oscians, Phoenicians, Albanians, and Greeks. In no case did he provide empirical data as a basis for his system of classification. His approach in a book written specifically about the South, entitled *In Calabria*, appears at first glance more scientific. Here he divided the Calabresi into two types: Semites with long heads (*dolicocefalo*), eyebrows that almost met over arched noses, and either black or dark brown eyes; and Greco-Romans with short heads (*brachicefalo*), high broad foreheads over aquiline noses, and lively, conspicuous eyes.[49] The attempt to identify races based on the measurement of skulls was typical of the period throughout Europe. But even in this study, Lombroso muddied the waters by alluding at times to Albanians without defining their cranial type or explaining whether they fit into either of the two major groups.

On this scientifically unsteady base of racial classification, Lombroso built elaborate and colorful typologies of criminal behavior. At times, he would generalize about the predominance of crimes against the person in the South or, in this case, the region of Calabria: "To murder someone here with a gun . . . is considered a joke and not very serious; and everyone therefore carries a gun, and he who has two barrels is more respected."[50] But more often he provided a criminal geography of southern Italy by ethnic group. Thus, the areas populated by Greeks were the least criminal, at least in crimes of blood, while the Albanian regions showed high rates of vendetta and brigandage. In Sicily, brigandage was concentrated around Palermo,

where the rapacious Berber and Semitic tribes took up an early and long-lived residence. . . . When one thinks that here, like in the Arab tribes, cattle and sheep stealing is the preferred crime, it is easy to convince oneself that blood of these people—who are acquisitive and rapacious, hospitable and cruel, intelligent but superstitious, always mobile, restless and disdainful of restraints—must have its part in . . . perpetuating brigandage.[51]

Such barbaric behavior was less common in eastern Sicily, like Catania, where a richer mixture of "Aryan blood" could be found.[52] In Sardinia, Lombroso found less homicide and more property crime than in the rest of the South and attributed this more evolved or northern profile of deviancy to the Phoenician—rather than Arab—stock of its inhabitants.[53] How the Phoenicians were racially different from Arabs was never explained.

The crudity of Lombroso's racial analysis was combined uneasily with an often more subtle psychological and social analysis of the etiology of southern crime. In *Criminal Man*, he admitted that individual temperament limited the determinism of race on behavior. Even among "the most barbarous savages" like the "hottentots" and the "kaffirs" could be found both relatively honest and industrious people and "more savage individuals who are incapable of any type of work and live on the labor of others like vagabonds."[54] Perhaps more important for southern Italy, he admitted that vestiges of feudalism were partially responsible for the high rates of southern crime. He pushed this idea much further in the conclusion to his study of Calabria, where he argued for breaking up the large estates and redistributing the land by a "collective action of the State."[55] Disappointed with the results of the *risorgimento* in which he had believed so fervently as a youth, he sadly observed that in Calabria unification had profited only the rich while for the poor it had added "the drawbacks of civilization to those of barbary."[56]

Lombroso's analysis of anti-Semitism provides an interesting counterpoint to his writings on the Italian South, since he explained Jewish behavior more in environmental than racial terms. When asked by two foreign journals to express his opinion on anti-Semitism, he hesitated, feeling "that disgust which hits even the least impatient scientist when he must study the most repulsive human secretions."[57] But he agreed to make an impartial study, publishing the results in Italy in 1894 under the title *Anti-Semitism and Modern Science*. In this book, he began by labeling Jews as a race, but later defined them as a mixture of Semitic and Aryan blood. Based on his studies in Venice and Piedmont, he concluded that Jews came in all sizes, body types, and hair color, since they took on the characteristics of the peoples with whom they lived. In terms of craniology, "the Jew [is] more Aryan than Semitic," from intermixing with other Europeans.[58] He pronounced this race mixing as quite normal, arguing that "a mosaic of the most diverse races" inhabited each European nation.[59] Race mixing was not only normal but good, for Darwin had shown the benefits of cross-fertilization on plants. Alternately, where Lombroso had found "the most complete uniformity of race, as in Abyssinia and Sardinia . . . the people demonstrated an inferior intelligence to those who had a variety of cranial forms. Therefore the Sardinians are infinitely inferior to the Sicilians," since the latter region had Norman, Greek, and Semitic blood.[60] Despite their mixed blood, Jews did, according to Lombroso, exhibit a constellation of distinctive traits. For instance, they tended to cloak obstinate tenacity with humility and apparent flexibility leaving them open to the charge of duplicity. But this flaw in character was neither heredity nor racial, but necessary for survival through the centuries in hostile environments. Similarly, he admitted that Jews had traditionally been bankers, tax collectors, and wandering traders rather than exercising "honest occupations," but environment not blood had driven them to this choice.[61] As nations like Italy opened all professions to Jews, they had taken immediate advantage of the new liberty to move into the universities, state, and army. Thus, anti-Semitism was irrational and even atavistic, "an icy wind of savage hate running through even the most civilized peoples of Europe."[62] Anti-Semitism would finally cease when "little by little, in five or six centuries, the Jew will disappear" through intermarriage with Christians.[63] For Lombroso, intermarriage was just another example of healthy mixing of the races, which would also promise the end of religious fanaticism in both Jewish and Christian communities.[64]

In contrast to the Jews, Lombroso found blacks to have a mental and emotional life almost entirely determined by biology. As we have seen, in *White Man and Colored Man* Lombroso argued that great inequalities marked the races, with Negroes being "the most imperfect" and whites the "most perfect."[65] According to his evolutionary theory, blacks represented the lowest and most primitive race, from which all others—including intermediary groups like the Semites and the Asians—had sprung under the positive influence of temperate climates. But the African had changed little for millennia, still displaying "that infantile and monkey-like manner of smiling and gesturing."[66] For Lombroso, this intellectual weakness sprang directly from physical inferiority: "The brain is undeveloped in the back and weighs less than ours. As for the skull which holds it, . . . the face predominates over the forehead as [their] passions drown [their] intelligence."[67] Thus, blacks were closer to monkeys than whites in language, art, and, of course, science.

Enrico Ferri

A defense attorney and law professor, Ferri formed part of the triumvirate of the founding fathers of positivist criminology along with Lombroso and Garofalo. As evidenced in the title of his most famous work, *Criminal Sociology*, Ferri stressed sociological factors more than Lombroso did. Although it was Ferri who actually coined the term "born criminal," his eloquence on the importance of factors like poverty and illiteracy in the etiology of crime convinced Lombroso continually to reduce his estimate of the percentage of crime caused by atavism through the various editions of *Criminal Man*. Yet Ferri believed there was a small but dangerous group of born criminals, and considered race an important element in their behavior. Only race could explain the wide variations in patterns of crime in areas with similar physical and social environments like southern Italy.

Like most criminal anthropologists, Ferri claimed to base his definition of race on cephalic indices that divided peoples into long-headed and short-headed types. Asserting that the distribution of races in Europe was generally understood, he identified three main groups: the Germans, Slavs, and Greco-Latins.[68] While Italy fell into the third group, he admitted a host of subgroups could be found within the peninsula: Ligurians in the North, Umbrians and Etruscans in the Center, and Oscians in the South with later migrations of Germans, Celts, and Slavs to the North and Phoenicians, Arabs, Albanians, and Greeks to the South.[69] Two of these groups— the Germans and the Slavs—corresponded to his major races; the classification of the others was never clarified. Ferri also at times employed the broad categories of the "white race" and the "colored races."[70]

For Ferri, race was most important as the cause of serious crimes like homicide, that is, those crimes most likely to be committed by the born criminal. He agreed with other criminal anthropologists that violent crime was giving way to property crime since "civil evolution consists in man's continuous stripping-off of the most deep and ancient traces of his animal and savage origin."[71] In a work entitled *Homicide in Criminal Anthropology*, he traced this evolution beginning with a chapter on "Murders among animals" followed by "Homicide among primitive humanity." Asking why "inferior races" were more prone to homicide, he speculated that "the Negro does not have a bad but only an unstable character like a baby, but with the difference that it is linked with mature physical development; thus this instability is the consequence of an incomplete cerebral development."[72]

As for the differences between patterns of crime in northern and southern Italy, Ferri correlated these partly with economic disparities but also with the particular "racial energies and attitudes" of each region.[73] Only the North had reached the modern pattern of a predominance of property crimes like theft and fraud so that "from the provinces of southern Italy and the islands to the northern regions one sees a progressive diminution of barbaric and violent crime."[74] Yet even the South was dotted with oases of low homicide, where Greek, Albanian, and "Longobard" blood was common.[75] Elsewhere, the predominance of Semitic blood assured high rates of crimes against persons.

Like Lombroso, Ferri tempered his racial analysis with the disclaimers that individual temperament could limit racial determinism and that environment also accounted for a large amount of crime. In fact, Ferri, a more committed and consistent socialist than Lombroso at the turn of the century, suggested a future in which socialism might eliminate most lawbreaking. He rejected the rosy picture painted by some of his political colleagues in which socialism would wipe out crime entirely. For Ferri, "isolated cases of acute pathology" in born criminals could never be mitigated by benign environmental change and as such would always be dangerous to social order.[76] But when a future socialist society guaranteed work to all citizens, the "struggle for existence" would be eased and most crime would cease. How socialism would erase the racial stigmata of entire regions was not clear.

Interestingly, Ferri also wrote on anti-Semitism, perhaps out of deference to his friend and colleague, Lombroso. In an article published in the *Nuova rassegna* in 1893, he minimized description of Jews as a race and concentrated on a political analysis of the rise of anti-Semitism in Europe.[77] Although anti-Semitism was not new, it had reappeared with a new virulence fueled by conservative governments bent on diverting attention from present injustices and the new socialist parties that promised to right these injustices. For Ferri, it was not coincidental that those nations with the strongest reform movements—Germany, Russia, and Austria—exhibited the most hysterical outbursts of anti-Semitism. As a type of Christian revivalism meant to overshadow the "supreme ideal" of socialism, anti-Semitism, according to Ferri, was becoming "a huge fire" that threatened to escape control of its conservative creators.[78] In a chilling and unwitting prognostication of the future, he warned that "if, by a neronian hypothesis, we could imagine the destruction of all the Jews of Europe," the intellectual level of the continent would decline sharply.[79] As a non-Jew, he declared his agreement with Lombroso that "anti-Semitism, as an individual sentiment, represents an atavistic residual of medieval barbary and ignorance."[80]

Alfredo Niceforo

Alfredo Niceforo represented the third generation of students who eagerly took up the tools and theories of positivist criminology. He dedicated an early book entitled *Crime in Sardinia*, published at the age of twenty-one, to his "affectionate teacher Enrico Ferri" and Ferri returned the compliment in a laudatory preface.[81] Based on a visit to the island two years earlier, this work seemed to refute Lombroso's assertion that Sardinia was the only part of the South relatively free of violent crime. Citing statistics on homicide, arson, armed robbery, kidnapping, and extortion, he claimed that Sardinia rivaled and often surpassed Sicily in these felonies. He concluded that "these statistics are terribly eloquent; they indicate—in Sardinia—a vast and acute morbid process, a cancerous erosion that corrupts the moral life of that island."[82]

Yet, like his older colleagues, he found a variation in crime rates across geography and asserted that "the predominance of crime in certain regions is surely dependent, for the most part, on race."[83] Again like his colleagues, he failed to clearly define race. In one passage he divided Italy into two major groupings: the European or Celtic race that characterized northern Italy and the Mediterranean race, originally from Africa, that occupied the South and the Islands. Yet in Sardinia he found over four different "zones" of crime—for example, vendetta, in the Gallura, theft in Alghero, and slander in Bosa—but the correlation between this criminal geography and his two races is never entirely clear. He noted that Galluran women were blond and blue-eyed, so that even tourists could tell they were "perfectly celtic types."[84] But he was most interested in Nuoro, which he labeled the "delinquent zone" for its high rates of armed robbery, kidnapping, extortion, vendetta and other violent crimes. Not surprisingly, he found that the inhabitants of Nuoro exhibited more "atavistic stigmata" than other Sardinians.[85] His study of Nuorese skulls turned up some new types, which he found to correspond with those of Canary Islanders, that is, Africans.

Although Niceforo offered an unsatisfactory definition of race, he was more explicit than his colleagues in linking race to behavior. The physical atavisms common to the Nuorese corresponded to moral deficiencies, since "the moral sense . . . [is] organized by a series of molecular variations."[86] Thus, moral, like physical, traits were inborn, and this "psychological heredity is quite stable and will not disappear . . . [even] when confronted with other models to imitate or with education; this is the psyche which is transmitted fatally from father to son, with all its accumulation of defects."[87] Here, Niceforo was explicit about the materialist root of psychological phenomena.

Niceforo presented a variety of evidence that the delinquent zone of Nuoro had "atrophied on the road to civilization and [had] retained the moral ideas of primitive society."[88] These mountaineers, like Africans, organized "armed raids against other villages, with the same enthusiasm as primitive tribes drawn up before their symbolic totems."[89] Echoing Herbert Spencer, Niceforo condemned such violence as atavistic, since modern society was evolving from egoism and war to altruism and peace. Niceforo also condemned Nuoroese men for the degradation of their wives, forced to perform the "most menial work" like women in "ancient tribes."[90] The latter judgment takes on a bit of irony in light of Niceforo's unabashed misogyny in other writings. Even the music of Nuoro showed "great similarity to savage singing. This singing is oppressive; it penetrates the brain, rasping, whirring, and boring through it with sharpness, tenacity and insistence. It is nothing but dissonant variations on a few notes."[91]

Although Niceforo admitted that crime sprang from social as well as biological causes, he gave the former much shorter shrift in his book on Sardinia than Ferri or even Lombroso. This was also true of another work notoriously entitled *Contemporary Barbarian Italy*, in which he argued that the South represented "a real and actual social atavism" compared to the North.[92] Citing statistics on education, industry, suicide, and crime, he sought to establish the existence of "two Italies" divided by race. Because of their discipline and educability, the Aryans of the North deserved a form of government based on liberty, while the Mediterraneans of the South "need energetic and at times dictatorial action to tear them away from the shadows" of traditionalism.[93] Niceforo thus concluded that only a highly decentralized government would allow the two Italies to devise political systems consonant with their racial differences.

Niceforo's racial analysis takes on much more complexity and subtlety in a slightly later work entitled *The Germans: History of an Idea and a Race*. Clearly irked by the German claims to racial purity and Aryan superiority, he denied the equivalence of the terms "German" and "Aryan." Now identifying three races in Europe, the Nordic, Alpine, and Mediterranean, he argued not only that the Nordic race— blond, long-headed Aryans—could be found in many other countries, but also that only about half of Germany was Nordic. Thus, Germans were wrong to equate their nation with the Aryan race. He also defended Italy from German charges of "ethnic chaos" and "extensive racial mixing," asserting that Italy had a simple racial map with one group each in the North and the South.[94] Furthermore, he ridiculed the German notion that all great men in European history had been Aryans. In his chapter entitled "Did all Greek heroes really have blond hair?" he answered that this was "a poetic fiction" as was the absurd theory that all Renaissance geniuses, like Dante, had been German and that this Aryan blood had later been submerged in that of lower races.[95]

For our purposes, it is perhaps most interesting that Niceforo softened his stance on the determinist link between race and psychology in *The Germans*. In an attempt to deny the possibility of a superior race, he pointed out that the psychology of each people is complex, influenced by history and environment as well as race. He now pronounced it difficult to define the particular psychologies of the Nordic, Alpine, and Mediterranean peoples. Niceforo's conversion to environmentalism in the case of Aryans clearly reflected political changes in the relationship between Italy and Germany. As Germany became an overweening senior partner in the Triple Alliance and finally an enemy in World War I, Niceforo's admiration of Aryans paled. Bristling at their claims of racial superiority, he modified a belief in biological determinism previously held to be scientifically objective.

CRITICS

It is not surprisingly that the main opponent of the positivist doctrine on race and crime was Colajanni, the "sociological" criminologist who never tired of ridiculing biological determinism and the notion of the born criminal. Furthermore, as a parliamentary deputy for many years from Sicily, he passionately denounced reductionist stereotypes of southern behavior based on race. In *Latins and Anglo-Saxons (Inferior and Superior Races)*, he offered a direct response to the positivist analysis of the Southern Question.

Colajanni pointed out confusion in racial classification despite the general agreement among anthropologists on a tripartite division into Germans, Alpines or Celts, and Mediterraneans. He quoted a variety of experts to show the myriad discrepancies among descriptions of these three simple categories as well as the existence of multiple subcategories. According to the generally accepted scheme, Italy harbored two races, the Alpine in the North and the Mediterranean—"the cursed race"—in the South. He was amused that the Alpine race could be considered so culturally and economically superior in northern Italy while being bemoaned as ragged, ignorant mountain folk in southern France. He was especially delighted to show that experts could not even agree on the appropriate racial categorization of great men anymore than could "the inmates in an insane asylum."[96] For example, one theorist labeled Lord Byron "a real German" while another dismissed him as "a vulgar Celt."[97] Colajanni concluded that while pure races may have existed in the distant past, today "peoples," or "nations" were the proper terms for groups with a collective psychology, behavior, and history.[98]

Even if races could be identified, Colajanni rejected a key proposition in the Lombrosian analysis: the correspondence between "anatomical characteristics and psychological characteristics."[99] The modern world showed this correlation to be absurd, since most nations harbored a variety of races and yet all citizens felt, thought, and acted in the same way. Furthermore, no race was superior, although "anthro-sociological fantasy" had assigned to Anglo-Saxons "the *character* of *characters*, the highest trait which assures their superiority: educability."[100] For Colajanni, racial theorists were like the defenders of slavery in the time of Aristotle who believed that "men's internal nature made them *free* or *slaves*."[101] That slaves in Aristotle's time were from northern Europe, now considered superior, made the notion of racial hierarchy even more absurd. Surely Aryans or even Celts had not been needed to build the marvels of Agrigento, Syracuse, Segesta, and Selinute in his own Sicily.

When turning to statistics on crime, Colajanni admitted that Italy held "very sadly, first place in violent crime."[102] But he refused to see the high homicide rate as "a measure exclusively of the greater *ferocity* of the Italians, especially those of the South."[103] Since he claimed that assault rates were higher in Germany and Scotland than Italy, violence was not inevitably linked to one race but common in different forms to all races. Even specific types of murder, like infanticide, were higher in northern Europe than Italy. And homicide in general had declined in Sicily and Sardinia to almost one-half of what it had been twenty years previously, a rapid change incompatible with racial determinism. Even the blot of the mafia and camorra in the Italian South were not unique, since bands of whites who lynched blacks similarly dishonored the United States. Dismissing the positivist racial theory as "pseudo-scientific," Colajanni saw homicide rates "simply as an index of the level of social and intellectual evolution" reached by a society.[104] For him, the denial by criminal anthropologists of the primary influence of environment and education on crime constituted "a real madness."[105]

ANTHROPOLOGY IN ITALY

That Colajanni was almost alone in criticizing the positivist doctrine of scientific racism points to a widespread consensus across the political spectrum on the superiority of white Europeans. While a diversity of voices found fault with the notion of the born criminal and even with the theory of women's inferiority, the idea of racial hierarchy received little challenge. Critiques of criminal anthropology by classical penologists, Catholic spiritualists, and feminist activists rarely referred to race, seeming to accept the backwardness of southern Italians or black Africans as self-evident. The positivist emphasis on the fundamental role of biology in determining the psychology and intelligence of human groups was particularly important in shaping the emerging discipline of anthropology.

What was the relationship of criminal anthropology to the general discipline of anthropology? Anthropology today, with its emphasis on cultural analysis, seems to have little in common with the biological determinism of Lombroso and his followers. Yet from its establishment as an academic profession in the late nineteenth century until at least World War II, Italian anthropology shared a passion for physical measurement of skulls and other parts of the body with criminal anthropology. The latter, therefore, was a recognized and integral subdivision of the former and certainly better known among the general public. The close connection between the development of anthropology in general and its criminological variant is clear from the writings of the two founders of the discipline in Italy, Giuseppe Sergi and Paolo Mantegazza. Sergi worked closely with criminal anthropologists on topics like female sensitivity while Mantegazza, who had differences with Lombroso, nevertheless echoed the positivist doctrine on race in his writings.

Of the generation of Lombroso, Sergi had fought with Garibaldi during the wars of unification before becoming a pioneer in the discipline of anthropology. He was appointed to the one of the first Chairs of Anthropology, at the University of Bologna, in 1880 and four years later moved to the University of Rome where he founded the Institute of Anthropology. Known for his work on the typology of human races, he was quoted by the other positivist criminologists already discussed, although not always accurately. Sergi collaborated actively with Lombroso in the *Archives* and shared key positivist assumptions that, for example, physical racial characteristics determined internal psychological traits. But his work on race was more careful than that of other criminal anthropologists, and he tried to sort out many myths and misconceptions about Aryans and their relation to Italy.

In the preface to his work entitled *Aryans and Italics*, published in 1898, Sergi warned that his opinions opposed common wisdom about the Aryans. He criticized the reliance of traditional Italian anthropology on linguistics and ethnography to try to classify races; in this vain endeavor, "the principle defect . . . was to try to establish ethnological rules without anthropology, which is quite a curious phenomenon."[106] Although linguistics pointed to the unity of most Europeans based on the Indo-European roots in their languages, he believed that all these groups could be considered "neither a race nor a people."[107] Italian intellectuals needed to get over their disdain for anthropology, by which he meant physical anthropology, and accept the tools it offered for solving this puzzle.

Despite his allusions to cultural practices such as burial, Sergi relied mainly on the shapes of skulls and faces to categorize race. Claiming to have compared ancient and modern skulls of groups like Egyptians and American Indians, he concluded that "the forms of the skull are *persistent*," unchanging over many thousands of years.[108] For Sergi, this persistence of physical type was consistent with the "laws of animality," and only "extremist evolutionists" could believe that physical characteristics such as the shape of the skull could have changed in the short time since humans appeared on earth.[109] By "extreme evolutionists," Sergi probably meant monogenists, since he subscribed to the rival theory, polygenism. Based on his belief in the persistence of cranial types, he argued that races could not have descended from one ancestor in Africa, but evolved independently in several geographical locations. Although he differed on this point with the monogenist Lombroso, he held the father of criminal anthropology in high esteem, praising him as "a man whose powers of intuition and sharp eyes of observation are worth a thousand others."[110]

Sergi filled his book with tables of cephalic indices and photographs of skulls to underpin his classification of races in Italy. Based on his evidence, Sergi tackled the confusing multiplicity of groups found in Italian history such as the Italics, Terramare people, Umbrians, Latins, Etruscans, and Ligurians. After measuring skulls from each group, he concluded that all of Italy—in fact all of Europe—was populated by two general races: the long-headed Italics and the short-headed Aryans. According to his theory, the Italics had their origins in Africa and had spread throughout Europe in Neolithic times. Labeled "Euroafrican" by Sergi, they varied widely in skin color because of differing climates. In the bronze age, the Aryans invaded Europe from the east, pushing most Italics either to the south or the north. These "Euroasians" included the Germans, Slavs, and Celts, the last two of which entered northern Italy and penetrated as far as the Tiber River. But the late Etruscans and the Romans were Italic, so that Italy remained a mixture of Aryans and Italics in the north while being almost homogeneously Italic in the South. Even within the North, Aryan influence varied, so that it was quite weak in Rome but "the Po valley can consider itself predominantly Aryan."[111] It is noteworthy that while Sergi based his classification on biological measurement, he rejected skin color as indicative of fundamental racial differences.

In the conclusion to his book, Sergi left his careful and closely reasoned analysis of physical evidence to leap into ungrounded speculation about the psychological differences between Aryans and Italics. Based partially on anecdotes from his own trips to northern Europe, he asserted that Aryans were more socially connected and orderly than the individualistic, anarchic Italics. During ancient Rome and the Renaissance, Italic individualism produced great military leaders and artistic geniuses, so that Italy had triumphed over the rest of Europe. But in modern times, the social solidarity of the Aryans had allowed them to create stronger institutions like schools, industry, and families, and thus European leadership had passed to them. Undocumented by any rigorous data, this analysis showed that Sergi was as careless as his colleagues in assuming that biology determined psychology.

Ten years older than Sergi, Mantegazza was also a committed patriot, having fought against the Austrians in 1848. Trained in medicine, he taught pathology before being invited in 1869 to take the new Chair of Anthropology at the Institute of Advanced Studies in Florence.[112] Originally housed in the division of philosophy, the chair was transferred to the faculty of science under Mantegazza's positivistic influence. He quickly founded the "Society for Anthropology and Ethnology" with its own journal, as well as a "National Museum of Anthropology." As a pioneer in institutionalizing anthropology, Mantegazza made Florence the intellectual center for the discussion and propagation of Darwin's ideas in Italy.[113]

Although not a criminal anthropologist like Sergi, Mantegazza was a passionate positivist in the general sense of the term. As a liberal deputy and senator, he championed science as the key to progress for the newly united state. A popular author in Italy and abroad, Mantegazza was best known for a trilogy of widely translated books on the "physiology" and "hygiene" of love published between 1872 and 1885.[114] While bold in their intent to apply a scientific approach to sex, these works were neither systematic nor empirical. Instead, they offered a jumble of anecdotes about strange and lurid sexual practices drawn from past and present societies around the globe. Presented in "rhetorical and decadent prose," these pioneering works in "sexology" drew a large audience more for their titillating than scientific nature.[115]

In many ways, Mantegazza's books resembled the sections of Lombroso's works in which he eschewed tables and statistics in favor of data comprised of popular sayings and secondhand anecdotes. This is only one of the several parallels that can be drawn between the two men, which include their training in medicine, their role as propagators of Darwinian evolution, and their intense interest in psychology. As Lombroso included "psychiatry" in the title of his journal, Mantegazza added the phrase "comparative psychology" to his *Archives of Anthropology and Ethnology*. Yet Mantegazza did have differences with Lombroso and Sergi and gradually severed his relations with criminal anthropology. He criticized Lombroso's early theory of the born criminal, claiming that it failed to distinguish between atavism and pathology as the cause of psychological anomalies. In the case of Sergi, he accused him of relying too heavily on craniometry, or the measurement of skulls, for classifying individuals and groups. But Mantegazza himself never abandoned the practice of physical measurement, gathering an extensive collection of skulls for his museum.

That Mantegazza's distance from criminal anthropology was only one of degree is clear from his theory of race. He set out its principles in a "letter on race" published in 1876 and reiterated them in later works like *Physiognomy and Expression*. In this letter, he offered his "confession of faith" on the existence of many races, some of which had disappeared.[116] Of the still existing races, the lowest were "black or brown" and the highest were "white or almost white."[117] In *Physiognomy and Expression*, he illustrated this racial hierarchy as a series of trees—a "morphological tree," an "aesthetic tree," and an "intellectual tree" of human races—on which the branch labeled "Aryans" was always at the top.[118]

Mantegazza's classification not only of races but also of facial features resembled that of criminal anthropology. Despite his critique of craniometry, he shared the positivist assumption that exterior physical features constituted signs of mental development. In a passage reminiscent of Lombroso, he asserted that "One of the most important characters of a human face is the possession or non-possession of prominent jaws, thick lips, and a receding forehead. In the first case the face is said to be *prognathous*; it is the type met with in negroes, the Australians, and some Papuans. In the second case the face is *orthognathous*; this is the face of all the higher races."[119] Furthermore, "no high race has a very small skull, or very large ears, or a flat nose, or a retreating chin," so that Mantegazza was able to provide his reader with a table identifying the "anatomical characters" of an "intelligent face" versus a "stupid face."[120] The author assured his readers that his table offered "a *resumé* of the actual state of science relative to the value of the anatomical guides taken for the determination of the place of a human face in the intellectual series."[121]

As is clear from Mantegazza's inclusion of an "aesthetic tree" next to his morphological and intellectual trees of racial hierarchy, he believed beauty correlated with
mental ability. He thus made explicit an assumption that often went unacknowl-
edged by criminal anthropologists that the European standard of beauty guided the
ranking of physical characteristics on the evolutionary scale. Never offering any
empirical proof that white skin, small ears, or a strong chin were inherently superior
to their opposites, racial scientists fell back on aesthetic prejudices embedded in
their culture. In analyzing human expressions, Mantegazza clearly addressed this issue, although he claimed that his standards of beauty were universal rather than
European. According to Mantegazza, "Many centuries before there was any study
of morphological rank according to the evolutionist scale, the wide and lofty brow
was universally considered beautiful, the low and receding brow, ugly. This appreci-
ation absolutely conformed to nature, since the former was peculiar to the more intelligent races, while the latter characterized the inferior races, and an intelligence
of a low order."[122] That beauty correlated with evolution only reinforced the notion
touted by criminal anthropology that a criminal—marked by atavisms reminiscent
of "primitive" peoples—could be identified by physical measurement or even an educated glance.

Despite the proximity of Mantegazza's racial analysis to that of Sergi, the two giants of early Italian anthropology had a falling out in 1893. Sergi, now at the University of Rome, founded his own association, the "Roman Society of
Anthropology" with its journal.[123] Yet the two founders of the field had much in
common.[124] Both Sergi and Mantegazza demanded that the discipline of anthropology be moved to the Faculty of Science, underlining the centrality of biological
analysis to their endeavors. Consequently, the study of cultural practices like linguistics, religion, and customs was relegated to the subsidiary fields of ethnology
and folklore. Ethnology had a long tradition in Italy and was composed of researchers, like Marzolo, who focused on "primitive" societies like Africa. But ethnologists
tended to teach within the Faculties of Humanities and had no clear institutional
identity until 1967, with the establishment of the first chair at the University of
Rome. Folklore explored the popular customs of Italy, especially in the South,
which, as in physical anthropology, was considered backwards. As early as 1910, the
first chair of folklore was created for Giuseppe Pitrè, the famous doctor and collec-
tor of arts and crafts made in his native Sicily.[125] Until World War II, ethnology and
folklore remained wedded to the humanities and were heavily influenced by
Crocean idealism that disparaged economic and political analysis.

From its founding, the academic location of Chairs of Anthropology was usually
in the Faculties of Science, inhibiting the growth of social or what is now called
"cultural" anthropology. Thus, before World War II, Italy lacked a tradition of the
social science of anthropology, which would have firmly located the study of culture
within a social, economic, and political context. The continuing domination of a
biological perspective into the twentieth century is clear from the first textbook of
anthropology, published by Fabio Frassetto in 1913 and reissued in 1918. Frassetto
wrestled with the definition of anthropology, since it was "still a young science."[126]

But he argued for limiting anthropology to "the zoology of Man," that is, "reserving the term . . . for only the physical aspect."[127] Comparing anthropology to a tree, he pronounced the study of morality, customs, and psychology to have branched out from the main trunk to the extent of now constituting independent disciplines. He was pleased that most of his colleagues, like Sergi, agreed that physical anthropology constituted the core of the discipline; the only exception was the unclassifiable Mantegazza "who gives a completely personal stamp to his teaching, combining physical Anthropology, Ethnology, Ethnography, and also Psychology."[128]

For Frassetto, criminal anthropology naturally fell within the wider field of anthropology, and in his list of the first nine chairs of anthropology in Italy, he included three in criminal anthropology. Frassetto did admit frustration at the notoriety of positivist criminology, complaining that the public ignored anthropological studies of "normal" human behavior in favor of having their heads or characters "read" for criminal tendencies.[129] In consequence, "a bit for fun and a bit seriously, the concept of Anthropology is associated with crime and insanity, and in our society the anthropologist is often regarded with a certain curiosity and mistrust, as perhaps were necromancers and alchemists in the past."[130]

Although Frassetto may have envied the popularity of criminal anthropologists, his definition of "general physical anthropology" echoed their program, albeit extended to the entire population:

General physical anthropology, which we can also call morphology, studies the origins of Man, his place in the animal kingdom, his probable place of origin, his age and his evolution; it classifies Men according to zoological criteria, determining the limits within which oscillate the anatomical, physiological and pathological characteristics of different natural human groups, of the two sexes, and of various age groups, and searches for an explanation based on a series of morphological and environmental factors; finally, it studies all aspects of heredity, including cross-breeding [and] atavism.[131]

To pursue such studies, Frassetto emphasized the methods dear to criminal anthropology, devoting over half of his textbook to a detailed explanation of the methods of anthropometry, or the measurement of the body. Thirteen out of his thirty-nine chapters, or "lessons," were devoted to craniometry, showing the importance that he attributed, *pace* Mantegazza, to the size and shape of the head for human classification.

Under fascism, the classification of individuals and groups according to physical criteria continued to dominate the discipline of anthropology. A good illustration is provided by the entry for "anthropology" in the *Treccani Encyclopedia*, the reference work that is still admired today for its scholarly rigor despite its compilation during the fascist dictatorship. The third volume, published in 1929, devoted sixteen densely printed pages to the rubric "anthropology." Except for a short historical introduction of two pages, the entire article is devoted to three subsections: "anthropology as a natural science," "the instruments of anthropology," and "criminal anthropology." Little mention is made of ethnology or folklore, which were relegated to separate articles.

Unlike ethnology and folklore, criminal anthropology was still considered an integral part of the larger discipline by the authors of the *Encyclopedia*. Such a link was especially clear in the *Encyclopedia's* definition of criminal anthropology as "the study of criminal man conducted with the same naturalistic methods with which general anthropology studies normal man, that is, by elaborating and employing notions of anatomy, physiology, psychology, ethnology, demography, and even philology."[132] Despite the seemingly wide net cast by this list of subjects, the article gave no examples of research by positivist criminologists on ethnology or philology. Similarly, while the article cautioned that criminal anthropology had always admitted that social factors caused crime, none of these was mentioned. Instead, the *Encyclopedia* touted that criminal anthropology had "a clearly Italian origin" that emphasized "the physical, anatomical and organic anomalies" of criminals.[133] It then reviewed the standard Lombrosian atavisms, including cranial capacity, size and angle of the ears, left-handedness, tattoos, and insensitivity. Institutionalized with its own university chairs and journals like the *Archives* and *The Positivist School*, criminal anthropology, according to the *Encyclopedia*, had a secure future in Italian intellectual life.

The subsection on "anthropology as a natural science" was also devoted almost entirely to physical measurement, mostly for the purpose of defining racial categories. It still recognized Sergi's scheme of five races—composed of two extinct groups and "American man," as well as Euroafricans and Eurasians—as authoritative, but not unchallenged. In addition, the author of the article, Giocchino Sera, noted the importance of a theory of V. Giuffrida-Ruggeri that posited eight races and his own recent effort to develop a new "craniological system, based on the study of the relation between the skull and the base of the cranium."[134] Other scientific developments also promised to clarify racial categories, including Mendelian genetics, endocrinology, and blood analysis. But he cautioned against expectations that these new approaches would quickly establish definitive results, warning that races had not yet been clearly defined and that racial mixing was widespread.

Other Italian anthropologists employed less measured tones when analyzing African blacks, especially after the conquest of Ethiopia in 1936. In his reflections on the history of anthropology, Giulio Angioni writes that almost all Italian anthropologists of the 1930s and early 1940s were complicit in the imperialist enterprise of the fascist state.[135] They served as researchers in the colonies and apologists for Italian policy at international academic congresses. In 1938, for example, the eminent ethnologist Lido Cipriani declared at the Conference of Moral and Historical Sciences that

We Italians have already irrevocably fixed our attitude toward the colored races in Africa. We are convinced that a fundamental inferiority, linked to biological causes and therefore transmittable from generation to generation, distinguishes these races from Whites. Therefore, it is necessary to avoid mixtures of blood. . . . It is our firm opinion that breeding with Africans constitutes an outrage against European civilization because it encourages degeneration.[136]

Cipriani admittedly constituted an extreme case of anthropological complicity with fascism, even contributing to the infamous journal, *Defense of the Race*, founded by the ideologue Julius Evola. But he was not unique, as collaboration with the dictatorial regime came from the ranks of physical anthropologists, ethnologists, and folklorists alike. Part of the explanation for this willingness to participate in the construction of fascist propaganda lay in the personal and professional links between interwar anthropologists and the founding fathers of criminal anthropology. The well-known folklorist Raffaele Corso, for example, had been the student of Giuseppe Sergi, while other interwar leaders of the discipline, like Giovanni Marro and Sergio Sergi, were literally sons of positivism.[137] Thus, as part of their early professional training, they had imbibed the principles of scientific racism as propounded at the turn of the century.

In 1938, Benito Mussolini enacted the first unified racial policy of his regime, under the specious title of "The Manifesto of Racist Scientists."[138] It began with familiar propositions that had been enunciated by Lombroso in 1871 and become articles of faith within mainstream anthropology. These were that "human races exist," that there are greater and lesser races, and that race is a purely biological concept.[139] The last part of the manifesto, however, went far beyond positivist orthodoxy by proclaiming the existence of only one race in Italy. Arguing that Italy had suffered no contamination of its blood since the Longobard invasions a thousand years earlier, Mussolini pronounced the single Italian race to be Aryan. Thus, "contemporary Italians have their origins in the same races that constitute and will continue to constitute the living fabric of an eternal Europe."[140] With this new twist to nationalistic propaganda, the regime turned to folklorists to document the ancient and rich traditions of the "Italic" people.

Not coincidentally, the publication of "The Manifesto of Racist Scientists" appeared during the same year as the promulgation of a series of "Racial Laws" by Mussolini. While fascist propaganda, often dressed up in anthropological clothing, had always denounced intermarriage between Italians and Africans, the Racial Laws of 1938 targeted another group; the new enemy was the Jews, who were now defined as being outside of the "Italic race" of Italian Aryans. The Racial Laws not only forbid marriage between Jews and "Aryans" but also excluded Jews from military service, state employment, public schools, and ownership of large amounts of property. They defined Jews biologically, as anyone born of Jewish parents. Thus, in an official discourse that pronounced all Italians as being descended from Aryan stock, the Southern Question disappeared. Jews now replaced southerners as the "inferior" and "degenerate" race that threatened to weaken Italy. Although the Racial Laws have often been explained, and partially excused, as the result of Italy's increasingly close alliance with Nazi Germany, it is clear that Mussolini also drew on an indigenous intellectual tradition of racial thinking and vocabulary constructed fifty years earlier by criminal anthropologists.[141]

CONCLUSION

Were criminal anthropologists of the late nineteenth century the precursors of the racist ideologues of the fascist period? Most of the evidence points to an affirmative answer. Lombroso and his followers formed the vanguard of scientific racism in Italy. They popularized the notion that race was a biological fact that could be measured and classified. It constituted a fundamental characteristic of both individuals and groups, determining their potential for moral and intellectual prowess. Not only polygenists like Sergi but even monogenists like Lombroso emphasized the importance of studying racial differences rather than the biological and psychological aspects that united humanity. In the positivist version of social Darwinism, these differences expressed themselves as a clear hierarchy, with the "white" races at the top and the "colored" races below.

Criminal anthropology also set a precedent for the kind of slipshod research methods that typified fascist pronouncements on race. As our analysis of the writings of Lombroso, Ferri, Niceforo, and Sergi illustrates, no consensus existed even on a general classification of races. Lombroso categorized Italians as Latins and Semites, Ferri as Greco-Latins, Niceforo as Mediterraneans, and Sergi as Aryans and Italics. Furthermore, each writer except Sergi contradicted himself within his own writings, referring to smaller groups like Umbrians, Greeks, or Phoenicians that seemed to lie outside of the larger categories. Only Sergi was careful about defining his racial groups; others were so cavalier in their racial classification that they even misused Sergi's categories.

Confusion in racial classification arose from incomplete or unpersuasive data. Sometimes positivists substituted skin color (white and black) or language (Albanian or Greek) for rigorous empirical evidence of fundamental physical differences. The most persuasive data, the cephalic indices, were used consistently only by Sergi; other writers supplied them for some categories and not for others. Yet, the cephalic index, with only two categories of long-headed and short-headed, was too blunt a tool to create the detailed racial maps of the South proposed by Lombroso, Ferri, and Niceforo. Without a clear definition, the concept of race slipped among biological, cultural, and political categories in their writings.

Perhaps even more disturbing was the assumption, central to criminal anthropology, that biology determined psychology and morality. While the cephalic indices might have correctly distinguished inherited physical differences among humans, this type of data did not prove that the shape of the skull had any effect on morality. Of our writers, only Niceforo explicitly addressed this connection by asserting that thought is a function of molecules. This assertion proved inadequate when positivists admitted that environment also influenced criminological behavior. Except for Ferri, who at least differentiated between violent crime springing from race and property crime arising from social influences, most writers never attempted to explain the interplay of race and environment in the etiology of crime.

In the writings of positivist criminologists before the fascist period, the weight of race or environment in the crime equation seemed to shift, depending on the groups studied. This became especially clear in the writings of Lombroso and Ferri on anti-Semitism or of Niceforo on the Aryans. Here, environmentalism almost triumphed over the authors' usual racial analysis as they pursued the political aims of defending Jews or criticizing Germany. On the other hand, blacks were compared to monkeys, both incapable of escaping biological instincts. Implicitly, positivists constructed a sliding scale with heredity at one end and environment at the other: Africans and other "savages" were placed near the pole of heredity while Jews, and, after the rise of a threatening Germany, Aryans were placed near the pole of environment. Southerners in Italy were assigned a place near the pole of heredity, but with a slight shift toward environment. Thus, prejudices or political passions underpinned a supposedly scientific analysis of racial determinism.

Fascist ideologues inherited a solid intellectual tradition of scientific racism from the late nineteenth and early twentieth centuries. Yet in several important ways they distorted the lessons of criminal anthropology. Most obviously, they redefined Jews as a biological race and relegated them to the bottom of the evolutionary scale. Jews now shared the same opprobrium as African blacks, both groups being officially prohibited from intermarrying with Italian "Aryans." On the other hand, southerners were elevated to the exulted ranks of northerners, as fascism increasingly insisted on the existence of one "Italic" race on the peninsula. By the 1930s, the supposedly scientific hierarchy of races had changed significantly in ways unforeseen by the first positivist criminologists. Lombroso never intended for Jews to be "biologized" as a race, although we have difficulty today understanding why he did not foresee such a logical application of his own theories on southerners and blacks.

Fascist racial theory also ignored the generally positive evaluation of race mixing by positivist criminologists. Despite the crudity of their racial classifications, criminal anthropologists agreed that nineteenth-century Italians were descended from more than one race. Most, like Lombroso, were enthusiastic proponents of race mixing, comparing the crossbreeding of people with that of plants and animals. From his Darwinian perspective, crossbreeding created hardier and, in the case of humans, more intelligent strains that were superior to the dull reproductions of identical characteristics in an isolated group. Admittedly, criminal anthropologists did not encourage race mixing between contemporary "white" Italians and the "colored races." But all agreed that Semitic groups like Phoenicians and north Africans had migrated in the past to southern Italy and were among the ancestors of present-day Italians. They would have found preposterous the fascist claim that one race, especially the Aryan race, united the peninsula.

Finally, fascist propaganda of the 1930s ignored the subtleties and internal contradictions that often unintentionally softened the rigidity of racial categorization in the writings of early criminal anthropologists. First, Lombroso and Ferri allowed for psychological variation within all races, so that some individuals might escape the general characteristics assigned to a group. They believed that, for example, in exceptional cases some Africans might be honest and some southerners industrious. More important, a strong humanitarian streak marked positivist thinking before World War I, so that the failings of most racial groups were attributed to environment as well as biology. This was most evident in the case of Jews, whose behavior was almost entirely attributed to sociological causes, but also to a lesser extent to southerners. Thus Lombroso, Ferri, and Niceforo—all members of the socialist party—combined a seemingly cold logic of racial determinism with heartfelt denunciations of the wretched conditions of life in the South. This uneasy mixture of biological and sociological causation left open potential spaces for change and progress among southerners, although less so for blacks. Such ambiguities were lost under fascism, whose ideologues denounced both socialism and humanitarianism as incompatible with the virility and militarism of the regime.

NOTES

1. The *Nuova antologia* is comparable to today's *New Yorker*, with articles on politics, art, and science as well as examples of new fiction. It is still being published.

2. Cesare Lombroso, "L'ultimo brigante," *Nuova antologia* (Feb. 1, 1902), p. 508.

3. Ibid., p. 509.

4. Ibid., p. 510.

5. Ibid., p. 509.

6. Ibid.

7. Ibid., pp. 509–10.

8. Ibid., p. 510.

9. Ibid., p. 511. Lombroso uses the word "mafia" in reference to Musolino's Calabrian gang, although its use is generally limited to Sicily.

10. Ibid., p. 512.

11. Ibid., p. 509.

12. Ibid., p. 508.

13. Ibid.

14. Ibid.

15. Ibid., p. 513.

16. C. Lombroso, *L'uomo bianco e l'uomo di colore: Letture sull'origine e le varietà delle razze umane* (Padua: F. Sacchetto, 1871), p. 121. Lombroso's use here of "pigmy" to indicate intellectual inferiority is itself racist.

17. Ibid., p. 7.

18. Ibid., pp. 7, 5.

19. Ibid., p. 88.

20. Ibid.

21. Ibid., p. 127.

22. Ibid., p. 135.

23. Ibid., pp. 172–73.

24. Ibid., pp. 120–22.

25. Ibid., p. 106.

26. Ibid.

27. Ibid., p. 70.

28. Ibid., p. 20.

29. Ibid.

30. Ibid., p. 21.

31. Ibid., p. 222.

32. As a later section argues, Lombroso was never clear on the number of existing races; in *L'uomo bianco* he variously refers to two races, white and colored (p. 222), three races, white, bushmen, and black (p. 23) or White, Yellow and Black (p. 170); or more than three, including Semites, Australians, American Indians, and Mongols.

33. C. Lombroso, *L'uomo bianco*, p. 25. In Italian, the last phrase was "sua poco gentile metà," which implies that, unlike in civilized Europe, an African wife was neither the "gentle sex" nor the "better half" of her husband.

34. Ibid., p. 55.

35. Ibid., 222.

36. See, for example, Nancy Stepan, *The Idea of Race in Science: Great Britain, 1800–1960* (Hamden, Conn.: Archon, 1982) and William B. Cohen, *The French Encounter with Africa: White Response to Blacks, 1530–1880* (Bloomington: Indiana University Press, 1980).

37. See Marta Petrusewicz, "Before the Southern Question: 'Native' Ideas on Backwardness and Remedies in the Kingdom of the Two Sicilies, 1815–1849," in Jane Schneider, ed., *Italy's "Southern Question": Orientalism in One Country* (New York: Berg, 1998), pp. 27–49.

38. Silvana Patriarca, "How Many Italies? Representing the South in Official Statistics," in Schneider, ed., *Italy's "Southern Question*," pp. 81–87.

39. General information on developments in the South are found in Di Scala, *Italy* and Martin Clark, *Modern Italy*.

40. Di Scala, *Italy*, p. 140.

41. Ibid., p. 141; Clark, *Modern Italy*, p. 166.

42. Several new books have begun to analyze how different types of nineteenth-century discourse created the perception that the South was a problem or "question." See Claudia Petracone, *Le due civiltà: Settentrionali e meridionali nella storia d'Italia dal 1860–1914* (Rome-Bari: Laterza), 2000; Petrusewicz, *Come il Meridione divenne una Questione* (Soveria Mannelli: Rubbettino, 1998); Schneider, ed., *Italy's "Southern Question*"; and Robert Lumley and Jonathan Morris, eds., *The New History of the Italian South* (Exeter, Devon, UK: University of Exeter Press, 1977).

43. Quoted in Nelson Moe, "The Emergence of the Southern Question in Villari, Franchetti, and Sonnino," in Schneider, ed., *Italy's "Southern Question*," p. 66.

44. Patriarca, "How Many Italies," p. 85.

45. For an excellent overview of research on brigandage and the mafia, see John Davis, *Conflict and Control: Law and Order in Nineteenth-Century Italy* (Atlantic Highlands, N.J.: Humanities Press, 1988).

46. On anti-Semitism in popular literature, see Lynn M. Gunzberg, *Strangers at Home: Jews in the Italian Literary Imagination* (Berkeley: University of California Press, 1992).

47. C. Lombroso, *L'uomo delinquente*, 5th ed., vol. 3, pp. 38, 28.

48. Ibid., p. 29.

49. C. Lombroso, *In Calabria (1862–1897)* (Catania: Niccolò Giannotta, 1898), pp. 53–54.

50. Ibid., p. 95.

51. C. Lombroso, *L'uomo delinquente*, 5th ed., vol. 3, pp. 26–27.

52. Ibid., p. 27.

53. Ibid., p. 33.

54. Ibid., vol. 1, p. 85.

55. C. Lombroso, *In Calabria*, p. 151.

56. Ibid., p. 146.

57. C. Lombroso, *L'antisemitismo e le scienze moderne* (Turin: Roux, 1894), p. 5.

58. Ibid., p. 41.

59. Ibid., p. 10.

60. Ibid., p. 56.

61. Ibid., p. 18.

62. Ibid., p. 9.

63. Ibid., p. 98.

64. Such comments raised controversy in the Jewish community in Italy. See Delia Frigessi, "Cattaneo, Lombroso e la questione ebraica," in Alberto Burgio, ed., *Nel nome della razza: Il razzismo nella storia d'Italia, 1870–1945* (Bologna: Il Mulino, 1999), p. 262.

65. C. Lombroso, *L'uomo bianco*, pp. 220–21.

66. Ibid., p. 84.

67. Ibid., pp. 27–28.

68. Ferri, *L'omicidio nell'antropologia criminale* (Turin: Bocca, 1895), vol. 1, p. 251.

69. Ibid., pp. 259–60.

70. Ibid., p. 247.

71. Ferri, *Sociologia criminale* (Turin: UTET, 1929), 5th ed., vol, 1, p. 347.

72. Ferri, *L'omicidio*, vol. 1, p. 250.

73. Ferri, *Sociologia criminale*, 5th ed., vol. 1, p. 347.

74. Ibid., p. 348.

75. Ferri, *L'omicidio*, vol. 1, p. 265.

76. Ferri, *Sociologia criminale*, 5th ed., vol. 1, p. 351.

77. Ferri's article "L'antisemitismo" was reprinted in *Studi sulla criminalità* (Turin: Bocca, 1901), pp. 533–42.

78. Ibid., pp. 538, 542.

79. Ibid., p. 540.

80. Ibid., p. 541.

81. Niceforo, *La delinquenza in Sardegna* (Palermo: Sandron, 1897), n.p.

82. Ibid., p. 6.

83. Ibid., p. 30.

84. Ibid., p. 32.

85. Ibid., pp. 29, 21.

86. Ibid., p. 68.

87. Ibid.

88. Ibid., p. 41.

89. Ibid., p. 43.

90. Ibid., p. 54.

91. Ibid., p. 51.

92. Niceforo, *L'Italia barbara contemporanea* (Milan: Sandron, 1893), p. 14.

93. Ibid., p. 297.

94. Niceforo, *Les Germains: Histoire d'un idée ed d'une race* (Paris: Bossard, 1919), 2nd ed., p. 74.

95. Ibid., pp. 107.

96. Colajanni, *Latini e anglo-sassoni (Razze inferiori e razze superiori)* (Rome-Naples: Rivista popolare) 2nd ed., p. 18.

97. Ibid.

98. Ibid., p. 25.

99. Ibid., 14.

100. Ibid., 42–43.

101. Ibid., 75.

102. Ibid., 99.

103. Ibid., p. 94.

104. Ibid., pp. 97–98.

105. Ibid., p. 158.

106. Giuseppe Sergi, *Arii e italici* (Turin: Bocca, 1898), p. 4.

107. Ibid., pp. 2–3.

108. Ibid., p. 102.

109. Ibid., p. 103.

110. Ibid., p. 104.

111. Ibid., p. 188.

112. While Mantegazza is often held to have occupied the first Chair of Anthropology in Italy, Fabio Frassetto, in his textbook of anthropology, cites two earlier chairs: the first established at the University of Pavia in 1860 for Giovanni Vincenzo Giglioli and the second established at the University of Turin in 1867 for Giuseppe Allievo. See his *Lezioni di antropologia* (Milan: Hoepli, 1918), 2nd ed., v. 1, p. 89.

113. On Mantegazza in Florence, see Landucci, *Il Darwinismo a Firenze.*

114. They are entitled *Fisiologia dell'amore* (1872); *Igiene dell'amore* (1877); and *Gli amori degli uomini* (1885).

115. The description of Mantegazza's prose is from Landucci, p. 107.

116. Included in Mantegazza, *Physiognomy and Expression* (London: Walter Scott, n.d.), p. 73.

117. Ibid., p. 74.

118. Ibid., pp. 312–14 (Plates II–IV in the Appendix).

119. Ibid., p. 29.

120. Ibid., p. 288.

121. Ibid.

122. Ibid., pp. 33–34.

123. The title of the journal was the *Acts of the Roman Society of Anthropology.*

124. One of Mantegazza's students, Enrico Morselli, even joined the ranks of the positivist criminologists.

125. Pitrè's chair was labeled "demopsicologia," literally the psychology of peoples or races. On the early history of anthropology, see George Saunders, "Contemporary Italian Cultural Anthropology," *Annual Review of Anthropology*, v. 13 (1984), pp. 450–52.

126. Frassetto, *Lezioni di antropologia*, v. 1, p. 99.

127. Ibid., v. 1, pp. 102, 112.

128. Ibid., v. 1, p. 124.

129. Ibid., v. 1, p. 97.

130. Ibid.

131. Ibid., v. 1, p. 114.

132. *Enciclopedia italiana* (1929), v. 3, p. 590.

133. Ibid.

134. Ibid., p. 585.

135. Giulio Angioni, *Tre saggi sull'antropologia dell'età coloniale* (Palermo: S.F. Flaccovio, 1973), p. 44. As examples, he lists eminent names like Lidio Cipriani, Enrico Cerulli, Carlo Conti Rossini, Raffaele Corso, and Nello Puccioni.

136. Ibid., 45.

137. For an excellent exploratory article on the ideological role of Italian anthropology between the two world wars, see Sandra Puccini and Massimo Squillacciotti, "Per una prima ricostruzione critico-bibliografica degli studi demo-etno-antropologici italiani nel periodo tra le due guerre," in Pietro Angelini et al., *Studi antropologici italiani e rapporti di classe* (Milan: Franco Angeli, 1980), pp. 67–93; 201–39.

138. The "Manifesto" is reprinted in Luigi Preti, *Impero fascista, africani ed ebrei* (Milan: Mursia, 1968), pp. 250–52.

139. Ibid., p. 250.

140. Ibid., p. 251.

141. The author of a recent book, which came out after the completion of this manuscript, has made a similar point about the sciences in general. See Roberto Maiocchi, *Scienza italiana e razzismo fascista* (Florence: La Nuova Italia), 1999.

Guiteau.

Passanante.

Italian brigands. Photograph from Cesare Lombroso, *L'uomo delinquente*.

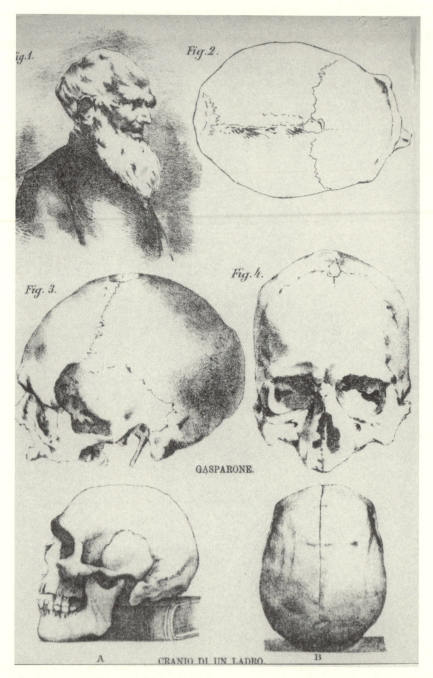

Skulls of criminals. Photograph from Cesare Lombroso, *L'uomo delinquente*.

Insane criminals. Photograph from Cesare Lombroso, *L'uomo delinquente*.

Female arsonist from Pesaro. Photograph from Cesare Lombroso, *L'uomo delinquente*.

Fig. 1. — SALVATORE A., brigante della Calabria.

Fig. 2. — G. SANA DI GALLUCCIO, brigante.

Fig. 3. — CAVAGLIÀ, detto *Fusil*, assassino.

Fig. 4. — G. B. VENAFRO DI CASPOLI, brigante.

Fig. 5. — O....., ladro napoletano.

Fig. 6. — CARBONE, capo-brigante

Criminal men. Photograph from Cesare Lombroso, *L'uomo delinquente*.

Delinquent child. Photograph from Cesare Lombroso, *L'uomo delinquente*.

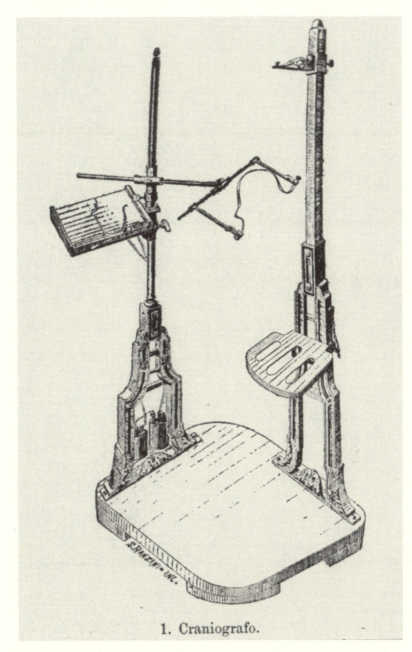

1. Craniografo.

Anfosso's craniograph. Photograph from Cesare Lombroso, *L'uomo delinquente*.

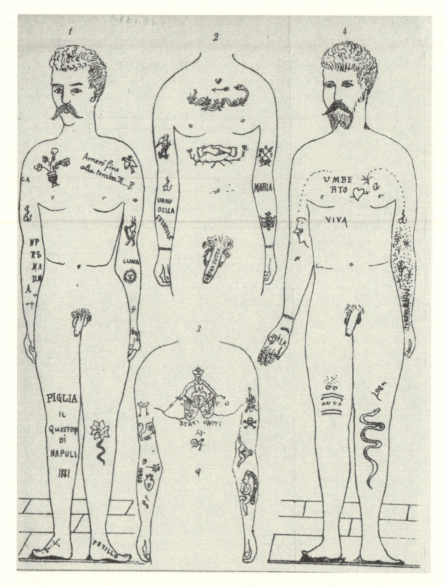

Tattoos of criminal soldiers. Photograph from Cesare Lombroso, *L'uomo delinquente.*

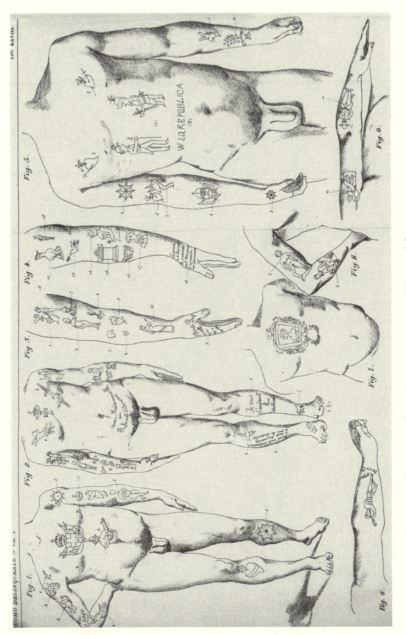

Tattoos of male criminals. Photograph from Cesare Lombroso, *L'uomo delinquente*.

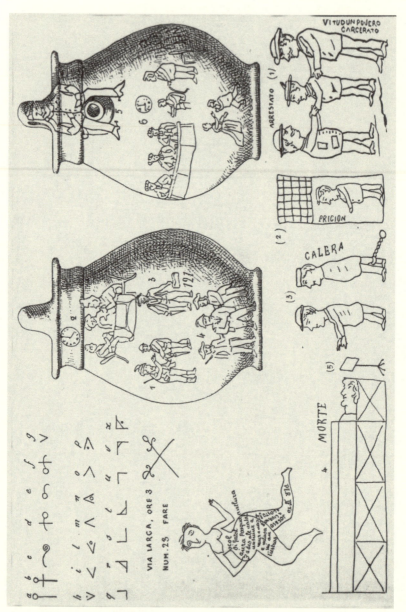

Art by prisoners. Photograph from Cesare Lombroso, *L'uomo delinquente.*

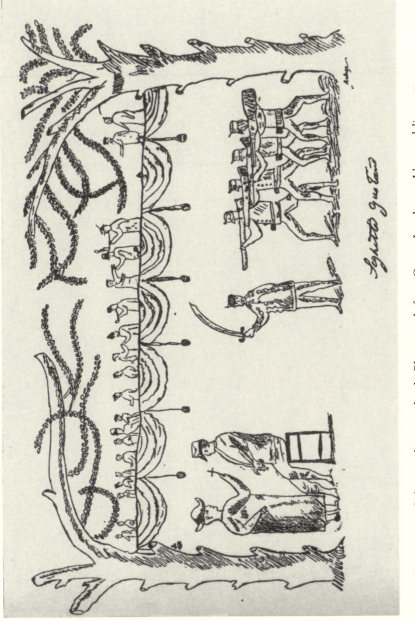

Carving by a criminal showing his own death. Photograph from Cesare Lombroso, *L'uomo delinquente*.

Chapter 4

"Scientific Police"

From its inception, criminal anthropology was never a discipline confined to the ivory tower of academia; it was meant to influence state policy. For Lombroso, the creation of a new positivist criminology was a calling that he received during the patriotic season of the wars of unification. By establishing the proper identification of certain classes of criminals—such as brigands, *mafiosi*, prostitutes, and thieves—he strove to protect the new and fragile nation of Italy from destruction by atavistic or degenerate subgroups in the population. As early as 1879 he published a book to explain the practical application of criminal anthropology to the Italian system of criminal justice. Entitled *On the Increase of Crime in Italy*, it began with a preface in which Lombroso explained why he, being neither a lawyer nor politician, dared to suggest legislative reforms. He was only "an honest man," inspired "not by love of a sect or party, but of the nation; he belonged to that handful of people who believe that it is best to have no party until one arises that prefers the gradual and continual improvement of the popular classes to personal and regional caprices."[1] As a psychiatrist who had studied crime for many years, he had a duty to address the problem of "the tide of crime that is always rising and rising, threatening to submerge as well as disgrace us."[2]

Twenty-five years later, shortly before his death, Lombroso penned an equally impassioned preface to a collection of his articles on social and political topics. As indicated by its title, *The Present Moment*, this work addressed an array of current issues, from the reform of police and prisons to free speech, parliamentary corruption, and imperialism. Again, Lombroso emphasized his obligation as a scientist to address practical matters, if only "to avoid becoming a living fossil in a world that stirs around him."[3] More important, the recent crisis of 1898–1900, when Italy became "the victim of militaristic and despotic power," had convinced him of the need for

academics to apply their expertise to current affairs.[4] He therefore offered this collection of essays, formerly published in popular newspapers and magazines, "without any other reason than as an outlet for a grieving soul, encouragement to the
oppressed, and a warning to those who rashly put Italy in immense dangers thanks
to their vast ignorance."[5] By this time Lombroso had found a party devoted to the
"improvement of the popular classes," the PSI, and he continued to pursue his vision, created during the *risorgimento*, of an Italy in which science would bring both
order and justice.

As we have seen, Lombroso was typical of criminal anthropologists in his effort to
popularize positivist theories about the boundaries between normalcy and deviancy. Many wrote for the socialist weekly *Critica sociale*, and for the more widely distributed *Nuova antologia*. In the series of volumes entitled *The World of Crime*,
Ferrero, Sighele, and Bianchi interpreted famous court cases, like that of Ernesta
Bordoni, into positivist terms. The Turinese publisher, Fratelli Bocca, put out a series devoted exclusively to positivist criminology, while the PSI included titles by
leading criminal anthropologists among the list of publications available from the
party. In addition, proponents of positivism were tireless in giving lectures, whether
to ladies' clubs in the case of Lombroso's lesson on race or throughout South America like Ferri. By the death of Lombroso, the anthropologist Frassetto complained
that the public, enamored with the notion of detecting criminals from physical appearance, identified anthropology as a whole with its criminological subfield.

Despite such monumental efforts to disseminate the positivist message,
Lombroso complained throughout his life that few politicians listened. The
Zanardelli Criminal Code of 1889 caused his greatest disillusionment, as it retained
the theoretical underpinnings of the Classical School despite his own enormous efforts to persuade Parliament to infuse it with the tenets of positivism. In later editions of *Criminal Man*, he repeatedly criticized his own government for failing to
implement experiments—like parole, criminal insane asylums, and reformatories
for youth—that were consonant with his theories and already being tried in other
nations. Exasperated with legislative and bureaucratic immobility, he bewailed the
fate of his beloved Italy, which could be saved only by the modern dictates of his
own criminological science. Thus, while his pronouncements on the theoretical advances of positivist research carried a triumphal and self-congratulatory tone, his
assessment of Italy's system of criminal justice—including law, courts, police, and
prisons—was pessimistic and despairing.

Most scholarship has agreed with Lombroso's assessment, declaring that his ideas
not only had little practical influence but also were outmoded by the time of his
death in 1909. After the turn of the century, a younger generation championed idealist philosophies over positivism, which was denounced as mechanistically materialistic, anti-aesthetic, and devoid of spiritual values. This "revolt against
positivism" included a diverse array of figures including Benedetto Croce, who introduced neo-Hegelian idealism into Italian philosophy; Giuseppe Prezzolini and
Giovanni Papini, who extolled a mystical nationalism; Gabriele D'Annunzio, who
exulted aesthetic decadence in his poetry, plays, and novels; and Filippo Marinetti,

who founded the anti-bourgeois movement of futurist art. For these young rebels, Lombroso was a "well-known little charlatan," who continued to cling to the outdated doctrines of scientific determinism, evolution, and socialism.[6]

Lombroso's latest and best biographer, Villa, similarly concludes that positivism, the premier "scientific product for export" from Italy in the last decades of the nineteenth century, lost its hegemony over intellectual life by the twentieth.[7] He frames his book with the Conference of Criminal Anthropology held in Turin in 1906 to commemorate the life and work of Lombroso. For Villa, this conference represented the death knell of positivism, where Lombroso's colleagues and students pretended to honor ideas that they knew were no longer sound. Thus, at Lombroso's death three years later, "criminal anthropology, understood as a 'lombrosian' discipline, died with him."[8]

I would like to offer an alternative perspective and argue that Lombroso's ideas had a deep and lasting impact on the Italian criminal justice system. The last half of this book will develop this new perspective, which diverges from the traditional historiography on Lombroso in several ways. First, it focuses on a longer chronological sweep, because the institutionalization of criminal anthropology occurred for the most part after the death of Lombroso. Second, it expands its lens from the isolated figure of Lombroso to the large and active group of his followers who were well known in Italy and abroad. Their corpus of work, while within the general positivist framework, suggested a multiplicity of directions for future policy. At times it was their ideas, rather than those of Lombroso, that were chosen as the basis for penal reform. Third, this new perspective lowers its sights from the lofty plane of high culture to the more middle-brow arena of bureaucratic policy. Although the artistic and intellectual avant-garde may have rejected and belittled criminal anthropology after 1900, the lessons of positivism had already become common sense among much of the educated classes. Members of Parliament, for example, routinely employed the vocabulary of criminal anthropology in debates about law, police, and prisons. Finally, the new perspective acknowledges that the state never implemented positivism as a complete program, but introduced bits and pieces into specific areas of the state administration. Thus, while the "Positivist School" was never triumphant in converting the entire criminal justice system to its principles, it nevertheless left an indelible imprint on certain sectors.

With the death of Lombroso and the intellectual ascendancy of idealism, why did positivist criminology finally receive recognition by the state? In the academic world, criminology remained a subdiscipline within medical schools, assuring a continuing emphasis on the biological origins of crime. New support for the hereditary nature of deviancy was found in the developing fields of endocrinology and constitutionalism, thus assuring vitality in scholarly theorizing.[9] These insights were often translated directly into administrative policy by the large numbers of criminal anthropologists now ensconced in the Ministries of the Interior and Justice, responsible for the police, prisons, and courts. By Lombroso's death, the second and third generations of criminal anthropologists had finally reached a critical mass and constituted a network of believers reaching into the universities, Parlia-

ment, public institutions like prisons, hospitals, insane asylums, and the state bureaucracy. They did not need Lombroso's prodding to become missionaries of
positivism within their own spheres of influence.

While political opposition and bureaucratic immobility continued to hamper the
efforts of these positivist apostles, a succession of "moral panics" offered opportunities for them to shape criminal justice policy. The Italian parliament, fragmented
among a multiplicity of parties, made passage of major reform legislation difficult,
while the large size of Italy's centralized ministries of the Interior and Justice en-
sured a certain amount of inertia even after the adoption of new laws. Thus, positivist criminology made its greatest impact on institutions perceived to be in crisis. The
following chapters will investigate three of these: the Public Security police, juvenile justice, and criminal law. They will range over the first four decades of the
twentieth century, since many positivist ideas were not implemented until the fascist period. This may seem curious, given that the fascist state raised idealism to an
official philosophy and rejected both materialism and socialism. But the dictatorship found a useful tool in positivist criminology, with its emphasis on surveillance,
classification, and control, and thus assured its survival until World War II.

CONTEXT

After the unification of Italy in 1861, consensus existed across the political spectrum on the need to reform the police. In the states of the old regime, police had
earned popular hatred for their arbitrary and ruthless implementation of the repressive laws of princes, kings, and popes. Most commentators warned that respect for
the new Italy would come only when police no longer resembled *sbirri*, the unprofes-
sional thugs who repressed any movement for political change during the Restora-
tion. Thus, in 1868, the patriot Augusto Aglebert called on the new government
"to *change course*, abandoning error and the memories of despotism in order to walk
on the path of reason and experience and take refuge in the arms of liberty."[10] For
Aglebert, author of a comparative treatise on European police, the English
"bobbie," organized into local, civilian units, provided an apt model for Italy.
Giovanni Bolis, the *questore* or provincial police chief of Bologna in 1871, also
called for police reform, insisting that "the most accurate thermometer for gauging
good government in a State is the degree of public and private safety enjoyed by its
citizens and the protection extended to the free exercise of their rights."[11] In words
ringing of *risorgimento* sentiment, he argued that "it is the police officer who guaran-
tees the weak against the oppressor."[12]

Despite such grand hopes, popular hostility to police remained unchanged. Bolis
himself had to admit that, even after "the tricolor flag was unfurled from the towers
of Italy," police officers "did not yet generally inspire that respect and confidence
which they nevertheless highly deserve."[13] Even where "the populace is distinguished by common sense, almost all refuse to furnish authorities with evidence and
insights for their investigations and, in certain cases, even offer resistance and opposition to police officers."[14] Over twenty years later, little had changed according

to the Roman lawyer, Giuseppe Leti. In an article of 1893, he reported that "respectable citizen[s] keep as far away as possible from police officials; few embrace that career; and all hold their noses if they find themselves, by accident, in the office of the *questura*."[15] So lacking was the police force in intelligence and morality, that it constituted "a seedbed of criminals."[16]

This chorus of lament over the inadequacy of the police continued after the turn of the twentieth century, through World War I, and up to the advent of fascism. In 1912, for example, the Deputy Rosario Pasqualino-Vassallo complained that "for many years, the judicial police in Italy has acted with very little respect for . . . private, personal liberty."[17] In vocabulary reminiscent of criminal anthropology, he declared that police behavior seemed "profoundly, almost irremediably, tainted by a type of constitutional disease."[18] As late as 1919, the Prefect of Genoa reported that the "old defects" persisted in police officers, so that the public retained its "prejudices" against them, based on "odious memories of traditional police practices."[19] The seizure of power by Mussolini silenced public criticism of the police, but only because it quashed free speech in general.

Unanimously agreeing that policing was in crisis, politicians, police administrators, and journalists debated the causes. Some pointed to the inefficiency of the national police, which was composed of two forces.[20] The oldest was the *Carabinieri*, founded in 1814 as a royal guard for the Piedmontese king. It gradually developed as a force to patrol rural highways for bandits and brigands in coordination with the Ministry of the Interior. But the *Carabinieri* was not a modern police force, being entirely militarized in structure, commanded by the Minister of War, and mandated to fight alongside other army units in the case of international conflict. With unification, the *Carabinieri*, like most other Piedmontese institutions, was integrated into the new Italian state.[21] Its military tradition attracted many aristocrats to its officer corps, making the *Carabinieri* generally admired in the strongly class-based society of late nineteenth-century Italy.

The Public Security police, referred to as the PS, was established to patrol the growing cities of the nineteenth century. Formed as recently as 1852 in Piedmont and commanded by administrators in the Ministry of the Interior, the PS was meant to be a civilian force in some ways modeled on the English bobbies. The comparison was not exact, since the PS was national rather than local in scale and its lower, uniformed ranks were in fact organized along military lines. The civilian administrators, called functionaries, came from the middle classes and had university degrees, usually in law. Functionaries began their careers in the administrative hierarchy at the level of delegate, rising gradually to that of commissioner and then *questore*. The uniformed cops on the beat, called guards (*guardie*) or agents (*agenti*), came from the lower classes and were commanded by officers with military titles of marshal, brigadier, and finally commander.[22] *Questori* directed the activities of both the functionaries and the uniformed forces and formally reported to regional inspectors and finally the Director General in Rome. In practice, however, *questori* were also answerable to the prefect, who represented the interests of the central government, and thus the ruling parties, in each province. *Questori*, then, were vulnerable to political pressure, forcing them to expend much of the PS's energies on patrolling strikes and demonstrations or intimidating parties of the opposition at election time.

By the late nineteenth century, the *Carabinieri* had also taken up duties in the cities, so that confusion ensued as to the division of labor between them and the PS. To further complicate matters, each city employed a third force, the municipal police, to enforce local regulations like those on traffic. Some critics traced inefficiency in policing to this overlapping structure. In an article in *Nuova antologia*, Senator Giovanni Codronchi, for example, commented ironically on the mixture of civilian and military units in the PS: "the present organization has the merit of originality; it was invented in Italy, but has been imitated by no-one; this unhappy experiment has not inspired any other State to copy it."[23] He called for the demilitarization of the lower ranks of the PS, who were unfairly required to live in a barracks and prohibited from marriage. Claiming that the Italian policeman need not be "an armed monk," Codronchi suggested that the PS be merged with the municipal police into a decentralized, civilian force.[24] Liberated from military discipline, this new single force would possess the flexibility to catch urban criminals, who were more astute than violent. In short, Codronchi recommended the following "axiom" for police: "Civil officers in the city, military officers in the countryside."[25]

Other critics advised a more radical solution to the duplication of police forces in Italy—unite the *Carabinieri* and the PS in the investigation of crimes. In the present dual system, citizens could report a crime to the local station house of either force. In consequence, as the lawyer, Pietro Nocito, pointed out, "often a kind of rivalry or antagonism develops in a city between the brigadier of the Royal *Carabinieri* and the delegate of the PS. Each of them collects evidence on his own [and] witnesses are often questioned two times by different officials to gain information."[26] He compared this chaotic process to a pack of police dogs who, rather than working together, block each others' paths and bite each other. Although Nocito recommended that PS functionaries, because of their legal education, command any member of the *Carabinieri* involved in urban judicial investigations, other commentators counseled the complete unification of the two forces.

In addition to overlapping jurisdictions, police suffered from understaffing, according to experts like Giuseppe Alongi. A delegate and later inspector in the PS, Alongi lamented in his book—*Police and Crime* in Italy, published in 1887—that the populace experienced "a unanimous feeling of aversion for police personnel, whether high or low," referring to functionaries and guards, respectively.[27] They yelled "*SBIRRO!*" at police officers, while "every region, every province adds its own disdainful little name."[28] But according to Alongi, the small size of the police forces explained their inefficiency, especially in comparison with those of France and England.[29] A series of parliamentary deputies made the same point in their yearly discussion of the police budget. The situation was worse for the PS than for the *Carabinieri*, who not surprisingly were the target of fewer complaints. In 1891, the size of the PS was 7,525 as opposed to the *Carabinieri* with 25,605 men.[30] Thus, the PS composed only 22 percent of all national police.[31] After continual complaints in Parliament, Giolitti doubled the size of the PS, bringing it to 12,212 by 1914.[32] As the *Carabinieri* had also grown, the PS represented only 28 percent of national police, still a distinct minority. The PS experienced an even larger spurt of growth in 1919, when their numbers reached 33,000.[33] They now constituted 35 percent of Italy's national police force.

Official statistics on police, however, did not always reflect reality, because many jobs were never filled. As Eugenio Forni explained in 1877, as former *questore* of Naples he had received few applicants for the position of PS guard, and those who did apply were often unqualified and quickly fired.[34] This situation continued into the twentieth century so that calls for reform paradoxically combined a request for more PS with a lament about the inability to fill available jobs. In 1910, Deputy Giuliano Corniani confirmed to Parliament that the situation remained unchanged, with most of the prospective guards coming from the impoverished South. Even the more prestigious administrative levels of the PS failed to attract the best candidates, with qualified lawyers often preferring careers in other Ministries.[35] By 1911, over 1,000 jobs went begging in the PS guards, nearly one-tenth of the total. In 1916, the government reported to Parliament that the PS was short 250 functionaries.[36] The war understandably worsened shortages of personnel, as younger administrators and guards left for the front, but the armistice failed to bring an influx of police recruits. In 1919, a parliamentary subcommittee on the PS budget was still citing the need for recruits of higher intelligence and morality, in order to remold the "figure of the policeman from one of a laughing-stock to that of a beloved guardian of public safety."[37]

According to many commentators, the problem of recruitment stemmed from the low pay accorded both administrators and the uniformed ranks of the PS. As early as 1877, Forni criticized the failure to remunerate fairly both tiers of the urban force, declaring that "*policing is more difficult than astronomy,*" because the latter was predictable while the former was not.[38] Ten years later, Alongi expressed satisfaction that the salaries of functionaries no longer depended on the "caprice" of the Minister of the Interior, but were pegged to those of administrators in other departments.[39] But he argued that they deserved higher pay than the average sedentary bureaucrat, since they endured longer hours and more danger. In 1910, Deputy Rudolfo Molina was still making this argument to Parliament, pointing out that the PS functionary was responsible for "the entire social and economic life of the country."[40] Why should a university graduate in law choose to enter the PS, when other ministries offered careers with well-defined tasks, limited hours, and circumscribed responsibility? He doggedly pursued the same subject a year later, claiming that "the PS functionary is always in service; it is said that he does not have a family, does not have a home, that he can not decide how to spend his time."[41] During his tour of Rome in 1916, the American expert on police, Raymond Fosdick, was more concerned with the uniformed cops, whom he declared could not live on their wages.[42] In 1919, PS functionaries complained to a parliamentary commission that their salaries had actually fallen below those of equivalent positions in other ministries; according to the Director General, this explained why he recently received only thirty applicants for 250 jobs.

Official statistics confirmed that improvements in wages for all levels of the PS were modest during the first two decades of the twentieth century. The entering annual salaries of guards, who composed the numerical bulk of the PS, remained almost stationary, at 1,100 lire in 1901 and 1,200 lire in 1917.[43] Their commanding officers—the brigadiers, marshals, and commanders—did better, with increases during the same period of one-third. On the other hand, delegates, the entry level for administrative functionaries, saw no increase, staying at 2,000 lire over the sixteen-year period. The same stagnation characterized most of the upper civilian levels. Delegates were particularly irked that their salaries were no higher than those of uniformed marshals and commanders, who were not required to have a university education.

Finally, many supporters of police reform condemned the political role of the PS for hampering recruitment or hastening resignations. Predictably, the socialists were most vociferous, but deputies of various political stripes raised the issue in Parliament. The socialist deputy Claudio Treves criticized the government's handling of strikes, charging that it "mistakenly made it a point of honor always to say that [PS] guards were right, especially when they were wrong."[44] He claimed that even PS administrators recognized that many guards were too young and inexperienced to police demonstrations and often became "little novice soldiers" who overreacted.[45] According to Luigi Gasparotto, the PS was discredited in the eyes of all parties; both the socialists and the rightwing nationalists were wont to cry "Down with the police spies (*sbirraglia*)!" when their demonstrations were broken up.[46] Burdened with breaking strikes and fixing elections, the PS was seen as "a class of servants . . . the long arm of the Government for constraining the popular will."[47] Deputy Giuseppe Marchesano agreed, claiming that functionaries who resisted the political will of their mayors or local members of parliament were promptly fired. This had the "frightening effect of a long artificial selection in reverse," assuring that corrupt officers survived and the innocent were purged.[48]

Perceived to be in a prolonged crisis, policing offered fertile ground for positivist analysis and reform. This chapter will examine three issues where positivist theory affected police practice: education of the PS; the disciplinary measures of *ammonizione* (warning) and *domicilio coatto* (internal exile) wielded by the PS; and the movement to unionize the PS. It will focus on the PS, which had a worse reputation than the *Carabinieri* and was responsible for controlling common crime in the burgeoning cities.

Positivist ideas influenced each case differently. In the case of education, criminal anthropologists themselves organized a new school for PS administrators and fought successfully to have it recognized by the Ministry of the Interior. The second case was more complicated; while Lombroso and his disciples opposed *ammonizione* and *domicilio coatto*, their theories created an atmosphere conducive to the retention of these special disciplinary powers of police in successive versions of PS legislation. Finally, police officers themselves adopted criminal anthropology as a weapon in their struggle to form a union, a struggle not organized by criminal anthropologists themselves. These examples show a variety of paths by which a criminological theory may affect a system of criminal justice. Proponents of a specific criminological school may implement their ideas directly or have those ideas coopted and perhaps distorted by other political forces. Thus, theories often have unforeseen consequences once they enter public debate and must be turned into concrete policy.

"SCIENTIFIC POLICING"

Criminal anthropologists turned the seemingly intractable problem of policing to their advantage, fashioning a set of reforms based on positivist theory. They focused their proposals on the PS, partly because it suffered a particularly low reputation for solving crimes. As a newer and less militarized force than the *Carabinieri*, it also promised to be more open to change, especially at the hands of university professors. Yet the centralized structure of the PS assured a degree of immobility in policy, so that positivist criminologists campaigned for years before their ideas were integrated into police practice.

Lombroso was the first to suggest that positivist theories might offer to members of the PS "a prestige that unfortunately they do not have, or perhaps do not merit."[49] As early as 1879, in his book *On the Increase in Crime*, he called for making the police "a scientific instrument . . . which employs photography, the telegraph, notices in newspapers, and above all knowledge of criminal man."[50] He amplified these ideas in an article in the *Archives*, most of which was later integrated into the last edition of *Criminal Man*. Noting that only 20 percent of all criminals were ever identified, he called for the application of statistics and criminal anthropology to police work. To replace torture, which the Old Regime had used to elicit information, he counseled the creation of "a scientific police that knows, with mathematical exactness, the physical characteristics of criminals."[51] He hoped that such suggestions for strengthening the police would counteract the false impression among some statesmen that criminal anthropologists—because of their denial of moral responsibility in criminals—"were dangerous to the safety of the country."[52]

Although Lombroso coined the term "scientific police," Ottolenghi was primarily responsible for developing the concept and putting it into practice. Trained in medicine, Ottolenghi served as an assistant to Lombroso at the University of Turin from 1885 to 1893. A dedicated apostle of criminal anthropology, he took its message first to the University of Siena, where he was appointed to the Chair of Legal Medicine in 1893, and later to the University of Rome. Although not a particularly innovative thinker, Ottolenghi deserves attention as an intermediate-level bureaucrat who successfully introduced positivist criminology into government administration.

Ottolenghi dedicated his life to promoting "scientific police," a term that he generously attributed to "that titanic figure, Cesare Lombroso."[53] But it was Ottolenghi who took the unsystematic hints of his teacher and elaborated them into a new philosophy of policing. The key to reforming the PS was science, a term he infused with a cluster of meanings. First, science meant the application of new technologies to the collection of evidence or what today is called criminalistics. In the late nineteenth century, most western European nations relied on anthropometry, or the measurement of body parts, as the most accurate method of criminal identification. In 1887, Lombroso praised this so-called Bertillon method, named after its French inventor, and lamented that it was "probably unknown to all the *questori* in the kingdom," and if not, "little used."[54] By the turn of the century, Ottolenghi added the even newer technique of fingerprinting to the catalogue of expertise needed by police. Science also offered the tools of forensic photography and laboratory analysis to aid in the investigation of crimes.

For Ottolenghi, scientific policing went beyond mundane technology to embrace the theories of criminal anthropology. Methods like fingerprinting had to be combined with a deeper understanding of the etiology of crime to produce an efficient and humane official in the PS. At an international conference in 1911, he declared that "the only real Scientific Police" were those who "did not limit themselves to ascertaining the identity of the accused, of his fingerprints and his crimes—but orient their activities toward an anthropological-psychological understanding of the individual and his environment."[55] Once imbued with the positivist insight that criminals were sick rather then sinful, police would be less brutal and more humane in their enforcement of the laws. As Ottolenghi explained, "Criminal anthropology teaches us that there are human beasts who will lose their ferocity and even show a glimpse of another nature if treated according to criteria that take into account the nature of their degeneration and the determinism of their actions, rather than being tormented by the old police methods."[56] With positivist training, police officers could instantly categorize suspects and handle gently those who did not pose a danger to society.

Armed with criminal anthropology, police officers would become modern and "rational" rather than old-fashioned and "empirical." In Ottolenghi's terminology, "empirical" carried a negative connotation and referred to investigative methods that were haphazard and based merely on hunches. Positivist criminology, on the other hand, was "rational," based on scientific theory. He predicted that, armed with this rational foundation for everyday work, each police official would attain "the greatest probability of success, whether or not he has the intuition of Sherlock Holmes."[57] Gone would be the despised police of the past who, except for the odd brilliant detective, were incapable of solving crimes and keeping order. In this way, criminal anthropology would restore respect to the police for, as Ottolenghi promised, "we aspire to making the action of the Public Security force stronger and always more noble, thanks to the rigor and value of the new methods, and therefore to increase its esteem among the public."[58]

To replace empiricism with science in Italian policing, Ottolenghi proposed the establishment of a national school for PS functionaries. A reliance on education to promote social reform came naturally to a university professor, especially to one in the field of legal medicine. Experts in legal medicine already interpreted scientific evidence for the courts, but Ottolenghi believed that similar methods needed to be utilized earlier in the investigatory process, that is, at the time of arrest. Like legal medicine, scientific policing should inculcate the theories of criminal anthropology as well as more technical skills needed to preserve and analyze evidence. Thus,

Ottolenghi envisioned his school as the wedge that would open the PS bureaucracy to new scientific methods.

Ottolenghi first developed a course in "scientific policing" after he was appointed to the Chair of Legal Medicine at the University of Siena in 1895. He brought this course to Rome on an experimental basis in 1902. When he joined the Faculty of Medicine at the University of Rome in 1903, Ottolenghi quickly convinced the Director General of the PS, Francesco Leonardi, to let him establish a permanent "School for Scientific Policing." Initially located in two rooms of the New Prison (*Carceri nuovi*) in central Rome, the school moved in 1907 to a three-floor facility in the newly constructed Regina Coeli jail. Locating the school within a prison was consistent with positivist theory, since prisoners were close at hand to serve as empirical illustrations to classroom lectures. As Ottolenghi put it, the prison provided the students with "precious didactic material" for practicing the skills of "knowing" the individual offender and "individualizing" the punishment.[59]

Under the direction of Ottolenghi, the school became the locus from which scientific policing was infused into the PS. Most obviously, the staff developed a curriculum dedicated to molding a modern police trained in positivist ideas and methods. In addition, the school carried out various tasks for the PS administration such as fingerprinting, forensic laboratory testing, and compiling criminal dossiers. As these services became more central to everyday police work, the school functioned increasingly as a department within the police administration. Ottolenghi proudly published the floor plan of the school, after it was expanded in 1907, to illustrate its many activities; the plan included rooms for classes, fingerprinting, and photography, as well as a forensic laboratory, library, and criminological museum. The last was modeled on that of Lombroso in Turin and contained drawings of tattoos, photographs of crime scenes, writings of criminals, weapons, fake documents, and instruments for picking locks.[60] The rest of this section will examine each of these functions separately in order to better understand what "scientific policing" meant to Ottolenghi and his staff.

The School

The school's primary mission was to transform the traditional officials of the PS into "modern functionaries."[61] Ottolenghi drew his original students from the university-trained civilian administrative ranks of the PS rather than the subordinate, uniformed patrolmen. Although well educated, these delegates, vice-commissioners, and commissioners lacked acquaintance with the new advances of scientific policing. The "modern functionary," according to Ottolenghi, needed to learn not only technical skills such as fingerprinting but also the theories of criminal anthropology. Since these theories taught that deviance stemmed from an individual's physiological and psychological makeup, Ottolenghi explained that "we aspire to base measures of prevention and repression on the *knowledge of the delinquent and the environment in which he lives*."[62] Ottolenghi frankly admitted to "vulgarizing" the new positivist criminology in order to prepare functionaries to more readily put it into practice. After graduation from the school, they would be equipped with "a rational method of investigation and work based on the objective scientific method and on the most modern concepts of justice and humanity."[63]

According to Ottolenghi's lesson plans, positivist criminology did indeed constitute the central focus of education at the school. His course entitled "Applied Anthropology and Psychology" promised to train students to recognize in a criminal "his precise hereditary, physical, ethnic, psychological, and pathological characteristics (like a doctor learns to know a patient in a hospital)."[64] Ottolenghi subtitled his course "Criminality clinic," because inmates were brought from their cells to be examined before the class. After being measured and interrogated, the inmates were then divided into categories similar to those of Lombroso and Ferri. For those of sound mind, the classifications included "born or instinctual criminals," criminoloids, habitual criminals, criminals by passion, and occasional criminals. Ottolenghi's major innovation on this familiar scheme was to add a category of collective crime, which had been studied extensively by Sighele and included "criminal couples," criminal associations like the mafia, and criminal crowds.[65] He also refined the classification of insane criminals, dividing them between the congenitally mad (including imbeciles, idiots, epileptics, and the morally insane) and those with an acquired sickness (including manic-depressives, alcoholics, and the demented). This multiplication of psychological categories typified a general trend among Lombroso's successors to emphasize the mental rather than the physical anomalies of born criminals.

Ottolenghi's collaborators during the early years of the school were Giovanni Gasti, who taught fingerprinting, and Pietro Ellero, who gave courses in forensic photography. Ottolenghi himself taught a third technical course, "judicial investigation," which focused on the appropriate methods for collecting evidence at the scene of the crime. Since such evidence included dead bodies, Ottolenghi conducted several classes in the city morgue, attached to his own department of legal medicine at the University of Rome. Ottolenghi was assisted by his student Giuseppe Falco, a young PS functionary who devoted his entire career to the school. Other important figures who joined the staff later were Ugo Sorrentino and E. Giri, from the ranks of the PS, and Di Tullio, like Ottolenghi a university professor. Devoted to the director and his vision, this group dominated the school for its first forty years and assured continuity in its curriculum even after Ottolenghi's death.

The student body grew rapidly from the first course of thirty-five functionaries that was conducted on an experimental basis in 1902. As early as October 25, 1903, with the institution of the school in the New Prison, the Minister of the Interior, Giuseppe Zanardelli, made attendance mandatory for all new PS functionaries. In 1909, the new "Regulation for the officials and administrators of the PS" added to the existing requirements for acceptance into the administrative ranks of the PS the successful completion of a three-month course at the school.[66] By 1912, Ottolenghi and his staff had offered twelve courses for a total of 730 administrators.[67] Since the PS was a national, centralized police force, the school drew students from all regions of Italy and returned them, it was hoped, as apostles of scientific policing. As Ottolenghi put it, "If the propaganda of the word in any just cause creates converts, then we will not fail to get good results from sowing this seed [of scientific policing] across our entire Nation."[68]

To spread his message, Ottolenghi also founded the *Bulletin of the School of Scientific Policing* in 1910. In the first issue, he complained that many still harbored suspicion about the school because they did not fully understand the new investigative methods. In response, the *Bulletin* included a section entitled "Criminology clinic," which reproduced a class in which Ottolenghi measured and interviewed a prisoner, followed by his own positivist analysis. The *Bulletin* also delighted in recounting current criminal cases that the staff of the school had solved by matching fingerprints at the scene of the crime with those in their files. Widely distributed by the Director General of the PS, the *Bulletin* was sent to all prefects, *questori*, judges, district attorneys, and prison administrators.[69]

Ottolenghi's success in establishing both the school and its *Bulletin* owed much to the support of Giovanni Giolitti, prime minister during most of the decade before World War I. Serving also as his own minister of the interior, Giolitti periodically intervened in parliamentary debates to praise the work of Ottolenghi. In 1910, he called the school "an excellent institution" that was teaching police officers to consider the lawbreaker "like a sick or mentally ill person, rather than like a vulgar criminal."[70] It represented "great progress in the organization of our public safety," because criminal anthropology had proven that "the criminal is not normal, but abnormal and in many cases a degenerate."[71] Three years later he defended the school against the charge of Deputy Domenico Cavagnari that the PS was unable to catch criminals. Cavagnari provoked laughter in Parliament when he pointed out that, while fingerprinting was all very well and good, "to get fingerprints, one needs to have the suspect in custody, unless he thinks to send his hands [to police] so that they can see the prints."[72] In response, Giolitti suggested that Cavagnari's opinion would change if he visited the school, where he would observe PS functionaries collecting evidence "not casually, but according to fixed scientific norms."[73]

With the end of World War I, Ottolenghi pleaded for increased support from the Director General of the PS for the school, "an institution which is envied abroad and continually offers moral and economics advantages to the State."[74] Despite Giolitti's prewar support, the school had never been regularized in law. In 1919, Ottolenghi finally obtained his goal, when the government of Prime Minster Francesco Savario Nitti issued legislation recognizing the school as an official subdivision within the PS.[75] The school continued to flourish under fascism, undergoing only a nominal change, that of being renamed the "Advanced School of Police." It continued to increase in prestige, as gauged by its budget. Excluding personnel, this budget more than doubled from 12,669 lire in 1907, the year of its move to the three-floor facility in Regina Coeli to 30,000 lire in 1910, the first year of the *Bulletin*. This sum remained steady throughout the war years, when the general PS budget was curtailed, then rose to 55,000 lire by 1921. Mussolini more than doubled this allotment to 136,000 lire in 1925.[76] While admittedly a minuscule percent of the overall expenses for the PS, the budget for the school rose at roughly the same rate, illustrating its acceptance by both liberal, conservative, and fascist prime ministers.

While he sought increased official recognition for the school, Ottolenghi expanded the circles of his proselytizing, offering courses not only for the civilian but also the militarized ranks of the PS. From the school's early years, he offered an abbreviated curriculum for PS guards, although their numbers always remained rather small. Since educational requirements were low for their ranks, most were not capable of following courses in anthropology or psychology. Each PS office, however, needed a corps of experts in criminal identification, so the brightest patrolmen were sent to Rome for training in fingerprinting and photography.

Always a missionary, Ottolenghi also went outside the PS to convince other bureaucracies of the benefits of the new positivism. Select groups of *Carabinieri* attended the school from its early years, so that by 1912 a total of 260 uniformed police from the PS and *Carabinieri* had been trained in criminal identification.[77] Always seeking to expand the school's student body, Ottolenghi convinced both the railway and navy administrations to send selected personnel.[78] After the advent of fascism, the student body became even more varied, with training provided for prison guards, officers and doctors at military prisons, the colonial police, and even the fascist militia, the MVSN. According to the *Bulletin*, "All of the gentlemen officers [of the MVSN] took the course with the greatest interest and enthusiasm and furthermore have shown in the two final examinations to have gained much profit from the lessons."[79]

This proliferation of courses for different branches of state administration shows that Mussolini believed fascism and scientific policing to be compatible. Near the end of the interwar period, positivist criminology seemed to be on the verge of bringing one of its traditional enemies into its fold, the judiciary. Magistrates, loyal to the Ministry of Justice, had generally shown skepticism toward criminal anthropology and protected their independence from encroachment by the Ministry of the Interior and specifically the PS. But, in a circular of September 18, 1937, the fascist government announced that the school would host "special post-graduate courses for all Judges for the purpose of contributing to their integration of, and specialization in, professional, technical knowledge."[80] Perhaps only the advent of World War II prevented the further subordination of the judiciary to the principles of scientific policing.

Why did the fascist dictatorship accept and even promote scientific policing at the same time that it denounced the philosophical principles on which it was based? In its rise to power, fascism had rejected all materialist philosophies in the name of creating a new "ethical" and "spiritual" nation. In this endeavor, the regime denounced determinism as passivity and glorified action and the human will. It also identified criminal anthropology with another type of materialism—socialism— with which most of its early members had identified. A former member of the PSI before World War I, Mussolini savaged the socialists and communists with the excessive fervor of an ex-believer. He blamed the Left for promoting class warfare while refusing to recognize the beauty and morality of nationalism and imperialism.

One answer to this question is provided by the figure of Ottolenghi, who joined the fascist party at an early date. According to his obituary in the *Bulletin*, "the revolutionary genius, Salvatore Ottolenghi, walked with youthful boldness in formation with the Fascists during the March on Rome and sang with them the songs of fascist youth."[81] Already sixty-two years old, Ottolenghi may have joined the party more out of expediency than political commitment. Yet he did not hesitate to flatter Mussolini, describing himself in 1927 as "absolutely devoted to the Duce with the pure faith of a fascist."[82] With such words, he received an audience with Mussolini to explain "the application of sound technical means for more effective prevention and repression by judicial and political police."[83]

In an article of 1928 entitled "Police and Fascism," Ottolenghi again praised Mussolini, this time for working toward "the moral and civil education of the Country."[84] He continued, in words that recalled the title of Lombroso's book of complaint published thirty-five years earlier, that "we are Italians worthy of the present moment," because the "Regime . . . will propel the Country to the most noble conquests."[85] As we will see, Ottolenghi was not the only positivist criminologist who supported fascism during the interwar years; another famous example was Ferri, who slid across the political spectrum from his position a revolutionary socialist in the 1890s. More striking was the fact that Ottolenghi, like his teacher, was Jewish and would therefore seem unlikely to have become a fascist of the "first moment," that is, a participant in the March on Rome. But he was not alone in being a Jewish fascist, especially during the 1920s when anti-Semitism was not yet prominent in the official discourse of Italian fascism. Ottolenghi was fortunate enough to die in 1934, four years before the racial laws would have stripped him of the directorship of the school.

Members of the fascist regime returned Ottolenghi's admiration. Leonardo Arpinati, while Mussolini's Minister of the Interior, praised the school for contributing to the improvement of the PS, a force "really admirable for its spirit of sacrifice and for its understanding of the times."[86] Because it had offered modern and scientific tools to police officers, "the Advanced School of Police has proven itself to be very useful."[87] At Ottolenghi's death in 1934, Arturo Bocchini, Director General of the PS, sent his personal condolences to the family. He expressed "real grief at the loss of Prof. Salvatore Ottolenghi, who gave such luster to the Advanced School of Police, which he directed for many years with the fervid love of a scientist."[88]

A second reason why fascists looked kindly on scientific policing was their ability to adopt parts of its theory to their ends. This may seem ironic, since Ottolenghi and his staff neither repudiated criminal anthropology as a materialist doctrine nor its founder, the socialist Jew, Lombroso. In the same article of the *Bulletin* that promised to "raise our thoughts and our hearts to the Duce," Ottolenghi recalled the greatness of Lombroso.[89] He reminded his readers that Lombroso first enunciated the principle that "one cannot understand the crime if one does not study the criminal."[90] Even after Ottolenghi's death, Di Tullio, his student and colleague in teaching the course on "Anthropology and Psychology," kept Lombroso's name alive as the founding father of his discipline.[91] According to Di Tullio, the essence of criminal anthropology was "a biological orientation in the fight against crime," and he attributed to Ottolenghi "no little importance for developing and spreading this biological orientation."[92]

Di Tullio was not alone in crediting Italy with a unique emphasis on imbuing police officers with positivist theory. Emilio Saracini, a retired PS functionary, wrote in 1931 that "The Italian Police, compared to all the others, has given priority to a biological orientation, having first studied the personality of the delinquent, and then applied a rigorous, scientific methodology to every police function."[93] On the eve of World War II, Falco, the successor of Ottolenghi as the director of the school, reaffirmed the centrality of criminal anthropology to the education of police. In an address to the First Congress of Criminology, held in 1938 at Rome, he explained that the school devoted only half of its curriculum to technical skills like fingerprinting. The other half, taught originally by Ottolenghi and now by Di Tullio, consisted of the presentation of "cases" for the students: "the lesson is a real, clinical demonstration in which the subject has his body examined and is interrogated."[94] According to Falco, "Hundreds and hundreds of subjects have been presented [to classes] from 1902 to today."[95]

Despite the continuing allegiance of Ottolenghi and his staff to positivism as the fundamental philosophy of the school, the fascist regime found it convenient to cultivate any institution that promised to strengthen the police. As we will see in subsequent sections, the state could frequently use criminal anthropology as a theoretical underpinning for disciplining dangerous individuals. Not only political dissidents but also unruly groups like prostitutes, juvenile delinquents, alcoholics, and drug users became subject to special norms of surveillance and punishment. In most cases, Ottolenghi and other criminal anthropologists were cooperative and even enthusiastic about new fascist regulations that increasingly loosened civilian and judicial control over police discretion. Although many early positivists, like Lombroso, never intended to destroy individual rights or the rule of law, their theories lent themselves easily to manipulation in nondemocratic hands. Fascist apologists ignored the materialistic and socialistic origins of scientific policing or simply proclaimed the opposite. In 1936, for example, Corso Bovio favorably compared Ottolenghi and Mussolini in their emphasis on the "spiritual" mission of the police. He claimed to recall Ottolenghi's warning that "spiritual elements must prevail in the crusade against crime."[96] While these words do not have the ring of Ottolenghi's standard pronouncements, which varied little over the decades, he could have uttered them to prove his fascist credentials.

A third attraction of scientific policing to fascism was its national and especially international reputation. By founding the school, Ottolenghi brought Italy into line with other European nations that already educated their police administrators. Before Ottolenghi, Italy had seen only one experiment in offering courses to police, under the leadership of Director General Bolis in 1883. But they were dropped after his premature death in 1885, leaving experts like Alongi and Saracini to bemoan their demise.[97] As early as 1882, Alongi called on the government to catch up with England, France, and the United States by equipping police with cameras and telegraphs, which were not simply "a novelty or creations of a self-interested fantasy."[98] Almost twenty years later, he was still bemoaning the "mute opposition to anthropometric identification, because of that suspicious hatred of anything new, which obstructs every innovation that in the least disturbs the habitual routine of bureaucratic life."[99] Saracini, one of the PS functionaries to take the courses introduced by Bolis, greeted the opening of the school with enthusiasm. Praising Ottolenghi as an "impassioned apostle of the new science," he approved the positivist insistence that police learn to analyze "criminal man in all his physical, physiological and psychological particularities."[100] Saracini continued to promote the school throughout his long career, which included the editorship of the fascist police magazine, *The Magistrate of Order* (*Il Magistrato dell'Ordine*).

Ottolenghi, his staff, and admirers were tireless in spreading the reputation of the school outside Rome. In 1920–21, for example, Falco gave public lectures on scientific policing in Pisa and Lecce. According to the *Bulletin*, Falco used "easy and clear words" to explain the purpose of the school to the audience, "which was always very large."[101] Manuals of scientific policing also proliferated, like that of Luigi Tomellini, a professor of legal medicine in Genoa. Having studied with Bertillon in Paris, Tomellini was enthusiastic about the new investigative techniques "that seemed born out of the fantasy of a novelist but now have become reality!"[102] Because of Ottolenghi, Italy had a police school comparable to other nations, which trained "many worthy functionaries" and then "scattered them throughout the peninsula, even in the most remote villages."[103] Even at the rather small University of Modena, the Law School instituted a "Course in Scientific Police and penal practice" in 1924, open to "students, professionals, officers in the *Carabinieri* and the judicial police, [and] the Director of Prisons."[104]

Even more than his national reputation, Ottolenghi's international prestige impressed Mussolini. From its founding, the school had been involved in a variety of international conferences and expositions, seeking to establish its credentials as the Italian equivalent of prestigious foreign schools of police. Ottolenghi and his staff in turn used the international arena to promote criminal anthropology as the appropriate basis of domestic policing. For example, the *Bulletin* announced that the school had enjoyed "a real triumph" in 1911 at the International Exposition in Brussels, where its exhibit had won a gold medal and attracted the attention of foreign journalists.[105] The exhibit included diagrams, photographs, technical instruments, and an explanation of "The Ottolenghi classification of cranial-facial types of criminals."[106] A year later, the Italian government appointed Ottolenghi and Ferri to organize the criminology section at the International Exposition of Social Hygiene, which was meeting in Rome.[107] In 1914, Ottolenghi, with Niceforo, was again a representative of Italy in Munich at the Congress of Judicial Police; he felt vindicated in his mission when, following his speech, the international body voted to support "the teaching of scientific policing in universities and in police schools."[108]

When foreign travel resumed after the war, Ottolenghi was awarded "the Officer's Cross in the Order of Leopold" by the King of Belgium.[109] Ottolenghi's prestige grew in 1921 when he founded a second journal, named *Zacchia*, which became the official organ of his Institute of Legal Medicine at the University of Rome. Of the many international conferences attended by Ottolenghi or his staff, the International Congresses of Criminal Police provided the most prominent platform for the Italians. At Washington, D.C., the delegates applauded the elaborate anthropological-biographical dossier drawn up by Ottolenghi, and at Antwerp in 1930, they agreed to promote "criminal biology" as the core of policing. "Criminal biology" had already been defined by Ottolenghi's lecture, in which he argued that "real criminality" is always attributable to "a degenerative element in the individual."[110] After Ottolenghi's death, the school remained active in international fora, like the First International Congress of Criminology held in Rome in 1938.[111]

Such strenuous attempts at publicity brought the school foreign students and visitors. Most attention came from police officials in Europe, with Switzerland, Bulgaria, and Turkey, for example, sending visitors in 1910.[112] The school received praise from two American experts touring Europe: Fosdick in 1916 and the criminologist Sheldon Glueck in 1926. Praising the work of "the renowned Dr. Ottolenghi," Fosdick was most impressed that PS functionaries were required to have a university degree before entering the school.[113] Glueck was even more glowing in his report, evaluating the school as "one of the best schools for detectives and higher police and judicial officials in the world."[114] He reproduced the curriculum, which had changed little since 1903, and compared the Italian identification bureau favorably to those in the United States, pronouncing it "absolutely objective and scientific."[115] In 1931, a Portuguese expert in legal medicine published a similarly enthusiastic review, writing that "the School of Ottolenghi was the first to be founded, and it serves as a model for all the others. Its influence is reflected in everything that is done in all the nations of all the continents."[116]

Criminal Identification

Besides its fame for offering rigorous education in scientific policing, the school gained an international reputation as the seat of Italy's first bureau of identification. When chasing a suspect across international lines, foreign police officials directed their inquiries to Ottolenghi and his staff. By organizing Italy's first "technical services" of identification, Ottolenghi cleverly made the school indispensable to the state. It equipped the PS with expertise in criminalistics, which included fingerprinting, photography, and laboratory analysis of evidence. In addition, Ottolenghi set up the Central Identification Office, called the *Casellario Centrale*, which kept files of criminal suspects. Focused on common crime, this archive differed from the notorious *Casellario politico centrale* founded in 1894 by Crispi to gather information on political opponents and reorganized by Mussolini to track anti-fascist organizations.[117]

The technical services of the school were popular with Parliament, where sensible tools like fingerprinting appealed even to those deputies hostile to positivist theories about born criminality. Ottolenghi promised to improve the efficiency of police, who were simultaneously feared as repressive and ridiculed as comically inept. Deputy Cavagnari, for example, complained that "when there's a crime, the police are always right on the case but know less about it than anyone else."[118] Condemning both the PS and *Carabinieri*, he expressed no surprise if their own wallets were stolen. Another member of the Chamber of Deputies, Giovanni Indri, agreed, charging that 40 percent of all criminal cases remained unsolved, because police failed to identify a suspect. He urged that the school provide recruits with more practical training and "the direct knowledge of our criminal world."[119]

To meet such criticisms, Ottolenghi built on Lombroso's early suggestion that police begin to employ modern technology in their investigations. In 1894, he enthusiastically reviewed Alphonse Bertillon's book, *Anthropometric identification*, commenting that it would show "our statesmen how scientific discoveries can and must be used for the benefit of society."[120] Employed by the Parisian Prefecture of Police, Bertillon was famous for having developed a set of instruments for measuring a standard set of body parts of suspected criminals. With their measurements on record, these individuals could be identified if re-arrested, even if using a false name. Bertillon's method aroused such interest in Italy that the criminal anthropologist Luigi Anfosso devised a simplified and cheaper version that employed only one measuring device, the *tacheo-antropometro*, which was much admired by Lombroso.[121] Although the Ministry of the Interior showed little interest in adopting either method for the PS, the Ministry of War allowed the antropometric measurement of recruits, sometimes by criminal anthropologists looking for control groups to compare with lawbreakers.[122]

By the time that Ottolenghi opened his school in 1902, however, many police forces in Europe and the Americas were replacing *bertillonage* with fingerprinting. While France for nationalist reasons clung to the former, Ottolenghi made the decision to base the identification bureau at the school on the latter for several reasons. Bertillon's method was useless on minors who had not reached their full growth, yet fingerprints remained constant from infancy into adulthood. Fingerprinting was a relatively quick and easy technique, able to be learned by functionaries and guards alike. On the other hand, anthropometry required careful and exact measurement by highly trained officials on a variety of instruments. Finally, the ever practical Ottolenghi realized that the equipment for fingerprinting cost much less than Bertillon's instruments, a great advantage when arguing for its adoption by the state. As head of the Central Identification Office he chose Gasti, who devised a new Italian system for classifying fingerprints.

To complement fingerprints, Gasti requested additional information on the standardized "identification form" (*cartellino segnaletico*) issued to local PS offices. Affixed to the forms were photographs, long understood to be useful to police work. Yet they remained secondary to fingerprints, since the former had to be filed alphabetically while the latter, as organized by Gasti, allowed the identification of suspects using false names. Ellero was director of forensic photography at the school, training students to place their subjects in uniform poses, facing front and in profile. Finally, the identification forms asked for the physical attributes of the suspect, including—in the spirit of Lombroso—marks like tattoos and calluses. Although anthropometric measurement was not required, police officers were expected to point out features that were particularly large or small—that is, "abnormal."

With his usual enthusiasm, Ottolenghi bombarded the director general of the PS with propaganda in favor of fingerprinting. The response was positive, with the Ministry of the Interior agreeing in 1907 to establish provincial fingerprinting laboratories (*gabinetti*); their number rose quickly, from seventeen in 1910 to fifty-eight in 1933.[123] Cities too small to support a special laboratory began to fingerprint at the local precincts by 1910.[124] By this year, the Central Identification Office had gathered a total of 13,908 sets of prints and added 10,962 more by 1910 alone.[125] The number collected yearly continued to rise throughout Ottolenghi's tenure, fluctuating only during and immediately after World War I.[126] In 1934, the year of Ottolenghi's death, 23,931 additional records with fingerprints were added to the central files. By 1915, most fingerprinting went on in the PS laboratories or precinct offices rather than the school itself. After nurturing the new technique in the school, Ottolenghi had effectively insinuated it into the PS and turned it into a routine procedure of police work.

Ten years after introducing fingerprinting and photography into the PS, Ottolenghi triumphantly wrote that "it is now tempting to affirm, without fear of being contradicted, that, although in 1902 our country was behind other nations in this field, today it possesses an identification service that is perhaps less ostentatious but more practical."[127] His success had not come without problems. When the Director General of the PS balked at the cost, Ottolenghi agreed to delay the distribution of forensic cameras in favor of the cheaper "fingerprinting box" which cost only 5.5 lire.[128] Local PS and *Carabinieri* also complained that they lacked the time and expertise to fill out the identification forms, problems that Ottolenghi minimized. Short of attending the school, uniformed cops could simply follow his "illustrated handbook" with pictures of normal heads, noses, and ears for comparison with suspects in custody.[129] At Ottolenghi's urging, the director general of the PS issued a series of circulars prodding local PS offices to improve the quantity and quality of the identification records sent to Rome.[130]

Despite these problems, Ottolenghi boasted that the school functioned "as a real observatory of the most dangerous criminality."[131] But who was being observed? Police initially focused on fingerprinting foreigners, considered suspicious for their nationality alone, at the time of arrest. Such files allowed the school to raise its profile by answering requests from foreign governments for information on suspects who had fled their native countries.[132] Railroads were closely watched, with Gasti composing pocket-sized "identification albums" with descriptions of notorious train robbers for conductors.[133] To facilitate international communication, in 1921 Ottolenghi pioneered the technique of telegraphing fingerprints between cities and marked it another triumph for Italy.[134]

The school also routinely fingerprinted political suspects, supplying the director general of the PS with a list of "subversives" every two months. In 1912, Ottolenghi even included the name of Primo Fagioli who, although not a known subversive, had *Viva l'anarchia* (Long Live Anarchy) tattooed on his forearm.[135] In Parliament,

the socialist deputy Turati protested the automatic fingerprinting and photograph-
ing of political protesters who, after arrest, were rarely brought to trial much less
convicted of breaking the law. When asked for a response from the Minister of Justice, Gasti defended the process of identification as completely innocent as it left no
traces on the body, required no undressing, was not prohibited by law, and was
aimed only at ascertaining the truth.[136] The right to question the treatment of political prisoners died with the advent of fascism, as the government reminded prefects
of the importance of compiling identification records on all "subversive and suspected elements" in the population.[137]

   Although government ministers may have been most interested in tracking foreigners and political opponents, Ottolenghi and his staff expressed more worry over
common crime. They sought the cooperation of other institutions in fingerprinting
as many Italians as possible, at least those with "deviant" tendencies. This urge
sprang less from political ideology than a technician's desire to perfect the perfor-
mance of the identification bureau. But the government was happy to endorse a
policy that gave police license to draw up an identification record on any suspicious
person. In a circular of 1912, the director general of the PS, Giacomo Vigliani,
urged local police to go beyond foreigners and make records on "dangerous individuals with criminal records, professional criminals, and likewise those arrested or
stopped by police who, for the type of crime committed or for other circumstances . . .
show characteristic criminal attitudes or can be presumed to have recidivist tendencies."[138] Thus, anyone who appeared deviant was liable to be stopped by police
and fingerprinted, even if police lacked enough evidence to make an arrest, much
less an indictment. For functionaries trained in Lombrosian criminology, measures
of deviancy included physical features, psychological traits, or simply tattoos. After
this circular, the number of identification records submitted to the school from local PS offices soared, because, according to Ottolenghi, "the apathy and indifference" of many policemen had disappeared once fingerprinting received such strong
support from high administrators.[139] In the following year, 1913, the Ministry of the
Interior also launched a daily bulletin of wanted criminals, with fingerprints, photographs, and physical descriptions provided by the Central Identification Office at
the School.[140]

   To enlarge their pool of identification records, Ottolenghi early on sought the
cooperation of the Direction General of Prisons. Prison officials, often themselves
criminal anthropologists, viewed the initiative favorably and, by 1911, already sixty
prisons were equipped with "fingerprinting boxes." Prison policy allowed the fingerprinting of only convicted criminals, so the school began a campaign in 1910 to the
pool to include *imputati*, or those awaiting trial. The number of *imputati* was large, as
Italian criminal procedure generally prohibited release on bail. Partial victory came
in 1920 when the director general of the PS issued a circular requiring that "all prisoners accused of serious crimes" be fingerprinted, so that any who escaped could be
identified.[141] In 1918, Ottolenghi also requested that insane asylums compile identification records for all inmates who were considered dangerous or liable to escape.

Despite the opposition of some psychiatrists in these institutions, the government ordered all to comply in 1918.[142]

War brought new subjects for identification. In 1917, the military authorities requested that the PS fingerprint all deserters once recaptured. Because desertion was frequent during this year of disastrous defeats for Italy, the number of such records was "considerable" and were welcomed by Ottolenghi because of "the frequency with which common criminals are found among deserters."[143] After the war, the school began to receive identification records from Trent, a northeastern city newly annexed to Italy as a member of the winning coalition. Delighted with the "quality" of the fingerprints and photographs on its records, Ottolenghi predicted that the identification office in Trentine PS would become "one of the best and most important" in the nation.[144]

Imperialism also became a font of new records, with an identification office being established in Tripoli in 1912. According to the *Bulletin*, the purpose of submitting Libyans to the identification process was "to gather knowledge of the population of the new colony, knowledge that will be useful both from a scientific and from a practical standpoint."[145] These records of the physical attributes of its subjects would benefit Italy, whose colonial policy should take into account "the biological and social laws of all societies, especially exotic ones."[146] Despite the opposition of some criminal anthropologists, in the tradition of Lombroso, to Italian imperialism, they were nevertheless delighted to have new data to bolster their racial arguments on the inferiority of Africans.

Ottolenghi was not as immediately successful in convincing the PS of the need for a second technical service—the investigation of the scene of the crime (*servizio di sopraluogo*). Although this function was not officially assigned to the school until 1919, Ottolenghi had begun to develop a technical office of judicial investigation as early as 1904. On request, the office sent specially trained functionaries to the scene of any crime to take fingerprints, photographs, and samples of blood and body tissue for analysis at the school's forensic laboratory. At first, requests from the judiciary, *Carabinieri*, and even the local PS offices were few. Finally, in 1919, Ottolenghi convinced the government to make the technical description of the scene of the crime a mandatory part of any PS report. For this purpose, he drew up a special "speaking portrait of the scene of the crime" (*ritratto parlato del sopraluogo*) inspired by Bertillon's *portrait parlé* of the human body. According to Ottolenghi, the speaking portrait promised "the exact, faithful, and precise reconstruction of the scene of the crime, that is, identification not dependent on the time or person making it."[147] Furthermore, it would constitute "a real imprint of the delinquent that will serve to give a glimpse of his personality [and] his specific criminal activity."[148] Again, positivism emphasized not only technical expertise, but also the importance of knowing the individual criminal.

Analysis of the scene of a crime formed part of the school's curriculum from its founding. The school "always had a bag packed and ready" with the necessary equipment for emergency calls from police or judicial authorities, and students were sometimes taken along to witness science in action.[149] On April 27, 1907, for example, as Ottolenghi was beginning his lesson in applied anthropology and psychology, "the PS Commissioner of Trastevere telephoned to alert the Director of the School that a burglary had occurred on Via S. Dorotea . . . and he invited the School to come to the site because an investigation would be of great interest."[150] The servant of the household, who claimed to have been hurt during the robbery became a suspect after the stolen goods were found in the house covered with her fingerprints.

This type of training was extended to the uniformed patrolmen after 1919 so that even a precinct too small to warrant an administrator would have experts proficient in judicial investigation. Although Ottolenghi continually bemoaned the small number of magistrates who called on the services of these experts, the numbers of interventions by the PS at the sites of crimes to take fingerprints, photographs, or laboratory samples rose significantly under his directorship. This intervention occurred seventy-one times in 1914, the first year that the *Bulletin* devoted a special section to this service and increased to 457 in 1933. Most gains occurred during the 1920s and 1930s and were attributed by the *Bulletin* to the recognition by the fascist regime of the value of technological modernization of the police.[151]

Perhaps the most ambitious of the services performed by the school for the PS was that of compiling "anthropological-biographical dossiers" (*cartelle antropobiografiche*) of suspected and convicted criminals. Not content with simple fingerprinting and photography, Ottolenghi devoted his life to developing a series of increasingly complicated forms intended to capture and record the distinguishing characteristics of each individual delinquent. Although the PS law of 1889 required that local police keep dossiers of dangerous residents, these originally contained little more than a legal history of past arrests. In 1903, Ottolenghi and his staff began to expand this form to include physical and psychological traits as well as a family history. In 1914, the dossier was updated to include anthropometric measurements. According to Ottolenghi and Gasti, the Bertillon method "had fallen from an exaggerated height of enthusiasm into unjustified discredit."[152] While they still preferred fingerprinting for quick identification, they urged that it be complemented with corporal measurements, since some criminals tried to mutilate their fingertips. Furthermore, other nations like France, Germany, and Switzerland still used anthropometry and requested such information for international criminals. Warning that ignorance of anthropometry left a "harmful gap that needs to be filled" in policing, the staff at the school ignored their own leading role in replacing it with fingerprinting.[153] To cut the cost of the Bertillon system, which depended on a group of instruments, Gasti developed a single *pantropometro* able to measure all parts of the body. Proudly displaying photographs of the *pantropometro* in the *Bulletin*, he pronounced it "simple, elegant and I would say almost perfect."[154]

The increased length of the new biographical dossier only strengthened the resistance of local PS guards, who claimed that they had neither the time nor the training to fill it out. Frustrated that the PS left most forms incomplete, Ottolenghi turned to the prisons for a source of human material. In 1915, he began drawing up biographical dossiers on the inmates of the Regina Coeli jail, where the school was located. Within a year, this "anthropological-biographical service" had been extended to prisons in nine other major cities, often directed by followers of Lombroso like Mario Carrara in Turin.[155] Although the service was initially restricted to prisoners already convicted of serious offenses, the Minister of the Interior Antonio Salandra readily approved the inclusion of suspects accused of breaking the terms of *ammonizione*.

With the coming of fascism, Ottolenghi and his staff continued to promote the anthropological-biographical dossier with positivist arguments. For them, it was an essential tool for both police and prison administrators, needed to classify offenders "anthropologically (normal, abnormal), clinically (healthy, sick), [and] criminologically (occasional, habitual, congenital)."[156] Like a patient in a hospital, the prisoner needed to be diagnosed and "the anthropological-biographical dossier must constitute the first and indispensable element for understanding [his] individual personality and for the prevention and treatment of the biological factors of crime."[157] In a handbook 1932, the school continued to stress a technical and objective approach to completing the dossiers: "the functionary must gather this information following a fixed order, according to practical and scientific dictates, leaving out prejudices and direct or indirect intimations, and limit himself to the listing of facts, incidents, events, and information that he has verified."[158] Such a neutral and rigorous methodology seemed to leave little room for the political considerations dear to Mussolini.

Yet the fascist regime supported the expansion of the school's anthropological-biological services, with the Minister of the Interior, Luigi Federzoni, giving his name to the revised dossier of 1924. What interested the regime most was its last page, which evaluated the degree of dangerousness posed by the offender to the social order. For Ottolenghi and his staff, a properly compiled dossier would lead automatically to an objective assessment of dangerousness, which was held to be inherent in a person's "somatic-psychic constitution."[159] Crime was only one symptom of "dangerousness," and a well-trained functionary could scientifically evaluate suspects even before conviction. Ottolenghi admitted that such a task was delicate and campaigned throughout his life for the employment of doctors of legal medicine in each precinct to evaluate everyone brought in for arrest.

What attracted fascist administrators to the anthropological-biographical dossiers was not a dedication to science but the prospect of collecting vast amounts of data on a widening circle of individuals. Those convicted, or even suspected, of crimes could be labeled dangerous and kept under surveillance or admitted to an institution for "treatment." While not particularly interested in the political use of the dossiers, the staff of the school seized the opportunity to expand the anthropological-biographical service by emphasizing its compatibility with fascism. For example, they boasted at international conferences of the *italianità* of the dossiers, using a favorite fascist term connoting an Italian heritage stretching back to the glories of the Roman Empire. In this nationalist vein, they claimed that "our police is the leader of other Nations" in its emphasis on "knowing the criminal personality."[160]

By praising fascism and willingly implementing its policies, the staff of the school became politicized in a way that was incompatible with the original vision of positivism as the objective pursuit of scientific truths. How deeply did fascist ideology penetrate the workings of the school? The theory of scientific policing changed little with the advent of fascism, with Falco's address to the first International Congress of Criminology in 1938 constituting almost a plagiarism of Ottolenghi's earliest articles in the Bulletin.[161] Ottolenghi's conception of scientific policing was fully formed in 1903 and remained unchanged throughout his long career at the school, where he had imbued his students, like Falco, with unswerving faith in his vision. But Ottolenghi and his colleagues served all governments with equal fervor, taking advantage of the authoritarian power offered them by Mussolini to strengthen the position of the school within the PS bureaucracy. They welcomed a regime that accepted their premise that biology was the key to human behavior and cooperated in using the tools of scientific policing to identify "inferior" racial groups, like blacks and Jews, as socially dangerous.

Although the entire staff of the school was complicit with the dictatorship, their individual commitment to fascism varied. Ottolenghi joined the party earliest, with younger members of his staff—like Falco, Sorrentino, and Giri—following suit. At Ottolenghi's death in 1934, Falco succeeded him as Director of the School, only to retire from ill health in 1940.[162] He in turn was succeeded by Sorrentino, who later claimed to have joined the PNF in 1932 only to keep his job. In 1945, he was absolved of collaboration, partly because he organized the identification of the dead after the notorious massacre by the Nazis at the Fosse Ardeatine.[163] Giri did not escape censor by the purification committee, having joined the Fascist Party as early as 1926 and having sworn allegiance to the Republic of Salò in 1943.[164] Although claiming to have joined Salò primarily to save the technical equipment in the Central Identification Office from German plunder, Giri was transferred from the school in 1945.

Thus, commitment to fascism varied among the instructors of the school, many of whom collaborated with fascism more out of professional opportunism than ideological commitment. But they had created a "scientific" rationale for the identification and surveillance of all "dangerous" individuals and were willing let fascism use it to destroy civil liberties. They applauded the proliferation of the anthropological-biographical dossiers, even when they were applied to opponents of the regime. After the Ethiopian War, the Bulletin promoted the extension of the dossiers to the colonies "for racial purposes."[165] According to Pietro Bianconi, a young instructor at the school, it was of "the highest importance" to record the "anthropological, organic, psychological, cultural, social, [and] moral characteristics" of criminals in the colonies.[166] Equipped with these dossiers, "the Colonial Police Corps could improve their service, contributing efficaciously to the defense of the Italian race against possible infiltration from elements of different and inferior races."[167] Support by the school of fascist imperialism flowed logically from the scientific racism of early positivists like Lombroso and shows the deep complicity of Ottolenghi and his staff in the repressive policies of Mussolini. Never simply technical and neutral as Ottolenghi claimed, scientific policing revealed its political compatibility with fascism as both strove to identify and discipline enemies of social order.

AMMONIZIONE AND DOMICILIO COATTO

While the School of Scientific Policing constituted the main avenue for the introduction of criminal anthropology into the PS, positivism also shaped legislative debates on the proper extent of police powers. From the time of unification, Italian police exercised wide discretion in applying "administrative measures" to control or punish behavior deemed too petty for a court trial. Most controversial of these administrative measures were *ammonizione* (warning) and *domicilio coatto* (internal exile), both of which could be applied to suspicious persons even if they had not been convicted of any crime. By the late nineteenth century, both practices had come under severe criticism by liberals, democrats, and socialists as conducive to arbitrary abuses against the civil rights of individuals whose innocence had never been disproved in court. The first generation of positivist criminologists also opposed *ammonizione* and *domicilio coatto* less on theoretical than practical grounds, since neither had proven successful in reforming criminals. Instead, they outlined alternative institutions for instilling industriousness and good moral habits in social deviants. Yet the more general and well-known message of criminal anthropology ironically weakened opposition to these two police powers since it fanned public hysteria about the need to defend society against born criminals. Although the number of individuals assigned to *ammonizione* and *domicilio coatto* decreased before World War I, these two institutions remained legally alive and available for expanded use by Mussolini.[168]

Administrative rather than judicial punishments, *ammonizione* and *domicilio coatto* were defined not in the Criminal Code, but in the laws defining the powers of PS officers. In the Public Security Law of 1889 that governed the last decades of the liberal monarchy, both were discussed in Section III entitled "Dispositions concerning the dangerous classes of society."[169] While "dangerous classes" was a label predating Lombroso, it also evoked the positivist criterion of "dangerousness" as the proper measure for assigning punishment. For *ammonizione*, the law defined dangerousness broadly to include vagabonds, the unemployed, and reputed criminals.[170] The last need not have been convicted of a crime. Thus, the definition of "reputed criminal" was fuzzy, and PS officers therefore had wide discretion in choosing candidates to undergo *ammonizione*.

The procedure for applying *ammonizione* involved the magistracy only marginally. Although a PS officer had to officially present his charges to the *pretore*, or local judge, the *pretore* examined them "summarily" rather than granting the defendant a regular trial.[171] If the accused could not clearly refute such vague charges, the judge "warned" him not to engage in certain behaviors for a period of two years. Vagabonds and the unemployed had to find work immediately, establish a fixed address, and advise PS authorities of their whereabouts. Reputed criminals had "to live honestly, respect persons and property, avoid suspicious behavior, and remain in their present neighborhoods."[172] The PS law prescribed curfews for both groups and forbade them to carry arms, hang out with bad characters, or frequent taverns and brothels. Any infraction of this list of regulations would lead to arrest and imprisonment for up to a year. On release, those who had violated the conditions of *ammonizione* were subject to "special surveillance" (*vigilanza speciale*) that, in addition to the behavioral norms of *ammonizione*, required periodic visits to the local police station.

The more severe administrative measure was *domicilio coatto*, or the exile of dangerous individuals to an internal penal colony for one to five years. Meant to isolate recidivists from urban centers, this punishment could be applied by police to anyone convicted of two or more crimes. Yet these crimes might consist simply of violations of the conditions of *ammonizione*, so that a vagabond who was twice caught in a tavern, for example, could be sent to a penal colony. According to critics, the vagabond was punished without due process, because he had no right to court review and his offense did not constitute a crime according to the Zanardelli Criminal Code. They thus charged that rather than preventing crime, *domicilio coatto* created criminals. Furthermore, the provincial committee assigned to review PS application of this punishment was dominated by administrative rather than judicial personnel.[173] Although inmates might shorten their sentences by good conduct, only the Minster of the Interior, not of Justice, had the power to give them "conditional freedom." Thus, sentences of *domicilio coatto* received even less judicial review than those for *ammonizione*.

Exposés by opponents of *domicilio coatto*, like the democrat Jesse White Mario, as well as information collected by the Ministry of the Interior attested to the dismal conditions in the penal colonies. In 1896–97, White Mario published a series of articles in the *Nuova antologia* describing her visit to the penal colony at Favignana, an island off the coast of Sicily. An Englishwoman who, after marrying an Italian, had worked for democratic and feminist causes since the time of unification, White Mario was appalled at the conditions at Favignana. Although a champion of individual rights against the centralizing tendencies of the Piedmontese monarchy, she did not blindly condemn the entire prison system on principle. Upon visiting San Giacomo, a prison for those with life sentences, she pronounced the warden to be "a man endowed with intelligence and energy," who had created "order, discipline, and cleanliness everywhere."[174] Nor did she idealize the inmates, noting that many had "receding foreheads, protruding cheek-bones, swollen lips, enormous ears, squashed noses; a few had such narrow and depressed skulls that it was doubtful that they could hold an average-sized brain."[175] Her attention to physical features and use of Lombrosian language shows the wide appeal of the criminological theory of positivists, even to a feminist who rejected their doctrine of male superiority.

In contrast to the prisoners in San Giacomo, White Mario described the men condemned to *domicilio coatto* as "the most vile and despicable mixture of human beings that I have ever set eyes on."[176] They roamed the island, "without discipline and without work," terrorizing the inhabitants and preying on each other.[177] In discussions with Alongi, who had once been warden of a penal colony, she learned that his charges had spent most of their time in drinking and gambling. The strong had transplanted the methods of the camorra to the island, shaking down the weak after the distribution of the daily allowance.[178] White Mario also noted the disproportionately high percentage of Sicilians in the penal colonies, showing the continuing prejudice and even outright persecution they endured at the hands of the central government.[179] She concluded that the system of *domicilio coatto*, "while evil in and of itself and harmful to all, is deadly for Sicilians."[180]

Official reports echoed the criticisms of White Mario. In 1909, there were eight colonies located on the islands of Favignano, Lampedusa, Lipari, Pantelleria, Ponza, Tremiti, Ustica, and Ventotene. The small and weak economies of such locations offered little opportunity for employment. According to a report of 1913 from the Prefect of Agrigento to PS headquarters in Rome, only sixty of 200 inmates on the island of Lampedusa had found jobs, although almost all of them were able-bodied. The work, primarily on the docks or in agriculture, was unskilled and seasonal, paying only about one lira per day. Over 50 percent of the men were alcoholics, with 15 percent having acquired their bad habit since arriving at the colony. Drunkenness was punished with banishment to an isolation cell, but—by his admission—"such measures are for the most part totally useless."[181] About 10 percent of the convicts had tuberculosis or syphilis, exacerbated by the filthy dormitories that needed disinfecting. Fights between inmates were frequent, including "violent acts typical of the Camorra, that is, of organized crime."[182] He concluded pessimistically that the colony of Lampedusa was "a preparatory school for the perpetuation and execution of future crimes since the infectious germ of criminality is disseminated with the exchange of ideas."[183] He asked for more dormitories, in order to separate the prisoners, and funds for disinfecting them weekly.

Criminal anthropologists joined the chorus of criticism of both *ammonizione* and *domicilio coatto*, finding them inhumane and, more important, ineffective. As usual, Lombroso laid the groundwork for the positivist argument, condemning both as early as 1879 in his book, *On the Increase in Crime*. Instead of being "remedies" for crime, he found these two administrative measures "not particularly legal and not particularly useful" and "like palliatives in general, always ineffective and sometimes harmful."[184] Those subjected to *ammonizione* were "slaves in the hands of [PS] guards," liable for arrest if they simply greeted a fellow suspect or missed their nightly curfew.[185] The law also put PS guards themselves in a bad position; they were forced to arrest even those *ammoniti* who were sincerely looking for a job and even pleading with them for help. *Domicilio coatto* was as bad, since the islands offered little opportunity for work, the essential component of rehabilitation.

Ferri agreed, writing in an article on *ammonizione* for the *Archives* that it was "absolutely inefficacious in protecting public order," although it lulled citizens into feeling safe.[186] More than his colleagues, he worried about civil rights, arguing that it was inappropriate for a civilian government at peace to maintain "this exceptional institution in quite normal times."[187] Yet he boasted that he opposed *ammonizione* from an "absolutely practical point of view."[188] First, those under police warning could rarely find a job, because employers routinely turned down such applicants as untrustworthy. Rather than being reformed through steady work, the condemned had to turn to crime in order to survive. Second, *ammonizione* also discouraged serious investigations by police, since they tended simply to turn to the list of those under warning rather than going after the real culprits. That 50 percent of all criminal cases had to be dropped in the first phase of the trial (*istruttoria*) for lack of evidence proved that keeping a phalanx of men under surveillance did not help police solve crimes.

Even Ottolenghi, a champion of strong police powers, accused *ammonizione* of "strongly contributing to the *creation* of crime."[189] Based on years of interviewing at the school those who had broken the terms of their *ammonizione*, he concluded that several parts of the regulation were "contrary to the most essential laws of life."[190] For example, the evening curfew not only interfered with some jobs, but made it impossible for those under warning to properly relax. Instead of being confined to "that restricted and often unhygienic environment that constitutes their house," they should be allowed to frequent certain popular restaurants and other places of amusement.[191] After all, even prisons had begun to offer entertainment to their inmates! In addition, the law should not permit police to enter the house of any person under warning at night to check up on his behavior. This irritated those subjected to *ammonizione*, who have a "right to sleep," and forced them to live alone so that such intrusions would not disturb their families.[192] Instead of reforming a suspect, *ammonizione* "embitters him, inflames him and puts him in the same condition as micro-organisms that a biologist heats so that they grow and reach their maximum virulence."[193] His readers need only "put themselves for a moment in the shoes of someone who is under surveillance" to see that *ammonizione* "is in clear conflict with the laws of biology and psychology."[194]

While Ottolenghi was not as sweeping in his criticism of *domicilio coatto*, he warned that only appropriate subjects should be sent to the penal colonies. Because work was the basis of reform, the physically and mentally ill should be exempt from this type of punishment and sent to special hospitals or asylums. True to the positivist penchant for classification, he also opposed the sentencing of all recidivists to *domicilio coatto*, because only criminals with inborn tendency to crime need be separated in such a radical way from society. Even the author of a single crime, if a born criminal, might be eligible for internal exile, since "dangerousness can be inferred . . . from many other criteria and especially from rashness, intellectual deficiency, impulsivity, bad behavior, an instinct for rebellion, inability to work caused by psychological inertia or dependence, [or] ties with organized crime."[195] One had only to study the "face" of the suspect to gather such "data."[196]

Despite the specific arguments of the Positivist School against *ammonizione* and *domicilio coatto*, the more general and well-known lessons of criminal anthropology contributed to their longevity. In a seemingly contradictory way, the popularization of criminal anthropology after the turn of the century—among both statesmen and the general public—gave these two hated measures a new lease on life and combated the liberal and socialist sentiment that had been building against them for several decades. Two general aspects of positivist theory helped to perpetuate *ammonizione* and *domicilio coatto*, despite specific criticisms of them by Lombroso, Ferri, and Ottolenghi.

First, the figure of the born criminal became a stumbling block for reformers, few of whom dared suggest complete abolition of police surveillance on recidivists or other groups thought to have an inherited predisposition to crime. It had become common sense to believe that a hard core of congenital deviants threatened the honest citizenry and that the doctrine of "social defense" required their discipline. Thus, rather than abolishing the two administrative measures, parliamentary deputies suggested new institutions to replace them, and these institutions in turn created controversies that delayed decisive action.

Ottolenghi and his school actively contributed to the construction of an equation between those subjected to police surveillance and born criminals by eagerly seeking the former as candidates for identification records and anthropological-biographical dossiers. Part of the reason was practical, as *ammoniti* and *coatti*, as the two groups were called, provided a literally captive population for experimentation. The *Bulletin* admitted as much, calling them "precious human material" exhibiting "a thoroughly antisocial essence."[197] Thus, *ammoniti* were one of the first groups brought regularly to the school for fingerprinting, while Ottolenghi convinced the Director General of the PS in 1913 to have identification equipment sent to the internal colonies.[198] With the regularization of the anthropological-biographical service at the school in 1915, the staff eagerly accepted *ammoniti* as candidates for dossiers and exhibits for classes of PS administrators.

Ottolenghi and his colleagues used positivist theory to defend their use of *ammoniti* as research material. Criminal dossiers highlighting information on biology, psychology, and family history would promote "penal individualization," that is, treatment tailored to each suspect.[199] The *Bulletin* went so far as to claim that many of the *ammoniti* "willingly underwent the . . . exam, showing that they sympathetically welcomed our interest in their regard."[200] But the staff of the school used the results of the examinations not to challenge the legality of *ammonizione*, but to outline the similarities between the *ammoniti* and born criminals. They therefore reinforced the popular belief that *ammoniti* deserved to be under surveillance since, according to the *Bulletin*, they exhibited high rates of "social diseases" like tuberculosis and syphilis, insanity, and alcoholism. Ottolenghi and his staff also eagerly counted tattoos and scars, proclaiming "the utility of these physical examinations for being able to glimpse on the very skin of the individual . . . the principle events of his life."[201] Official reports from the school labeled *ammoniti* as "those who constitute the foundation of the criminal underworld" and *coatti* as "the most fearful part of habitual criminality"[202] Thus, in their eagerness to get new human material for research, Ottolenghi and his staff became complicit in the perpetuation of *ammonizione* and *domicilio coatto* in a manner that contradicted and made less forceful their simultaneous criticism of these same policies.

A second part of the general positivist message that strengthened support for *ammonizione* and *domicilio coatto* was its emphasis on preventive policing. The distinction between "repressive" and "preventive" policing was common in nineteenth-century treatises like those of Alongi; the first referred to solving crimes already committed and the second to hindering prospective lawbreaking. In a rough way, the organization of the PS mirrored this division of labor, with the judicial police aiding prosecutors in solving criminal cases while the administrative police were responsible for granting licenses and monitoring demonstrations. As early as 1882, Alongi suggested that preventive police continue to wear uniforms, as a warning for the public to behave, while repressive police adopt plainclothes, to make them inconspicuous when collecting evidence.[203]

The idea of preventive policing began as a liberal one, championed by writers like Bolis as a method of reducing the number of citizens subjected to arrest and prison. As he wrote in 1871,

A police that is well-organized to correspond to its principle purpose—which is indeed not revenge by an injured society nor the punishment and repression of criminals—must above all prevent evil and impede it from happening . . . . The duties of a policeman under a liberal government are to make citizens more moral, give them the means of making an honest living, [and] to hinder the poor from turning to crime in order to save the country from distress and to save humanity from the sorrow of witnessing the rise of prisons and scaffolds.[204]

For Bolis, prisons and scaffolds symbolized the repressive police of the old regime, who kept peace through indiscriminate arrests without concern for civil rights. In contrast, the new preventive police would form part of a broad political program to better the lives of the masses so that crime, and therefore the opportunity to mistreat prisoners, would diminish.

Thus, criminal anthropologists built on an earlier concept with a patriotic pedigree when they used preventive policing to underpin many of their innovations. On the one hand, they strengthened the liberal vision of social renewal, by including police as one of the many "penal substitutes" that would divert people from entanglement in the criminal justice system. For example, Leti, in his article indicting the PS for themselves being criminal, did not deny the necessity for police who, once reformed, would constitute "a powerful penal substitute."[205] Not coincidentally, Leti's article appeared in Ferri's journal, *The Positivist School*, since among the triumvirate of founding fathers, Ferri most fervently promoted a variety of measures to cut crime including higher wages, improved education, and divorce. Faith in penal substitutes fit into his "criminal sociology," which gave greater weight to environmental factors in the etiology of crime than the positivism of Lombroso or Garofalo. Yet all three criminal anthropologists subscribed to the positive role of penal substitutes in combating the conditions that nurtured occasional crime.

On the other hand, preventive policing could have a more foreboding aspect, embodied clearly in *ammonizione* and *domicilio coatto*. Measures like these—which promoted surveillance over innocent people—could also be characterized as preventive policing, since they purportedly defended society from potential crime. By arguing that born criminality was visible on the body, criminal anthropology encouraged the idea that police could correctly identify deviants even before they broke the law. In their passion for identification, Ottolenghi and his staff lobbied for permission to compile identification records and anthropological-biographical dossiers on not just convicted but also suspected criminals. According to positivist doctrine, it was not behavior but personality that marked an individual as dangerous, and that personality could be measured at any stage in life. That the positivist prescription of isolating dangerous individuals—that is, born criminals—from the rest of society sounded suspiciously like *ammonizione* and *domicilio coatto* only strengthened these measures among politicians and the public. They tended to ignore the positivist niceties about careful measurement and rehabilitation, whether from inattention to specifics or more purposely, as in the case of police officials loathe to lose such powerful tools of social discipline.[206]

These two positivist themes—the born criminal and preventive policing—were instrumental in shaping debates in Parliament about the reform of *domicilio coatto*. During the twenty-five years before fascism, a series of proposals for new legislation tackled this problem in different ways. The Finocchiaro–Aprile–Pelloux proposal of 1899 substituted indeterminate relegation to isolated agricultural or industrial prisons or exile from Italy entirely for *domicilio coatto*, while the Gianturco plan of 1900 suggested relegation or deportation for an indeterminate time. In 1904, the Ronchetti proposal echoed that of Emanuele Gianturco but added parole (*liberazione condizionale*) as a mechanism to encourage good behavior and rehabilitation on the part of inmates. The authors of all three plans had learned the positivist lesson that punishment should be individualized to suit the biological and psychological makeup of each offender by refusing to dictate the appropriate length of punishment, whether relegation or deportation. Wide discretionary power was left in the hands of judges who, on the advice of prison administrators and other experts, would determine when—if ever—a recidivist was sufficiently normalized to rejoin society.

Since none of these plans was approved by parliament, Prime Minister Luigi Luzzatti proposed a further variant to the Chamber of Deputies in 1910. He retained the principle of indeterminate sentencing, which could be "prolonged in perpetuity for incorrigible criminals, thus putting into practice the eliminative principle of natural selection as society has been demanding."[207] He rejected Gianturco's idea of deportation to penal colonies in Africa, since a previous experiment in Assab had proven too costly to the state and too hard on convicts taken long distances from their families. Yet Luzzatti was unwilling to give up the hope of an African scheme, since "current criminology," meaning criminal anthropology, taught that "individuals unable to adapt to our civilization will adjust and feel at home in a semi-savage environment."[208] Adopting the positivist equation of criminals and "barbarians," he suggested sending convicts and their families to colonize Africa, a plan that would provide the maximum social defense of Italian society at a minimum cost, since families would be self-supporting. Anticipating objections that such forced colonization would punish innocent family members, Luzzatti quoted the positivist maxim that "inborn criminality is almost never limited to one member of a family but rather is one of the types of anomalies that effects the entire stock."[209]

Realistically, however, most habitual criminals would not be sent to Africa but to six new "colonies of confinement" (*colonie di relegazione*) that would replace the present facilities for *domicilio coatto*. Luzzatti did not clearly define how the new colonies would avoid the abuses of the old, except to insist that they be situated where work would be available to all inmates. Relying on the positivist faith in the reformative value of work, he trusted that steady employment in agriculture or commerce would rehabilitate some recidivists and at least keep them from harassing the local "honest and free population."[210] He argued that convict labor would not depress wages on the capitalist job market if the new colonies were located in areas such as Sardinia, Basilicata, and Calabria, where emigration had emptied rural villages. To placate whatever population was left, the proposed law forbade convicts from frequenting public places.

Consistent with its earlier pattern, Parliament failed to pass this modification of *domicilio coatto*. The proposal was doomed both by outright opposition from many on the Left, who insisted on total abolition of the colonies, and by bickering among moderates over the shape of a new institution to replace them. After the fall of Luzzatti's short-lived government, successive prime ministers could not summon the political will to modify a policy that bolstered the power of the state to discipline the population. As the war interrupted further discussion of the issue, *domicilio coatto* as well as *ammonizione* remained on the books until the fascist seizure of power, when they were eagerly appropriated by the new regime. The new fascist PS Law of 1926 retained both administrative measures with modifications, changing the name *domicilio coatto* to *confino*, or internment. It weakened the scraps of due process contained in the old law that were supposed to protect individual rights. Police no longer brought evidence for *ammonizione* before a judge but before the Prefect, an administrative and political figure likely to concur.[211] If declared "dangerous to public security," *ammoniti* could be automatically sent to *confino*, without the PS any longer having to argue that they had contravened the regulations twice.[212] The new law also explicitly extended the application of the two administrative measures to political opponents of the regime, so that the penal colonies became integral to the totalitarian aspirations of the fascist state.

The 1926 law expanded powers of police discretion in other ways. PS officers could order that all "dangerous or suspect persons" carry identity cards and be subjected to fingerprinting. Other citizens could request similar documents, presumably to be able to prove their respectability if stopped by police.[213] Thus, the modern identity cards carried by all Italians had their roots in the fascist era. Even more radical was the blanket declaration in Article 4 that the PS could execute administrative measures independent of judicial review.[214] Thus, the police had broken their subservience to the courts in a variety of areas beyond *ammonizione*. According to Federzoni, the fascist Minister of the Interior, Article 4 created a type of autonomous police power that had "a clearly preventive character."[215] Police were to serve "the State and consideration of the individual is secondary."[216]

Not surprisingly, the numbers interned under *domicilo coatto* increased under fascism, even before it became *confino* in 1926. This reversed the previous trend, as the number of penal colonies had shrunk from eight to four and the number of prisoners from 1513 to 114 between 1910 and 1921. After Mussolini became prime minister, the sum of *confinati* jumped exponentially to 439 in 1925 and 4,500 in 1930.[217] Not all the *confinati* were assigned to penal colonies, whose number had expanded again to six by 1930, because some political prisoners were exiled individually to small towns in the South. But fascism succeeded in resurrecting an institution that had almost died from disuse in order to banish troublesome individuals from the cities. These individuals were not only political opponents of the regime but also representatives of social groups—like prostitutes, homosexuals, and alcoholics—who were seen as threats to the morality and health of the Italian race. That common crime preoccupied the dictatorship is clear from a letter of 1925 from Francesco Crispo Moncada, Director General of the PS, to his superiors in which he pleaded for the reopening of Favignana as a penal colony. He argued that "the general interest" demanded the expansion of *domicilio coatto*, because "in the last few years, a remarkable resurgence of criminal activity has occurred, which has made it indispensable to resort more often to removing from their normal residences those disorderly elements who are notoriously dedicated to lawbreaking."[218] Favignana was reopened, as the PS gained ever increasing authority to cleanse the urban areas of those whom they deemed common or political criminals.

With the rise of fascism, the staff at the school muted, but did not drop, its criticism of *ammonizione* and *domicilio coatto*. In 1923, Falco announced in the *Bulletin* that "we" are against the abolition of the two police measures, as long as they are applied only to "the individual who, because of his somatic-psychological constitution, has the misfortune of being dangerous, that is, of having the inclination to hurt others or himself."[219] In 1931, Di Tullio reminded the readers of the *Bulletin* that the state was not yet individualizing treatment for different categories of *confinati*. Upon visiting the colony of Ventotene, he found a conglomeration of various types of inmates including alcoholics, those with tuberculosis or syphilis, and the mentally ill. Recalling "the teachings received from our master, Salvatore Ottolenghi," he called for the expansion of health facilities, the establishment of a school, and the provision of work in order to cure and rehabilitate common criminals.[220] Less outspoken than his positivist predecessors before the advent of fascism, Di Tullio skirted the delicate topic of political prisoners and muted his criticism of Ventotene with tactful praise of Bocchini and the fascist regime. But it was clear that criminal anthropology had failed to reform *confino* in its own image. Instead, they had provided the dictatorship with the theoretical tools to revive and expand a repressive institution.

The strong positivist climate of late nineteenth- and early twentieth-century Italy helped to prolong unnaturally the life of *ammonizione* and *domicilio coatto*, two measures that seemed directly in conflict with the liberal principles at the basis of Italian unification. In many other ways, Italy became more democratic during the half-century preceeding World War I as male suffrage was expanded, strikes legalized, and mayors became elected rather than appointed. Yet proposals for the reform of *ammonizione* and *domicilio coatto*, measures that were considered a blot on Italy's constitutional character, never even got to the stage of being voted on in Parliament. Although individual criminal anthropologists, who for the most part opposed these police measures, were not directly responsible for perpetuating such a contradiction, misinterpretations of their theories were. At the moment when public support for the complete abolition of the two measures was increasing, positivist criminologists raised the spector of the born criminal as an eternal enemy of civilized society. Thus, growing liberalism was countered by a fear of atavistic and degenerate delinquents who, according to the dictates of criminal anthropology, had to be separated from normal men and women. The fascist regime used this fear, alongside the threat of political subversion, to rehabilitate *ammonizione* and *confino* as part of the general expansion of police power over the civilian population.

NATIONAL FEDERATION OF THE PS

A third aspect of the PS that scientific policing shaped was the campaign for unionization. In 1919, activist functionaries founded the National Federation of the PS, initially limited to the administrative ranks, including white-collar clerks (*impiegati*). The union was fostered by a new publication, *Social Defense* (*La difesa sociale*), which carried the subtitle "monthly journal of applied sociology for the subjects of policing and prisons." This designation was intended to emphasize the educational aim of the new magazine over its role as a mouthpiece for economic demands. As a review of the contents of the articles makes clear, criminal anthropology provided the intellectual foundation of *Social Defense*, whose very name evoked the positivist philosophy of punishment.

Unlike the School of Scientific Policing, however, the federation and its journal were not the direct creation of the Positivist School. The founding editors of the *Defense* included a judge, a retired prefect, and two retired PS administrators, one being the ubiquitous Alongi.[221] Its list of "principle collaborators" did include Ottolenghi, Ferri, and Umberto Ellero, who contributed articles on criminal anthropology as applied to police, prisons, and law. Because these essays did not address the issue of unionization, it appears that these positivist stalwarts were sympathetic to, but not the prime movers behind, the push by PS functionaries to improve their lot.

From an international perspective, the drive for unionization among the Italian PS was not unusual, as similar struggles were occurring in England and several American cities in 1919. By that time, workers in other occupations were organized and had markedly improved their economic status, while police were legally forbidden to unionize by governments citing reasons of national security. After the war, police began challenging these restrictions as the cost of living had risen sharply while their wages had stagnated. Extreme economic hardship provoked police throughout the Western world to shed their traditional submissiveness to superiors and follow the example of other occupational groups by forming labor unions.

As we have seen earlier, the complaints of the Italian PS about low salaries predated the war and had been raised repeatedly in Parliament. Some PS officials like Alongi and Saracini had publicized the problem in books and articles, and, not surprisingly, both were active in the new Federation. In 1920, the *Defense* exposed the plight of "homeless Functionaries," reputedly 300 in Rome alone, who could not afford permanent housing for themselves and their families.[222] Hours were also long, as police—considered "always on duty"—received no overtime pay. Exaggerating the point, the *Defense* claimed that "according to Italian law, there are only two categories of persons who do not have the right to the eight-hour day . . . the PS and servants!"[223]

Besides salaries, PS administrators also demanded expanded opportunities for promotion from the lower rank of delegate to those of commissioner and *questore.* Parliament had also considered this issue, with Gasparotto in 1914 pointing out that less than twenty percent of all PS functionaries held a title above that of delegate, while almost 50 percent did in the prison administration.[224] Consequently, many candidates who successfully passed the examination for the rank of Commissioner never received a promotion with its higher salary. In a cover story, the *Defense* also protested the frequent transfers of functionaries from one region to another "without regard to length of service, family, health, time of year, or children's schooling."[225] It concluded that "the transfer of police is a weapon of the state, and tyrants at every level use it."[226]

Resentment of government authorities ran through the pages of the *Defense,* which insisted that PS administrators needed to gain autonomy from the political whims of prefects. Comparing the PS to the Prussian bureaucracy, one article condemned "the draconian system that converts the human functionary into an automaton."[227] Citizens would come to respect the police only when they "were completely and clearly convinced that the PS is not an instrument to further the interests of the governing parties" but instead was dedicated to protecting "the common interest."[228] For this purpose, the Federation called for the demilitarization of PS guards, elimination of the authority of prefects over *questori,* and the appointment of outstanding *questori,* rather than political allies of the government, to the post of Director General of the PS.

To justify their demands for better working conditions and increased autonomy, the Federation adopted Ottolenghi's argument that education was essential to professionalization. Calling for improved training at all levels of the PS, the *Defense* praised the School of Scientific Policing and reprinted the regulation of 1919 that integrated it officially into the PS. It carried articles by Ottolenghi on technical services of the school, Ferri on legal reform, and Ellero on "graphology," or the identification of suspects through handwriting. That union organizers seriously believed in the value of education for their cause is clear from their request for more rigorous examinations. Because the tests for promotion to Commissioner were so easy that too many candidates passed, the Minister of the Interior—that is, a political official—made the final choice. In a deprecating tone, the Federation criticized this process, because "the ministerial Olympus . . . does not take theoretical learning into much account, as is revealed by the fact that eminent functionaries, who are applauded as illustrious sociologists in the academic world, are relegated to lower offices and viewed with suspicion and dislike, while mediocrities, who are quick to adore any sun which rises, make it to the top."[229] This had happened during the war, when the government suspended examinations and based promotions "on merit." In short, the Federation saw education in scientific policing as the best instrument for professionalizing the PS and securing its autonomy from political authorities.

From its founding, the Federation was viewed by the government with ambivalence, if not downright hostility. The PS functionaries defended their right to organize, calling themselves the "new Cinderella" who had been left behind in the movement toward unionization that already included other groups of public employees.[230] Administrators in the departments of railroads, the post office, prefectures, prisons, and justice had their own federations, which had lobbied successfully for increased salaries. Only the policeman remained unorganized and passive, "like a dog, with its ears cocked, waiting for the morsel of bread that the master is getting ready to throw him."[231] According to the *Defense*, wages of PS functionaries now fell below those of PS guards and the *Carabinieri*, who were lower ranking but had protested "a bit noisily."[232] It was a "fact" that only agitation led to improvement in working conditions, and, as Lino Ferriani, one of the founders of the Federation pointed out, "the good positivist has the duty never to ignore a fact, which—as Lombroso taught—is the real master in life."[233] The PS thus had no choice but to organize.

Despite this combative tone, the *Defense* also tried to soothe government officials by pointing out that the right of association had a long history in Italy, going back to the Piedmontese *Statuto*. If forbidden to organize, the PS would be reduced to the status of *ammoniti*, who, it claimed, were the only other group not allowed to congregate. On the other hand, a legal Federation would pursue "noble and altruistic ends" leading to improvements in policing and society in general.[234] Stronger and more professional police were especially needed in the cities, which were plagued by "that plethora of people who are restless, uncontrollable and in continual ferment and who constitute the most shadowy and turbulent level of the social underworld."[235] Unlike unions of manual laborers, the Federation promised to eschew violence and class hatred and instead become "an inextinguishable source of reason founded on law."[236] Its founders pleaded with ministry officials to accept the principle of unionization, promising cooperation rather than confrontation.

Prospects for the Federation initially looked promising. Founded in February 1919, its membership reached 1,000 within five months and included, according to the *Defense*, almost every functionary in many provincial capitals in the South as well as the North.[237] The Federation won the approval of Prime Minister Vittorio Emanuele Orlando, who appointed a commission to write legislation reforming the PS. Headed by Camillo Corradini, the commission formulated a bill that would have increased the number of *questori* and given them, rather than prefects, complete control over both functionaries and guards. But Orlando's government fell in June, leaving the reform bill unpassed.

After a short government headed by Nitti, the Federation was heartened at the return of Giolitti as prime minister and his appointment of Corradini as deputy secretary of the Interior. Complaining that Nitti had unjustly labeled PS functionaries as "rebellious" and "seditious," the *Defense* appealed to Giolitti to consider "police, in a democratic regime, not as the old jailers of shameful memory nor as an instrument of oligarchical and reactionary vendettas, but as an impartial and calm arbitrator of a law that is really equal for all."[238] But the Federation irked even its friend Corradini by its activism; in response, Corradini declared that the Federation had become "an organization of resistance to the Government" and ordered it to disband.[239] In an article entitled "we obey," the Federation agreed, noting that "great events are developing for the Nation, which today more than yesterday needs a police that is strong and, let us say it, blindly disciplined to accept even the most painful and humiliating sacrifices."[240]

It is not clear to which "great events" the Federation was referring. But Italy was experiencing a variety of crises during the short life of the union, which explains the rapid succession of prime ministers with which it negotiated. Called "the red two years (*biennio rosso*)," the period of 1918–20 witnessed a series of strikes by rural and urban workers experiencing similar economic hardships to police. Peasants occupied land, which had been promised to them as combatants during the war, while factory workers struck to improve wages that had not kept pace with wartime inflation. From the other end of the political spectrum, radical nationalists formed in 1919 the first fascist paramilitary groups dedicated to destroying the new Italian Communist Party. Loathe to lose control of a force that had traditionally been its political servant, the government was fearful of any displays of police autonomy during this period of extreme instability.

For our purposes, the Federation, although short-lived, is of interest for its reliance on criminal anthropology as the intellectual justification for unionization. This choice shows that, far from being superseded by idealism, positivist criminology was well known and respected by the founders of the Federation, which included prefects, magistrates, and PS administrators. It offered to improve the reputation of PS functionaries, by providing them with skills in scientific policing. It also promised to give the police a supposedly scientific and neutral body of knowledge on which to base their claim to professional status. Once recognized as professionals, PS administrators could claim independence from political pressures and turn their attention to what they perceived as Italy's real problem, common crime.

The PS's attempt at unionization also shows the political elasticity of criminal anthropology. Championed by all voices in the Federation, positivism—in its flaunted objectivity—united members of various political stripes. As the Federation was officially apolitical, writers for the *Defense* never openly discussed their party allegiances. But the tone was liberal, contrasting the subservience of the PS to the liberal principles of Italy's constitution, especially the right to association. Some articles showed socialist sympathies and called on the PSI to extend its support to unions of white-collar workers, like the Federation. That many of the leaders of the Federation later converted to fascism may partially be attributed to their disillusionment with a succession of Liberal prime ministers—like Giolitti, Nitti, and Orlando—who for decades failed to substantially reform the PS or improve the abysmal working conditions of police. In Mussolini they found a leader who was eager to strengthen police, and union members like Saracini, Ottolenghi, and Ferri became supporters of fascism while retaining their faith in positivism. Rather than objective and apolitical, criminal anthropology proved to be malleable and able to serve a variety of political masters.

CONCLUSION

In 1931, Mariano D'Amelio, senator and president of the Supreme Court of Appeal, wrote in the *Corriere della Sera*, the most eminent Italian newspaper, that, "in fewer than twenty years, the infant science of scientific policing—which, like all academic fields taking their first steps, was received with smiles of skepticism and a few jokes—has distinguished itself in practice and is very well known."[241] These words greeted the publication of a book by Ottolenghi, volume two of his *Treatise on Scientific Policing*.[242] In the same year criminal anthropology, as applied to police, received another vote of confidence. At the request of the Minister of Justice, Arturo Rocco, a Museum of Crime (*Museo criminale*) was established in Rome, based on the collections of the School of Scientific Policing. Thus, as he entered his thirtieth year as Director of the School, Ottolenghi could congratulate himself on the success of his long campaign to introduce the principles of positivist criminology into the everyday practice of the PS.

Why was Ottolenghi successful? Cleverly taking advantage of a crisis in policing, Ottolenghi proposed a solution that did not require immediate legislation or a large outlay of public funds. Working with a small staff in his school, he trained increasing numbers of functionaries who carried their new positivist faith back into the ranks of the PS throughout the peninsula. With foresight, he developed an array of technical services—like fingerprinting and photography—that were becoming essential to modern police work and were gradually embraced even by the most traditional bureaucrats in the PS. Admired for his willingness to teach even the most basic courses for guards, unusual for a member of the university elite, Ottolenghi also drew the admiration of police reformers like Alongi and Saracini. Such allies, while not criminal anthropologists themselves, vouched for the utility of scientific policing and made it an essential component of the campaign to unionize the PS in 1919.

Ottolenghi was also careful to draw on the prestige of criminal anthropology in his campaign to infiltrate scientific policing into the PS. He never tired of vaunting Italy's glorious legal tradition, stretching from Beccaria to Lombroso and stressed the *italianità* of scientific policing because it formed part of this evolution.[243] Because he made biological and psychological theories of crime integral to his vision of scientific policing, he could genuinely claim to form part of the "Italian School" that was so well known in international criminological circles. He shared with other criminal anthropologists the tendency to oversimplify and sensationalize certain notions, like the dangerousness of born criminals and the need for preventive policing. This willingness to "vulgarize" a complex theory made it more accessible to the public but raised fears about abolishing police powers like *ammonizione* and *domicilio coatto*.

Managing to adapt scientific policing to a variety of political agendas, Ottolenghi assured its survival from liberalism to fascism in Italy. In the Giolittian period, the penchant of Ottolenghi and his staff for drawing up identification records and classifying ever larger groups of the population reimposed a web of surveillance over the lower classes reminiscent of the old regime. During the liberal era, this technocratic zeal was tempered by pleas for better treatment of *ammoniti* and *coatti*, especially those considered occasional criminals. Under fascism, the more authoritarian impulses of scientific policing dominated the school, which applauded the strengthening of the "preventive" powers of the PS in the name of social defense or even, in the words of Di Tullio, "the betterment and strengthening of the Race."[244]

In his famous Ascension Day speech of 1927, Mussolini declared that "it is time to say that the Police are not only respected but honored."[245] Six years later, the Italian delegate to the Congress of the International Commission of Criminal Police told his audience in Chicago that "thanks to the Fascist Government, there is no more crime in Italy" and that "in Italy live 43 million Italians who are all ready to die for the Duce."[246] Similar myths were mouthed regularly in Parliament, but further research is needed to uncover the true conditions of criminal justice in fascist Italy. Clearly, political opponents of the regime hated the police, and it is doubtful the uniformed cops on the streets suddenly elicited increased respect. But current research has suggested that the administrative ranks of the PS, outside of the political police, retained a certain autonomy from the fascist party and developed a strong professional identity.[247] According to Giovanna Tosati, high positions in the PS were more often filled by functionaries than political appointees under fascism than during the earlier liberal monarchy. If this hypothesis proves true, scientific policing was an important component of this new professional identity.

NOTES

1. Cesare Lombroso, *Sull'incremento del delitto in Italia* (Turin: Bocca, 1879), p. iii.

2. Ibid.

3. C. Lombroso, *Il momento attuale* (Milan: Moderna, 1903), p. 10.

4. Lombroso is referring to the attempt by General Luigi Pelloux, prime minister during these years, to suspend many civil rights guarenteed by the *Statuto*, the Italian constitution. These attempts were successfully resisted by Parliament and the electorate, which voted Pelloux's government out of office.

5. C. Lombroso, *Il momento*, p. 11.

6. The phrase is from the nationalist journal, *Leonardo*, edited by Papini and Prezzolini and is quoted in Landucci, *Darwinismo a Firenze*, p. 253.

7. Villa, *Il deviante*, p. 233.

8. Ibid., p. 234. Although Villa does outline briefly developments in Italian criminology during the first decades of the twentieth century, he believes that these can only be loosely traced to Lombroso (pp. 233–241).

9. See Chapter 6 for the development of Italian criminology after Lombroso's death.

10. Augusto Aglebert, *Della polizia in Inghilterra, in Francia e in Italia: Frammenti* (Bologna: Monti, 1868), p. 13.

11. Giovanni Bolis, *La polizia e le classi pericolose della società: Studii* (Bologna: Zanichelli, 1871), p. 5.

12. Ibid., p. 8.

13. Ibid., pp. 11, 10.

14. Ibid., p. 14.

15. Giuseppe Leti, "La delinquenza nella PS," *Scuola positiva*, v. 3, n. 19 (1893), p. 879.

16. Ibid., p. 887.

17. Italy, Camera dei Deputati, *Discussioni* (hereafter *Disc.*), Legis. 23:1, 1909–13, v. 15, p. 17759.

18. Ibid., p. 17758.

19. ACS, M. Int., DGPS, Div. Personale PS, 1912–46, b. 5.

20. A good overview of police organization since unification can be found in Richard Collin, "The Blunt Instruments: Italy and the Police," in John Roach and Jürgen Thomaneck, eds., *Police and Public Order in Europe* (Dover, N.H.: Croom Helm, 1985), pp. 185–214. For more detailed treatment of shorter periods, see Steven C. Hughes, *Crime, Disorder and the Risorgimento: The Politics of Policing in Bologna* (New York: Cambridge University Press, 1994); Richard Bach Jensen, *Liberty and Order: The Theory and Practice of Italian Public Security Policy, 1848 to the Crisis of the 1890s* (New York: Garland, 1991); Giovanna Tosatti, "La repressione del dissenso politico tra l'età liberale e il fascismo: L'organizzazione della polizia, *Studi storici*, v. 38 (Jan.–March, 1997), pp. 217–55, and Jonathan Dunnage, *The Italian Police and the Rise of Fascism: A Case Study of the Province of Bologna, 1897–1925* (Westport, Conn.: Praeger, 1997). These works focus on the policing of political, rather than common, crime.

21. The Kingdom of Piedmont led the movement for unification, imposing its king, laws, and administrative structure on the new Kingdom of Italy.

22. As part of the continual efforts to reform the corps of uniformed cops, the government changed its title periodically, from "public security guards" to "city guard," in 1890, to "royal guards" in 1919, and back to "public security guards" in 1925. In popular speech, the guards were also referred to as "agents."

23. Giovanni Codronchi, "Sul riordinamento della pubblica sicurezza in Italia," *Nuova antologia* (Sept. 1, 1895), p. 219.

24. Ibid.

25. Ibid., p. 218.

26. Pietro Nocito, "Polizia giudiziaria: Studi di riforma legislativa," *Rivista penale*, v. 50 (July, 1899), p. 13. Nocito's article was taken from his report to the Commission for the Reform of the Code of Criminal Procedure.

27. Giuseppe Alongi, *Polizia e delinquenza in Italia: Saggio* (Rome: Ufficio dell' "Agenti di PS," 1887), p. 9.

28. Ibid., p. 10.

29. Jensen, who has done the most careful analysis of the size of Italy's police, believes that Alongi's statistics exaggerate the disparity between Italy and the rest of Europe. See "Police Reform and Social Reform: Italy from the Crisis of the 1890s to the Giolittian Era," *Criminal Justice History*, v. 10 (Westport, Conn.: Meckler, 1989), p. 180.

30. Jensen, "Police Reform," p. 180.

31. This statement is not entirely correct, since other corps like the Finance Guards (*Guardie di Finanza*) and the Forestry Guards (*Guardie campestri*) also had police powers; these powers, however, were limited to a restricted area.

32. Ibid.

33. Jonathan Dunnage, The Italian Police, p. 95. His numbers seem to include only guards and not functionaries.

34. Eugenio Forni, Dei criteri d'investigazione nei segreti dei reati (Naples: Antonio Morano, 1877), p. 313.

35. Italy, Parl., C.D., Disc., Legis. 23.1 (1909–1910), v. 7 , p. 7688.

36. Italy, Parl., C.D., Disegni di leggi (hereafter Disegni), Legis. 24:1 (1913–19), v. 14, 444A and 444bis-A, p. 10.

37. Ibid., v. 23, 902A, p. 12

38. Forni, Dei criteri, p. 299.

39. Alongi, Polizia e delinquenza in Italia (Rome: Cecchini, 1882), p. 45.

40. Italy, C.D., Disc., Legis. 23:1 (1909–13), v. 7, p. 7685.

41. Italy, C.D., Disc., Legis. 23:1 (1909–13), v. 12, p. 14345.

42. Raymond Fosdick, European Police Systems (New York: Century, 1916), p. 243.

43. Most job titles had several levels, so that salaries rose slightly with seniority. Italy, C. D., Disegni, Legis. 23:1 (1909–13), v. 19, n. 940, pp. 4–5; ACS, M. Int., PS, Div. Pers., 1912–46, b. 4.

44. Italy, C.D., Disc., Legis. 23:1 (1909–13), v. 20, p. 24274.

45. Ibid., p. 24275.

46. Italy, C.D., Disc., Legis. 24:1 (1913–19), v. 3, p. 2828.

47. Ibid., p. 2829.

48. Ibid., p. 2653.

49. C. Lombroso, Sull'incremento, p. 134.

50. Ibid., p. 135.

51. Archivio, v. 7 (1886), p. 612 [C. Lombroso].

52. Ibid.

53. Ottolenghi, "L'opera di Cesare Lombroso e la polizia scientifica," L'opera di Cesare Lombroso nella scienza e nelle sue applicazioni (Turin: Bocca, 1908), p. 220.

54. Archivio, v. 7 (1886), p. 611 [C. Lombroso]

55. Bolletino della Scuola di Polizia Scientifica (hereafter Boll. SPS), v. 1 (1911), p. 32 [Ottolenghi].

56. Ibid., v. 2 (1912), p. 74 [Ottolenghi].

57. Boll. SPS, v. 4 (1914), p. 187 [Ottolenghi].

58. Boll. SPS, v. 1 (1910), p. 4 [Ottolenghi].

59. Boll. SPS, v. 14–15 (1924–25), p. 182 [Ottolenghi].

60. Boll. SPS, v. 1 (1910), pp. 26–27. The museum, now administered by the Ministry of Justice, is still in existence.

61. Boll. SPS, v. 4 (1914), p. 185 [Ottolenghi].

62. Boll. SPS, v. 1 (1910), p. 4.

63. Ibid.

64. Ottolenghi, L'insegnamento della Polizia Scientifica (Rome: Mantellate, 1914), p. 4.

65. Ottolenghi, Polizia Scientifica: Quadri sinettici delle lezioni tenute nella Scuola di Polizia (Rome: Società Poligrafia, 1907), pp. 108–12.

66. Boll SPS, v. 1 (1910), pp. 5–6 gives a short history of the early years of the school.

67. Boll SPS, v. 3, (1912), p. 79.

68. Boll. SPS, v. 21 (1931), p. 240. Ottolenghi's phrase echoes that of his anarchist opponents, "the propaganda of the deed."

69. ACS, PS, Pol. Giud., 1916–18, B. 205, f. 12985.4.

70. Italy, C.D., Disc., Legis. 23:1, (1909–13), v. 2, p. 1369.

71. Ibid., p. 1517; 1519.

72. Italy, C.D., *Disc.*, Legis. 23:1 (1909–13), v. 20, p. 24299.

73. Ibid., p. 24340.

74. ACS, M. Int., DGPS, Div. Personale PS, 1912–46, b. 5.

75. This official recognition of the school formed part of a radical overhauling of the PS and apparently part of a plan to strengthen the police in the face of working-class protests as well as the rising violence of fascist squads after World War I. Nitti's reform further militarized the uniformed ranks of the PS and renamed them the "Royal guards"; Mussolini reversed this decision in 1923.

76. For 1907, see Italy, C.D., *Disegni*, Legis. 23:1 (1909–13), v. 16, n. 636–A, p. 31; for 1910, Ibid., v. 8, N. 288, p. 13; for 1921, Ibid., Legis. 25:1 (1919–21), v. 10, n. 1014, p. 17; for 1925, ibid., Legis. 27, (1924–27), v. 8, n. 289, p. 32. Beginning in 1926, expenses for the school were not listed separately in yearly legislation on the PS budget.

77. *Boll. SPS*, v. 3 (1912), p. 79 [Ottolenghi]. Relations between the PS and *Carabinieri*, however, remained uneasy, with Gasti charging that a former student from the *Carabinieri* had plagiarized his lessons and published them in 1913 under the title *Compendium of Scientific Police*. Nevertheless, *Carabinieri* continued to attend courses at the school and, after World War I, Falco began commuting to Florence to teach courses in scientific policing at a new school for *Carabinieri* officers. ACS, Pol. Giud., (1913–1915), b. 153, f. 12985–4 and (1916–18), b. 34, f. 19599A.

78. *Boll. SPS*, v. 3 (1912), p. 2; v. 19–21 (1919–21), p. 4.

79. *Boll. SPS*, v, 16–17 (1926–27), p. 8.

80. *Boll. SPS*, v. 27–29 (1937–39), p. 160.

81. *Boll. SPS*, v. 22–23 (1932–33), p. 14 [Falco].

82. ACS, PS, Personale, vers. 1963–65, b. 199.

83. Ibid.

84. *Boll. SPS*, v. 18 (1928), p. 167 [Ottoleghi]. Reprinted in the *Bulletin*, this article appeared originially in *Echi e Commenti*, a magazine read by the general public.

85. Ibid.

86. Italy, C.D., *Disc.*, Legis. 28 (1929–34), v. 7, p. 8412.

87. Ibid.

88. ACS, PS, Personale, vers. 1963–65, SSR, b. 199.

89. *Boll. SPS*, v. 18 (1928), p. 159 [Ottolenghi].

90. Ibid., p. 157.

91. For example, see *Boll. SPS*, v. 22–23 (1932–33), p. 171 [Di Tullio].

92. Ibid.

93. *Boll. SPS*, v. 19–21 (1929–31), p. 260 [Saracini].

94. Falco, "La profilassi criminale nell'attività della polizia italiana," *Atti del 1. Congresso internazionale di criminologia* (Rome: Mantellate, 1938), v. 5, p. 119.

95. Ibid.

96. Corso Bovio, *Commento alla legge di pubblica sicurezza: Testi di legge-dottrina-giurisprudenza* (Naples: Eugenio Jovene, 1936), p. xiv.

97. Emilio Saracini, *I crespuscoli della polizia: Compendio storico della genesi e delle vicende dell'amministrazione di pubblica sicurezza* (Naples: SIEM, 1922), pp. 74–78.

98. Alongi, *Polizia e delinquenza* (1882), p. 51.

99. Alongi, *Progetto di legge e di regolamento sulla pubblica sicurezza* (Rome: Ludovico Cecchini, 1901), p. 64.

100. Saracini, *I crespuscoli*, p. 163.

101. *Boll. SPS*, v. 9–11 (1919–21), p. 222 [Sorrentino].

102. Luigi Tomellini, *Manuale di polizia giudiziaria* (Milan: Ulrico Hoepli, 1912), p. xv.

103. Ibid., xvi.

104. *Boll. SPS*, v. 14–15 (1924–25), p. 227.

105. *Boll. SPS*, v. 3 (1912), p. 147.

106. *Boll. SPS*, v. 2 (1911), p. 54 [Ottolenghi].

107. ACS, PS, Uff. Ris., 1912, b. 52, f. L4.

108. *Boll. SPS*, v. 4 (1914), pp. 209–10.

109. *Boll. SPS*, v. 9–10 (1919–21), p. 221.

110. *Boll. SPS*, 19–20 (1929–30), pp. 184–85 [Ottolenghi].

111. *Boll. SPS*, v. 27–29 (1937–39), p. 78 [Falco].

112. ACS, PS, Uff. Ris., 1910, b. 5, f. 5071.

113. Fosdick, *European Police*, p. 192.

114. Sheldon Glueck, *Continental Police Practice* (Springfield, Ill.: Charles C. Thomas, 1974) p. 7; orig. published 1926.

115. Ibid., p. 8.

116. Joáo Alberto Pereira de Azevedo Neves, *Médecine légale et police criminelle (France, Belgique, Allemagne, Autriche et Italie)* (Lisbon: Imprimerie Nationale, 1931), p. 352. Police officials from Columbia and Chile took courses at the school in 1928, illustrating the special interest that Latin countries had in criminal anthropology. See the *Boll. SPS*, v. 18 (1928), p. 6.

117. On the founding of the Casellario politico centrale, see Tosatti, "Il Ministero degli interni: Le origini del Casellario politico centrale," in ISAP, *Le riforme crispine* (Milan: Giuffré, 1990), pp. 447–85.

118. Italy, CD, *Disc.*, Legis. 24:1 (1913–19), v. 3, p. 2445.

119. Italy, CD., *Disc.*, Legis. 23:1 (1909–13), v. 7, p. 7667.

120. *Archivio*, v. 14 (1893), p. 599 [Ottolenghi].

121. *Archivio*, v. 10 (1998), p. 222 [Anfosso].

122. See the excellent article by Bernardino Farolfali, "Antropometria militare e antropologia della devianza, 1876–1908," *Storia d'Italia, Annali*, v. 7 [*Malattia e medicina*, ed., Franco della Peruta] (Turin: Einaudi, 1984), pp. 1179–1219.

123. *Boll. SPS*, v. 1 (1910), p. 15; v. 3 (1912), p. 10 [Ottolenghi and Gasti]; and v. 22–23 (1932–22), pp. 27–28.

124. Ibid., v. 1 (1910), p. 15.

125. Based on statistics published yearly in the *Bolletino SPS*.

126. Ottolenghi speculated that fingerprinting decreased because potential criminals were being drafted and PS offices were short of personnal. See ACS, PS, Pol. Giud. (1916–18), b. 205, f. 12985.4.

127. *Boll. SPS*, v. 3 (1912), p. 11 [Ottolenghi and Gasti].

128. ACS, Pol. Giud. (1910–12), b. 357, f. 12985.4.

129. ACS, Pol. Giud. (1910–12), b. 271, f. 11200.8.

130. These circulars were reprinted in the *Boll. SPS*. The PS administration also demanded frequent reports from each province on its success in expanding its capacity to send fingerprints to Rome. See ACS, Pol. Giud., 1913–15, b. 153, f. 12985.4. The increase in the school's budget in 1913 went specifically to support its investigative services, another sign of government support. See Italy, C.D., *Disegni*, Legis. 23:1 (1909–13), v. 29, n. 1230, p. 12.

131. *Boll. SPS*, v. 1 (1910), p. 16.

132. For examples of such requests, see ACS, PS, Uff. Ris. (1911), b. 62, f. L4 and PS, Comm. Int. P. Cr. (1930–35), b. 1.

133. Giuseppe Falco, *"Identità": Metodo scientifico di segnalamento e identificazione* (Rome: P. Maglione & C. Strin, 1922), p. 330.

134. *Boll. SPS*, v. 9–11 (1919–21), pp. 92–106. Ottolenghi collaborated with a Frenchman, Belin, in the first transmission, which was from Lyon to Paris (rather than in Italy).

135. ACS, PS, Uff. Ris. (1912), b. 52, f. L4.

136. ACS, PS, Pol. Giud. (1913–15), b. 153, f. 12985.4.

137. *Boll. SPS, v. 18 (1928), p. 112.*

138. *Boll. SPS*, v. 4 (1914), p. 19 [Gasti].

139. ACS, PS, Pol. Giud. (1916–18), b. 205, f. 12985.4.

140. This was named the *Bolletino delle richerche*, not to be confused with the *Bolletino SPS*.

141. *Boll. SPS*, v. 9–11 (1919–21), p. 20 [Ottolenghi].

142. ACS, PS, Pol. Giud., 1916–18, b. 205, f. 12985.4; *Boll. SPS*, v. 7–8 (1917–18), pp. 17–18 [Ottolenghi].

143. *Boll. SPS*, n. 7–8 (1917–18), p. 15 [Ottolenghi].

144. *Boll. SPS*, v. 9–11 (1919–21), p. 221.

145. *Boll. SPS.*, 1914, p. 114 [Ottolenghi].

146. Ibid., p. 148.

147. *Boll. SPS* (1922–23), p. 125 [Giri].

148. Ibid., p. 126.

149. *Boll. SPS*, v. 3 (1912), p. 53 [Ottolenghi].

150. *Boll. SPS*, v. 1 (1910), pp. 52–53 [Falco].

151. *Boll. SPS*, v. 21 (1931), p. 176. [Giri].

152. *Boll. SPS*, v. 6 (1916), p. 110 [Ottolenghi].

153. *Boll. SPS*, v. 3 (1912), p. 94 [Gasti].

154. Ibid., p. 97.

155. *Boll. SPS*, v. 6 (1916), pp. 219–20 [Ottolenghi]. The other cities were Milan, Venice, Florence, Bologna, Cagliari, Palermo, Naples, Turin, and Genoa.

156. *Boll. SPS*, v. 12–13 (1922–23), pp. 91–92 [Di Tullio].

157. Ibid. p. 93.

158. Scuola Superiore di Polizia, *Nozioni per la compilazione della cartella biografica del pregiudicato* (Rome: Istituto Poligrafico dello Stato Libreria, 1932), p. 18.

159. *Boll. SPS*, v. 14–15 (1924–25), p. 142 [Falco].

160. *Boll. SPS*, v. 16–17 (1926–27), p. 133 [Ottolenghij]; ibid., v. 21 (1931), p. 241.

161. Falco, "La profilassi criminale nell'attività della polizia italiana."

162. ACS, PS, Div. Pers., vers. 1963–65, b. 200.

163. ACS, PS, Div. Pers., vers. 1963–65, b. 124.

164. ACS, PS, Div. Per., vers. 1963–65, b. 129. A second committee later overturned the censor of Giri, who became a *questore* in 1948.

165. *Boll. SPS*, v. 26–27 (1937–39), p. 135 [Bianconi].

166. Ibid.

167. Ibid., p. 136.

168. For statistics on *domicilio coatto* before World War I, see Jensen, "Italy's Peculiar Institution: Internal Police Exile, 1861–1914," *Essays in European History*, ed. June K. Burton (Lanham, MD: University Press of America, 1989), pp. 99–114. Contemporary commentaries on *domicilio coatto* include Guglielmo Filipponi, *La legislazione italiana in materia di*

polizia giudiziaria ed amministrativa: Guida teorico-pratica (Forlì: Romagnole, 1909) and Augusto Ferraro, *Delinquenti abituali e le colonie penali* (Naples: Veraldi, 1910).

169. Testo unico della Legge di Pubblica Sicurezza, n. 6144, 30 June 1889.

170. Arts. 94–95.

171. Ibid., Art. 97.

172. Ibid., Art. 104.

173. The chair was the prefect and members included representatives of the PS and Carabinieri as well as a local judge and prosecutor.

174. Jesse White Mario, "Il sistema penitenziario e il domicilio coatto in Italia," Parte 1, *Nuova antologia*, v. 148 (July–Aug., 1896), pp. 16, 18.

175. Ibid., p. 16.

176. Ibid., p. 19.

177. Ibid.

178. Each prisoner in the penal colonies received a pittance of fifty *centesimi* each day for food.

179. White Mario was writing only three years after the brutal repression of protests by the the Sicilian *fasci*.

180. White Mario, "Il sistem penitenziario," Parte II, *Nuova antologia* v. 149, (Sept.–Oct., 1896), p. 320.

181. ACS, PS, Pol. Giud. (1913–15), b. 68.

182. Ibid.

183. Ibid.

184. C. Lombroso, *Sul incremento*, p. 64.

185. Ibid., p. 65.

186. *Archivio*, v. 10 (1889), p. 21 [Ferri].

187. Ibid., p. 26.

188. Ibid., p. 21.

189. *Boll SPS*, v. 9–11 (1919–21), p. 176.

190. Ibid.

191. Ibid., p. 177.

192. Ibid.

193. Ibid., v. 6 (1916), p. 210 [Ottolenghi].

194. Ibid., p. 209.

195. Ibid., v. 1 (1910), p. 63 [Ottolenghi].

196. Ibid.

197. *Boll. SPS*, v. 7–8 (1917–18), p. 197 [Trombetti].

198. ACS, PS, Pol. Giud., 1913–15, b. 68.

199. *Boll. SPS*, v. 6 (1916), p. 204 [Ottolenghi].

200. *Boll. SPS*, v. 7–8 (1917), p. 65 [Ottolenghi and Falco].

201. Ibid., p. 66.

202. *Boll. SPS*, v. 6 (1916), p. 216 [Ottolenghi] (referring to *ammoniti*); ACS, PS, Pol. Giud., 1913–15, b. 68 (referring to *coatti*).

203. Alongi, *Polizia e delinquenza* (1882), pp. 37–38.

204. Bolis, *La Polizia*, p. 19.

205. Leti, "La delinquenza," p. 878.

206. Dunnage has also concluded that the concept of "preventive policing" provided continuity from liberalism to fascism in relation to political crime. See *The Italian Police*, p. 163.

207. Italy, CD, *Disegni*, Legis. 23:1 (1909–13), v. 12, n. 599, p. 5.

208. Ibid., p. 4.

209. Ibid.

210. Ibid., p. 6

211. Legge di Pubblica Sicurezza, n. 1848, 6 Nov. 1926, Art. 166.

212. Ibid, Art. 184.

213. Ibid., Arts. 3, 159. These personal identity cards did not themselves carry finger-prints; separate records with fingerprints were filed at local police stations. These police files, according to a law of 1940, were to contain not just fingerprints but also photographs and anthropometric measures. See R. Decreto 6 maggio 1940, n. 635, Art. 7.

214. Ibid., Art. 4.

215. Quoted in Saracini, *Nuova pratica di polizia amministrativa* (Naples: Elpis, 1929), p. 31.

216. Ibid.

217. Italy, CD, *Disc.*, Legis. 27 (1924–27), v. 6, p. 5472, (for 1910), p. 5515 (for 1920 and 1925); ACS, PS, Div. Pol. 1895–1945, b. 1, f. 2. (for 1930).

218. ACS, PS, Div. Pol., 1894–1945, b. 1, f. 2.

219. *Boll. SPS*, v. 12–13 (1922–23), p. 199 [Falco].

220. Ibid., v. 21, 1931, p. 212 [Di Tullio].

221. The founding editors were Edoardo Armò of the Supreme Court of Appeal in Palermo; Giuseppe Alongi, retired Inspector General of the PS; Costantino Taranto, re-tired Prefect; and Antonino Candia, retired Commissioner of the PS.

222. *Difesa Sociale* (hereafter *Difesa*), v. 2, n. 1 1920, p. 13–14; the issue was again raised in a front-page story in v. 2, n. 11, 1920, p. II.

223. *Difesa*, v. 2, n. 3 (1920) [A. Saieva].

224. Italy, C.D., *Disc.*, Legis 24:1 (1913–19), v. 3, p. 2827.

225. *Difesa*, v. 1, n. 7 (1919), p. ii.

226. Ibid.

227. Ibid., v. 1, n. 8 (1919), p. 2 [Lino Ferriani].

228. Ibid., v. 1, n. 5 (1919), p. 10 [Fanelli].

229. Ibid., v. 2, n. 3 (1920), p. 43.

230. Ibid., v. 1, n. 1 (1919), p. 6 [Alongi].

231. Ibid., v. 1, n. 3 (1919), p. iii.

232. Ibid., v. 1, n. 1 (1919), p. 10 [Corsi].

233. Ibid., v. 1, n. 5 (1919), pp. 5–7 [Ferriani].

234. Ibid., v. 1, n. 3 (1919), p. 5 [Edoardo Armò and Candia].

235. Ibid., v. 2, n. 7 (1920), p. 103. [Saieva].

236. Ibid., v. 2, n. 4 (1920), p. 49 [Biagio Di Pietra].

237. Ibid., v. 1, n. 4 (1919), n.p. (supplement).

238. Ibid., v. 2, n. 7 (1920), p. 99.

239. Ibid., v. 2, n. 11 (1920), p. 163.

240. Ibid., p. 165.

241. Quoted in *Boll. SPS*, v. 21 (1931), p. 259.

242. The first volume of his *Trattato di polizia scientifico* was published in 1910; volume one was subtitled, "physical identification" and volume two, "psychological and biographi-cal identification in legal investigations."

243. He uses the word "*italianità*" as early as 1907 in *Polizia Scientifica*, p. vii.

244. *Boll. SPS*, v. 16–17 (1926–27), p. 185 [Di Tullio].

245. Quoted in Romano Canosa, *La polizia in Italia dal 1945 a oggi* (Bologna: Il Mulino, 1976), pp. 72–73.

246. ACS, M. Int., P.S., Comm. Int. P. Cr., 1930–35, b. 2.

247. Collin suggests that "Bocchini was never more than a *pro forma* fascist" who "carefully maintained the political independence of the police from the Fascist Party" in "The Blunt Instruments," p. 194. More recently, Tossati concludes that "indeed the period of fascist power seems to have been the only one in which police enjoyed a real autonomy and decision-making power" because so many career officers, as opposed to political appointees, were promoted to the higher ranks. See "La repressione del dissenso politico," p. 255.

Chapter 5

Juvenile Delinquency

In 1894, the *Criminal World* opened its second volume with a case entitled "The Drama of Mezzojuso," referring to a small town outside Palermo. It is appropriate that Sighele, the positivist criminologist best known for his research on "criminal couples" and rebellious crowds, narrated the events of this "drama," because it involved a cast of characters. All belonged to a single extended family and were inspired by, in his words, "collective atavism."[1] Because the main protagonists were youth (*giovinotti*), the case also fit into a second category of interest for Sighele, that of the criminality of children.

Sighele's account followed the common positivist pattern, which first narrated the "facts" and then offered a *perizia*, or expert evaluation. His description of the events of 1890 in Mezzojuso was fairly straightforward, although colored by a northerner's tendency to see "mysticism," "bigotry," and "superstition" pervading southern life.[2] At the center of the story was the Carnesi family, composed of a father, mother, and seven children. After the Feast of the Madonna on December 8, the oldest son, Biagio, began to exhibit strange behavior. Rather than going to work in the fields, he spent all day and night crying and praying to be pardoned for his sins. Gradually, his sister Lucia, who was taking care of him, and three other brothers were also seized by religious delusions. According to Sighele, the mood of Lucia was remarkably different from that of her brothers; while they displayed "a melancholy delirium with fears of damnation, tears, and prayers," she showed "a simple religious exaltation that apparently left her intellectual faculties intact but multiplied her moral energy and physical strength."[3]

A number of events followed, culminating in a gruesome scene in the second-floor room in the Carnesi's house. After a *vecchietto*, or old man with magical powers, failed to cure Biagio, the son tried to murder his father, who was saved only by the superhuman strength of the exultant Lucia. At the house of her cousins, Lucia later "cured" another brother, Giacomo, of spirits that were clutching at his throat. A series of signs—like a falling tree and restless mule—seemed to confirm that the devil was punishing the Carnesi family, for whom Lucia would be the savior. In the final scene of the drama, Lucia, at three in the morning and surrounded by her relatives, tried to exorcise Biagio of his inner demons. When words failed, she began to beat her brother with "St. Antonio's log," a piece of wood left over from the saint's fire kindled on his feast day and believed to protect the house. Her parents, aunt, and brother Salvatore remained mute, while her two cousins held down Biagio during the blows. After more than an hour, with Biagio certainly dead, Lucia used her nails and teeth to rip off the foreskin of her brother's penis, displaying, according to Sighele, "a kind of necrophilia that until now was thought to be exclusively male."[4]

In the second half of his article, Sighele used positivist methods to analyze the causes of this horrible chain of events. Beginning with environmental factors, he noted that the agrarian crisis, especially acute in the South, "had favored and nourished mysticism and superstition among the peasants" of Mezzojuso.[5] Plagued with high rates of emigration, the town was going through a period of instability and transition that encouraged superstition in the populace. Since "religiosity is in inverse proportion to education," the minimal amount of schooling available to the inhabitants also encouraged a flight from reason.[6] Furthermore, the Carnesi children "fed on a double ration of liturgy and religious practices" because they attended both churches of their parents, one employing the Latin rite and the other the Greek.[7] Thus, poverty, illiteracy, and religious rivalry helped to explain the collective psychology of Mezzojuso, which atavistically recalled the primitive superstition of past times.

Yet these environmental factors, said Sighele, only triggered the hideous behavior of the Carnesi family. Like other criminal anthropologists, Sighele emphasized inborn pathology as the necessary root of the insanity of the four brothers, the criminality of Lucia, and the passivity of the onlookers. Based on a physical and psychological analysis of the extended family, he concluded that "each member has anomalies or is degenerate, with a heredity that makes him a candidate for insanity or at least group psychosis."[8] The father had "a skull full of prominent anomalies" including a long head, protruding forehead, large ears, a crooked nose, and huge lips. In short, he "is really the grotesque figure of savage man."[9] His wife, in addition to physical anomalies, suffered from "hysterical epileptic convulsions" during which she ground her teeth and barked like a dog.[10] Their son Salvatore was an imbecile, possessing a skull that Sighele dubbed "a museum of anomalies."[11] Even the cousins shared "exaggerated religiosity" and "degenerative anomalies" with the Carnesi family, as their mothers were sisters and their father "suffered a nervous disorder."[12]

The greater part of Sighele's analysis was devoted to the "sad heroine of the drama," that "virago" Lucia.[13] At twenty years of age, she had a "coarse and savage physiognomy with slightly Chinese eyes, swollen lips which expressed disdain, and a pronounced protrusion of the upper teeth which gave her face the appearance of an animal. . . . The whole face is shaded by light down and from time to time her soft eyes give out flashes of evil."[14] These physical anomalies signaled that Lucia, although having led the exemplary life of a religious and chaste daughter, was in fact degenerate. Having inherited an "epileptic neurosis" from her mother, her diseased constitution weakened during the days filled with fasting and praying before her brother's death.[15] For Sighele, it was also significant that Lucia was menstruating when her hidden degeneracy finally broke out into what he termed religious mania (*teomania*). Through this "divine orgasm," she not only began to believe in her own supernatural powers of exorcism, but brought her relatives under her spell in a type of collective psychosis.[16]

Not unsympathetic to the plight of Lucia, Sighele approved of her internment in an insane asylum rather than a prison. Comparing her to Joan of Arc, he characterized them both as possessed by religious mania that simply exhibited itself differently. Yet the overall impression left by his portrait of Lucia is one of a monster, doubly stunted in body and mind by her identity as both a southerner and a woman. Primitive and sexually abnormal, she had no control over the eruption of her baser instincts. These had been passed down to her from her parents, although Sighele mentions no evidence that they had previously exhibited unusual, much less insane, behavior. Criminal anthropologists predicted that deviant behavior would cluster in families. When they found no supporting data, they pointed instead to physical anomalies shared by family members as signs of their underlying abnormality.[17]

Interest in inheritance thus led Sighele and other criminal anthropologists to conduct research on juvenile delinquency. As we have seen, family history was integral to the interviews performed by Ottolenghi on *ammoniti* and, therefore, to a complete anthropological-biographical dossier. According to positivists, parents might be a cause of their offspring's crime in several ways. As in the case of Lucia, they might have passed on enough physical and psychological anomalies to give their child the constitution of a born criminal. Or they might have infected their children with a pathology like syphilis, tuberculosis, or alcoholism that left them degenerate from birth. Families might also create such an immoral environment that even "normal" children were enticed into crime. Criminal anthropologists claimed to be able to predict which children were prone to crime, since signs of atavism and degeneracy were legible on the body from the earliest years.

As in the case of police, positivist criminologists were able to influence legislation because of a moral panic, in this case over the perceived explosion of juvenile delinquency. In the late nineteenth century, concern about criminal behavior among children was widespread throughout Europe and the United States, and, in response, most Western nations devised new types of reformatories and courts for minors. Despite Lombroso's continual carping on the backwardness of the Italian treatment of juvenile delinquency, little changed during his lifetime. But his successors continued the campaign for reform through World War I and into the fascist era. In fact, it was only under Mussolini that Italy established a code of juvenile justice, in many ways reflecting positivist principles. This chapter will analyze the context of the moral panic over juvenile crime, positivist theories about children, and finally the development of a network of special reformatories and courts for minors.

CONTEXT

The heightened anxiety about deviant youth evident in Parliament and the press between 1890 and 1940 cannot be attributed simply to an increase in juvenile delinquency. According to the government's own reports, the number of persons under the age of twenty-one convicted by Italian courts dropped from 30,108 in 1890 to 24,471 in 1930.[18] Admittedly, much fluctuation occurred between these dates. The total rose noticeably during the 1890s, peaking at 44,172 in 1898.[19] But as adult rates of crime also increased significantly in that decade, the percentage attributable to minors remained steady, at 23 to 24 percent of the total. Furthermore, as the statistician Alfredo Spallanzani pointed out in an article in *The Positivist School*, the figures for the 1890s inflated the number of juvenile delinquents compared to later figures, since the first counted an individual each time he or she was convicted of a crime while the second documented only the last crime of those committed each year by recidivists.[20] Nevertheless, as the high figures for 1896–1900 were published only in 1909, they fueled a moral panic that lasted until World War I. To compound the misperception, the Ministry of Justice failed to publish any statistics broken down by age for the years 1901–1905, a period during which juvenile delinquency was apparently falling.

This hypothesis that juvenile crime was decreasing after the turn of the century is based on the figures for 1906, which showed the number of convictions of minors at 38,867. Totals continued to drop, with the low point at 22,117 in 1918. While juvenile delinquency rose after the war, numbers during the twenties remained far below the high point of the 1890s. Because adult crime was falling even faster between 1900 and 1922, the percentage of minors among the total population of offenders fluctuated during this period, sometimes reaching almost one-third. But after 1922, juveniles made up on average only 22 percent of all convictions.

The pattern becomes more complicated if one compares the subcategories presented in official criminal statistics. Because children under nine years old could not be held responsible for crime, the three subcategories by age were 9–14, 14–18, and 18–21. For most of the four decades after 1890, the youngest group was responsible for only 8 to 10 percent of all juvenile delinquency, the middle group 42 to 48 percent, and the oldest group, 45 to 50 percent. The only significant alteration to this pattern came during World War I, when the participation of the older group in lawbreaking declined sharply. This drop mirrored that of adults and probably occurred for the same reason, the drafting of young men, including potential delinquents, for military service. Yet commentators pointed to a rise in convictions among the youngest group as proof that the war had aggravated the problem of juvenile delinquency. Even though this surge abated in the 1920s, the fascist regime remained obsessed about deviancy in children throughout the interwar period.

In terms of sex, the average percent of girls convicted of juvenile crime fluctuated between 11 percent and 13 percent of the total. The only major exception occurred during the war when girls represented up to 41 percent of all lawbreakers between eighteen and twenty-one years of age. In absolute numbers, however, convictions remained steady, probably because girls of this age were welcome in the booming economy of wartime. They had little need to participate in theft, the dominant crime of children. Therefore, girls made up a larger contingent of all juvenile delinquents not because they were committing more crimes, but because boys of draft age were committing fewer.

Not reflecting an unambiguous increase in crime by children, official statistics cannot account for the moral panic about juvenile delinquency that spanned the fifty years after 1890. More general uneasiness about the changing definition of childhood and social roles of children lay behind the tendency to categorize children as increasingly deviant and immoral. Demographically, the Italian population was bulging with children by the late nineteenth century because of a sharp decline in the mortality rates, especially among infants and children. As we saw in Chapter 2, Italians adopted birth control only slowly and with great regional variation after 1890, so that family size remained rather large. On the eve of World War I, the median number of children per family was still close to four.[21] Although this number of siblings had been normal for upper-class children in preindustrial Italy, lower-class children after unification faced the novel situation of competing for economic support and emotional sustenance with a large number of brothers and sisters. Even more disadvantaged were children born outside of marriage. Rising from the end of the eighteenth century, the illegitimacy rate peaked in the 1880s, when 7.5 percent of all babies were born to unwed mothers.[22] Most unwanted children of single mothers were abandoned at foundling homes, established by the Church and state to discourage infanticide.

Traditionally, most Italian children, whether legitimate or not, began to work at a young age either as part of the productive unit of the family or as apprentices or servants outside their homes. This pattern began to change after Italian unification, as the new state organized a system of public schools, and education became compulsory. The need for education was overwhelming; 69 percent of the population aged six and over were illiterate in 1871 when the acquisition of Rome completed unification.[23] Legislation was inadequate. When the Casati Law of 1877 made school compulsory, it required attendance for a mere two years, a figure raised to three in 1888. Since the funding and organization of elementary education was left to the local communal government, many rural areas could only gradually introduce the facilities required by national law. Truancy was widespread and encouraged by parents, especially in the South, who needed the labor of their children to augment the family budget. With these impediments, it is not surprising that many children lapsed back into illiteracy, especially if they came from areas that spoke a dialect and were therefore learning Italian as a foreign language. The situation was bleakest for girls, since the Casati Law segregated schools and curricula by gender. While primary education for boys included geometry and linear drawing, girls were

to supplement their alphabet only with non-academic *lavori donneschi* or female domestic skills.[24] That the Italian government, the Church, and even parents were
unwilling to devote resources to female education is clear from the disparity in illiteracy rates: while those of men fell from 62 to 42 percent between 1871 and 1901,
those for women began at a higher 72 percent and fell only to 54 percent during the
same period.[25] Girls, therefore, entered the workforce with many fewer skills then
boys.

With industrialization, patterns of child labor began to change. Domestic service
continued to employ a large number of adolescents in northern and central Italy,
but the gender composition of the workforce changed dramatically. Most servants
had been male in the eighteenth century, yet the profession became increasingly
feminized during the nineteenth.[26] Although the majority of children, like women,
probably remained in the unmodernized sectors of the economy, a significant number were drawn into the early stages of industrialization. Women and children out-
numbered adult men in the textile workshops and factories, the mainstay of the
Italy's late nineteenth-century industrial economy. Employers could pay children
even less than women and believed that their small hands and bodies were especially dexterous in trades such as textiles and mining. Child labor was perhaps
heaviest in silk manufacturing, which employed over 64,000 children, or almost a
third of the workforce, in 1876.[27] By 1890, despite the proliferation of schools, the
percentage had dropped only to 21 percent. Rates of child labor in the cotton and
wool industries were lower, but also significant: in 1894 minors made up 12 percent
of all wool workers and in 1901 they made up 13 percent of all cotton workers.[28]
Most of them were female as was the large preponderance of adult workers. Sulfur
mining, an important export industry in Sicily, also employed large numbers of children. When Sicily was annexed to united Italy in 1861, 50 percent of its 10,000
workers were minors,[29]

Protective legislation, while weak and badly enforced, gradually redefined childhood as a period devoted to education rather than work. Attendance at school was
increasing, and the percentage of the wage earners who were children dropped from
24 percent in 1876 to 14 percent in 1903, and to 10 percent in 1911.[30] According to
Louise Tilly's statistics for Milan between 1894 and 1911, even migrants—the most
economically unstable portion of all urban residents—pulled their children out of
the workforce and began to send them to school.[31] Probably the law alone could not
have produced this dramatic rewriting of the life cycles of Italy's youth. Legislation
requiring elementary education and restricting child labor was reinforced by a
changing economy, one that was moving away from a heavy reliance on textiles.
Like women, children were less in demand as Italian industry became increasingly
dependent on heavy industry and an adult, male workforce.

Although children had no political rights, their position in family law was set
forth in the Civil Code of 1865. Legitimate children fell under the rule of the father
according to the traditional doctrine of *patria potestà*. He had the right to control
the property of his offspring, make decisions about their education, and decide
when they could marry or be "emancipated" from his control. With his permission,

daughters could marry at fifteen and their brothers at eighteen.[32] Before reaching legal majority at twenty-one, both could be emancipated by their fathers at the age of eighteen.[33] At marriage or emancipation, children took control of their own property, although the assets of married daughters passed into the management of their husbands.

Sons and daughters entered adulthood with more legal equality than in the preunification states of the peninsula. At twenty-one, both reached legal majority if they were not already married or emancipated by their fathers. Single girls could, like boys, choose their place of residence, own and manage property, and join the labor force. The law no longer required that girls receive a dowry, an innovation that was intended to facilitate marriage and free women from being wooed simply for their property. In return, sons and daughters were to inherit equally upon the death of parents. Less fortunate were illegitimate children, who had no claim on their father's property. Gender equality dissolved at the time of marriage: sons gained control over their wives' property, while daughters once again became legal minors in the houses of their husbands. From its passage, the Civil Code was contested by female emancipationists, who felt that it had not gone far enough in bringing equality to the family. They demanded that mothers share with fathers the power of *patria potestà*, and that girls retain control over their own property after marriage.

Such debates over education, child labor, and family law were occurring during a period of demographic flux and economic change. Most migrants to Italy's burgeoning cities were young and many under twenty-one, the legal age of minority according to the Civil Code. Rather than forming part of families, as children or servants, an increasing number of youth lived alone on wages from factories, construction, or piecework. Such a radically new pattern frightened middle-class observers, who perceived an increasing number of children as abandoned and potentially criminal. Thus, despite steady or declining rates of juvenile crime, the state turned to experts like positivist criminologists to explain and curtail deviancy among youth.

POSITIVIST VIEWS OF CHILDREN

Criminal anthropologists challenged many traditional views of children in their attempt to trace the seeds of born criminality back to infancy. Unlike their contemporaries, they were not surprised that children could commit delinquent acts for, as Lombroso always insisted, "crime . . . appears to be a natural phenomenon; in the language of philosophers, it is a necessary phenomenon like birth [and] death."[34] "Instinctively cruel acts," therefore, were common not just to animals, but to humans of all ages.[35] That Lombroso believed children to be closer to their atavistic origins than adults was clear from the organization of the last edition of *Criminal Man*, which opened with a chapter on crime in plants and animals, followed by a second on "savages," and a third on children. This intuition that children occupied the same evolutionary stage as primitive peoples was present in his writings as early as *White Man and Colored Man*, in which he proved the cultural inferiority of Africans and Asians by arguing that their language and art resembled that of European children.[36] He also compared both groups to the insane, another group arrested in its physical and psychological development.

Sighele agreed, writing in his collection of essays, *The Ideas and Problems of a Positivist*, that "the public believes that infants are *angels*, while they are nothing but *savages*."[37] The explanation for this shocking truth lay in Haeckel's biogenetic law, which held that ontogeny reproduces philogeny. In other words, as Sighele elucidated for his general audience, "from the moment of conception until that of birth, the individual reproduces all the phases through which the species has evolved. . . . As we reproduce in our fetal development the physiology of our prehuman ancestors, similarly during the first years of life we reproduce the psychology of our human ancestors."[38] For Sighele, as for his positivist colleagues, Haeckel's law implied that "the germs of crime thus exist not as a rare exception, but as the rule, in all children."[39]

In an article in the *Archives* of 1883, Lombroso and his fellow positivist Antonio Marro listed the many ways in which children were morally depraved. Such a notion was revolutionary in that it contradicted the prevailing view that babies were born innocent. Such had been the belief since the Enlightenment, when Jean-Jacques Rousseau's *Emile* counseled that children be left to follow their natural instincts, which were good and healthy.[40] It was society, usually in the form of authoritarian mothers or brutal nurses, that promised to corrupt and cripple the innate sense of justice and morality in infants. Victorian culture perpetuated this belief in the innocence of babies, simply wrapping it with sentimentality. Lombroso and Marro flatly contradicted the widespread faith in innate benevolence, asserting that "the germs of moral insanity and criminality are found normally, and not as an exception, in the early years of man."[41] Rather than emerging pure, children were born without moral sense and with emotional traits similar to the born criminal. Youthful vices included anger, cruelty, dishonesty, vanity, and idleness.

The crying of newborns showed that anger came naturally to babies. Lombroso and Marro quoted approvingly an expert on child psychology who argued that "by their first birthdays, the anger [of babies] has grown to the point that they hit people, break dishes, and throw them at those who displease them, precisely like those savages the Dakota [Indians] who go into a fury when they kill bison and the Fiji [Islanders] who exhibit very excitable but not enduring emotions."[42] Much of this anger expressed a sense of revenge against nurses when they finished breast feeding or mothers when they disciplined bad behavior. In such cases, children reacted to adults by scratching, screaming, hitting, or even biting like "bears in a cage."[43] For Lombroso and Marro, such behavior proved that "anger is therefore an elementary emotion in man that can be controlled but never be hoped to disappear."[44]

Linked to anger was the exquisite cruelty of youth. According to Garofalo, "Almost all children during the first years of their life seem destitute of moral sense. Their cruelty to animals is well known, as is also their propensity to seize what belongs to others."[45] Lombroso and Marro enumerated the favored pastimes of one child: "He delights in poking animals, in drowning flies, in beating his dog, [and] in suffocating sparrows."[46] They concluded that children indulged in cruelty and anger because they lacked the higher faculties needed to control such passions.

Impulsiveness also led children to tell lies without shame. Lombroso even recalled a case in his own young life when he had tricked the family doctor into believing that he had a stomachache to avoid learning his arithmetic lesson. More appalling, however, was the fickleness of youthful affections. At the age of seven, "Children can forget their own mothers whom they appear to love very much. Often one can also see two or three-year-old children who cause [their mothers] serious pain by their insults."[47] In short, children resembled "prostitutes, who are attached to you only by the gifts given to them and the hope of receiving more and cease to love you when there is less hope of gain."[48] Lombroso admitted that there were exceptions, including his own late son, "my angel whose sweet and bright eyes still shine at me from the grave."[49] But, as in the case of the few "good savages," the exception confirmed the rule that young bodies could not thrive with such sensitivity.

The vanity of children, or their preoccupation with themselves at the expense of others, also reminded criminal anthropologists of megalomaniacs and born criminals. According to positivist anecdotes, children rejected equality by always wanting to be first; the sons of the rich lorded over those of the poor. Even babies cried if they were not dressed in their favorite clothes. A related moral lapse was jealousy, which was "common to all animals."[50] Jealousy led to rivalry among children, especially siblings, for both material possessions and love.

Finally, children resembled savages and criminals in their tendency to idleness and abhorrence of sustained work or learning. Criminal anthropologists did not deny a seemingly contradictory characteristic of youth, "that of changing position continually, of wanting new toys, of wishing to be among many friends . . . [and] participating together in orgies of movement and noise."[51] But like criminals, children took part willingly only in activities that gave them pleasure and did not require thinking. Among these activities was masturbation, since "all abnormal and monstrous sexual, like almost all criminal, tendencies begin in the first years of life."[52]

Despite this grim picture of childhood, positivist criminologists promised that most youth would mature into normal adults. For boys, this meant losing atavistic, criminal traits like cruelty, vanity, dishonesty, and idleness and joining the elite group at the top of the evolutionary ladder, adult males. Girls never lost these unfortunate characteristics so that they would continue to resemble children all their lives. They would, however, develop countervailing virtues like piety, modesty, and maternity that would keep their dangerous and delinquent tendencies under control. To explain how normal adults could emerge from the cocoons of "semi-criminals," Garofalo recalled the biogenetic law, that "the evolution of the individual is an epitome of that of the species."[53] As the black and brown races had supposedly evolved into the white race, children would mature from atavism to adulthood.

Yet a significant minority of adults committed crimes, indicating that they had not successfully completed the transition from childhood. Positivist criminologists puzzled over the mechanism of this transition, and their writings contain a number of hypotheses as to why certain individuals experienced "a state of *prolonged child-hood*," that is, why they remained deviant.[54] Numerous studies made the point that criminal children inherited their traits from their parents and could be identified through similar physical anomalies. Lombroso and Marro estimated that up to 58 percent of all juvenile delinquents were born criminals, a rate higher than that for adults. The *Archives* regularly reported studies of inmates in various juvenile refor-matories, listing their physical anomalies and those of their parents.[55] Raffaele Gurrieri, a follower of Lombroso, even measured the rate of tattooing among 170 youth in the Reformatory of Bologna, finding "the not unimportant percent of 31.76."[56] Popular designs included letters, numbers, hearts, hands, and crosses. Ac-cording to the director of the reformatory, "the tattooed youth always stood out as undisciplined; and in the recent riot they were among the ringleaders in the tenac-ity of their resistance."[57]

Although such reports generally counted anomalies among groups of delinquent youth, some studies focused on especially sensational and exemplary cases. In 1886, for example, a doctor Stura published in the *Archives* his detailed examination of G.B. di M., "a case of moral insanity." Stura identified in his patient a series of anomalies like facial asymmetry, a deformed nose, and "a wild look."[58] The boy seemed a throwback in evolution with his "ape-like hands," while his atrophied genitals and "female-shaped breasts" threw his masculinity into doubt.[59] Yet he was sexually active, having begun to masturbate at the early age of nine. The boy's life at home was marked by traumas like falling into a well, experiencing convulsions, and undergoing a blow to the head. After taking up drink at a young age, the boy began to run away from home and school, leading the life of a vagabond and thief. Stura clearly held the boy's parents responsible for passing down an abnormal heredity. The father, a tavern owner, had "a very bad character" that expressed itself in "bloody acts of ferocity and lust" toward his mate like plucking out all of her pubic hairs.[60] Noting that the father often became drunk, Stura attributed such bizarre behavior to "alcoholic insanity."[61] Stura had little more sympathy for the mother, whom he described as a prostitute harboring so little affection for her son that she interned him immediately after birth in a foundling home.

As in the case of G.B., criminal anthropologists classified parents as abnormal on the basis of a variety of criteria. The most obvious included criminality, insanity, and alcoholism. But unmarried parents, especially those who gave up their children as foundlings, were assumed to pass on degenerate genes to their offspring. Claiming that 18 to 20 percent of all juvenile delinquents were orphans, Lombroso affirmed, "with the greatest certainty, that the greater part of the foundlings that es-cape death abandon themselves to crime. Doubtless heredity enters largely into this result."[62] The last phrase constitutes a case of slippery logic, since the bad environ-ment in orphanages could just as easily have led their charges toward a life of crime. But from the middle-class perspective of Lombroso, only parents suffering from moral insanity could be so insensitive as to abandon their children.

As the doctor of the regional jail [*carcere giudiziario*] of Turin, Marro hypothe-sized that the age of parents determines the biological makeup of their offspring. He praised the eugenicist Francis Galton for having explained how a brilliant father might have a mediocre child if the mother's "gemmule[s]" or genes were inferior to his.[63] Yet why were there such differences between siblings in the same family? From observation of his childhood friends, he began to suspect that children of either extremely young or old parents could inherit "anomalous physical and psychological characteristics."[64] Based on his research at the Turin prison, he claimed to have confirmed his theory, finding that children of young parents tended to be thieves while those of older parents committed crimes of violence. His reasoning became convoluted, since parents were not always of the same age, and the teachers he consulted praised the children of young mothers. But he partially discounted the hereditary role of mothers, since "the mother enjoys greater power to transmit her emotional than intellectual faculties to her children."[65] Lombroso found Marro's argument so convincing that he included a table correlating types of crime with parents' age in his *Atlante*, the appendix to the fifth edition of *Criminal Man*.[66]

Despite the weight of heredity in the writings of positivist criminologists on childhood, they did not discount the role of education. They were most convinced of the value of early moral training by mothers. According to Garofalo, in a passage repeated approvingly by Lombroso,

The children of a loving mother, affectionate or severe as the case demands, become accustomed to watch for the approbation or blame in her look. What penalty can be greater than the grieved reproof which the mother gives the child who has lied or maltreated a companion? Such a child will acquire, month by month and year by year, an instinct opposed to falsehood, theft, and cruelty, a physiological aversion, thanks to which crime will be for him no longer possible.[67]

Such maternal education would be most successful in a home also offering a healthy physical environment, that is, one free from debilitating diseases like syphilis, alcoholism, and tuberculosis.

Criminal anthropologists were less convinced of the value of formal schooling, believing that "the family can accomplish far more than the teacher."[68] Ferri railed against "the sentimental declamations of popular writers" who promised that universal education would solve all social problems.[69] Classifying human beings into the very good, the very bad, and those of an "average nature," he singled out the last group as most affected by education. The very good did not need education to act morally while criminal anthropology had established the intractability of inborn criminality. Only the middle group, admittedly the largest, might benefit from education, although he warned that human progress would always be slow. Citing Galton and Darwin, he put more faith in natural selection than education to weed out the unfit and gradually improve the moral level of society. For Ferri and his colleagues, advanced literacy always held the danger of making criminals more astute, especially in carrying out modern economic crimes, like fraud and graft, that relied on intelligence rather than violence.

As in the case of adults, positivist criminologists recommended different treatment for juvenile delinquents with hereditary taint than for those formed by an immoral environment. To identify the former, they recommended tight surveillance over children in the home, in school, and on the streets. Such troublemakers needed to be removed from such environments where they might contaminate their innocent peers, even before committing any infraction of the law. As Lombroso explained, "Preventive isolation of the criminal is considerably facilitated by new advances in anthropology; for the characteristics of physiognomy and cranium, taken together with biological characteristics and the excess of tendencies to evil-doing, assist powerfully in distinguishing the dominant and always increasing criminality of the born criminal from that which is found temporarily in the case of all children."[70] He warned that "children of this type, notwithstanding their tender age, are a social danger, and the moral disease from which they suffer should be taken in hand at once."[71] With such preventive measures, the state could assure that schools did not become "criminal centers."[72]

Criminal anthropologists counseled that only "antisocial, harmful, [and] incorrigible elements"—that is, born juvenile delinquents—should be sent to prisons.[73] There, according to Ferri, they should be "segregated from society, without false humanitarianism and without useless cruelty."[74] Lombroso warned against intellectual education in prisons, saying that it only created more crafty criminals. But he and his colleagues approved of training in manual labor, preferably in agriculture. In seeming contradiction to their belief in biological determinism, positivist criminologists always held out the hope that a born juvenile delinquent might reform if kept under surveillance from infancy and disciplined by work. Reform might be rare, but the penal system should always be ready to release the exceptional child who overcame his inborn, evil tendencies.

Despite their sensational rhetoric about the evil in all children and the incorrigibility of "born" juvenile delinquents, criminal anthropologists were generally optimistic about the possibility of diverting most minors from crime. Since most juvenile lawbreakers were occasional criminals, they would be susceptible to a range of "penal substitutes." Not only the sociologically oriented Ferri, but also Lombroso recognized that poverty, hunger, and homelessness encouraged begging, theft, and violence among youth and called on the state to improve the living conditions of lower-class families. In Lombroso's words, the family was "that preservative against crime" which, in most cases, provided the best environment for children.[75] But what about orphans, or, "children who have a family, but a perverse family, at whose dinner table sits dishonor and crime?"[76] The next best option was adoption, which would plunge an endangered youth into "a veritable moral bath in the middle of an honest family."[77] As adoption was rare in late nineteenth-century Italy, Lombroso cited evidence from other nations to support his case. He also urged lay charities to organize nurseries and day schools to help families as well as orphanages to raise abandoned children. Criticizing the Church's domination of most philanthropy in Italy, he expressed a socialist conviction that in the future it would be based "on cooperation and finally collectivism."[78]

Even if such preventive measures failed, criminal anthropologists warned against sending children to prison. They recommended innovative and progressive alternatives, like suspended sentences and parole, to keep youth out of reformatories, the so-called "houses of correction."[79] Dubbed "houses of corruption" by Sighele, reformatories admitted a combustible mixture of delinquents convicted of crimes and disobedient youth interned by their fathers, and thus did not allow the individualized punishment so dear to positivists. Considering reformatories as a last resort, Lombroso demanded that they "admit a small number of individuals and divide them into categories of class, age, habits, attitudes, [and] morals."[80] Citing models from Europe and the United States, he advised that reformatories be reorganized as industrial or agricultural schools, whose purpose would be reform rather than punishment.

JUVENILE JUSTICE, 1900–15

Having already developed a theory about deviancy among children, criminal anthropologists were in a strong position to influence the debate about juvenile delinquency that developed during the first decade of the twentieth century. Positivist research was well known to Giolitti, prime minister during most of the era, and to Alessandro Doria, his new and dynamic director general of prisons. Although Lombroso was less active at the national level during his last years, disciples like Ferri, Garofalo, and Bianchi sat in Parliament and participated in the frequent debates about the problem of juvenile crime. Other positivists, like Sighele and De Sanctis, were appointed, in their capacity as university professors, to a special parliamentary committee to study juvenile delinquency, which began meeting in 1909. Having themselves raised fears about exploding rates of crime by young born criminals, criminal anthropologists now put themselves forward as experts offering "scientific" solutions to the problem. As with the issue of police, they raised their professional visibility and stature by creating a moral panic that would encourage the state to implement their own agenda for legislative reform.

As with the issue of police, positivist criminologists were able to find political allies for the implementation of their ideas. To do so, they tended to emphasize the "soft" or liberal side of their theory, that is, the part that held most children to be occasional criminals and therefore malleable to reform. Their well-known views that children should be diverted from prison won approval from others in the new movement for the protection of children that was forming in the early years of the century. Usually liberal or socialist, these advocates included feminists, who often shared the views of criminal anthropologists on child welfare while continuing to reject their ideology of female inferiority. Measures for reforming Italy's system of juvenile justice thus formed part of a larger national debate about how far the state should intervene to protect children in the home, on the streets, at school, and at work.

Parliament took up first the issue of juvenile reformatories, at the behest of Giolitti and Doria. That Giolitti took a personal interest in juvenile crime and often defended his legislation in Parliament attests to the importance that the question had taken on even at the highest reaches of the state. He could rely on support from many in Parliament, like Deputy Pilade Mazza who warned in 1902 that "an innumerable army of abandoned adolescents are growing up in the poisoned atmosphere of the streets and tomorrow will become the advanced contingent of a phalanx of habitual criminals."[81] Mazza's use of the label "habitual criminal" echoed criminal anthropology, which taught that bad environment could turn even normal children into occasional criminals and finally into such severe recidivists that they would be unable to break the habit of crime.[82] By adulthood, such individuals posed as much threat to society as born criminals.

Before the passage of new legislation on reformatories during the decade prior to World War I, legal prescriptions for minors were simply appended to more general laws. According to the Zanardelli Criminal Code of 1889, individuals under twenty-one were to receive special consideration in sentencing.[83] The choice of twenty-one as the age of majority was consistent with the Civil Code that allowed fathers to exercise *patria potestà* until the same age. Children under nine years of age were totally exempt from criminal prosecution as were children between nine and thirteen when a judge ruled that they had acted without *discernimento* or the maturity to distinguish right from wrong. For convicted minors under fourteen who had understood the illegality of their offense as well as for those aged 14–17 and 18–20, the law prescribed reduced sentences. Leniency was inversely correlated with age, so that sentences for the age group of 18–20 most closely approximated those of adults.

Judges could assign children under nine years of age or those who had acted without *discernimento* to internment in what was termed a reformatory, but was usually no more than a jail.[84] In the early years of the twentieth century, Italy already had forty-six reformatories.[85] The state ran only eleven; private organizations, mostly religious charities, administered the majority. The disparity was most marked for girls who had access to only one government reformatory, that of Perugia. The total number of beds in all reformatories—8,355—was significantly higher than the number of young delinquents. The majority of the inmates had not been sentenced in court but were admitted at the request of fathers who could use *patria potestà* to turn disobedient sons and daughters over to the discipline of Church and State.[86] In 1901, for example, 60 percent of admissions to public reformatories and 67 percent to private ones followed paternal petitions to judges.[87] Thus, the heterogeneity of Italian reformatories extended to their inmate populations, which included both delinquents and children who had never broken the law. Government reformatories were often annexed to regular prisons, and no statutes required that children be treated any differently from adults.

Beginning in 1904, the Italian state began to issue a series of legislation to reform and unify the principles undergirding the treatment of incarcerated minors. A law of 1904 split reformatory personnel from prison guards, requiring that the former be teachers rather than simply custodians of their charges.[88] By 1907, all reformatory personnel were required to be certified in primary education, further emphasizing the mission of reforming minors. To specialize the training of reformatory instructors, the law promised future courses in criminal law, pedagogy, and "the elementary principles of anthropology."[89] These moves to change reformatories from prisons to schools were in line with the opinion of Lombroso and his colleagues that traditional prisons were schools of nothing but crime. Most children promised to grow out of their youthful deviance if encouraged by teachers rather than infected by more vicious criminals as was customary in regular penitentiaries.

The physical separation of reformatories from prisons was presaged in a brief decree in 1905 mandating two separate bureaucracies within the Ministry of the Interior.[90] The process was finally complete in 1907 with the issuance of a detailed "Regulation on Government Reformatories." This law stipulated four categories of youth eligible for admission to public reformatories: "corrupted minors who have rebelled against paternal authority" under the age of twenty-one; beggars and prostitutes under the age of eighteen who had been picked up by police; juvenile delinquents under the age of nine or those under the age of fourteen who acted without *discernimento*; and first offenders between nine and thirteen years old at the recommendation of a judge.[91] As in the past, the reformatories were to house a curious combination of criminal, homeless, and rebellious youth. Again, mostly minors who had not broken the law would populate the reformatories, since convicted minors over thirteen were not admissible under the law. They would remain in adult prisons even though civil law defined them as minors.

The Regulation on Reformatories made few distinctions between the sexes, devoting only four articles specifically to girls and declaring that "the same system of education and discipline would be applied" in male and female reformatories.[92] Yet the few exceptions to this rule, made to accommodate "the special necessities of the [female] sex," promised to vitiate this equality in practice.[93] In addition to elementary education, girls over the age of fourteen had to learn "domestic tasks" by working "in the kitchen, in the laundry, in the supply room, in the storerooms, and in the general cleaning of the institution."[94] Boys were under no such obligation. In addition, girls were unlikely to enjoy the special training envisioned for boys, which included military exercises, gymnastics, industrial design, music, and even a course for firefighters. Such special skills would have been considered inappropriate for girls or outside the competence of the nuns staffing their institutions. For the personnel at girls reformatories—whether public or private—was to be religious, unlike the civilian teachers provided for boys at state-run institutions. Even the positivist and anti-clerical Lombroso approved of surveillance by nuns over deviant girls whose "great susceptibility to suggestion" made them more pliant to religious conversion than boys.[95]

Besides the general movement toward separating minors from the contamination of adult felons, early legislation on juvenile delinquency also incorporated two specific proposals that had long been touted by criminal anthropologists. The first was the penal substitute of the "suspended sentence" (*condanna condizionale*), which in 1904 was granted only to children under the age of eighteen.[96] If convicted of a crime carrying a penalty of six months or less in a reformatory, a minor could be released under the supervision of certain benevolent societies (*patronati*) newly organized to help delinquent youth. In 1913, the new Code of Criminal Procedure expanded eligibility of this program to minors sentenced to one year of incarceration.[97] Second, the Regulation on Reformatories of 1907 required that a "biographical dossier" (*cartella biografica*) be compiled on each inmate, recording his or her "anthropological and anthropometric characteristics."[98] Based on this information, prison personnel could assess the "dangerousness" of interned children, categorizing them into born and occasional criminals. To implement this reform, Doria turned to Ottolenghi, who, with the help of positivist colleagues like Sergi, provided reformatories with a series of increasingly detailed forms.[99] Again, children were the object of positivist experimentation, as Ottolenghi had not yet successfully convinced prison officials to require biographical dossiers of all adults. Not willing to tamper with traditional legal procedures for adults, Parliament was more willing to apply positivist innovations to minors in the name of protection. The benefits of this protection were double-edged. On the one hand, suspended sentences lightened punishment for children. On the other hand, the collection of extensive personal information in the biographical dossiers invaded the privacy of minors in a way that was as yet inadmissible for adults.

After the passage of his Regulation on Reformatories in 1907, Giolitti boasted that officials would now be able to distinguish between "reformable offenders and others for whom it is useless to do anything," categories paralleling the positivist ones of occasional and born criminals.[100] Based on the biographical dossiers,

we . . . have adopted a system of separation, putting to one side those least susceptible to reform, because we can have no illusions about some youth assigned to reformatories. We have therefore adopted a system of separation: those with better conduct are kept away from those with worse conduct; the latter are put in special reformatories so they do not corrupt the former. And I can assure you that all those reformatories that admit reformable youth have given really splendid results.[101]

The last statement implied that Giolitti's legislation had quickly solved the pervasive problems in Italy's system of juvenile internment.

Many members of Parliament supported the principle of separation between incarcerated juveniles and adults, but did not agree that the new reformatories ran smoothly. In 1910, during a debate in the Chamber of Deputies, for example, the jurist Alessandro Stoppato praised the idea of reformatories for bringing together "popular sentiment" and "scientific perceptions" about how to combat the "riotous nature of delinquent youth."[102] But he added that the number of government reformatories was so inadequate that 9,000 minors remained in adult penitentiaries at the end of 1909, mixed with "assassins, thieves, pimps, swindlers, and similar filth."[103] In 1914, on the eve of World War I, another deputy, Camillo Peano, was still complaining that about half of all youth sentenced to reformatories could not be admitted for lack of space. According to his statistics, over 2,000 youth remained in regular prisons.[104] Others complained that judges often refused to convict minors, since they knew that few openings existed in the reformatories.

Despite the problems with implementation, the law of 1907 at least brought Italy into line with other Western nations on the issue of juvenile reformatories. Separated from adults, delinquent youth were now sent to institutions that, at least in principle, had a mission to educate and reform rather than punish. Less progress was made in establishing juvenile courts, where minors would be tried according to less rigid and legalistic procedures than those prescribed for adults. Embarrassed that Italy lagged behind other European nations and the United States in establishing a separate code of criminal procedure for children, Giolitti issued a circular to magistrates in 1908, recommending that each district designate a single judge to handle all cases in which the defendant was a minor.[105] This judge was to make inquiries about the defendant's family and friends, for the purpose not only of establishing guilt or innocence but also of prescribing the best type of corrective measures for the child. The circular also requested that trials of minors and adults be held at different hours, to avoid contamination of the former by the latter. Several major cities complied with the circular, while most ignored a directive that did not yet have the approval of Parliament.

The circular constituted only a prelude to what Giolitti and his Minister of Justice, Orlando, hoped to be a radical overhaul of Italy's system of juvenile justice. In 1909, Orlando appointed a "Royal Commission to study juvenile crime," usually called the Quarta Commission after its president.[106] Oronzo Quarta, a senator and public prosecutor of the Supreme Court of Appeal (*Corte di cassazione*) in Rome, assembled a committee dominated by members of the positivist school, including the deputies Ferri and Luigi Credaro, the professors Sighele, De Sanctis, and Antonio Martinazzoli, the lawyer Antonio Guarnieri-Ventimiglia, and the judge Raffaele Majetti. Doria, Director General of Prisons, also participated as did two women, Ersilia Majno Bronzini and Lucy Bartlett. The two women, a rarity on parliamentary committees, had relevant expertise: Majno Bronzini directed a lay charity for "endangered" girls, the Mariuccia Refuge (*Asilo Mariuccia*), while Bartlett had founded a network of benevolent institutions (*patronati*) to supervise youth released on suspended sentences.[107] President of the National Female Union (*Unione Femminile Nazionale*), an organization of bourgeois and socialist feminists, Majno Bronzini brought a perspective to the commission that emphasized the rights of women as well as children.

Although the Quarta Commission also included members of the classical school, like Senator Lucchini, positivist terminology pervaded its proceedings. Some of the dicussion reflected the "hard" or conservative side of positivist theory, that is, the warning that a growing phalanx of young and monstrous born criminals posed a dire threat to Italian society. In his report to the king explaining the need for such a commission, Minister Orlando cited the rapid rise in crime during the first decade of the century, an increase that Lucchini and many classical criminologists contested.[108] Orlando went on to credit "the sociological and anthropological sciences" with having focused public attention on the problem of juvenile delinquency, one of whose principle causes lay in "pathological degeneration which, by way of heredity, aggravates the anomalies typical of puberty and adolescence."[109] Similarly, in the introduction to the final report of the commission, Quarta warned that some juvenile delinquents were "descended from convicts, alcoholics, vagabonds, or beggars, miserable offspring who have in their blood original sin, the hereditary *virus* of degeneration."[110] Even Majno Bronzini, in her report to the commission on female delinquency, used the language of biological determinism, warning that failure to protect girls from corruption and prostitution would lead to "the degeneration of the race" and "generations of criminals and perverts."[111] Concerns about physical and psychological anomalies led the commission to recommend in its final report that biographical dossiers be prepared on all juvenile defendants.[112]

But most of the work of the Quarta Commission echoed the "soft" or liberal side of criminal anthropological theory. As the final report explained, the underlying principle of their new code was "*less to repress than prevent, less to punish than to educate and rehabilitate.*"[113] Therefore, its members found consensus around positivist concepts like the prevention of crime, individualization of punishment, and diversion from prison. That they wished to fashion a truly innovative approach to juvenile delinquency is clear from the integration of both civil and criminal matters in the new code. It proposed to consolidate all legislation relating to minors—including that on orphans, education, work, emigration, and criminality—into what today would be called a "Bill of Rights" but then was termed a bill to protect the interests of children.

At least half of the articles in the Quarta Code addressed the prevention of juvenile delinquency, especially among children who were either orphans or had been abandoned economically or morally by their parents. Although many private, mostly religious, charities already existed to take care of foundlings, orphans, and "endangered" youth, they would now be coordinated by a "Central Council" headed by a judge from the Court of High Appeal in Rome. State power would be strengthened in regard to not only philanthropic institutions but also fathers, who would forfeit *patria potestà* over neglected or abused children. The Commission blamed drinking for the bad behavior of many parents for, as Majno Bronzini pointed out, "the youth about whom we most worry are almost always children of alcoholics."[114] To counter the bad example of such parents, the code prescribed that primary and secondary schools give several lessons each year on the dangers of drinking. It also proposed that a special delegate from the PS conduct surveillance on all places frequented by children—like schools, workshops, and cinemas—to prevent mistreatment and detect abnormal behavior that might presage delinquency.

If such preventive measures failed, the principle of "individualization" would regulate the disciplining of deviant youth. A "district judge" (*magistrato distrettuale*) for juveniles would oversee the trial and punishment of defendants under the age of eighteen, although he had the power to turn those between sixteen and eighteen over to the regular courts. Criminal anthropologists on the commission opposed this exception, because, as Ferri argued, they wished to see "youth rescued from punishment and prisons; this is an approach that is scientific and must not be ignored."[115] De Sanctis added that "abnormal children with biopathologies" matured slowly, so that their adult personality often did not emerge before the age of eighteen.[116] But the commission finally compromised at sixteen, partially for the pragmatic reason that the present number of reformatories was inadequate for taking in older youth.

To assure the individualized treatment of defendants under sixteen, Ferri recommended that qualifications for the district judge include specialization in criminal anthropology, because "an ordinary judge is too much a jurist and not enough an expert in psychology and education."[117] Other members of the commission objected, either from a fear of separating the new juvenile courts too radically from the traditional system or more pragmatically for financial reasons, since most sitting magistrates would not meet such criteria. Article 3 of the Code thus offered a compromise, asking that district judges "possibly have a special training in the disciplines of biology, pedagogy, and sociology."[118] In addition, the "supreme court" located in the Ministry of Justice and charged with overseeing both the juvenile courts and philanthropic institutions was to include among its members "an official professor of the University of Rome, who has a special expertise in psychiatry and educational sociology."[119] To protect children from the rigors of judicial procedure, the code stipulated that all trials be held privately, behind closed doors. Rather than public prosecutors and defense attorneys, only relatives and representatives of schools and charity organizations would accompany the child to court. In a cooperative rather than adversarial atmosphere, these adults would help the judge fashion an appropriate strategy for reforming the defendant. The judge would also rely on information provided by the anthropological-biographical dossier that would accompany all minors into the courtroom.

Unlike regular magistrates, the district judge had wide discretion in prescribing punishment, so that he could tailor it to each defendant regardless of the crime. The code prevented him only from putting a minor in an adult jail. While awaiting trial, children were either returned to their families, assigned to a charitable institution, or, as a last resort, held in a special ward strictly separated from adults. At the end of the trial, the district judge alone decided whether to acquit or pronounce a sentence, which might range from mild measures like a warning or house arrest of several days to the more rigorous discipline of parole (*libertà sorvegliata*). Like suspended sentences, parole was a penal substitute long called for by criminal anthropologists. Most servere was internment in a philanthropic refuge for minors or, finally, one of the new reformatories. All sentences were conditional—that is, they could be revoked by the district judge if convinced that a child had been properly rehabilitated.

After three years of work, the commission published a five-volume report including a detailed "Juvenile Code" ready for the consideration of Parliament. The principles underlying the code—prevention, individualization, and penal substitutes—carried the endorsement not only of criminal anthropologists, but also other leading experts on juvenile delinquency who did not wholly identify themselves with the positivist school, like Quarta, Edoardo Majno (son of Ersilia Majno Bronzini), Ferriani, Stoppato, Luigi Ordine, and Bernardino Alimena.[120] The writings of Guarnieri-Ventimiglia, a lawyer active in the movement for the protection of children, had evolved from ambivalence to a full embrace of criminal anthropological theory by the time of his appointment to the commission.[121] Ottolenghi, after having received a copy of the Quarta report, sent his approval to the Director General of the PS and assured him that special approaches to juvenile delinquency "will constitute one of the principal parts of the educational program" for future functionaries.[122] Judges on the Courts of Appeal, usually loyal to the Classical School, voted in favor of the proposed Juvenile Code.[123] Even feminists, who denounced positivists for their pronouncements on the inferiority of women, shared their prescriptions for the prevention and rehabilitation of juvenile delinquency.

Despite such a formidable and perhaps unprecedented alliance of legal experts, Parliament never discussed the Quarta Commission's report, much less translated the Juvenile Code into law. On the eve of World War I, reform of the juvenile justice system had gone no further than the Regulation on Reformatories of 1907. Why did Italy fail to put in place a system of juvenile courts similar to those already functioning in most other Western nations? As always, legislative immobility prevented timely discussion and efficient implementation of major reforms. According to a predictable pattern, the careful work of a dedicated parliamentary commission remained a "dead letter," in the parlance of the day. In this case, however, the procrastination of the Chamber of Deputies amounted to more than mindless inefficiency. Fierce opposition to the Juvenile Code came from the Catholic Church in the name of family values. According to the leading Catholic newspaper, the Osservatore romano, the Code threatened "the rights that parents have over the education of their children" by weakening patria potestà.[124] By giving district judges the power to remove "endangered" children from their families and widening the grounds of legal culpability for unfit parents, the code authorized unwarranted intrusion by the state in private matters. Behind this defense of the authority of the father lay a more tangible concern of the Church, control over its charities. Coordination of all philanthropic institutions for children under the new "Central Council" appeared, to religious authorities, to be a thinly disguised attempt by the state to take over a sector traditionally in their domain. In the conflict between Church and state that raged from unification until Mussolini's Concordat of 1929, charities, like schools, were battle grounds for ideological control. Already under criticism for failing to introduce the new pedagogic approach in their reformatories, Catholic officials feared further erosion of their authority over orphanages, refuges, and other philanthropies for children. The prominence of criminal anthropologists on the Quarta Commission strengthened the opposition of the Catholic Church, which had denounced the materialism and socialism of positivist analysis from its earliest days.

JUVENILE JUSTICE, 1915–40

In the short run, the outbreak of World War I preempted parliamentary discussion of domestic legislation, including that on the establishment of juvenile courts. From a long-term perspective, however, the war accelerated the institutionalization of positivist ideas on juvenile crime, both directly, by heightening popular fears of family breakdown, and indirectly, by preparing the political ground for the triumph of fascism. With the overthrow of all vestiges of democracy in 1925, the dictatorship overcame the traditional obstacles to changes in the system of juvenile justice: ideological bickering between the Classical and Positivist Schools, immobility in Parliament, and opposition by the Catholic Church to state interference in the family and its own network of charities. By 1934, Mussolini's regime had implemented almost the entire agenda of criminal anthropology for the treatment of delinquent youth, including reeducation centers and juvenile courts.

World War I led directly to increasingly hysterical warnings that the Italian family was in disarray. In part, such fears were inevitable in the immediate postwar period, since the political system and economy in general seemed to be collapsing. Peasant conscripts had been promised land as a reward for military service and, when the government reneged after the war, they began unilaterally to occupy large stretches of farmland. In the cities, factories were hit by waves of strikes by workers angered by the freezing of wages during the war and, in some cases, insistent on increased proletarian power on the shop floor. Thousands of discharged soldiers, finding no jobs in the weakened economy, joined groups of roving paramilitary organizations, often of the extreme right. Government was unstable as several short-lived ministries were unable to forge successful coalitions in an atmosphere of accelerated radicalization on both the Right and the Left.

Within this general climate of upheaval, criminologists and politicians pointed to children as one group that was particularly out of control. Most obviously, the war had orphaned many children who would now need state support and protection. But, according to the statistician Spallanzani, even children with parents had been abandoned, "on account of the absence of both the father, drafted into the military, and the mother, forced to work outside of the home."[125] Left alone during the day, many children, according to Spallanzani, had developed bad habits that might develop into full-blown delinquency. These habits included drinking, using narcotic drugs, watching pornographic films, and frequenting prostitutes. Such behavior could lead to "social diseases" like alcoholism and syphilis, which, by weakening both the body and the mind, culminated in degeneration and a propensity for crime.

Blame fell particularly hard on mothers, whose visibility as workers was heightened by World War I. Women already participated widely in the wage economy, including the textile industry. But the war brought them into previously male-dominated sectors like metals and weapons. The image of the "new woman" patriotically taking the place of men on the shop floor of munitions factories became familiar to the public through photographs in mass publications.[126] But for experts on crime, like Alessandro De Paolis, director of the prison administration, the entrance of large numbers of women into the industrial sector had a darker side. Writing in *Defense*, he warned that wartime production in factories had promoted "dangerous promiscuity between the two sexes. The enervating work, the high wages and the consequently exceptional availability of resources, united with the absence of husbands, have led many women into an exceptionally libertine and dissolute life that . . . has powerfully contributed to the worsening conditions of the abandonment and related criminality of children."[127] Such invective against working women foreshadowed fascist initiatives to return women to the home in the name of protecting children.

In the face of increased moral panic about juvenile delinquency, voices in Parliament continued to call for the passage of the Quarta reforms. When Ferri was appointed to preside over a parliamentary commission to write a new criminal code, he incorporated many of the Quarta proposals into his report issued in 1921.[128] Consistent with the dictates of criminal anthropology, Ferri recommended an elaborate categorization of minors according to their degree of dangerousness to society; the separation of juveniles from adults during court proceedings; and the replacement of traditional punishment with education for all but those few diagnosed as harboring "a persistent tendency to crime."[129] With six governments following in close succession between the end of the war and the appointment of Mussolini as prime minister in 1922, however, Parliament was too preoccupied to consider the codes of either Quarta or Ferri.

After the fascist seizure of power, government officials continued to lament the rise in juvenile delinquency. The percentage of children among all convicted criminals had already peaked in 1918 at 31 percent. It then steadily declined, reaching 22 percent in 1923, a figure that had not been that low since the previous century. Even though statistics failed to support his hysteria, Deputy Alberto Geremicca in 1926 warned that Italy was being swamped by "that amorphous, indeterminate mass [of abandoned children] who, especially in the large cities, are dedicated to vice, live on the margins, and within whom the seed of crime is rankly growing and waiting for an occasion to bloom."[130] Such cries of alarm show that the fascist regime perceived threats to its authority not only from political opponents, but also from common criminals, in this case deviant youth.

Legislation on juvenile delinquency formed part of the broad initiative by Mussolini to regulate the family for the good of the state. Fascist interest in youth stemmed partly from its demographic campaign to increase the birthrate and produce soldiers for Italy's glorious imperialist future. Thus, in addition to outlawing birth control and abortion, taxing bachelors, discouraging female employment, and rewarding mothers of large families, the state became increasingly protective of infants and their health. Wanting not just quantity but quality, Mussolini devised a series of institutions to mold youth into the fascist "new man" of nationalism, militarism, and obedience. For this purpose, the party inserted fascist ideology into the educational curriculum and devised a series of youth groups, called *Balilla*, to dominate the free time of both boys and girls.

Central to the fascist policy on children was the creation in 1925 of ONMI, the National Commission for the Protection of Maternity and Childhood (*Opera Nazionale per la protezione della maternità e dell'infanzia*). Located within the Ministry of the Interior, ONMI was mandated to give assistance to "pregnant women and mothers who are poor or single; nursing and weaned infants up to five years old from needy families; children who are physically or psychologically abnormal; and minors under eighteen years of age who are materially or morally abandoned, deviant, or delinquent."[131] By giving ONMI the power to coordinate all existing programs dedicated to mothers and children, the fascist government succeeded in breaking the traditional opposition of the Catholic Church to state interference in religious charities. This opposition had been partially responsible for the failure of Quarta's juvenile code, which had proposed placing private religious reformatories under the control of district judges. Once Mussolini assumed dictatorial powers in 1925, however, he was able to enact legislation that the more democratic parliaments of the earlier liberal monarchy, with their countervailing interest groups, had been unable to pass.

Usually analyzed within the context of the development of welfare legislation for women and children, ONMI also deserves an important place in the history of juvenile justice. That deviance among children was a central focus of ONMI from the beginning is clear from its journal, *Maternity and Childhood*. Its directors, with the approval of fascist authorities, appropriated the theories of criminal anthropologists on the identification and treatment of juvenile delinquency. In 1928, for example, an editorial in *Maternity and Childhood* repeated the positivist maxim that "today we try to interpret delinquency and criminality like a pathology and, rather than despising it, try to investigate and cure it."[132] Explaining that all babies are born with "a substratum of tendencies, instincts, [and] inherited anatomical and psychological characteristics," the editors warned that children of parents infected by syphilis, tuberculosis, or alcoholism would be predisposed to deviancy.[133] The article expressed cautious optimism that these children could be cured, but only if their tendency to crime was identified early. Therefore, it recommended that teachers and police exercise strict surveillance over schools, playgrounds, and families, a policy previously recommended by criminal anthropologists and readily accepted by a regime seeking totalitarian control over its citizens.

To complement the views of the editors, *Maternity and Childhood* published three articles by Di Tullio, Ottolenghi's student and colleague at both the School of Advanced Policing and the Department of Legal Medicine at the University of Rome. Although emphasizing the biological roots of criminality, he held that "all children prone to crime (*delinquibili*), even if truly abnormal, are always, at least in part, susceptible to education and re-adaptation to social life."[134] This cautiously optimistic view underpinned his endorsement of "Observation Centers" where a "medical criminologist" (*medico criminalista*) would examine not only convicted delinquents but any child who exhibited physical or psychological anomalies. Using Ottolenghi's biographical dossiers, medical criminologists would record "all salient facts related to the physical and psychological personality" of delinquents and assess their "corrigibility and dangerousness."[135] According to Di Tullio, "this dossier could and should . . . accompany the child always and everywhere," so that teachers and welfare workers could adopt the appropriate treatment.[136] Like other criminal positivists, he never worried that children might be classified incorrectly and stigmatized as a delinquent even before committing any crime.

To implement the new observation centers, positivist criminologists worked closely with the fascist regime. Di Tullio praised the new fascist initiatives for children, like Balilla and ONMI, and promised that the centers would promote "the defense of the race, which has so justly become the aim of the cleansing social policy of the National Fascist Government."[137] Criminal anthropologists were responsible in 1926 for establishing the first experimental observation centers: in Rome, Ottolenghi and De Sanctis established the "Medical-pedagogical clinic for antisocial minors" and, in Genoa, Pende founded his "Institute of biotypology and genetics."[138] Regarded favorably by the regime, their doctors were recruited by ONMI to examine members of fascist youth groups.[139]

The fascist Criminal Code of 1930, usually called the Rocco Code after the Minister of Justice, constituted the next step in institutionalizing the Quarta reforms. It raised the age of *discernimento* from nine to fourteen and lowered the age of full legal responsibility from twenty-one to eighteen. Thus, all children under fourteen were exempt from prosecution, while those over seventeen were presupposed to be fully aware, like adults, of the criminality of their behavior. For minors between fourteen and eighteen, judges had the discretion to decide if defendants had acted with *discernimento*. Raising the age of *discernimento* was consistent with the "soft" side of criminal anthropology, which advocated judicial leniency for children.

Yet the Rocco Code favored the "hard" message of positivism, that some children posed a danger to society and merited strict discipline. Article 226 made special provisions for "minors who are habitual criminals, professional criminals, or criminals by tendency." Also applied to adults, the phrase "criminal by tendency" echoed the "born criminal" and constituted a victory by criminal anthropologists in influencing the new criminal code.[140] The law required that these youth be incarcerated in a special reformatory for at least three years. Fascist authorities thus possessed a legal tool for branding children as dangerous and submitting them to strict discipline. Because the Rocco Code classified reformatories under the rubric of "security measures," Article 226 applied even to children under the age of *discernimento*, who were theoretically free from punishment. Positivism had already supplied fascist lawmakers with a rationale for such contorted logic by arguing that reformatories, because they aimed at education and reform, constituted a "penal substitute" rather than punishment.

In 1934, a "Law on the Institution and functioning of juvenile courts" provided the keystone of fascist policies on deviant children. Consistent with the Rocco Code, the new juvenile courts had jurisdiction over all crimes committed by youth under the age of eighteen. Three judges presided over these courts, two from the regular magistracy and one private citizen "chosen from the practitioners of biology, psychiatry, criminal anthropology [or] education."[141] Before each trial, the state was to collect information about the "physical, psychological, moral, and environmental factors" that might explain the youth's misbehavior and was authorized to "hear the opinions of experts without any formal [judicial] procedure."[142] Once the trial had begun, all proceedings were held behind closed doors; of the general public, only the parents or guardian of the defendant, a local official of ONMI, and representatives of benevolent associations for the protection of children were allowed in the courtroom. Testimony by various types of experts was expected, and the judge could rule that the defendant leave the courtroom during presentation of such evidence or discussions of the causes of his or her deviancy.

Once convicted, minors qualified for a variety of alternative punishments to prison. In line with positivist recommendations of "penal substitutes" for youth, the law allowed judges to replace imprisonment with a judicial pardon (*perdono giudiziale*) or suspended sentence (*sospensione condizionale della pena*) in the case of less serious crimes.[143] They also had wide discretion to grant "conditional release" or parole (*liberazione condizionale*) at any time to a minor, followed by internment in a low-security reformatory or a period of "supervised liberty" (*libertà vigiliata*). Reformatories continued to receive disobedient children at the request of parents and "predelinquent" youth stopped by police. The new law also granted personnel from ONMI and Balilla the explicit right to refer any individual under eighteen who showed "obvious signs of corruption and seem to need moral reformation" to the juvenile courts for internment.[144] In this way, the Law of 1934 implemented the recommendation of criminal anthropologists and other members of the Quarta Commission that surveillance over youth begin in the home and at school to detect any predisposition to crime. But a measure that was initially benevolent in its intention to protect children from abuse now offered a further weapon to fascists against enemies of social and political order, in this case delinquent children.

In the Law of 1934, types of reformatories proliferated to a ridiculous degree. The first type, "reeducation homes" (*case di rieducazione*) took in the least "dangerous" cases, on the recommendation of parents, police, or fascist officials. Most inmates of the reeducation homes were "predelinquent," that is, they had never been convicted of a crime. "Special" reeducation homes were reserved for those who misbehaved in the regular homes. Second, the judicial reformatories (*riformatori giudiziari*) were to receive minors considered "dangerous," whether or not they had committed a crime. Finally, youth convicted of serious crimes served their sentences in juvenile prisons (*case di pena*). Alongside the reformatories were "observation centers," modeled on the experimental institutions pioneered by positivists like Ottolenghi, De Sanctis, and Pende. According to the new law, the principle purpose of these centers was to "carry out scientific examination of youth, ascertain their true personalities, and prescribe the best methods for assuring their reintegration into social life."[145] The observation centers would now form part of new regional complexes labeled "reeducational centers," which would also house the juvenile courts and reformatories. These reeducational centers were clearly intended to separate children from adults within the criminal justice system in both procedural and spatial terms.

Proud of their new institutions of juvenile justice, fascist officials publicized them both home and abroad. The Italian Library of Information distributed a book in English by Pietro Corsi to tout its programs for children to foreign readers. Entitled *The Protection of Mothers and Children in Italy*, it opened with the assertion that "biologists, economists and politicians are today fully endorsing the opinion that numbers are the strength of the nation."[146] Corsi thus placed the entire package of legislation on women and children, including the Law of 1934 on juvenile courts, within the context of Italy's demographic campaign. In the positivist tradition, he blamed tuberculosis, syphilis, and alcoholism for creating juvenile delinquents: "such children are street urchins, vagrants, little beggars and girl prostitutes, a veritable army of subjects predisposed to crime."[147] Citing De Sanctis, he advised that deviant youth be sent to the observation centers for classification, "taking into account the morphological, physiological, psychical, moral and educational development of the child."[148] He claimed that between 1931 and 1934, Italy's observation centers had examined 1,464 minors, creating anthropological-biographical dossiers for each one. Quoting Di Tullio, he predicted that the observation centers would be able to cure most physical and psychological anomalies in children.

For Italian readers, the Minister of Justice, Dino Grandi, issued a two-volume survey of Italy's prison system in 1941, devoting a large portion to the new observation centers and centers of reeducation for youth.[149] Entitled *Human reclamation* (*Bonifica umana*), this government publication equated penal reform with the well-publicized fascist "battles" of land reclamation. According to Grandi, youth should welcome the new institutions of juvenile justice, because they "all comprise one school: a school that is differentiated and more or less difficult but one that always emphasizes honesty, duty, courage, and the love of country."[150] The volumes are filled with photos of happy children at work and play. Grande boasted that the fascist state had "moved the frontier of intervention . . . forward" by including predelinquent youth in its "struggle against physical and moral degeneration."[151] Through screening by Balilla, children who had committed no crime but appeared "abnormal" could be interned in the observation centers. Such a policy promised ominous consequences in a totalitarian regime, where "abnormality" could simply include resistance to fascist indoctrination. This increasing criminalization of youth did not bother fascist functionaries, but instead evoked pride.

Such a plan brought more children into the web of the criminal justice system. While rates of juvenile crime were holding steady or even falling, the number of institutions for minors jumped from forty-six in 1907 to 126 in 1941. Of the 126, thirty-six were observation centers, sixty-eight were houses of reeducation, sixteen were judicial reformatories, and six were juvenile prisons.[152] Clearly, the expansion in incarceration affected mostly predelinquent youth, that is, those interned in the observation centers and houses of reeducation. In order to promote order, discipline, and social homogeneity, the fascist regime took advantage of positivist ideas to justify widespread preventive detention of minors just as the special political tribunals sent adult dissenters to prison or internal exile.

Statistics on the population of juvenile reformatories also document an increase of incarceration during the 1930s. The number of children in detention rose from fewer than 4,000 in 1930 to nearly 6,000 in 1935 and 10,000 in 1941, the year of Grandi's boastful publication on fascist institutions of juvenile justice.[153] Girls were imprisoned in higher rates than boys, a pattern that had also characterized the preceding liberal monarchy. Although the percentage of juvenile crime committed by girls hovered around 11 to 13 percent, they made up 20 to 40 percent of the population in reformatories.[154] Consonant with positivist theory, fascist legal experts diagnosed female deviance as primarily sexual and girls as weak-willed, necessitating their forced exclusion from the streets. Nuns continued to manage all institutions for girls, showing that fascists, like their predecessors, regarded religion as an effective and appropriate restraining force on female sexuality.

CONCLUSION

In 1936, Di Tullio explained the fascist policy toward juvenile delinquency, one that had been drawn explicitly from the theory of criminal anthropology: "It is necessary that the Police . . . operate in a way that will allow surveillance over all minors who, within the family, on the streets, in the schools, and at work, present signs of serious moral perversion and symptoms of a special predisposition to crime; they must be subjected with the greatest haste to the necessary measures of re-education."[155] Di Tullio's words came at a time when the Fascist dictatorship in Italy was at the height of its popularity after a successful imperialist war against Ethiopia. As a foundation for this expansionist foreign policy, Mussolini had already established aggressive domestic legislation to isolate and punish internal enemies of his regime. Although most research has focused on his persecution of political prisoners, fascists also perceived threats to their centralized authority from a variety of "nonpolitical" groups including juvenile delinquents. As Di Tullio's warning indicates, fascist authorities had no scruples about extending their surveillance from the streets into schools and even private homes to identify children who had not yet broken the law but were "predisposed" to disrupt the "new society" of fascism.

Mussolini's regime launched a series of policies for children, inspired by both the "soft" and "hard" aspects of positivist doctrine on juvenile delinquency. On the "soft" or liberal side, ONMI provided services too long neglected by earlier liberal governments, like health care for poor mothers and milk for babies. It overcame traditional prejudices, extending assistance to unwed mothers and illegitimate children. Its legislation on juvenile delinquency echoed the reformist language of the prewar Quarta Commission, calling for education and reform of youth. The Law of 1934 finally mandated the removal of children from adult courts and prisons.

The "harder" or conservative side of positivist theory led to the increasing incarceration of youth, whether in observation centers, reformatories, or juvenile prisons. Although technically labeled as "penal substitutes" or "administrative measures," these institutions indeed criminalized ever larger numbers of youth by subjecting them to examination and classification by the state. Labeled as predelinquent, many were interned in reformatories without benefit of due process. This tendency to institutionalize youth was not new, as most Italian cities since the Middle Ages supported an array of foundling homes, refuges, and conservatories for children.[156] After unification, parents and the police could also admit troublesome minors to the new government reformatories. Fascism continued this historical tradition of incarcerating deviant children, adding a more overtly political dimension to the selection process.

What was innovative in fascist legislation was the definitive separation of children from the traditional network of adult courts and prisons. Although criminal anthropologists had been at the forefront of the campaign to erect an autonomous system of juvenile justice, this policy was not unique to Italy. Instituted in other countries often under the aegis of liberal or socialist governments, juvenile courts received support across the political spectrum in the early twentieth century. Despite their progressive pedigree, however, they harbored contradictions that could, under an authoritarian regime, lead to the repression rather than protection of children. By replacing the adversarial system of due process with the paternalistic council of judge, experts, and parents, children lost the right to a full defense based on uniform procedures. Reformatories, after being labeled institutions of education rather than of punishment, could hold minors for long periods under indeterminate sentencing. Youth, unlike adults, could be interned for behavior that was simply "immoral" rather than illegal.[157]

Such outcomes were likely in a nation where the leading school of criminology had posited that all children were atavistic and that a significant percent of youthful born criminals would never outgrow their immoral and antisocial tendencies. The penchant of criminal anthropologists for classification led them to advocate that ever widening circles of children be submitted to physical and psychological examinations, culminating in Ferri's proposal of 1920 to require schools to draw up anthropological dossiers on all students.[158] With the advent of fascism, positivists like Di Tullio eagerly collaborated with fascists to subject youth to surveillance, discipline, and internment in the name of protecting them from the bad influence of family and friends. Positivists were thus complicit, in the name of science, in weakening the rights of children within a legal system intent on criminalizing any behavior perceived as a threat to the fascist state or social order. They also eagerly cooperated with the state in creating a potential gulag for youth, an autonomous array of institutions holding an ever growing number of children. The ease with which positivist criminology adapted to fascism laid bare its authoritarian tendencies, as the supposedly "scientific" techniques of examination and classification easily developed into regimentation and repression.

NOTES

1. Ferrero, Bianchi, and Sighele, Mondo criminale (1894), v. 2, p. 13.

2. Ibid., pp. 16–17.

3. Ibid., p. 21.

4. Ibid., p. 33.

5. Ibid., p. 40.

6. Ibid., p. 37.

7. Ibid., p. 16. The Catholic Church with Greek rites was associated with descendants of Albanian immigrants.

8. Ibid., p. 42.

9. Ibid., pp. 42–43.

10. Ibid., p. 43.

11. Ibid., p. 45.

12. Ibid., p. 45.

13. Ibid., pp. 46, 44.

14. Ibid., p. 46.

15. Ibid., p. 44.

16. Ibid., p. 51.

17. For an interesting use of the same technique by defense lawyers in an American court, see Idanna Pucci, *The Trials of Maria Barbella* (New York: Vintage Books, 1997).

18. Official statistics for juvenile delinquency were not published between 1930 and 1950, so that statistics for 1940 are not available.

19. The data and calculations in this section are based on ISTAT, *Somm. stat. storiche* (1958), pp. 98–99. The age of minority, as defined in the criminal codes, changed during this period. I am using here the most inclusive definition, consistent with the Zanardelli Code, of those under twenty-one years of age.

20. Alfredo Spallanzani, "Della delinquenza dei minorenni in Italia negli anni 1891–1917 secondo le statistiche giudiziarie," *Scuola positiva*, New series, v. 1 (1921), p. 384.

21. Manoukian, "la rappresentazione statistica," p. 444.

22. Ibid., p. 447. Figures for illegitimacy were somewhat inflated during the first few decades of unification, since after 1866 the new Italian state no longer recognized marriages formalized only in a religious ceremony. Until couples from all classes became accustomed to contracting civil marriages, many continued to contract only religious—and therefore legally unrecognized—unions, whose offspring were technically illegitimate.

23. Clark, *Modern Italy*, p. 36.

24. Simonetta Ulivieri, "La donna nella scuola dall'unità d'Italia a oggi," *Donnawomanfemme*, v. 2 (Jan.–Mar., 1977), p. 28.

25. Ibid., p. 35.

26. Agiolina Arrù, "Protezione e legittimazione: Come si usa il mestiere di serva nell'800," in Lucia Ferrante, Maura Palazzi, and Gianna Pomata, eds., *Ragnatele di rapporti: Patronage e reti di relazione nella storia della donne* (Turin: Rosenberg & Sellier, 1988), pp. 381–416.

27. Camilla Ravera, *La donna italiana del primo al secondo Risorgimento* (Rome: Edizioni di cultura sociale, 1951), p. 30.

28. Ibid., p. 32.

29. Denis Mack Smith, *Italy: A Modern History* (Ann Arbor: University of Michigan Press, 1959), p. 48.

30. Ravera, *La donna*, p. 66.

31. Louise Tilly, "The Working Class of Milan, 1881–1911" (Ph.D. dissertation: University of Toronto, 1973), pp. 210, 210a.

32. Civil Code of 1865, Art. 55.

33. Civil Code of 1865, Arts. 323, 311.

34. C. Lombroso, *L'uomo delinquente*, 5th ed., v. 2, p. 68.

35. Ibid.

36. C. Lombroso, *L'uomo bianco*, pp. 65, 75, and 198.

37. Sighele, *Idee e problemi d'un positivista* (Milan-Palermo-Naples: Remo Sandron, 1907), p. 188.

38. Ibid., pp. 188–89.

39. Ibid., p. 189.

40. Jean-Jacques Rousseau's educational tract, *Emile*, was published in 1762.

41. *Archivio*, v. 4 (1883), p. 7 [Lombroso and Antonio Marro]. An expanded version of this article was incorporated into Volume 1 of the Fifth Edition of *Criminal Man* (1897).

42. Ibid., p. 7.

43. Ibid., p. 9.

44. Ibid.

45. Garofalo, *Criminology*, p. 257.

46. *Archivio*, v. 4 (1883), p. 13.

47. Ibid., p. 12.

48. Ibid., p. 13.

49. Ibid.

50. Ibid., p. 9

51. Ibid., p. 14

52. Ibid., p. 16.

53. Garofalo, *Criminology*, p. 257.

54. C. Lombroso, *L'uomo delinquente*, 5th ed. v. 2, p. 67.

55. In the *Archivio*, for example, see v. 3 (1882), pp. 148–149 [Antonio Siffredi]; v. 3 (1882), pp. 151–153 [Riccardi]; and v. 8 (1887), pp. 83–84 [V. Rossi and A. Tardi].

56. *Archivio*, v. 12 (1891), p. 434 [Raffaele Guerrieri].

57. Ibid., p. 435.

58. *Archivio*, v. 7 (1886), p. 499 [Stura].

59. Ibid.

60. Ibid., p. 498.

61. Ibid.

62. Lombroso, *Crime: Its Causes and Remedies* (Boston: Little, Brown, 1912), 146.

63. *Archivio*, v. 7 (1886), p. 217 [Marro].

64. Ibid., p. 219.

65. Ibid., p. 230.

66. C. Lombroso, *L'uomo delinquente*, 5th ed., v. 4 (*Atlante*), p. lxxxvii.

67. Quoted in C. Lombroso, *Crime*, pp. 303–304.

68. C. Lombroso, *Crime*, p. 303.

69. *Archivio* , v. 4 (1883), p. 26 [Ferri].

70. C. Lombroso, *Crime*, p. 306

71. C. Lombroso, *Criminal Man*, pp. 177–78.

72. C. Lombroso, *Crime*, pp. 307–308.

73. *Archivio*, v. 4 (1883), p. 31 [Ferri].

74. Ibid.

75. C. Lombroso, *L'uomo delinquente*, 5th ed., v. 3, p. 415.

76. *Archivio*, v. 3 (1882), pp. 246–47 [A. Bargoni].

77. Ibid., p. 427.

78. Ibid., p. 364.

79. Sighele, *Idee e problemi*, p. 195.

80. C. Lombroso, *L'uomo delinquente*, 2nd ed., p. 409.

81. Italy, C.D., *Disegni*, Legis. 21:2 (1902–04), v. 6, pp. 20–21.

82. "Habitual criminal" was one of Ferri's famous five categories of criminality, and the label was adopted by Lombroso and the rest of the Positivist School.

83. Criminal Code of 1889, Arts. 53–56.

84. The law of 1889 reorganizing the prison system first used the term "reformatory" to distinguish juvenile jails from those of adults, but made no substantive change in their nature.

85. ISTAT, *Statistica dei riformatori (1908)* (Rome: Mantellate, 1909), p. 3.

86. According to Article 222 of the Civil Code of 1865.

87. ISTAT, *Statistica delle carceri (1901)* (Rome: Mantellate, 1902), p. clxxx.

88. Legge 3 Luglio 1904, n. 318.

89. R.D. 24 Marzo 1907, n. 122, Art. 24.

90. R.D. 10 Novembre 1905, n. 572.

91. R.D. 14 Luglio 1907, n. 606, Art. 1.

92. Ibid., Art. 165.

93. Ibid.

94. Ibid., Art. 167

95. C. Lombroso, *Crime*, p. 406.

96. Legge 26 Giugno 1904.

97. Code of Criminal Procedure of 1913, Art. 423.

98. R.D. 14 Luglio 1907, n. 606, Art. 65.

99. *Boll. SPS*, v. 12–13 (1922–23), p. 86 [Di Tullio].

100. Italy, C.D., *Disc.*, Legis. 23:1 (1909–13), v. 2, p. 1519.

101. Ibid.

102. Italy, C.D., *Disc.*, Legis. 23:1 (1909–13), v. 7, p. 7853.

103. Ibid., p. 7854.

104. Italy, C.D., *Disc.*, Legis. 24:1 (1913–19), v. 3, p. 2433.

105. Circolare 11 maggio 1908.

106. The commission was nominated by R.D. Nov. 7, 1909.

107. See Buttafuoco, *Le Mariuccine*.

108. See Chapter 1.

109. *Commissione reale per lo studio dei provvedimenti contro la delinquenza dei minorenni: Atti* (Rome: Stamperia reale, 1912), v. 1, p. 10.

110. *Comm. reale*, v. 5, p. 30.

111. Ibid., v. 2, p. 225.

112. Ibid., v. 5, p. 71.

113. Ibid., v. 5, p. 28.

114. Ibid., v. 1, p. 155.

115. Ibid., v. 1, p. 47.

116. Ibid., v. 1, p. 51.

117. Ibid., v. 1, p. 54.

118. Ibid., v. 5, p. 35.

119. Ibid., v. 5, p. 38.

120. See for example, Oronzo Quarta, "L'incremento e il trattamento della delinquenza dei minorenni," *Scuola positiva*, v. 18 (Jan., 1908), pp. 1–15; Edoardo Majno, "La difesa ed il giudice dei minorenni," *Congresso giuridico nazionale (VII): Relazioni* (Rome: Gianandrea, 1911), pp. 1–40; Lino Ferriani, *Minorenni delinquenti* (Milan: Kantorowicz, 1895); Alessandro Stoppato, "Per una magistratura special per i minorenni delinquenti," *Riv. disc. carc.*, v. 32 (1907), pp. 19–22; Luigi Ordini, "Il magistrato dei minorenni," *Rivista Penale*, v. 74 (1911), pp. 300–21; Bernardino Alimena, *I limiti e i modificatori dell'imputabilità* (Turin: Bocca, 1894, 1896, 1899), 3 vols.

121. For ambivalence, see Antonio Guarnieri-Ventimiglia, *La delinquenza e la correzione dei minorenni* (Rome: Nazionale, 1906), p. 146; for a full embrace of positivism, see "La tutela sociale dei minorenni e il progetto Giolitti per l'infanzia abbandonata," *Scuola positiva*, v. 18 (Mar.–Apr. 1908), p. 136 and "La difesa ed il giudice dei minorenni," *Congresso giuridico nazionale*, p. 8.

122. ACS, M. Int., PS, Pol. Giud., 1910–12, b. 357, fasc. 12985.4.

123. Domenico Izzo, "Il trattamento dei minorenni delinquenti dalla circolare Orlando al Progetto Ferri (1908–21)," *Rassegna di studi penitenziari*, v. 8 (Mar.–Apr., 1957), p. 177.

124. Quoted in ibid., p. 178.

125. Spallanzani, "Della delinquenza dei minorenni," p. 297.

126. See Paola Di Cori's fascinating analysis of these photographs in her article, "The Double Gaze: Visibility of Sexual Difference in Photographic Representation (1908–1918)," in Mirna Cicioni and Nicole Prunster, eds., *Visions and Revisions: Women in Italian Culture* (Providence, R.I.: Berg, 1993), pp. 89–116. These photographs appeared in popular publications like *L'Illustrazione italiana*, an equivalent of *Life* magazine.

127. *Difesa*, v. 1, n. 7 (1919), p. 12 [De Paolis].

128. See Chapter 6 for a wider discussion of Ferri's proposed criminal code.

129. Izzo, "Il trattamento dei minorenni," p. 87.

130. C.D., *Disc.*, Legis. 27 (1924–27), v. 6, p. 5473.

131. Legge 10 Dic. 1925, n. 2277, Art. 4.

132. La Redazione, "Profilassi della delinquenza dei fanciulli," *Maternità ed infanzia*, v. 3, n. 6 (June, 1928), p. 432.

133. Ibid., p. 434.

134. Di Tullio, "Sulla profilassi e terapia della criminalità minorile, *Maternità ed infanzia*, v. 3, n. 5 (May, 1928), p. 419.

135. Ibid.

136. Ibid.

137. Di Tullio, "I centri di osservazione per i minorenni delinquenti nei rapporti dell'igiene sociale e della difesa della razza," *Maternità ed infanzia*, v. 3, n. 11 (Nov., 1928), p. 960.

138. "Consultorio medico-pedagogico per minorenni antisociali" (Rome) and "Istituto Biotipologico-Ortogenetico" (Genoa).

139. La Redazione, "L'Opera Nazionale per la Protezione della Maternità e dell Infanzia e l'Istituto Biotipologico ortogenetico di Genova," *Maternità ed infanzia*, v. 3, n. 6 (June, 1928), p. 458.

140. See Chapter 6 for an expanded discussion of the Rocco Code.

141. R.D.-Legge 20 Luglio 1934, n. 1404, Art. 2.

142. Ibid., Art. 11.

143. Judicial pardon was applicable only to minors and deleted any criminal conviction from a youth's record. Suspended sentences, also applicable to some categories of adults, left the conviction intact on the minor's record. In neither case was a child automatically free from internment in some type of reformatory, since these institutions were considered educational and not penal.

144. Ibid., Art. 25.

145. Ibid., Art. 8.

146. Pietro Corsi, *The Protection of Mothers and Children in Italy* (Rome: Società Editrice di Noveissima, 1938), p. 7.

147. Ibid., p. 85.

148. Ibid., p. 61.

149. *Bonifica umana* was a kind of coffee-table book filled with pictures of smiling and energetic children in the process of reform.

150. Dino Grande, *Bonifica umana* (Rome: Mantellate, 1941), v. 1, p. 286.

151. Ibid., p. 284.

152. Grande, *Bonifica*, v. 2, pp. 25–26.

153. ISTAT, *Somm. stat. storiche*, p. 103.

154. Ibid., pp. 98, 103.

155. Benigno Di Tullio, "La profilassi criminale nella polizia," *Boll. SPS*, v. 24–26 (1934–36), p. 91.

156. The majority of these were for girls. For example, see Lucia Ferrante, "L'onore ritrovato: Donne nella Casa del Soccorso di San Paolo a Bologna (sec. XVI–XVII)," *Quaderni Storici*, v. 53 (August, 1983), pp. 499–527 or Sherrill Cohen, *The Evolution of Women's Asylums since 1500* (New York: Oxford University Press, 1992). Scholars who have begun to trace similar private institutions into the nineteenth and twentieth centuries include Angela Groppi, *I conservatori della virtù: Donne recluse nella Roma dei Papi* (Roma-Bari: Laterza, 1994) and Buttafuoco, *Le Mariuccine*.

157. This occurred until recently in the U. S., where minors could be arrested for "status offenses" like staying out all night, hanging out on street corners, or, in the case of girls, engaging in sex.

158. *Difesa*, v. 2, n. 4 (1920), p. iv.

Chapter 6

Theory and Law after Lombroso

In 1931, Di Tullio characterized the criminology of his day as directly descended from Lombroso: "It is evident . . . that beginning in 1879 the genius of Cesare Lombroso clearly traced the entire program of research necessary for efficaciously preventing crime, a program which in Italy, and throughout the whole world, has been gradually carried out by his best students who, like the Master, are men of genius and faith."[1] A student of Ottolenghi and therefore a third-generation criminal anthropologist, Di Tullio might be suspected of overrating the importance of positivism. After all, fascist Italy of the interwar period was markedly different from the newly united liberal state of Lombroso's heyday. But, five years later, the American criminologist, Elio Monachesi, confirmed Di Tullio's words, writing in the *American Sociological Review* that he "was amazed by the intense loyalty to and reverence for Lombroso displayed by students of crime in Italy."[2] After interviewing contemporary Italian criminologists and attending their lectures, he concluded that Lombroso's discovery of the cranium of Villella over sixty years earlier still dominated "all of the more important efforts of the present day Italian criminologists toward the understanding of criminal behavior."[3]

Both Di Tullio and Monachesi attested to the strong continuity that marked the discipline of criminology in Italy between 1875 and World War II. As late as the 1930s, criminologists like Di Tullio considered themselves direct heirs of Lombroso and evoked the name of the founding father with reverence. The continuity of the Positivist School was assured by the colleagues and students of Lombroso who, after his death in 1909, never flagged in their loyalty to his original vision of biological determinism. Ferri and Garofalo, the other two members of the positivist triumvirate, lived into the early 1930s and used their seats in Parliament to call for institutionalizing the principles of criminal anthropology. Recognized as internationally renowned experts on penal law, both were appointed to the parliamentary committee that proposed a new—and clearly positivist—criminal code in 1921.[4] Other second-generation criminal anthropologists, like Ottolenghi, Florian, Morselli, Viazzi, and Zerboglio, also outlived Lombroso and continued to champion his ideas.

Criminal anthropology could not have retained its preeminence in Italy without theoretical evolution, and this was supplied by a third generation of positivists like Di Tullio, De Sanctis, Pende, Patrizi, Giuseppe Vidoni, and Viola. Through their research, positivist criminology between 1910 and 1940 remained a living and changing academic discipline. This intellectual activity undergirded the successful positivist campaigns for the institutionalization of scientific policing and juvenile courts. It also provided the theoretical underpinnings for an array of changes in penal law inspired by criminal anthropology

Legal historians have generally denied that positivism significantly shaped the penal codes of united Italy. The Zanardelli Code of 1889 so clearly retained the classical principles first enunciated by Beccaria that Lombroso himself was moved to publish a cry of despair. Forty years later, his followers again crusaded to imprint the new fascist criminal code with the principles of criminal anthropology. The Rocco Code of 1930, however, incorporated only portions of their doctrine, and the final text represented an often illogical mishmash of the classical and positivist schools.

Criminal anthropologists were more successful in shaping "administrative laws" regulating moral behavior. Generally ignored because they did not form part of the unified penal codes, these administrative laws, nevertheless, criminalized a range of activities. Beginning in the decade of the 1910s and continuing through the fascist period, the state outlawed or restricted prostitution, pornography, drinking, and drug use. Positivists had long denounced each of these activities as not only immoral, but as threats to racial health. As we saw in the case of juvenile delinquency, anxiety escalated during World War I, which brought unstable conditions thought to favor vice. After 1922, the fascist regime used this moral panic as an excuse to clamp down on a range of hitherto private activities in the name of the state. It insisted on the need for moral cleansing in order to ensure population growth and the strength of the race.

Not surprisingly, the new laws targeted women and children as posing the gravest threat to the moral health of the nation. Criminal anthropology had long ago prepared the ground for stigmatizing these two groups, defining them as innately degenerate and possessing criminal qualities like vanity, jealousy, mendacity, and sexual viciousness. Only the family, and especially the control of the fathers through *patria potestà*, could neutralize the "semi-criminality" of wives and children. When World War I removed men to the front, women and children were thought to have gained an independence that bordered on anarchy and licentiousness. After the war, women received control over their own property with the abolition of *autorizzazione maritale*, but they were hounded from the workplace and deprived of the wages that might have afforded them autonomy. The patriarchal family was resurrected as an ideal to which women and children were to return.

Fascism built on the resentment against working women and the fears of juvenile delinquency that followed the war. Using the language of protection, it glorified the traditional family while at the same time maximized intervention by the state into domestic life. Told to reproduce rather than produce, women were barred by law from full participation in the educational or economic system. Although fascist propaganda touted women's affinity for motherhood, the state distrusted their supposed maternal instincts. It therefore established Balilla, the first youth organization outside the Church, to assure the proper socialization of children into fascist values. Another state program, ONMI, brought some benefits to women and children, but also increased surveillance over family life through a network of social workers chosen by fascist officials.

The new legislation on morality fit into this pattern of regimentation. It drew justification from a seemingly contradictory discourse that emphasized both the weakness and menace of women and children, a discourse inherited from criminal anthropology. As a context for this legislation, this chapter will begin by tracing the evolution of positivist theory from the death of Lombroso to World War II. It will then trace the evolution of laws on prostitution, pornography, alcohol, and drugs. Finally, it will weigh the contribution of criminal anthropology to the Rocco Criminal Code and the eugenics movement in fascist Italy.

POSITIVIST THEORY AFTER LOMBROSO

The quote that opens this chapter came from Di Tullio's *Manual of Criminal Anthropology*. Published more than fifty years after the first edition of *Criminal Man*, it did not simply parrot the original Lombrosian formulations. Indeed, positivist criminology could not have retained its preeminence in Italy without theoretical evolution. What remained fixed was an emphasis on the importance of heredity in determining the etiology of crime in deviant individuals. Two main trends characterized developments within the positivist camp after the death of Lombroso. First, many of his followers put an increasing emphasis on inborn psychological rather than physical abnormality as the defining feature of the born criminal. This "psychologizing" of positivism, however, never involved a complete abandonment of physical anomalies as signs of mental deviance. Second, criminal anthropologists tended to downplay morphological atavisms or irregularities in skeletal measurements as the most important signs of physical abnormality. Instead, theorists developed additional categories based on hormones and body types as the predictive basis for criminology.

The heirs of Lombroso modified his original formulations for several reasons. First, they continued the master's own policy of adjusting his theories in response to criticism, whether internal to the movement like Ferri's or from foreign opponents. Second, the younger generation took advantage of scientific advances to develop new tools for measuring anomalies. Rescuing criminal anthropology from the reputation of being a relic of the past, they employed and sometimes inspired new methods that were causing an international resurgence of interest in biological determinism in the interwar period. Thus, as criminology was establishing a niche in the traditional university, it was developing a certain intellectual autonomy. New approaches grew out of existing paradigms, giving the history of criminal anthropology its own internal logic.

No field of knowledge, however, is free of external influences, and this was especially true in Italy during the stormy period of World War I and the overthrow of parliamentary government by Mussolini. During this period, most positivist criminologists slid across the political spectrum from socialism to fascism. As we have seen, Ottolenghi participated in the March on Rome, while Ferri transformed himself from the leader of the maximalist wing of the PSI into a fascist sympathizer. The adherence of criminal anthropologists to fascism came partially from necessity, as professors, lawyers, and administrators of police and prisons could retain their jobs only by taking an oath of loyalty to the regime. Positivists—like Ottolenghi and Di Tullio—also took advantage of the demise of parliament to get their positivist programs institutionalized by fascist fiat.

But the cooperation of criminal anthropologists with Mussolini's regime was not entirely opportunistic since positivism and fascism shared ideological affinities. Both promoted surveillance, classification, and discipline. Both wanted to equip officials in the criminal justice system—whether police, judges, or prison wardens—with flexibility and discretion rather than binding them with the rule of law. And both were careless about individual rights in the name of social defense. Yet the two movements were not identical, as is clear from the early history of positivism and its close alliance with socialism. Although most criminal anthropologists discarded the humanitarian and progressive spirit that had tempered their biological determinism in Lombroso's day, several did not. Two of those were Lombroso's two sons-in-law, Ferrero and Mario Carrara who, as we will see, refused to cooperate with the fascist dictatorship.

Lombroso's family provides an important starting point for understanding why criminal anthropology did not die with him. He was survived by two daughters, Gina and Paola, and their respective husbands, Ferrero and Mario Carrara. Gina Lombroso, a physician who had served as her father's research assistant and secretary, continued to dedicate her energies to the dissemination of his ideas after his death. She prepared new and expanded Italian editions of *The Female Offender* (1911) and *Criminal Man* (1924), incorporating unpublished notes into the texts. In 1911, she issued the only English-language version of *Criminal Man*, although it was so short as to constitute only a summary. Based on a compilation of her father's articles on psychiatry, she put together an entirely new book in 1913 entitled *L'uomo alienato* (*Insane Man*). Most important, she used Lombroso's papers to write his intellectual biography, which was issued in 1915.[5]

In these projects, Gina Lombroso claimed to have neither inserted her own ideas nor tried to modify her father's theories to make them more palatable to changing intellectual fashion. In this sense she was even more rigid than many of his students, who saw the need to periodically update criminal anthropology. Her humility in front of her father's work also reflected an internalization of his teachings on the intellectual inferiority of women. According to Dolza, Lombroso always considered Gina as an essential but subordinate collaborator in his intellectual endeavors.

Two episodes illustrated Gina Lombroso's absolute loyalty to her father's original doctrines. The first occurred in 1913 upon publication of *The English Convict* by Charles Goring, touted as a definitive refutation of Lombrosian doctrines. Goring correctly criticized much of Lombroso's methodology for its statistical primitiveness and lack of control groups. Using "biometrics," or more sophisticated techniques like correlation and regression analysis, he showed that many of Lombroso's anomalies were no more frequent in criminals than in the general population.[6] Goring, however, found that convicts were deficient in height, weight, and intelligence. He concluded that:

A comparison of the results that have emerged from the present investigation ... leads to two very definite general conclusions. The one is that the criminal diathesis, revealed by the tendency to be convicted and imprisoned for crime, is inherited at much the same rate as are other physical and mental qualities and pathological conditions in man. [Second] the influence of parental contagion ... is, on the whole, inconsiderable, relatively to the influence of inheritance, and of mental defectiveness: which are by far the most significant factors we have been able to discover in the etiology of crime.[7]

This confirmation of the hereditary nature of criminality prompted Gina Lombroso to gloat that, rather than disproving her father, "Goring is more Lombrosian than Lombroso."[8] Goring's emphasis on mental rather than physical abnormalities in fact echoed the trend among many of Lombroso's heirs to psychologize criminology.

Eight years later in 1921, Gina Lombroso again displayed fierce loyalty to her father by publicly repeating the ritualistic and almost mythical story of the initiation of Cesare Lombroso's career. The occasion for her speech was the dedication of a memorial to her father in his birthplace of Verona. To celebrate the event, telegrams arrived from the King, Prime Minister, Ministers of Justice and Education, and presidents of the Senate and Chamber of Deputies. In attendance were state officials, leading criminal anthropologists from Italy and abroad, and members of the "Provincial Fascist Federation" of Verona. Ferri gave the memorial address, in which he noted that Lombroso had "the physiognomy and temperament of an Italian thinker."[9] Perhaps in deference to the contemporary reaction against materialism, most threateningly enshrined by the fascist delegation, he added ambiguously that Lombroso had been idealistic, but that his idealism had been grounded not in religion but in facts.

In her speech entitled "How my father came to criminal anthropology," Gina Lombroso recounted the professional stages of her father's career, beginning with the pivotal encounter with the skull of Villella. She characterized Lombroso as a practical man, gearing his scientific research toward solving social problems. After recounting his extreme disappointment with the Zanardelli Code, she urged passage of a new proposed penal code, drawn up by a parliamentary committee headed by Ferri. She praised other nations that had superseded Italy in implementing the recommendations of its own criminal anthropologists. Belgium, for example, had established juvenile courts based on the following positivist principle of social defense:

Since delinquency is a precocious disease that is difficult to hide during the early years of childhood, almost all of the most dangerous future criminals are brought before these judges; and as almost all born criminals are epileptic, morally insane and mentally deficient, from infancy they are—I would say mechanically—isolated and prevented from acting so that the public will be protected in the future from their behavior.[10]

Juvenile delinquency, she claimed, had immediately declined in Belgium after the institution of these measures.

Besides eulogizing her father, Gina Lombroso turned in the postwar years to the subject of women, both "normal" and criminal. It is surprising that she did not come sooner to this topic, since she must have felt some tension between the positivist dogma on female inferiority and her own personal experience as an educated and well-known member of Italy's cultural elite. Despite her own personal achievements, she had always remained faithful to her father's belief that women's intelligence was passive rather than creative and should remain subordinated to the superior projects of male genius. By 1920, her philosophy took an even more conservative turn, consonant with the general shift of popular opinion toward nationalism and fascism. In a series of books, Gina Lombroso declared that women were unsuited for any public roles.[11] This assertion, which would seem to condemn retrospectively her own early struggle to attend medical school, made her even "more positivist than the positivists" in the words of her biographer, Dolza.[12] According to Gina Lombroso, women's essential altruism or, as she called it, *alterocentrismo*, fitted them only for private life within the home. She now adamantly opposed feminism and supported the position of the more misogynistic male criminal anthropologists, like Niceforo who held that women's only appropriate and natural role was maternity.

Although Gina Lombroso's increasingly anti-feminist views echoed those of other women moving to the right during the teens and twenties, she and her husband remained committed to parliamentary democracy.[13] The co-author with his father-in-law of *The Female Offender*, Ferrero had given up research in criminology before World War I to concentrate on the study of history and politics. A prolific author, he gained an international reputation as a classicist and political philosopher. With his wife's support, Ferrero participated in anti-fascist activities during the early twenties and signed the famous anti-fascist manifesto of intellectuals, drawn up in 1925 by Croce. In retaliation, publishers, now under control of the dictatorship, no longer accepted his writings, and the state denied him a passport for lecturing abroad. After a struggle to secure permission to leave the country, Ferrero and his wife moved to Geneva in 1930, where he had been offered a chair at the university. He and Gina Lombroso never returned to Italy before their respective deaths in 1942 and 1944; repatriation would have been dangerous for Gina after the passage of the racial laws against the Jews in 1938.

Like Gina Lombroso, her brother-in-law Mario Carrara devoted his life to perpetuating the family legacy of positivism. He became Cesare Lombroso's assistant at the

University of Turin in 1893, working in his Laboratory of Legal Medicine and sharing his duties as doctor of the local prison. In 1903, Carrara took over the Chair of Legal Medicine, formerly held by Lombroso. During Lombroso's last years, he reorganized his father-in-law's museum and founded the Institute of Criminal Anthropology.

According to Dolza, Lombroso saw in Carrara "his spiritual heir, to whom he could entrust his scientific legacy."[14] Carrara fulfilled his expectation, taking over editorship of the *Archives* until his own death in 1937. He lost his Chair in Legal Medicine in 1931, however, when he refused to take the oath to the fascist regime required of all university professors. He was the only member of a medical faculty, and only one of twelve professors in the entire nation, to take such an independent and clearly adversarial stance to the dictatorship. In his letter to the Minister of Public Instruction, Carrara explained his decision in "scientific" rather than political terms. He argued that "if we wish to develop a 'scientific' approach in youth, we must be careful not to disturb educational spontaneity with doctrinaire dogmas and teleological preconceptions."[15] These words championed the scientific method over the idealism dear to fascist ideologues.

Carrara's refusal to take the oath was likely also political since he had been a committed socialist from his student days. Although he withdrew from political activism to academic pursuits by 1910, he remained committed, according to Dolza, to a reformist and humanitarian socialism throughout his life. She praises him as "the model of the positivist intellectual, who translated the rigor of his scientific thinking into an analogous rigor in his existential choices and conduct in life."[16] By refusing to cooperate with the fascist regime, he stayed true to the impulse among early criminal anthropologists to use their knowledge to help the poor of Italy. Paola Lombroso, although opposing the dictatorship like her husband, remained in Italy after his death and even after the promulgation of the racial laws in 1938. When the mass deportation of Italian Jews began in 1943, she finally fled to join her sister in Geneva. She returned to live in Italy after the war until her death in 1954.

Most of the work of perpetuating Lombroso's legacy fell to his disciples, who were more willing than his family to modify his theories to bring them into line with the general evolution of scientific research. Such reevaluations began as early as 1911, when Mariano Patrizi was appointed to the Chair of Criminal Anthropology at the University of Turin, vacant since the death of Lombroso. Patrizi explicitly outlined his deviations from the Master in his book entitled *After Lombroso*, published in 1916. Consistent with the growing interest in psychology, psychiatry, and psychoanalysis in the early twentieth century, Patrizi narrowed the search for the origins of crime to the emotions of deviant individuals. In a theory that echoed but simplified Sigmund Freud, Patrizi argued that two levels characterized the psychology of all people: the lower was regressive, egotistical, and impulsive in satisfying its appetites while the higher was altruistic, sociable, moral, and intelligent. In criminals, the lower, atavistic emotions predominated over their disorganized higher faculties. Because both levels existed in all humans, he denied the sharp break between normality and deviance that had been posited by Lombroso. Instead he proposed the image of an inclined plane, where all grades of deviancy blended into one another.

Because Patrizi traced all criminality to unbalanced and impulsive emotions, he refused to make distinctions among types of delinquency. Thus, "each crime is carried out by a born criminal," who is fatally marked by "insensitivity to others, egotism, [and] a predestination to crime."[17] In Patrizi's scheme, occasional criminality, prompted only by an evil environment, did not exist. Even the distinction between atavistic crimes and crimes by passion was specious, because both were carried out under the same emotional compulsion during the act of violence. Patrizi formulated his own system of classification to enshrine his new "monocausal" analysis of crime. By denying the influence of social factors on the etiology of crime, Patrizi admitted that "we could be teased as being more monarchical than the king, that is, more lombrosian than Lombroso."[18] Patrizi's theory, however, recalled Garofalo more than Lombroso in deemphasizing physical anomalies and ignoring sociological factors altogether. Both Garofalo and Patrizi narrowed the search for the etiology of crime to psychology, which they characterized as inherited and rigidly deterministic.

Patrizi found greater similarity between male and female criminals than the founders of criminal anthropology had. In his lessons at the University of Turin, he emphasized the "strong sexual drive" in all criminals, whether female prostitutes or male criminals, who tended to seek refuge from police in brothels. Lacking the ability to love, delinquents in general were marked by "sexual degenerations" like sadism, necrophilia, and homosexuality. He denied that women were "born" to prostitution any more than certain men were "born" to murder. As he explained:

Why does the female offender rarely commit crimes of force and violence? Why does she more often kill by poison than a knife? Why is she more often a thief and liar than a bully or robber? Because her bone structure is not solid and her muscular strength not great. Take the case of a woman, born to be immoral, who had the strong bones and bundle of muscles typical of the female figures of Michelangelo: she could easily be a brigand rather than a prostitute.[19]

Women's tendency to prostitution, then, lay more in their body type than in a specifically feminine psychology.

That Patrizi was conscious of working in an intellectual community that had not lost its coherence or vitality after the death of Lombroso is evident from the form of his book. After putting forth his own monocausal theory, he boldly attached an appendix with letters of both support and critique from positivist colleagues. Sighele, for example, congratulated him for having "really cleared up the thought of the Master, presenting it in the light of scientific rigor."[20] He agreed that all criminals were emotionally atavistic. The psychiatrist Enrico Morselli, on the other hand, charged Patrizi with obscuring "the exact remembrance of the final phase of lombrosian thought, substituting for the very correct concept of a plurality of causes and types of crime with a harmful return to an already surpassed simplistic unity of a unique origin."[21]

Ferri, who had crusaded for years to push Lombroso to recognize environmental determinants of crime, objected strongly to the theory of monocausality. He agreed with Patrizi that the differences among his own categories of criminality were those "of degree and of form," thus seeming to accept the image of the inclined plane.[22]

But he condemned an exclusive focus on psychology, stressing the importance not only of environment but also biology in the explanation of criminality. Decrying the absence of courses in physical morphology at Patrizi's Institute of Criminal Anthropology, he argued that "it is no longer acceptable to conceive of psychic functions without a somatic base (and I believe that biological chemistry reveals many concrete reasons for psychological processes) nor to differentiate criminals *only* by emotions or ideas or will."[23] For Ferri, Patrizi had gone too far in "psychologizing" the etiology of crime.

Many criminal anthropologists agreed with Ferri, rejecting Patrizi's monocausal analysis for one based on a combination of physical, psychological, and environmental factors. Achille De Giovanni, De Sanctis, Pende, Viola, and Vidoni, calling themselves the "constitutionalist school," emphasized the role of hormones in shaping both the physical body type and psychological character. The young science of endocrinology offered a new lease on life for Lombrosianism by supplementing the simple measurement of body parts with more sophisticated research on the metabolic functions of various glands. Vidoni proudly considered himself "among the defenders of criminal anthropology" and praised endocrinology for resurrecting positivism after many had declared it dead. Criticizing Lombroso for having been too prone to "materialize" his discoveries by overemphasizing the physical, Vidoni promised that endocrinology would restore a balance between the physical and psychological in penetrating "the essence of the human personality."[24]

Constitutionalists devised various classifications of body types or, as Pende called them, "biotypes." Early proponents of constitutionalism, like De Giovanni and his student Viola, followed Lombroso in making physical measurements, but based their analysis on the ratio between various parts of the body rather than absolute size. "Disequilibrium" between the length of the trunk and the arms, for example, signaled an abnormal constitution and therefore psychological deviancy. By adding endocrinological testing, Pende constructed more elaborate and complicated biotypes that linked body shapes to hormonal imbalance, a paradigm much admired by Vidoni.

According to positivists, criminals exhibited the most extreme disequilibrium of constitution and, therefore, temperament. Pende held that hot climates stimulated the thyroid gland, making southern Europeans emotional and sexually passionate. On the other hand, northern peoples had a more placid thyroid and a calm, if sometimes sluggish, disposition. He pointed out the continuity between his own research and that of earlier criminal anthropologists, noting that his endocrinological types "harmonize perfectly with the differing characters that Niceforo had found between Northern and Southern Italians."[25] More generally, Italian anthropologists were hopeful that constitutionalism would provide the tool necessary for finally classifying all human races and explaining how each race perpetuated its unique qualities.[26]

Vidoni, who applied Pende's theories to 400 criminals, claimed that certain constitutions correlated with types of crime. In his book, *The Value and Limits of Endocrinology in Criminal Anthropology*, he also confirmed the earlier racial theories of the late nineteenth century. Southern Italians most often expressed their deviancy in homicide, assaults, and kidnapping while the more placid northern Italians preferred theft, purse snatching, and other nonviolent crimes. He also blamed hormonal imbalance for sexual deviancy. Dominated by their genital glands, homosexual men were afflicted with "femininity" (*femminilismo*), as well as retardation in their "higher psychic life."[27] Vidoni triumphantly announced that gland transplants had cured many men of homosexuality.

Asserting that all women had overactive thyroids, Vidoni classified the entire female sex as fitting the "southern Italian" or "passionate" biotype. Instead of the ovary so important to earlier criminal anthropologists, he pointed to the thyroid as determining "normal" female behavior. According to Vidoni, "It is to this gland—whose secretions stimulate the release of energy accumulated in the nerve cells—that women principally owe their great emotionality. . . . Nothing is more true from the physiological point of view than the saying: man thinks, woman feels."[28] Despite dethroning the ovaries as the center of normal female biology, Vidoni nevertheless confirmed the classic positivist dogma on the intellectual inferiority of women. His innovation was in equating them with southerners rather than the more usual benchmark, children.

Like Lombroso, Vidoni identified prostitution as the typical form of female crime. In his book entitled *Prostitutes and Prostitution*, he claimed that prostitutes, unlike "normal" women, were indeed controlled by their sexual organs. This condition, called hyper-ovarianism (*iperovarismo*), created imbalances in the sexual glands leading to early menstruation, small breasts, virile tendencies, and even mongoloidism.[29] Lombroso had first proposed that female criminals were virile, and Vidoni replicated his results by finding that prostitutes exhibited masculine traits like muscular strength, sexual precocity, and lack of maternal feelings. He even entertained the hypothesis, put forth by the German positivist, Kurella, that "prostitutes are a subspecies of male homosexuals, having masculine habits and behaviors that in turn influence the physical structure of the body."[30] Thus, the counterpart of the "feminine" male homosexual was the "masculine" prostitute, both biologically flawed and a threat to an orderly society.

Although his language was reminiscent of Lombroso, Vidoni periodically tried to distinguish his theories from traditional positivism in a way that was typical of his colleagues in the 1920s and 1930s. Instead of arguing that certain glandular imbalances or certain biotypes directly caused crime, he claimed that they only predisposed certain individuals to abnormal behavior. Men and women who had inherited a morphological, endocrinological, and psychological disequilibrium were more prone to overreact when faced with negative external stimuli. In this way, constitutionalists claimed to incorporate environmental factors, although their description of them was usually brief and in passing. This disclaimer did not cancel the general impression left by their works, which was that biology determines behavior. They rarely evoked the "criminal sociology" of Ferri, except to condemn diseases like alcoholism and syphilis, which could trigger constitutional degeneration.

Building on the notion of biotypes, Di Tullio introduced the notion of the "constitutional criminal" in the late 1920s. As we saw at the beginning of the chapter, he had great reverence for Lombroso and "the figure of the born criminal [which] continues even today to constitute the base of Criminal Anthropology, despite the time that has passed and the continual and very severe critiques it has born."[31] Acknowledging a relative stasis, although not death, of positivist research during the teens, Di Tullio credited the constitutionalist school of De Giovanni, Viola, and Pende with providing a theoretical base for a reflowering of criminal anthropology. Their emphasis on the "vital unity" of biotypes had "served to confirm scientifically the fundamental concept of the Lombrosian theory, that is, the well-known relation between the body and the mind."[32] They had also confirmed the importance of heredity, since "constitution" meant "that part of individuality that is formed by hereditary and inborn characteristics (genotype or idiotype) and that are always easily distinguishable from those characteristics that come from the environment and are conditional, acquired or secondary."[33] For Di Tullio, this evolution of positivism had prepared the ground for his own research.

Like Vidoni, Di Tullio left his reader convinced of the overwhelming power of biological determinism, despite perfunctory warnings that abnormal constitutions only predisposed certain individuals to crime. Throughout his writings, he labeled the constitutional delinquent as alternately anomalous, abnormal, degenerate, or morbid. Di Tullio argued that only individuals with such "delinquent constitutions" committed "real crime."[34] This conviction led him to modify previous classifications of criminals, throwing out all intermediate categories like habitual criminals and criminals by passion. While he retained one category for occasional criminals or, as he called them, pseudo-criminals, he was more interested in erecting an elaborate categorization of "criminals from congenital inclination or constitutional predisposition," that is, "real criminals."[35] His system of classification resembled Patrizi's in its elimination of many of the categories originally proposed by Ferri. Di Tullio, like Patrizi, was thus "more lombrosian than Lombroso" and typified the trend among positivist theorists after 1910 to eliminate serious discussion of sociological and economic causes of crime like poverty, malnutrition, unemployment, or bad housing.

As a companion to the male "real criminal," Di Tullio was true to Lombroso in positing the "real prostitute." Based on his study of women in Roman prisons, Di Tullio concluded that "real prostitution . . . always originates in an abnormal, defective and irregular constitution, exactly like that of the delinquent."[36] With a tone of disdain, he enumerated the atavistic anomalies of prostitutes, already familiar from earlier positivist studies:

real prostitutes sometimes exhibit coarse physical features, little sensitivity to pain, a deadened epidermis, intellectual weakness, emotional frigidity and moral numbness and, therefore, are egotistical, insolent and lacking in modesty and prudence. Or they exhibit—besides physical anomalies (especially asymmetry)—accentuated neuro-muscular reactions, intellectual restlessness, strong fantasies, a tendency to lying, a notable inconstancy of moods, pronounced excitability to the point of irritability, a marked emotionality that becomes agi-

tation, a weak volition and impulsiveness; and they are therefore very capricious, uninterest-
ing, vain, mendacious, irritable, emotional and violent, as are hysterics and neuro-
psychopaths in general.[37]

After such a misogynist tirade, readers and students of his *Manual of Criminal Anthropology* could easily miss Di Tullio's passing mention of occasional or "pseudo-
prostitutes," who retained "the normal qualifications of femininity" and had been
forced into their profession by a bad environment.[38]

Yet prostitutes—whether regressive-atavistic, underevolved, hysteric, or neuro-
psychotic—were "if not indispensable, certainly useful" to modern society.[39] Di
Tullio echoed the standard regulationist argument that prostitutes were necessary
to protect those women who had chosen "virginal chastity and conjugal honesty."[40]
Useful as a sexual safety valve for men, prostitutes, nevertheless, required strict surveillance. Their antisocial natures were evident in their perverse sexual appetites,
which included lesbianism, sadism, and bestiality. In addition, real prostitutes were
predisposed to all types of "male" crime like theft, fraud, assault, and murder, sometimes carried out to please their criminal husbands.[41]

In 1943, criminal anthropology reached its theoretical culmination with the publication of a two-volume *Dictionary of Criminology*. It is significant that such a major
work of criminology—edited by three positivists, Eugenio Florian, Niceforo, and
Pende—should have appeared even in the midst of war. That it represented the
capstone to a movement stretching back to Lombroso was clear from the preface,
which attributed the *Dictionary*'s "conceptual unity" to its adoption of the "impartial, naturalistic-scientific point of view."[42] The editors also vaunted their project
for "making visible the preeminent place that Italian studies hold in modern scientific criminology, a science that is exquisitely Italian, and in which Italy must maintain the glory of its leadership first established by the celebrated work of the
founders and wise pioneers."[43] They characterized criminology as vitally important
to the fascist state, evidenced by the fact that Rome had just hosted the First International Congress of Criminology in 1938 and that the Minister of Justice, Grandi,
had recently issued *Bonifica umana*.

The roster of contributors to the *Dictionary* attested to the dominance of positivism
within Italian criminology as late as World War II. Its editors were Niceforo, who had
written extensively on the "Southern Question"; Pende, who had formulated the notion of constitutional biotypes; and Florian, who was best known for his studies of
vagabonds.[44] Other contributors included the few positivists left from Lombroso's era
like Zerboglio; second- and third-generation disciples like Di Tullio, Enrico Altavilla,
and Filippo Grispigni; constitutionalists like Viola and Vidoni; and faculty from
Ottolenghi's police school like Falco, Giri, and Sorrentino. Yet the *Dictionary* was not
simply an ideological mouthpiece for criminal anthropology, as authors were free to
express reservations about certain positivist findings and express their own views.
Thus, the *Dictionary* is useful for gauging the longevity of various positivist ideas as
they were reconfirmed, rejected, or simply ignored in the key articles.

The *Dictionary* comprised only a few biographical entries, but these included one on Beccaria. The author, Carlo Umberto Del Pozzo, described him not as the founder of the Classical School but as the font of all types of criminology. In deference, perhaps, to the fascist distaste for the rationalism of the Enlightenment, Del Pozzo, denied that Beccaria was a child of his times. According to this argument, *On Crimes and Punishments* was not based on the false eighteenth-century values of "abstraction, exaggerated individualism, optimism, [and] anti-historicism," but rather on the "immortal principles" of "creativity and history."[45] Del Pozzo characterized Beccaria as a precursor of the Positivist School, since his critique of punishment as retribution might be seen as foreshadowing the doctrine of social defense. This unprecedented appropriation of Beccaria to criminal anthropology may have been done to please the fascist regime, which tended to lump together all heroes of the past as similar in their *italianità*.

The *Dictionary* was more traditional in its biographical entries on "that glorious triad of the founders of the penal reform movement known under the name of the Italian Positivist School."[46] The editors did not neglect Lombroso despite the passage of the anti-Semitic legislation of 1938 and the opposition to the regime of his daughters and their husbands. Zerboglio, author of the entry on Lombroso and himself a former member of the PSI, downplayed Lombroso's stint as a socialist municipal counselor, explaining that the "Maestro" had not harbored sufficient "partisan cruelty" to make a good politician.[47] He did not mention his religion. This refusal to demonize or simply ignore Lombroso shows the continuing importance of what Zerboglio termed "his fundamental thought" for the criminologists of the decades of fascism.[48] Ferri and Garofalo received equally laudatory articles, although the former was much longer; it attributed many concrete changes in Italian law and prisons to Ferri's efforts. By his death, Ferri's ideas, according to his biographer, were no longer accepted only by positivists, "but were among the most widely-held principles of all students of crime."[49]

In the long article devoted to "criminal anthropology," Gian Giacomo Perrando reconfirmed the entire litany of positivist principles. He held that the Lombrosian theories of physical atavisms, degeneracy, and epilepsy were still valid and had been confirmed by the new constitutionalism. Reiterating a belief in biological determinism, he argued that "emotions, instinct, will, and, therefore, individual behavior are undoubtedly connected to constitution, age, sex, glands, menstruation, pregnancy, nursing, digestion, metabolism . . . [and] disease."[50] His genuflection to the influence of environment was brief, as was true of most interwar criminal anthropologists. True to Lombroso, his system of classification included born criminality, moral insanity, and epilepsy. He admitted that diseases like alcoholism, syphilis, tuberculosis, malaria, and pellagra could no longer be classified as hereditary atavisms in light of Gregor Mendel's genetic theories. These pathologies did, however, weaken the constitution and could predispose the individual to crime, insanity, or suicide. Perrando claimed that new devices like the American lie-detector test confirmed the positivist axiom that outward physical states reflect inner emotions and morality.

The article on "women," tellingly subtitled "sexual phases," devoted special attention to the influence of biology on female crime. The author, Vincenzo Mario Palmieri, emphasized "the somatic and psychological costs to women of their biological destiny."[51] He continued that "men, once they have reached adulthood, have only to provide for their own preservation, while women are dominated by their reproductive functions for about another thirty years of their lives, whether in the preparatory phase (ovulation, menstruation), in the phase of realization (pregnancy, childbirth), or in the phase of biologically supporting the product of conception (nursing)."[52] The new endocrinology claimed to have offered additional support to the traditional positivist assertion of radical gender differences. Proof of female inferiority no longer had to rest on disputed data such as brain size, since the hormones involved in conception and childbirth clearly distinguished women from men. Both Palmieri and Perrando warned that women tended to be especially unbalanced during "sexual phases" and predisposed to antisocial and even criminal behavior. Yet Palmieri found it impractical to release women from responsibility for their crimes because they were almost always in one of the many periods of female hormonal disequilibrium! Thus, like his positivist predecessors, he was willing to restrict the civil rights of women in the name of biology, but not to draw the logical conclusion that they should also be immune to criminal prosecution.

Perrando also dealt with juvenile delinquency in his overview of criminal anthropology. He followed Lombroso's lead in rejecting the "common assumption that children are innocent" and instead labeled them as mendacious, vane, cruel, and destructive.[53] In the article devoted specifically to "minors," the members of the constitutional school were credited with updating Lombroso's theories. According to Di Tullio and De Sanctis, during adolescence the endocrinological system developed "in a manner which is often tumultuously progressive or regressive."[54] Such hormonal instability helped to explain high rates of juvenile delinquency. To meet such problems, the article boasted that "Italy finally has a complete legal system for minors which, if it is not perfect, is certainly among the best and most scientific in the world."[55]

As the *Dictionary* made clear, positivism still dominated Italian criminology on the eve of World War II. Heaping praise on Lombroso, Ferri, and Garofalo, it credited the new endocrinological and constitutional theories with simply updating their original principles. Such theoretical continuity was complemented by institutional stability. The four major journals of the Positivist School were still in publication: the *Archives* founded by Lombroso; the *Positivist School* founded by Ferri; and the *Bulletin of the School of Scientific Policing* (now called the Advanced School of Policing) and *Zacchia*, founded by Ottolenghi. Within the universities, there were three chairs of criminal anthropology at Turin, Rome, and Naples; a chair of criminal sociology at Turin; a section of criminal anthropology in the Institute of Legal Medicine at Genoa; and many courses on positivist criminology for undergraduates in other medical and legal faculties. Besides Ferri's famous School of Juridical Application at the Rome Law School, two other postgraduate programs in positivist methodology were available in Turin and Modena.[56] Finally, the publishing house of Bocca continued to edit its series entitled the "Anthropological-Juridical Library," devoted to disseminating the findings of the Positivist School.

LEGISLATING MORALITY

Prostitution

Although special laws addressing pornography, alcoholism, and drug addiction were new to twentieth-century Italy, the regulation of prostitution was not. At the time of national unification in 1860, the Cavour Law had required that all prostitutes register with police, undergo biweekly health examinations, and, if found infected with venereal disease, submit to treatment in a special lock hospital for prostitutes, called the *sifilicomio*. Required to carry a special passport (*libretto*) containing a record of her medical examinations, each prostitute was subject to strict and unfettered police surveillance whether in the streets or in her licensed brothel. The Cavour Law minutely regulated the lives of prostitutes, prescribing when they could leave their brothels, where they could walk, and what they could wear.

Protest by civil libertarians, female emancipationists, and medical reformers had forced the state to liberalize laws on prostitution. According to the Crispi Law of 1888 and the Nicotera Law of 1891, police could no longer keep registers of individual prostitutes, which had been denounced as a violation of civil rights. The new laws also abolished the *libretto*, carried by no other group and considered a mark of second-class citizenship. Finally, health care was made less coercive, with prostitutes at registered brothels allowed to choose their own private physicians in place of state-appointed doctors. The repressive *sifilicomi*, in which sick prostitutes had been interned by force, were replaced with free and voluntary treatment for both sexes at outpatient dispensaries or special hospital wards for venereal disease. Finally, the Public Health Law of 1905 forbade police from interfering in the treatment of venereal disease, arguing that the sick—including prostitutes—would avoid the dispensaries and hospital wards if they feared identification and even arrest by PS agents.

The fascist dictatorship reversed this liberalizing trend toward abolishing special statutes on prostitutes and making them subject only to the Criminal Code. The prelude to Mussolini's return to repression came with the declaration of war by Italy in 1915. War gave the state the power and pretext for increasing surveillance over prostitution, as it had in 1860 when the wars of unification produced the Cavour Law. Fearing an epidemic of venereal disease, the army appointed special health advisors (*Consulenti medici d'armata*) and inspectors (*Ispettori*) to oversee the frequent examinations now required of both prostitutes and soldiers.[57] Although the military extended its control over prostitutes only in the North near the front with Austria, the Ministry of the Interior gave prefects similar powers in the rest of the country. As under the Cavour Law, prefects again ordered PS agents to patrol the health of prostitutes, using force to ensure compliance with examinations. That the aim of the new policy was the regulation rather than elimination of prostitution is clear from the government's contemporaneous establishment of "military brothels" and "health offices for post-coital disinfection" in the war zone.[58]

Contrary to expectations, World War I did not bring an epidemic of venereal disease. Syphilis rose only in the north near the front while it continued its prewar decline in central and southern Italy.[59] By 1918, the number of deaths from syphilis for the entire nation fell below prewar levels and declined even further in the years preceding the fascist takeover.[60] Such unexpected results led the noted expert on public health, Giorgio Mortara, to conclude that "the worsening [of venereal disease] during the war did not leave serious traces in the immediate postwar period; maybe the progress in the treatment of syphilis more than counterbalanced the damage from the previous spread of infection."[61]

Despite this decline in rates of syphilis, the fascist regime quickly reimposed police control over the health of prostitutes. This "Mussolini Law" of 1923 was reminiscent of the Cavour Law of 1860. Subsequent PS laws and the Rocco Criminal Code expanded police powers granted by the Law of 1923 over not only prostitutes but finally anyone with syphilis. Why Mussolini reimposed draconian surveillance over prostitutes when rates of venereal disease were actually falling involved a complex mixture of fears from the war, totalitarian and eugenic aims of the regime, and the availability of new positivist research confirming the dangerousness of prostitutes.

Politicians across the spectrum feared the demoralizing impact of World War I on youth. Left alone without the supervising influence of parents, who were either off to the front or working in wartime production, children were thought to have become free prey to pimps and procuresses. As proof of this danger, Federzoni reported to Parliament that in 1925 police had arrested over 1,000 panderers trying to lure women and children into brothels or the white slave trade.[62] He explained that "this campaign for moral defense is not the same as dewy puritanism, but represents the fruit of a healthy, bold, and efficient vigor that can and must be that of fascism."[63] Such words recast opposition to the white slave trade, previously the domain of the female social purity movement and Catholic Church, as a virile endeavor worthy of the fascist dictatorship.

In addition to moral breakdown, prostitution also promised to spread syphilis, a physical infection that could be passed down from mother to child. Declaring that "we consider it the definite task of the Government to come to the defense of children with all possible energy and zeal," Federzoni touted new laws that would control hereditary diseases like syphilis.[64] In the name of "positive" eugenics, the fascist state declared war on all such diseases that caused racial degeneration; it thus reversed the trend dating from the 1880s toward more liberal policies of public health. The rights of all individuals, including prostitutes, to choose when and where to get health care were curtailed in the interest of the state.

Conveniently for fascist policy makers, the new endocrinologists of the post-World War I period were reviving and modernizing Lombroso's concept of the born prostitute. As discussed previously, Vidoni was an instrumental figure in perpetuating the positivist theory that female criminality was fundamentally sexual. In *Prostitutes and Prostitution*, he claimed that prostitutes exhibited both Lombrosian atavisms and hormonal imbalance. Like many politicians, Vidoni warned that "the war . . . had been a great stimulus to moral corruption, a monstrous factory of public prostitutes."[65] He blamed it for inflaming the sexual instinct and multiplying sexual deviations including rape, illegitimacy, and marital separation as well as prostitution.

Older criminal anthropologists approved of the modernization by the constitutional school of Lombroso's original theory, despite the fact that the figure of the "born prostitute" had "not escaped sarcasm" from foreign commentators.[66] Morselli, for example, contributed a long and impassioned introduction to Vidoni's book, showing the continuities between the two theories. Rejecting the fashionable twentieth-century critique of biological determinism as materialistic, Morselli declared himself an "impenitent follower of the positivist method."[67] Only biology could provide the basis of "a scientific Sociology worthy of that name."[68] He accepted the endocrinologist's emphasis on "predisposition," because born prostitutes could logically be defined as "those women who harbor an individual 'predisposition,' which manifests itself precisely in morphological, physiological, and psychological characteristics of the sad tree of Degeneration."[69]

Like Lombroso, Morselli saw value in prostitution despite its basis in physical and psychological abnormality, since "the woman-prostitute is the safeguard of the woman-mother."[70] Prostitution had always existed and was still necessary to satisfy the male sex drive. In opposition to members of the social purity movement who would prohibit prostitution altogether, he reconfirmed the traditional positivist view that the male sex drive was uncontrollable. If prostitution were to be outlawed, male sexual impulses "would break out in masturbation or cause illnesses like genital neurasthenia and precocious dementia that, according to my clinical experience, rage more unrestrained among the chaste than the libertine."[71] Believing that war had unleashed the male sex drive, Morselli counseled toleration of prostitution.

Mussolini thus had the approval of criminal anthropologists when he reverted to the policy of nineteenth-century regulation, which had guaranteed men legal access to prostitutes who themselves were tightly disciplined by the state. The Mussolini Law of 1923 tightened restrictions on the civil rights of prostitutes in two areas.[72] In both cases, the new policy resembled the Cavour Law of 1860, whose more authoritarian aspects had been dropped under the succeeding Crispi and Nicotera legislation. First, it reimposed stricter surveillance over registered brothels. The state appointed its own "examining doctors" (*medici visitatrici*) to replace private doctors in carrying out routine medical examinations. Although the law supposedly forbade the use of "coercion" on women refusing examination, recalcitrant prostitutes were presumed to be infected with venereal disease. Along with other sick prostitutes, they were then reported to health authorities.

The second set of restrictions applied to "isolated" prostitutes, or those living and working outside of the tolerated brothels. The Mussolini Law reintroduced a licensing system, requiring isolated prostitutes to carry "health identification cards" (*tessere sanitarie*). Reminiscent of the *libretto* under the Cavour Law, the health identification cards contained a record of the dates and outcome of each vaginal examination.[73] While the law made possession of a health card nominally voluntary, those prostitutes without the card were subject to arrest by the PS. Thus, the declaration near the end of the legislation, that "health vigilance over prostitution is essentially the perrogative of the Provincial Health Authority" was ingenuous, since the Mussolini law again empowered the PS to arrest women whose health cards were not in order.

In addition to issuing his new law on prostitution, Mussolini also began in 1923 a campaign to round up and expel any foreign women working as prostitutes in Italy.[74] Giorgio Gattei, the first scholar to outline the fascist policy on prostitution, has analyzed this ethnic purification of Italy's brothels as part of Mussolini's general call for autarky, or national self-sufficiency, in the economy in general. The School of Scientific Policing helped Mussolini identify foreign prostitutes by reviewing its files in its Central Identification Office.[75] Mussolini claimed that he was simply cooperating with the League of Nations, which had called for ending the trade of prostitutes across national borders. Such zeal for cooperating with the League's policy sprang from the opportunity it afforded to increase police surveillance over a "dangerous" segment of the population. That Mussolini cared little for the League's moral position on prostitution is clear from his rejection of its call for the abolition of licensed brothels. In a gesture of contempt, he answered the League's inquiries about his legislation on prostitution by lying, that is, asserting that regulation did not exist in Italy.

That Mussolini had reasserted the control of police over prostitution was clear from PS legislation. The PS Law of 1926 included for the first time a special section on prostitution.[76] Composed of twenty articles, this section repeated the traditional prohibitions against dancing, gambling, and the sale of food and drink in brothels. It also reflected a new preoccupation with recreational drugs, an issue never before mentioned in prostitution legislation. According to Article 210, "[The PS] must order the permanent closure of any registered brothel which keeps or provides toxic narcotic drugs or harbors users of these drugs or even permits or favors their use." Narcotic drugs were labeled toxic less because of their immediate effect on an individual consumer than because of their degenerative effect on the race.

The PS Law of 1926 reiterated the duty of police to subject streetwalkers to health examinations. The law also expanded the definition of those situations in which police could accuse women of soliciting. Women were forbidden not only from "following people through the streets, seducing them with licentious acts or words" as they had been under the Nicotera Law, but also from "stand[ing] in public places in an alluring posture."[77] According to Gattei, framers of the law purposely chose this vague wording to give police the liberty to harass indiscriminately women on the street with accusations of prostitution. Before 1926, police claimed to have been hamstrung by many judges who inconveniently refused to interpret any female smile or glance as "licentious."[78] Now such women could be stopped and, if unable to show proof of employment, arrested for prostitution.

If the regime's policy on prostitution represented a reversion to nineteenth-century regulation, it went beyond the Cavour Law in submitting the general population to surveillance for venereal disease. The Law on Public Health of 1934, in addition to reconfirming requirements for examination and treatment of prostitutes, extended surveillance over other types of workplaces.[79] According to Article 294, state health authorities could order workers suspected of having venereal disease to undergo a health examination if they might spread that disease while carrying out their profession or craft. If the worker failed to produce a medical certificate attesting to good health within three days, he or she could be fired by order of the state. This was the first time that "respectable" citizens, outside of the military, had been required to undergo testing for venereal disease. Male clients of prostitutes had been shielded from similar proposals under the liberal monarchy, on the grounds that such government intervention constituted an infringement of civil rights.

Even more radical was the introduction into the criminal code of punishment for spreading syphilis or gonorrhea. The Zanardelli Code had contained no provisions on prostitution or venereal disease, relegating these "administrative" matters to a series of secondary statutes. The centrality of eugenics to fascism, however, prompted framers of the Rocco Code to include syphilis in a new section entitled "Crimes against the integrity and health of the race." According to the Rocco commission,

the reform of the criminal code could not refrain from dealing with the repression of sexual contagion, a problem that is joined to our active demographic politics intended to assure the health of the race and increase its potency. . . . The numerous preventative and social provisions contained in administrative laws do not by themselves represent a sufficient defense against the enormity of the evil; but they instead must be integrated with penal law, which fixes absolutely the prohibition for infected individuals to expose others to the danger of contagion.[80]

According to Article 554 of the Rocco Code, punishment for the "crime of venereal contagion" was imprisonment from one to three years.

The steps taken by the fascist regime to reimpose police control over prostitution and expand surveillance over the spread of venereal disease brought approbation and cooperation from positivist criminologists. Beginning in 1922 and continuing until the outbreak of World War II, the school made an agreement with the Director of Prisons to give "anthropological-biographical examinations" to all girls under the age of eighteen arrested for prostitution.[81] Such examinations would identify those girls who were "redeemable," based on their biological, psychological, intellectual, and social characteristics. Girls fortunate enough to be classified as "occasional" prostitutes were then turned over to the Italian branch of the International Abolitionist Federation and the Red Cross.

Positivists at the school also applauded the Rocco Code for criminalizing the spreading of venereal disease; according to the *Bulletin of the School for Advanced Policing*, this constituted a logical extension of "the propaganda, prevention, and foresight that the Fascist Government has fostered for the physical integrity and fertility of the race."[82] Falco emphasized that police surveillance of brothels was central to the protection of health, because "often the struggle against venereal disease is also the struggle against crime . . . police officers and doctors find themselves side by side" in the fight against the degenerative powers of syphilis.[83] Legislation on prostitution had thus gone full circle, returning to the Cavourian policy of eradicating disease not through public education but through police repression.

The willingness of fascist authorities to curtail the civil rights of prostitutes in the name of public health was consistent with their more general sexual politics. Like criminal anthropology, fascist ideology reduced women to their biological functions. Claiming that women were controlled by their sexuality, the dictatorship used a combination of rewards, propaganda, and force to channel dangerous female instincts into motherhood. Large families were given subsidies and preferences in housing, while a series of government regulations restricted women's access to education and employment. Those women who nevertheless shunned traditional marriage and continued to practice prostitution were considered threats to society and fair targets of police harassment. Positivist criminology had laid the theoretical ground for labeling prostitutes as so biologically and psychologically abnormal as to merit inhumane treatment by the state. As with much other fascist legislation, the Mussolini Law subordinated women's liberty to the needs of men, in this case the need for safe and efficient sexual satisfaction.

Pornography

Laws restricting access to pornography, alcohol, and drugs were newer than those on prostitution, but also formed party of the positivist campaign of "social defense." For decades, criminal anthropologists had blamed familial and racial degeneration on syphilis, alcoholism, and, in later years, drug addiction. Such diseases were purported to weaken the constitution of even "normal" individuals, causing physical and moral breakdown. Most positivist criminologists ignored the implications of Mendel's genetic theories and continued to insist, throughout the interwar period, that anomalies acquired from disease were inherited by future generations. The fascist government perceived all three as threats to its demographic policy, and, as in the case of prostitution, manipulated public fears growing out of World War I that youth were increasing prone to immorality.

Deputies in the fascist parliament were quick to link pornography to a bundle of other problems that were purportedly destroying the physical and moral fiber of the nation. In a commission report of 1927 recommending a new censorship law, Deputy Egilberto Martire warned that "pornography is assuming the technical and commercial character of a vast industry intimately linked to the more typical manifestations of the present crisis of family and social morals: alcoholism, prostitution, the white slave trade, juvenile delinquency, [and] crimes against family order and morality."[84] According to Martire, pornography incited men to visit brothels, thus encouraging the white slave trade and causing the spread of venereal disease. This was not the first time that legislators had made these connections. Four years earlier, Deputy Bortolo Belotti had argued for the establishment of a "Central Office for the Repression of Pornography" within the Ministry of the Interior by drawing a parallel with drugs. Reminding the chamber that they had recently approved a law against drugs because they constituted a "poison of the body," he characterized the various types of pornography as "poisons of the soul that are even more deadly, more horrible, [and] more devastating."[85]

Anti-pornography crusaders like Martire and Belotti pointed to youth as the group most susceptible to being seduced into a life of crime by pornography. Martire asserted that pornography was "the determining cause of *sexual precocity*," and, echoing criminal anthropology, he added that "sexual precocity is among the most characteristic signs and determinants of delinquency and perversion among minors."[86] Danger was greatest during "the crisis of puberty—which has a profound and often decisive importance on the moral life of the adult—in terms of the etiology of crimes against morality" including divorce, abortion, and birth control.[87] The fascist government held pornography to be anti-patriotic, anti-religious, and thus socialist, although representatives of a wide spectrum of parties feared future racial degeneration if pornography was allowed to infect the present phalanx of teenagers.

Both Belotti and Martire argued that Italy trailed behind other nations in recognizing the dangers of pornography. As early as 1893, an international convention signed in London established the International Bureau against Immoral Literature, with headquarters in Geneva. In line with these accords, Italy founded its own League for Public Morality in 1894. New conventions were signed in Paris in 1910 by fourteen nations, including Italy.[88] Inspired by this international movement, legislation to repress pornography had been introduced repeatedly in the Italian parliament: by Luzzatto in 1910 and 1914, Salandra in 1915, Orlando in 1916, and Nitti in 1919. All these proposals had failed to become law because of government instability or the precedence of larger issues like war.

In the opinion of Martire, liberalism was by definition incapable of fighting the "pornographic gangrene" enveloping the nation.[89] While he praised the authors of earlier legislative proposals, he indicted these liberals as being too tolerant of all values and timid in their prescriptions. Instead, "the method and doctrine of Fascism has given a new tenor to the struggle against pornography, by considering it as one aspect of a more vast and organic program of the State to defend the physical and spiritual vitality of the race and the established structure of traditional morality."[90] Martire welcomed the imminent adoption of Catholicism as the state religion, because it considered "the hierarchical, indissoluble family" as the basis of the state.[91] Thus, the "politics of good morals," including the fight against pornography, had become "for Fascism, a chapter in religious politics."[92]

Despite such alarm, comprehensive legislation to establish a central office of surveillance on all media was not forthcoming. Books and drawings already came under the purview of the criminal codes, which classified obscenity as a crime against "good morals" (*buon costume*). The Zanardelli Code punished "anyone who offends modesty with obscene writings, drawings or other objects of any kind" distributed or displayed in public with imprisonment up to six months and a fine of fifty lire; penalties were higher for those trying to sell obscene writings.[93] The law, however, made no attempt to define obscenity and passed over the matter rather quickly compared to other crimes against *buon costume* like rape and abduction. In 1930, the Rocco Code increased punishment for "anyone . . . who makes, brings into the national

territory, buys, receives, exports, or circulates" obscene writings and drawings.[94] It
defined obscenity as "acts and objects which offend modesty, according to general
sentiment."[95] With such vague wording, the law allowed police and judges wide
powers of censorship in the name of suppressing pornography.[96]

Most innovative in the Rocco Code was the inclusion of films, along with writings and pictures, as possible objects of censure. A form of public entertainment
that became widespread only in the first decades of the twentieth century, the cin-
ema worried legislators from its birth as potentially pornographic. As early as 1913,
Parliament passed a law authorizing state surveillance over domestic and foreign
films, mostly for tax purposes.[97] Only after the fascist seizure of power was the mechanism of censorship clearly outlined. A decree of 1924 instituted a commission to
view all films, with the power to require modifications or forbid distribution. Presided over by a PS functionary, the commission was to be composed of a judge and a
"mother." Revisions of this law in 1929 and 1931 expanded the commission to include a representative of the Fascist Party as well as members of other ministries. By
insisting on fascist participation in censorship, the regime showed a growing preoccupation with political subversion in films. Yet moral censorship remained equally
important, for the "mother" on the commission provided fascist propaganda with a
symbol of its concern for the protection of youth.

Alcoholism

As a legal dictionary published in 1914 pointed out, alcoholism was a "new term"
and not subject to special legislation before 1913. Yet by the turn of the twentieth
century, positivist criminologists had alerted the educated public, as well as lawyers,
doctors, and statesmen, to the degenerative effects of an overconsumption of alcohol on individuals and society. Mild concern about drinking had existed in the late
nineteenth century, but was restricted to bourgeois condemnations of working-
class dissipation as well as growing suspicions, often quite correct, that popular bars
were becoming havens of socialist education and activity. But most middle-class
Italians believed that widespread overindulgence in alcohol was confined to Anglo-
Saxon countries, and the few temperance societies in Italy remained small and
weak.[98] In her study of drinking in turn-of-the-century Genoa, for example,
Augusta Molinari found no evidence of local branches of the Anti-alcohol Leagues
(*Leghe anticooliste*) and Temperance Societies (*Patronati di temperanza*) that had begun to spring up in other cities of the peninsula and especially abroad.[99] The almost
universal consumption of wine among the middle and upper classes as well as the
central place of wine production in the economy contributed to the reluctance of
Italians to demonize alcohol.

Until 1913, Italy had no special statutes on liquor, regulating its sale only by a few
articles in the police laws and the Zanardelli Code. According to the PS Law of
1889, all "public establishments" selling liquor by the glass needed an official license
and were subject to surveillance.[100] "Public establishments" (*esercizi pubblici*) included billiard parlors, public baths, and hotels as well as bars and restaurants. The

PS, in accord with city councils, had the power to set hours for the opening and closing of bars. Permission to open a new bar could be denied if police believed that a
particular neighborhood already had enough drinking establishments. If taverns
became too disorderly or attracted criminals, the PS could suspend their licenses.
The Zanardelli Code added several other grounds for the suspension of liquor licenses: if a bar served a minor under fourteen years of age or someone who was already inebriated.[101] Police could also charge individual consumers with
misdemeanors if they displayed "troublesome and disgusting drunkenness" in public, fining them up to thirty lire. Repeated drunkenness could bring up to a month of
arrest in a workhouse or jail.[102]

By the twentieth century, positivist warnings about the degenerative effects of alcoholism had altered perceptions of drinking. Previously, while taverns were considered to be potential places of disorder and drunkards to be lazy and bothersome
to respectable city dwellers, alcohol was viewed as only a minor vice. Anyone might
give in to temptation and consume too much alcohol. Criminal anthropologists,
however, relabeled drunkards as alcoholics, infected with a hereditary disease that
set them apart from "normal" society. As Giolotti's Minister of Justice, Camillo
Finocchiaro-Aprile, explained, "the lethal effects of this disease do not stop at the
individual who is struck down by it, but have grave repercussions on his children
and descendents, making them more subject to tuberculosis, to epilepsy, [and] to
insanity."[103] Like syphilis, alcoholism also led to crime. According to Deputy
Umberto Gabbi, who served as a doctor in a reformatory at Parma, 50 percent of the
inmates at the male reformatory had alcoholic parents. According to his observations, these boys "no longer have a moral sense . . . [and] are inclined to crime, theft,
idleness, [and] violence."[104]

Based on such reasoning, Giolitti introduced the first law devoted solely to curb-
ing drink to Parliament in 1911 and succeeded in getting it passed by 1913. Entitled
"Provisions for combating alcoholism," the law sought to avert a crisis in which "alcoholism is becoming ever more widespread in Italy and is now expanding to include even groups that until now have been known for their exemplary sobriety."[105]
Finocchiaro-Aprile reported that mortality from chronic alcoholism had doubled
between 1887 and 1908, while alcoholic insanity had more than tripled. Correlating these frightening figures with the more than tenfold increase in the production of alcoholic beverages in Italy, he concluded that "the diffusion of the calamity
of alcoholism thus follows exactly and proportionally the rise in production."[106] He
also noted an increasing density of taverns, which had risen from one per 175 inhabitants in 1904 to one per 151 inhabitants in 1909. Finocchiaro-Aprile explained
that he would refrain from dwelling at length on the "damage" that arose from the
"abuse of alcoholism," since criminologists and doctors had already made them
known to everyone.[107]

Despite such inflamed language, the Law on Alcoholism of 1913 was far from one
of prohibition.[108] Establishments selling drinks by the glass now needed special authorization from the prefect, but only if they sold liquor with more than a 21 percent
content of alcohol, thus excluding wine. The prefect would base his permission on

the vote of a special provincial commission made up of health and police officials. The number of such establishments could not exceed one per 500 inhabitants, although producers who sold their own wine were exempt. Contrary to tradition, employers could no longer compensate their workers partly with hard liquor. The production, importation, or selling of absinthe, popularly called green poison (*veleno verde*) and considered the downfall of the poor, was totally forbidden. Sanctions against habitual drunks were strengthened, so that anyone arrested twice for "troublesome and disgusting drunkeness"—the phrase from the Zanardelli Code— or who had committed a crime while drunk would lose his right to vote or serve on a jury for five years after release from jail. Having just expanded suffrage to all adult men in 1913, Giolitti hoped that the lower classes would prize their new political power enough to refrain from inebriation. Finally, the law raised the age of minors who could be served hard liquor from fourteen to sixteen.

The fascist government decreed its own "Ordinances for Combatting Alcoholism" immediately upon taking power.[109] Complaining that the earlier ceiling on the density of taverns had not always been enforced, framers of the new legislation raised it to one per 1,000 inhabitants. They also spelled out the exact hours of opening and closing for bars, matters that had been formerly left to the discretion of the PS. When questioned about fascist policies to improve the health of the race, Federzoni boasted about this law as well as the Mussolini Law of 1923 on venereal disease. He added that "we consider it the precise duty of the national Government to work with all possible ardor and zeal to protect the child, the little Italian, not only in the area of health but also and above all in social matters and morality."[110]

For a nation proud of its wine and with a long tradition of drinking among adults, the legislation of 1913 and 1923 represented significant change. These laws recognized alcoholism as a disease and sought to combat it by limiting the sale of hard liquor. The impact of criminal anthropology is clear in the singling out of children as special objects of protection and of recidivist drunks as targets of punishment. The latter, according to recent studies, were mostly men, although neither law made any distinction between the sexes.[111] The only defeat for positivist criminologists came in response to their call for the institution of special "asylums" for the cure of criminal alcoholics. These asylums would ensure the individualization of punishment and take their place beside the hospitals for the criminally insane (*manicomi criminali*). But Giolitti opposed asylums for alcoholics on the grounds of cost; he held it too risky to proclaim "a rule that all the drunkards in the country could expect to be supported at the expense of the state."[112]

Narcotic Drugs

Unlike prostitution, pornography, and alcohol, use of narcotic drugs prompted little comment or parliamentary debate before the interwar period. But criminal anthropologists warned that drug addiction, like alcoholism, could lead to the degeneration of body and mind. The fascist government issued the first Law on Drugs in 1923. This law forbade the sale and consumption of cocaine, morphine, and "in general, poisonous substances that have a narcotic effect when taken in small amounts."[113] Most stringent of the morals legislation, it criminalized all use of recreational drugs, while prostitution, pornography, and drinking remained legal if carried out within guidelines set by the state.

Doctors and pharmacists could still prescribe and sell narcotics for medicinal purposes, although the law promised strict surveillance over their activities. Practitioners of both professions had to take care, since the former could be fined for not writing clearly the name and address of the patient on the prescription and the latter for filling such defective prescriptions. Punishment for pharmacists who sold narcotics without a prescription or increased the prescribed dosage was both jail time and a fine. Doctors and pharmacists faced suspension of their licenses if arrested more than once for any of these offences. The law required that pharmaceutical companies obtain special authorization from the PS to sell narcotic drugs, with their sale limited to medical or scientific uses.

Unlicensed vendors of recreational drugs also faced jail and a fine at the first arrest and harsher penalties for recidivism. Consistent with the general campaign to prevent the spread of immorality among children, punishment increased for anyone selling drugs to minors. Convicted drug dealers could be barred temporarily from public employment. Police could arrest anyone attending a gathering where drugs were being taken, even if the club or party was private. They were also authorized to shut down any such meeting place and confiscate its furnishings. Generally, penalties were heavier for sellers than consumers, with the former required to pay for the publication of their sentences in the newspaper.

As in the case of prostitution and pornography, Italy was not alone in its moral crusade against drugs in the interwar period. In 1931, Italy joined other nations in Geneva to sign an international convention to regulate the production and distribution of narcotic drugs.[114] Under the umbrella of this international effort, the fascist dictatorship strengthened its drug laws in 1934.[115] Drawing a strict line between dealers and consumers of narcotics, the legislation for the first time classified the unlicensed sale of drugs or the hosting of gatherings where drugs were consumed as felonies rather than misdemeanors.[116] Identical punishment fell on growers of marijuana or refiners of opium, two drugs left unnamed in earlier legislation. Police could consider repeated arrest for any of these crimes as sufficient grounds for declaring an individual to be a professional or habitual criminal or, in the new parlance of the Rocco Code, one "with a tendency to commit crime." As we will see in the next section, such a designation invited special police surveillance and harsher punishment.

Although the Drug Law of 1934 continued to label consumption as only a misdemeanor, it nevertheless strengthened surveillance of the state over drug users. Any participant in a public or private gathering who was "caught in a state of severe psychological impairment from drug abuse" was subject to not only a fine but also incarceration. Doctors were required to notify the PS of any patients suffering from chronic use of narcotics. Finally, the state could sentence anyone arrested for drug use to a hospital for "detoxification." Judges were to issue such sentences on the advice of police or psychiatrists.

To coordinate the repression of drug use, a "Consultative Committee on Narcotics" was established under the aegis of the Division of Public Health within the Ministry of the Interior. In the spirit of the eugenics movement, the Law of 1934 seemed most concerned over racial rather than individual health, emphasizing the links between drugs on the one hand and insanity or "the tendency to commit crime" on the other. Fear of degeneration is also clear from the repetition, in two different articles, of aggravated punishment for the sale of drugs to minors, even by licensed pharmacists following a legal prescription. It is not therefore surprising that positivist criminologists approved of the new fascist laws against, in Falco's terms, "the terrible ulcer of narcotics."[117] His only reservation was that the law might not be able to trap the "small sellers," often prostitutes and beggars, who worked at night. With these words, he added drug use to the list of behaviors that deserved to be criminalized in the name of positivist "social defense."

THE ROCCO CODE AND EUGENICS

Since the passage of the Rocco Code in 1930, lawyers and criminologists have debated the degree to which it, unlike the earlier Zanardelli Code of 1889, embraced the principles of positivism. Controversy has centered on the issue of free will versus social defense. Did the fascist code retain the classical principle of moral responsibility as the justification for punishment, or was it replaced by the positivist concept of dangerousness? Were penalties tailored to the crime or the criminal?

Efforts to replace the Zanardelli Code went back to 1921, when a parliamentary commission drew up a proposal for a new penal code. Criminal anthropologists were certain that their theories would finally triumph, for Ferri had been appointed to head the commission. With the help of colleagues like Garofalo, Ferri constructed a new code based on "general norms" that were clearly positivist.[118] Listed in a detailed introduction, these norms recommended that criminals be held legally but not morally responsible for their crimes; that punishment be based on the "dangerousness" of each defendant; and that sentences be conditional. Ample provisions were made for "penal substitutes" like suspended sentences and parole for less dangerous criminals, while penalties were compounded for those posing a high threat to society. The code offered a complex equation for measuring dangerousness, which included consideration of "abnormal organic and psychological conditions . . . that reveal a criminal tendency."[119]

In the tumultuous political atmosphere of 1921, Parliament failed to consider the "Ferri Code." In 1925 Mussolini appointed a new commission to study the question, which included Garofalo. But this commission had little power, simply rubber stamping the proposal of Alfredo Rocco, the fascist Minister of Justice. Rocco's Code mixed tenets of both the Classical and Positivist Schools. It claimed to be inspired by a new movement in legal philosophy that was labeled variously as the "Third," "Eclectic," or "Technical-juridical" School.

The Third School dated from a famous address given by Arturo Rocco, the brother of Alfredo, at the University of Sassari in 1910. In his speech, Arturo Rocco pronounced both classicism and positivism as outdated and explained their weaknesses. Foreshadowing the fascist critique of the Enlightenment, he ridiculed the Classical School's appeal to natural law or universal principles against which to measure "positive" or existing law. He called on legal scholars to shun philosophy and the vain search for timeless truths and concentrate on the meticulous dissection of the law as already codified for twentieth-century Italy.

On the other hand, he criticized the Positivist School for abandoning true legal research and immersing itself in the biological and social sciences. While supporters of the technical-juridical approach had no fundamental philosophical argument with criminal anthropology, they wanted empirical research strictly subordinated to the more pure and glorious analysis of legal categories and definitions. Interest in the criminal should not displace a fundamental focus on law itself. By the 1920s, even this Third School had found critics who ridiculed it for resting on "the minute logic of the scholastic dilettante" and offering nothing but an inconsistent hybrid of its predecessors.[120] Yet the technical-juridical approach gained wide prestige within law schools, partly because its adherents could avoid choosing between classicism and positivism.

Despite the eclecticism of the Rocco Code, criminal anthropologists declared it a triumph for their approach. In the *Bulletin*, Ottolenghi praised the code as "an obvious example of how science can be put into practice."[121] He was especially delighted at Article 108, which increased punishment for defendants exhibiting a "tendency to commit crime." Positivists considered the figure of the "criminal by tendency" in the Rocco Code to be the equivalent of the born criminal. Indeed, this article prescribed penalties based entirely on the character of the criminal rather than the nature of the crime. In the spirit of positivism, punishment was also increased for "habitual" and "professional" criminals. Unlike the Ferri Code, however, penalties for criminals outside of these three categories continued to be correlated to the severity of the crime.

Positivist influence was also evident in the section of the Rocco Code on "security measures" (*misure di sicurezza*). These were administrative measures that could be applied "to persons considered dangerous to society" even if they had committed no crime.[122] Security measures included internment in workhouses for adults, reformatories for juveniles, psychiatric hospitals for the insane, and special jails for "habitual" drunkards or drug users. Such sentences were indeterminate in length, lasting until "the persons subjected to them have ceased to be dangerous to society."[123] Judges had the discretion to add a period of "supervised liberty" (*libertà vigilata*) at the end of sentences. Thus, like the Juvenile Code, the Rocco Code promised to extend the reach of the criminal justice system over an ever larger proportion of the population as even noncriminals were subjected to security measures. Consistent with the positivist philosophy of preventive policing, security measures provided fascist officials with a legal method of isolating its enemies from the rest of society.

In addition to the concepts of "criminal by tendency" and "security measures," positivism also influenced the Rocco Code in its approach to eugenics. Twenty years earlier, criminal anthropologists had been among the first adherents in Italy of the international eugenics movement, already popular in nations like Germany, England, and the United States. Eugenicists believed in the power of heredity to transmit not only "social" diseases like syphilis and tuberculosis, but also "deviant" behavior like crime and insanity. They warned that governments must begin to take measures to cleanse their national populations from physical and moral taint. In 1913, Leonardo Bianchi, a positivist criminologist and member of the Chamber of Deputies, alerted his parliamentary colleagues to the importance of eugenics, which he defined as "control of structure, strength, and human attitudes for the purpose of obtaining the maximum number of industrious men to build civilization."[124] Feeling a duty to bring the issue to the chamber, he warned that "some statesmen from the North [of Europe] have expressed unfavorable opinions on the psycho-organic condition of the races of the Mediterranean basin and fear for their future, believing they are characterized by degeneration and obvious signs of deterioration."[125] While Prime Minister Giolitti congratulated Bianchi for bringing before the Chamber for the first time the need "to defend our race from weaknesses that could later become the cause of decadence," he was evasive about committing the government to new programs. Beyond the present legislation to control venereal disease and malaria and the proposed law on alcoholism, the state promised to do little more.

In addition to Bianchi, criminal anthropologists like Garofalo, Morselli, Niceforo, and Marro were active in the Italian eugenics movement. Brought together at the first International Congress of Eugenics held in London in 1912, Italian eugenicists lagged behind the British, Americans, and Germans in formal organization or concerted policy. World War I, however, accelerated fear over the degeneration of the Italian population, in both quantitative and qualitative terms. In 1922, concern about the "future of the race" led to the founding of the Italian Society of Genetics and Eugenics (SIGE) and the launching of its journal, *Social Defense*.[126] SIGE held conferences in Milan in 1924 and Rome in 1929, with Mussolini serving as honorary president of the latter. Eugenics gained academic legitimacy with the establishment in 1924 at the University of Milan of the first chair in the field.

During the 1920s and 1930s, criminal anthropologists continued to provide theoretical justifications for eugenics. In his *Manual of Criminal Anthropology*, published in 1931, Di Tullio defined eugenics as "that part of modern medicine that studies the causes of human degeneration, and therefore of physical and moral feebleness, in order to eliminate them and reduce the number of weak, unfit, and antisocial individuals in general and to secure a gradual improvement in future generations and a continual reinforcement of the race."[127] He argued that a strong eugenics policy would fight crime, since lawbreaking was an obvious sign of individual maladjustment. By weeding out the abnormal, eugenics promised to provide the fascist government with a population that "adapted easily to social life" and would become a "useful element for both the material and the spiritual life of the Nation."[128]

While such language echoed the rationalizations of Nazis to exterminate the elderly and sick in Germany during the 1930s, in fact Di Tullio opposed violent methods of eliminating the unfit. Instead, he urged the state to forbid marriage of psychopaths, epileptics, alcoholics, and carriers of syphilis and tuberculosis since all these diseases weakened the constitution and encouraged a predisposition to crime. He also recommended that criminals submit to hormonal treatment that promised to modify their physical and therefore psychological makeup. He claimed, for example, that endocrinologists had developed "antisexual hormones" to turn sex criminals into "sociable and altruistic individuals, incapable of doing wrong."[129] More generally, he reiterated his call for the prevention of crime through a combination of surveillance over and assistance to youth.

Obsessed as it was with demographic growth, the fascist dictatorship heeded the call of positivist criminologists for bringing Italy into the international eugenics movement. Debate about eugenics measures, rare before the March on Rome, became frequent in Parliament. In discussions of the budget of the Ministry of the Interior in 1924 and 1925, for example, Deputy Alessandro Guaccero made passionate pleas for new hospitals "to prevent and cure anomalies and deformities of the human body—whether they are constitutional or acquired—which cause predisposition to various organic diseases, abnormal moral developments, and criminality."[130] He explained that such efforts could be based on recent advances in endocrinology, pioneered by Italians such as Pende, and other techniques "in which the Italian school occupies the post of honor."[131] Although the Minister of Interior, Federzoni, went no further than accepting such "medical-sociological Institutes" as a recommendation for government study, they clearly presaged the future "Observation Centers for Youth."

By his famous Ascension Day speech of 1927, Mussolini had accepted eugenics as integral to his vision of increasing and improving the "Italian race." As Carl Ipsen has shown, Italy was a pioneer in fashioning a coherent demographic policy geared to serve primarily not the happiness of individuals or even the needs of the economy, but the military needs of an imperialist state.[132] Despite its willingness to persecute both political and common criminals, Italian fascists refused to practice "negative" eugenics, like sterilization and euthanasia, on individuals or groups considered inferior or deviant. Sterilization became widespread during the interwar period not only in Nazi Germany but also in England and the United States. Partly because of the strong opposition of the Catholic Church to even milder measures like birth control, abortion, and medical screening before marriage, neither criminal anthropologists nor fascist officials copied their Nazi ally in advocating extreme measures like sterilization and euthanasia.

Mussolini, however, was enthusiastic about "positive" eugenics that would increase the size of the Italian population. To encourage large families, the fascist regime imposed a tax on bachelors that confiscated at least 25 percent of the earnings of all single men between the ages of twenty-six and sixty-five.[133] It granted tax breaks to large families, allowances for children, and even interest-free loans to couples marrying before the age of twenty-six.[134] In 1933, the regime instituted a fascist

Mother's Day and inaugurated this new tradition by having each province send its female resident with the most children to a ceremony in Rome. Because fascism held that motherhood was the proper destiny for women, legislation imposed quotas on the numbers of women in universities and certain sectors of the workforce. Simultaneously, all non-fascist women's organizations were disbanded unless they agreed to restrict their activities to charity work and stay out of politics. Emigration, formerly a safety valve for Italy's burgeoning population, was discouraged.

A similarly disparate package of policies aimed at improving the physical and moral "quality" of the race. The regime sought to protect morality, especially of the young, by regulating prostitution, pornography, drinking, and drug use. ONMI was chartered not only to decrease infant mortality, but also to give food and medical care to poor, illegitimate, and abandoned children, who were thought to be prone to degeneration. If such positive measures failed, the observation centers and reformatories were available for isolating and remolding recalcitrant youth.

It is clear that women bore the brunt of such fascist initiatives, in that their bodies and physical power of reproduction were the locus for state intervention in the name of eugenics. As Victoria de Grazia has pointed out, women who heeded the fascist call to bear more children received no direct compensation; the state instead awarded tax breaks and family allowances to their husbands.[135] Not only did such policies fail to empower women who fulfilled their missions as mothers, but they ratified state intervention and surveillance over women's reproduction. Even if healthy and pure, women were now only breeding machines who were to give up their traditional role of moral and cultural education to the fascism, with its politicized schools, youth groups, observation centers, and reformatories. Such intervention was nowhere more clear than in the formulation of the crimes of birth control and abortion in the Rocco Code.

Early criminal anthropologists like Lombroso had opposed severe sanctions for abortion and even infanticide. But as in the case of *ammonizione* and *domicilio coatto*, positivist criminology had prepared the ground for repressive legislation against certain criminal types. In this case it was women, who had been defined since the publication of *The Female Offender* as semi-criminals, perpetually arrested on the evolutionary scale. Controlled by their sexual organs, women were too irrational to participate fully in political life. Only the instincts of motherhood would keep women's criminal tendencies in check. According to the famous formulation of Lombroso, atavistic or degenerate women automatically regressed to a state of sexual aberration, typified by prostitution. Such logic fed smoothly into the eugenics of fascism that wished both to increase the population and punish sexual deviancy. Fascist ideology appropriated the positivist lesson that motherhood represented the only normal and healthy state for women, while sexual deviancy threatened evolution as decreed by natural law. It simply extended the category of sexual deviancy to include birth control and abortion. Because criminal anthropology had never advanced the principles of women's rights in its defense of the decriminalization of abortion and infanticide, it offered a weak legacy for opposing fascist initiatives. Lombroso's argument that women who committed infanticide or abortion were occasional criminals and therefore posed little danger to society became less persuasive. Positivists during the interwar years, like Di Tullio, abandoned the pragmatic grounds proposed by their predecessors for leniency in cases of abortion and applauded the Rocco Code for its defense of the race.

Before 1926, birth control was not illegal in united Italy. Opposition to "neo-Malthusianism" was vocal, however, and made strange bedfellows. On the one hand, the Catholic Church continued its traditional condemnation of any type of sexuality not leading to procreation, which included masturbation, homosexuality, and marital intercourse employing *coitus interruptus,* condoms, and diaphragms. On the other hand, many gynecologists—a group that tended to be anti-clerical—condemned birth control on biological grounds. Defining the female role as motherhood, they predicted degeneration among women who avoided their fate. Especially dangerous was *coitus interruptus,* which they claimed left a woman with "serious nervous derangement from the 'failed discharge of sperm'" into her womb and lack of orgasm.[136] While many of these doctors echoed arguments of criminal anthropology about women's nature in their denunciations of birth control, they did not follow Lombroso's lead in preferring birth control and abortion to illegitimacy.

Not until the fascist era did birth control become the subject of government concern. As part of its campaign for population growth, the state gave police the power, in the PS Law of 1926, to arrest anyone printing or distributing information on "methods for impeding fertilization."[137] Newspapers and magazines risked confiscation for publishing advertisements mentioning birth control, even with a "medical or scientific pretext."[138] In 1930, the Rocco Code integrated this prohibition into its new and notorious rubric, "Crimes against the integrity and health of the race," that made eugenics central to criminal law. As one of the framers explained, "The penal code would not . . . conform to the directives on political demography of the new Italian State if it was not equipped with all the most energetic means of struggle against wicked practices to destroy fertility."[139] It prescribed punishment not only for "anyone who publicly incites to practices against fertility or makes propaganda in favor of them," as in the PS Law, but also for the consenting recipient of birth control and her accomplices.[140]

Fascist legislation against abortion also began with the PS Law of 1926, whose prohibition against the publication or distribution of information on birth control extended equally to abortion. But the tightening of penalties on abortion itself awaited the Rocco Code of 1930. Although the earlier Zanardelli Code had criminalized abortion, the fascist statute was harsher in three ways. First, it reclassified abortion, moving it from the rubric of crimes against the person to that of crimes against the integrity and health of the race. Such a redefinition put emphasis on the interests of society and the state rather than those of the individual or family. Second, punishment was increased for those who practiced abortion and the women who asked for their assistance; both were to be incarcerated for two to five years.[141] Accomplices received longer sentences if they belonged to the medical profession, if their patient was a minor (under fourteen), if she had not consented to the procedure, or if she died. Third, the Rocco Code proposed sanctions for attempted abortion, even if the female recipient turned out not to have been pregnant.[142] While the Zanardelli Code had been vague on this issue, most legal specialists and courts held that the crime of abortion could occur only if the necessary conditions were present, that is, the woman was pregnant and the fetus was successfully aborted. By criminalizing attempted abortion, the fascist code potentially subjected ever widening circles of women to surveillance and punishment by the state.[143]

CONCLUSION

Far from dying with Lombroso, positivism remained the dominant school within the academic discipline of criminology and a fundamental doctrine shaping Italian penal law throughout the interwar period. It represented one of the competing discourses that made up fascist ideology, an ideology that was neither unitary nor consistent. As shown by the Rocco Code, criminal anthropology never succeeded in defeating conclusively the free will doctrine of Classical and Catholic legal thinkers or the eclecticism of the "Third School." But the positivist doctrine of biological determinism had a much larger impact on fascist policy than has formerly been thought. Despite Mussolini's official rejection of materialism and socialism in favor of "action," "will," and the "spirit," the regime worked closely with criminal anthropologists and incorporated their views into legislation on police, juvenile justice, and morality. It drew on their prestige as members of the self-proclaimed "Italian School" that had attracted so much international attention for fifty years. While many fascist bureaucrats may have cared little for the philosophical substructure of positivist criminology, they appropriated its biological vocabulary to define certain groups as inferior and therefore deserving targets of surveillance and repression.

Those criminal anthropologists who so willingly collaborated with the fascist dictatorship were in some ways different from the founding fathers of the late nineteenth century. Early positivist criminologists tended to ally themselves with the socialist party and—despite a social Darwinism that pronounced women, southerners, nonwhites, and children as inferior to northern white men—expressed a humanitarian concern for the poor and oppressed. They felt a genuine if naive faith in the power of science to solve some of the problems that caused criminality. They can be faulted for sensationalizing lurid cases of born criminality, which fed moral panics and encouraged "hard" or conservative measures of "social defense." Yet many, like Ferri, were also tireless in campaigning for "penal substitutes" that would help to eliminate environmental causes of crime. No group was more committed to finding alternatives to prison, at least in the case of occasional criminals.

Yet the theory of positivist criminology needed to undergo little fundamental change when its proponents rejected socialism for fascism after World War I. Despite its birth in an era of liberalism, many of its basic tenets were in tension with democracy and individual rights. Emphasizing "social defense," Lombroso and his colleagues promoted the examination and categorization of all children for the purpose of identifying born criminals. Biology was destiny, and criminal anthropologists showed no reservations about interning children even before they had committed a crime. In their passion for classification, they advocated that police files document the physical and psychological characteristics of ever widening circles of the citizenry.

Positivist criminologists also created an intellectual environment conducive to dictatorship by labeling entire groups as biologically inferior and demoting them to lower rungs on the evolutionary scale. Such reasoning was finally turned against Lombroso after 1938 by the extreme racist ideologue, Evola. In his hate-filled magazine, *The Defense of the Race*, he denounced Lombroso and Freud as members of an international cadre of dangerous Jewish scientists. Turning the tools of positivism against Jews, he constructed pseudo-scientific charts that traced the transmission of "Jewish blood diseases," hereditary alcoholism, and insanity through successive generations of the Jewish "race."[144] Few of Lombroso's heirs subscribed to such a reductionist view, coming from a school of thought that rejected anti-Semitism, believed in the complexity of Italy's racial map, and held that social as well as biological factors determined human behavior. As war approached, fascist racial theorists increasingly ignored such subtleties, although their ideas remained distinct from the Nazi policies of elimination and extermination.[145]

NOTES

1. Benigno Di Tullio, *Manuale di antropologia e psicologia criminale applicata alla pedagogia emendativa, alla polizia ed al diritto penale e penitenziario* (Rome: Anonima Romana Editoriale, 1931), p. 295.

2. Monachesi, "Trends in Criminological Research in Italy," *American Sociological Review*, v. 1, n. 3 (June, 1936), p. 404.

3. Ibid., p. 396.

4. Commissione reale per la riforma delle leggi penali, *Relazione* (Rome: "L'universelle," 1921).

5. G. Lombroso, *Cesare Lombroso: Storia della vita e delle opere narrata dalla figlia* (Turin: Bocca, 1915). See Dolza, *Essere figlie*, for a fine discussion of Gina and Paola. Ironically, the two daughters of the man who had proven female inferiority were highly educated and well-known intellectuals in the Italy of their day.

6. Beirne, *Inventing Criminology*, pp. 194–99.

7. Quoted in ibid., p. 210.

8. Ibid, p. 213; Beirne agrees largely with Gina, seeing Goring as a contributor to the eugenics movement in England.

9. *Archivio*, v. 41 (1921), p. 722.

10. *Archivio*, v. 41 (1921), p. 435 [Gina Lombroso].

11. These books were *L'anima della donna* (1920), *La donna nella vita* (1923), and *La donna nella società attuale* (1927).

12. Dolza, *Essere figlie*, p. 230.

13. Other examples are Teresa Labriola and Margherita Sarfatti; before World War I, the first had been a leading bourgeois feminist and the second a socialist feminist. This shift to the Right was more widespread among bourgeois feminists than women on the Left.

14. Dolza, *Essere figlie*, p. 102.

15. Quoted in ibid., p. 104.

16. Ibid., p. 105.

17. Mariano L. Patrizi, *Dopo Lombroso: Nuove correnti nello studio della genialità e del delitto* (Milan: Società Editrice Libraria, 1916), p. 91.

18. Ibid.

19. Ibid., p. 99.

20. Ibid., pp. 184–85.

21. Ibid., p. 199

22. Ibid., p. 190.

23. Ibid.

24. Giuseppe Vidoni, *Valore e limiti dell'endocrinologia nell' Antropologia criminale* (Turin: Bocca, 1923), pp. 2, 86.

25. Ibid., pp. 98–99.

26. "Antropologia," *Enciclopedia Italiana*, v. 3, p. 587.

27. Vidoni, *Valore e limiti*, p. 108; Vidoni quoted in Thorsten Sellin, "A New Phase of Criminal Anthropology in Italy," *The Annals of the American Academy of Political and Social Science*, v. 125 (May, 1926), p. 239.

28. Vidoni, *Valore e limiti*, p. 98.

29. Vidoni, *Prostitute e prostutzione* (Turin: S. Lattes, 1921), p. 32.

30. Vidoni, *Valore e limiti*, p. 104.

31. Di Tullio, *Manuale*, pp. 10–11.

32. Di Tullio, *Manuale*, pp. 14–15.

33. Ibid., p. 16.

34. Ibid., p. 79.

35. Ibid., p. 288.

36. Ibid., p. 233.

37. Ibid., p. 232.

38. Ibid., p. 231.

39. Ibid.

40. Ibid.

41. Di Tullio, *Manuale*, p. 233; he repeated his defense of regulation at the International Congress of Criminology in 1938; see "L'organizzazione della profilassi criminale in Italia," *Atti del I. Congresso*, p. 88.

42. Eugenio Florian, Alfredo Niceforo, and Nicola Pende, eds., *Dizionario di criminologia* (Milan: Francesco Vallardi, 1943), v. 1, p. vii.

43. Ibid.

44. In recognition of his importance to criminal anthropology, Florian received a *festschift* at his retirement entitled, *Eugenio Florian: Maestro del positivismo penale* (Milan: Bocca, 1940).

45. Ibid., pp. 109, 110. [Del Pozzo].

46. Ibid., v. 1, p. 398 [F. Grispigni].

47. Ibid., v. 1, p. 514 [Aldofo Zerboglio].

48. Ibid., v. 1, p. 513 [Zerboglio].

49. Ibid., v. 1, p. 366 [Arturo Santoro].

50. Ibid., v. 1, p. 55 [Gian Giacomo Perrando].

51. Ibid., v. 1, p. 270 [Vincenzo Mario Palmieri].

52. Ibid.

53. Ibid., p. 67 [Perrando].

54. Ibid., v. 2, p. 556 [Silvio Brambilla].

55. Ibid., v. 2, p. 558 [Massimo Punzo].

56. "Antropologia criminale," *Enciclopedia italiana*, v. 3, p. 596.

57. Giorgio Gattei, "La sifilide: Medici e poliziotti intorno alla 'Venere politica,'" *Storia d'Italia, Annali*, v. 7, p. 789.

58. Ibid., p. 790. On the military brothels during World War I, see also Emilio Franzina, *Casini di guerra: El tempo libero dalla trincea e i postriboli militari nel primo conflitto mondiale* (Udine: P Gaspari, 1999).

59. Giorgio Mortara, *La salute pubblica in Italia durante e dopo la guerra* (New Haven: Yale University Press, 1925), p. 297.

60. Ibid., p. 226; rates of syphilis also declined markedly among soldiers according to Gattei, "La sifilide," p. 796.

61. Mortara, *La salute pubblica*, p. 360.

62. Italy, C.D., *Disc.*, Legis. 27 (1926), v. 6, p. 5516.

63. Ibid.

64. Ibid., (1924), v. 1, p. 701.

65. Vidoni, *Prostitute*, pp. 3–4.

66. Ibid., p. 22.

67. Ibid., p. xxiv.

68. Ibid.

69. Ibid., p. xix.

70. Ibid., p. xii.

71. Ibid., pp. xii-xiii.

72. Regolamento per la profilassi delle malattie veneree e sifilitiche, 25 March 1923, n. 846.

73. The identification of the *tessere sanitarie* with the old *libretti* was made explicit in T.U. delle leggi di PS, 21 Jan. 1929, which used the phrase *libretto sanitario* (health passport).

74. Circular, Direzione Generale della PS, 10 Oct. 1923, n. 6423.

75. *Boll. SPS*, v. 14–15 (1924–25), p. 7.

76. Testo unico delle leggi di PS, 6 Nov. 1926, n. 1848.

77. Ibid., Art. 213.

78. Gattei, "La sifilide," pp. 794–95. Later fascist laws on the PS (R.D. 18 June 1931, n. 773) and public health (Leggi Sanitarie 27 July 1934) retained identical provisions on prostitution.

79. Leggi sanitarie 27 July 1934.

80. *Codice penale* ed. Ruffo Mangini, Francesco Gabrieli, and Ubaldo Cosentino (Rome: L. Colombo, 1930), p. 432

81. *Boll. SPS*, v. 27–29 (1937–39), p. 62.

82. Ibid., pp. 159–60.

83. Ibid., p. 195 [Falco]

84. Italy, C.D., *Disegni*, Legis. 27 (1924), v. 6, n. 123, p. 1.

85. Italy, C.D., *Disc.*, Legis. 26 (1923), v. 10, p. 9612.

86. Italy, C.D., *Disegni*, Legis. 27 (1924), v. 6, n. 123A, p. 12.

87. Ibid, p. 13.

88. The conventions of 1910 were approved in Italy by R.D. 25 March 1911.

89. Italy, C.D., *Disegni*, Legis. 27 (1924), v. 6, n. 123A, p. 2.

90. Ibid., p. 4.

91. In 1929, Mussolini and the Vatican signed the Lateran Accords, which reconciled Church and state for the first time since unification and recognized Roman Catholicism as the sole religion of Italy.

92. Ibid., p. 8.

93. Criminal Code of 1889, Art. 339.

94. Criminal Code of 1930, Art. 528.

95. Ibid., Art. 529.

96. Works of art and science were exempted from the law unless distributed to minors outside of the classroom.

97. Legge 25 June 1913.

98. Tringali, Sabastiano, *Dizionario legale* (Milan: Hoepli, 1914), p. 51.

99. Augusta Molinari, "Alcool e alcoolisti a Genova tra Ottocento e Novecento: Una prima ricognizione," *Movimento operaio e socialista*, v. 11 (New series), n. 2 (May–Aug., 1988), p, 280.

100. See PS Law 1888, Arts. 50–58. for regulations on the sale of alcohol.

101. Criminal Code of 1889, Art. 489.

102. Ibid., Art. 488.

103. Italy, C.D., *Disegni*, Legis. 23:1 (1911), v. 19, n. 885, p. 2.

104. Italy, C.D., *Disc.*, Legis. 27 (1926), v. 6, p. 5500.

105. Italy, C.D., *Disegni*, Legis. 23 (1911), v. 19, n. 885, p. 1.

106. Ibid.

107. Ibid., p. 2.

108. Law of 19 June 1913, n. 632

109. R. D.-Legge 7 October 1923, n. 2208

110. Italy, C.D., *Disc.*, Legis. 27 (1924), v. 1, p. 701.

111. Michela Figurelli, "L'alcool e la classe: Cenni per una storia dell'alcoolismo in Italia," *Classe*, n 15 (June, 1978), pp. 116, 121; Molinari, "L'alcool e alcoolisti," p. 284.

112. Quoted in Figurelli, "L'alcool e la classe," p. 125.

113. Legge 18 February 1923, n. 396.

114. Signed July 13, 1931, this convention was approved in Italy by Legge 16 January 1933, n. 130.

115. Decreto-Legge 15 January 1934, n. 151.

116. The Italian categories, which are not exactly parallel, are *delitti* and *contravvenzioni*.

117. *Boll. SPS*, v. 9–11 (1919–21), p. 225.

118. Commissione reale per la riforma delle leggi penali, *Relazione sul progetto preliminare di Codice penale italiano* (Rome: "L'universelle," 1921), p. 149.

119. Ibid., Book 1, Art. 21.

120. Ugo Spirito, *Storia del diritto penale italiano da Cesare Beccaria al nostri giorni* (Florence: Sansoni, 1974; orig. published 1924), p. 200.

121. *Boll. SPS*, v. 19–20 (1929–30), p. 134.

122. Criminal Code of 1930, Arts. 202–203.

123. Ibid., Art. 207.

124. Italy, C.D., *Disc.*, Legis. 23 (1913), v. 20, p. 24283.

125. Ibid., p. 24282.

126. The scholar who initiated research into Italian eugenics is Claudio Pogliano. See his "Scienza e stirpe: Eugenica in Italia (1912–1939)," *Passato e presente*, v. 5 (Jan.–June, 1984), p. 71; and "Eugenisti ma con giudizio," in *Nel nome della razza*, ed. Burgio, pp. 423–42.

127. Di Tullio, *Manuale*, p. 299.

128. Ibid., p. 294.

129. Ibid., p. 316.

130. Italy, C.D., *Disc.*, Legis. 27 (1924), v. 1, p. 725.

131. Italy, C.D., *Disc.*, Legis. 27 (1925), v. 3, p. 2397.

132. Carl Ipsen, *Dictating Demography: The Problem of Population in Fascist Italy* (New York: Cambridge University Press, 1996).

133. Regio Decreto 19 Dicembre 1926.

134. Roberto Volpi, *Storia della popolazione italiana dall'Unità a oggi* (Florence: La Nuova Italia, 1989), p. 112.

135. Victoria De Grazia, *How Fascism Ruled Women* (Berkeley: University of California Press, 1992), p. 70.

136. De Longis, "'In difesa della donna e della razza,'" *Nuova Donnawomanfemme*, n. 19–20 (Winter-Spring, 1982), p. 161.

137. PS Law, 1926, Art. 113

138. PS law, 1926, Art. 115; it was replaced in 1931 PS law by similar articles (112 and 114).

139. *Codice penale*, ed. Mangini et al., p. 431.

140. Criminal Code of 1930, Art. 553.

141. Penalties remained the same only for women who aborted themselves without assistance; both the Zanardelli and Rocco Codes required one to four years of prison.

142. Criminal Code of 1930, Arts. 548 and 550.

143. Despite the severity of the Rocco Code, abortion remained frequent under fascism. See Denise Destragiache, "Un aspect de la politique démographique de l'Italie fasciste: La répression de l'avortement," *Mélanges de l'École francaise de Rome*, v. 92, pt. 2 (1980), pp. 691–735 and Luisa Passerini, "Donne operaie e aborto nella Torino fascista," *Italia contemporanea*, v. 151–52 (Sept., 1983), pp. 83–109.

144. Julius Evola, *Difesa della Razza*, v. 2 (1938), p. 7.

145. On the evolution of fascist racial policy and the debates among racial theorists, see Roberto Maiocchi, *Scienza italiana e razzismo fascista*.

Conclusion

During his lifetime, Lombroso succeeded in catching the imagination of artists and intellectuals throughout Europe and the Americas with his notion of the born criminal. Although the nuances of his theory were often ignored, his image of the atavistic deviant marked by telltale anomalies was widely appropriated. Characters in novels like *Resurrection* by Leo Tolstoy, and *The Secret Agent* by Joseph Conrad referred to Lombroso and his equation of criminality with savagery.[1] Even when authors mocked the Lombrosian conceit, they nevertheless expected their readers to be acquainted with the most sensational aspects of criminal anthropology.

This widespread familiarity with the theory of the born criminal was not coincidential, for Lombroso labored throughout his career to turn criminal anthropology into an international school of thought or, as one French scholar has put it, "a science without borders."[2] Although this book has focused on the impact of Lombrosian criminology within Italy, an evaluation of its impact abroad is warranted. This task is not easy, because serious histories of the development of criminology in Europe and the Americas are only beginning to appear. Several recent studies, however, allow an initial assessment of the popularity of biological determinism among criminologists outside of Italy in the late nineteenth and early twentieth centuries.

As the conclusion to Chapter 1 recounted, fervent opposition to Lombroso's theories of atavism and the born criminal arose as early as the second Congress of Criminal Anthropology, held in Paris in 1889. French criminologists, led by Alexandre Lacassagne and including Léonce Manouvrier, Paul Topinard, and Gabriel Tarde, instigated a bitter attack on the Italian School. This so-called French School (or Lyons School after the university of Lacassagne) rallied around the phrase "social milieu" as an alternative to atavism as the explanation of the etiology of crime. Attacking Lombroso's methodology, the French asserted the impossibility of proving that atavistic anomalies caused crime and therefore could serve as the basis for identifying born criminals. As we have seen, however, the proposed test was never implemented, leaving the Italian-French quarrel to simmer until World War I.

A recent collection of essays on French criminology argues that the opposition to Lombroso was more political than theoretical. Laurent Mucchielli believes that Lacassagne and his allies adopted the phrase "French school of social milieu" as "an appellation of combat" against the Italian domination of criminological discourse.[3] They disdained the hubris of Lombroso, who "had proclaimed himself as the pope of criminal anthropology." Exaggerating their differences with the Italian Positivist School, French criminologists sought to bolster their national reputation at home and abroad.

What distinguished the French from the Italian interpretation of the etiology of crime was more a question of emphasis than substance. Both schools were eclectic, combining social and biological causes of crime. Although the French proclaimed themselves the champions of social milieu, the Italians, most notably Ferri but also Lombroso, had always included education, poverty, and other environmental factors in their analyses. Similarly, the French never renounced biology or determinism as essential to a universal theory of crime. As Mucchielli points out, Lacassagne was, like Lombroso, a doctor and professor of legal medicine. While rejecting the notion of atavism, he nonetheless remained a fervent believer in phrenology throughout his career and accepted the classification of races based on biological criteria. Moreover, he believed in the significance of physical anomalies, simply differing from Lombroso in the explanation of their derivation. For Lacassagne, as for most French scientists, anomalies did not signal atavism but degeneration, or regression caused by social pathologies like alcoholism and syphilis. Although social in origin, these anomalies could become hereditary, leading to increasingly severe regression. The French, like the Italians, tended to dismiss Mendelian genetics and, in their case, relied on the Lamarckian theory that acquired characteristics, even if social in origin, could be passed down from generation to generation.

A recent study by Richard Wetzell of major German criminologists of the late nineteenth and early twentieth centuries reveals a similar pattern to the French. Franz von Liszt, the founder of the "modern school of criminal law" in Germany, rejected the notion of the born criminal, but nevertheless accepted many other major tenets of Italian positivism. Diagnosing crime as pathology, von Liszt advocated, like the Italians, that punishments be calibrated to the degree of dangerousness posed by the criminal. "Occasional" criminals thus deserved lighter retribution than "habitual" criminals. According to Wetzell, von Liszt was inspired by Lombroso to link biology to crime and by the 1890s classified "habitual criminals" as degenerates.[4]

As the subsequent development of German criminology moved into the field of psychiatry, Lombroso continued to inspire debate. Only Kurella, who translated Lombroso into German, defended the theory of the born criminal in its entirety. But other major figures in German psychiatry, like Emil Kraepelin and Gustav Aschaffenburg, while criticizing the notion of atavism, accepted the general research agenda set by Italian criminal anthropologists. For Kraepelin, the inborn traits that caused crime were psychological rather than physical, while Aschaffenburg blamed degeneration rather than atavism for deviancy. But both schools of thought followed the Lombrosian paradigm by focusing their research on the pathological and hereditary traits of individual criminals.[5]

Recent studies of the development of British criminology find less direct influence of Lombroso than on the continent, partially because *Criminal Man* was not translated into English until 1911 and then only in a brief and unrecognizable form edited by his daughter. Lombroso did have an English champion in Havelock Ellis, who reproduced the theories of the Italian school in his compendium, *The Criminal*, published in 1890. But, according to David Garland, Ellis's work did not fit within the indigenous tradition that rejected theory for pragmatic measures to manage criminals. The latter were developed by doctors in penal and psychiatric institutions rather than by university professors.[6] Yet this pragmatic approach, I would argue, was resolutely medical and fit within the international movement away from the Classical School and its emphasis on morality and character as the causative factors of crime. Like Italian criminal anthropologists, English prison doctors increasingly classified inmates as mentally incompetent and not entirely responsible for their actions. Even Goring, the prison doctor who claimed in 1911 to have rebutted definitively Lombroso's theory of atavism, substituted the clearly biological hypothesis of criminal diathesis to identify criminals.[7]

Although British criminologists may have greeted much of Italian positivism with relative indifference, they were eager to accept Lombroso's stereotype of the female offender as sick and degenerate. According to Lucia Zedner, although the impact of Lombroso's writings was limited in England, "in the case of female criminality it was obstinately enduring."[8] It promoted the image of the criminal woman as pathological and psychologically unbalanced. This psychological analysis was rooted in biology, because women's reproductive cycle and sexual organs were thought to control their minds. English reformatories for women, therefore, focused not on economic and social retraining but on psychological therapy. Special institutions were opened for the "feeble-minded" and other dangerous defectives. That "deviant" sexual behavior was considered a sign of feeble-mindedness was compatible with the Lombrosian conception of the prostitute as the typical female offender.

Compared to England, the United States was more receptive to the Italian school, although American criminal anthropologists redrew the image of the born criminal. According to a recent study by Nicole Rafter, most early nineteenth-century writings on American crime came from the pens of prison administrators or reformers, who did not consider themselves theorists. While this profile resembles that of England, Lombroso's impact was much greater, leading to the establishment of an American school of criminal anthropology by the 1890s.[9] Instrumental to the propagation of Italian positivism was the American Institute of Criminal Law and Criminology, which translated the major works of not only Lombroso but also Ferri and Garofalo. As we have seen, the publication in English of Lombroso began in

1895 with *The Female Offender*, assuring that his theories on female inferiority and sexual atavism had an early and lasting impact on American criminology. As in England, the Lombrosian notion that biological factors controlled the will and mind of criminals remained unchallenged for much longer in studies of female than male delinquency.

Under the influence of the Italian school, American criminologists began to identify themselves as scientists, committed to expanding the theoretical body of knowledge about the etiology of crime through empirical research. Rafter documents that these new criminal anthropologists did not add any startling new discoveries to the general Italian theory of the born criminal, but elaborated certain aspects. First, they warned of the hereditary danger of atavism, leading them quickly into the eugenicist camp. Second, they increasingly focused their studies on mental, rather than physical or psychological, anomalies. Thus, in the United States, criminologists developed new categories for the born criminal, including the criminal imbecile and the defective delinquent, both signifying low intelligence.

Pioneering studies on the history of criminology in Latin America have already documented the overwhelming impact of Lombroso's doctrines on both thinkers and public policy. According to Ricardo Salvatore and Carlos Aguirre, "positivist criminology impinged upon the Latin American imagination with stronger force than it ever did in Europe."[10] The route of transmission for Lombroso's ideas was partly though Spain and Portugal, where he had many admirers.[11] Several Italian positivist criminologists, most notably Ferri, had lectured in South America. Many aspects of criminal anthropology—like the emphasis on race as a factor in assessing dangerousness—appealed to criminologists trying to explain crime in countries with large numbers of indigenous Indians or descendents of African slaves. Adapting positivist theories to their national agenda, criminologists from Argentina, Brazil, Mexico, Peru, and Costa Rica leaned heavily on the positivist doctrine of social defense in shaping new penal institutions that reinforced racial hierarchy.

In conclusion, the influence of Lombroso and Italian positivist criminology had a greater international sweep than has been previously recognized. This is not to argue that alternative trends in criminology did not develop after the turn of the twentieth century, like the sociological approach of Emile Durkheim in France and the "Chicago School" in the United States. But even in countries where the biological approach did not remain dominant as in Italy, it continued to co-exist with sociological theories. Intrinsic to the birth of criminology, the notion of the born criminal and the hereditary nature of crime remained resilient in the face of critiques. Surviving World War I in their various national forms, biological theories of crime contributed to an intellectual and political atmosphere conducive to the policies of eugenics and even extermination of the 1930s and 1940s.

NOTES

1. Leo Tolstoy, *Resurrection* (New York: Washington Square Press, 1963), pp. 78, 353; Joseph Conrad, *The Secret Agent* (New York: Penguin, 1984; orig. published 1907), pp. 77–78.

2. Marc Renneville, "La réception de Lombroso en France (1880–1900)," in Laurent Mucchielli, ed., *Histoire del la criminologie française* (Paris: L'Harmattan, 1994), p. 110.

3. Laurent Mucchielli, "Hérédité et 'Milieu social': Le faux antagonisme franco-italien [et] la place de l'École de Lacassagne dans l'histoire de la criminologie," in Mucchielli, ed., *Histoire de la criminologie*, p. 203.

4. Richard Wetzell, *Inventing the Criminal: A History of German Criminology, 1880–1945* (Chapel Hill: University of North Carolina Press, 2000), pp. 34–37.

5. Wetzell, *Inventing the Criminal*, pp. 68–70.

6. Garland, "British Criminology Before 1935," pp. 2–5.

7. On Goring's study, see Chapter 1.

8. Lucia Zedner, *Women, Crime, and Custody in Victorian England* (Oxford: Oxford University Press, 1991), p. 83.

9. Rafter devotes an excellent chapter to the transmission of Lombroso's theories to the United States in *Creating Born Criminals*, pp. 110–28.

10. Ricardo Salvatore and Carlos Aguirre, eds., *The Birth of the Penitentiary in Latin America: Essays on Criminology, Prison Reform, and Social Control, 1830–1940* (Austin: University of Texas Press, 1996), p. 21.

11. See, for example, the praise for Italian criminal anthropology in Pereira de Azevedo Neves, *Médecine légale et police criminelle*.

Bibliography

GOVERNMENT DOCUMENTS

Archivio Centrale dello Stato (ACS), Ministero dell'Interno.

Codice Civile (1865); Codice Penale (1889, 1930); Codice di Procedura Penale (1913).

Commissione reale per la riforma delle leggi penali, *Relazione sul progetto preliminare di Codice penale italiano* (Rome: "L'universelle," 1921).

Commissione reale per lo studio dei provvedimenti contro la delinquenza dei minorenni, *Atti* (Rome: Stamperia reale, 1912), 5 vols.

Istituto Centrale della Statistica (ISTAT), *Sommario di statistiche storiche italiane, 1861–1955* (Rome: Istituto Poligrafico dello Stato, 1958).

ISTAT, *Statistica dei riformatori (1908)* (Rome: Mantellate, 1909).

ISTAT, *Statistica delle carceri (1901)* (Rome: Mantellate, 1902).

Parlamento, Camera dei Deputati, *Discussioni and Disegni Leggi*, Legislatures 21–28 (1900–1934).

Raccolta ufficiale delle leggi e dei decreti del Regno d'Italia (Torino: Stamperia reale, 1861–1947).

Scuola Superiore di Polizia, *Nozioni per la compilazione della cartella biografica del pregiudicato* (Rome: Istituto Poligrafico dello Stato Libreria, 1932).

Ufficio del Censimento, *Censimento della popolazione del Regno d'Italia al 10 giugno 1911* (Rome: G. Bertero, 1914), 3 vols.

JOURNALS

Archivio di antropologia criminale, psichiatria, e medicina legale
Bolletino delle ricerche
Bolletino della Scuola di polizia scientifica
Difesa della razza
Difesa sociale

Maternità ed infanzia
Nuova antologia
Rivista di discipline carcerarie
Rivista penale
Scuola positiva

PRIMARY SOURCES

Aglebert, Augusto, *Della polizia in Inghilterra, in Francia e in Italia: Frammenti* (Bologna: Monti, 1868).

Alimena, Bernardino, *I limiti e i modificatori dell'imputabilità* (Turin: Bocca, 1894, 1896, 1899), 3 vols.

Alongi, Giuseppe, *Polizia e delinquenza in Italia* (Rome: Cecchini, 1882).

Alongi, Giuseppe, *Polizia e delinquenza in Italia: Saggio* (Rome: Ufficio dell' "Agente di PS," 1887).

Alongi, Giuseppe, *Progetto di legge e di regolamento sulla pubblica sicurezza* (Rome: Ludovico Cecchini, 1901).

Anna Kuliscioff. Con gli scritti di Anna Kuliscioff "Sulla condizione della donna," eds. Marcla Boggio and Annabella Cerliani (Venice: Marsilio, 1977).

Antonini, Giuseppe, *I precursori di C. Lombroso* (Turin: Bocca, 1900).

Balestrini, Raffaello, *Aborto, infanticidio ed esposizione d'infante* (Turin: Bocca, 1888).

Beccaria, Cesare, *On Crimes and Punishments* (Indianapolis: Hackett, 1986; orig. published 1764).

Berardi, Vito Antonio, *La donna e la imputabilità giuridica* (Bari: Gissi, 1881).

Bolis, Giovanni, *La polizia e le classi pericolose della società: Studii* (Bologna: Zanichelli, 1871).

Bonis de Nobili, Irene de, *Per il voto alle donne* (Rome: Righetti, 1909).

Bosco, Augusto, *La delinquenza in vari stati d'Europa* (Rome: R. Accademia dei Lincei, 1903).

Bovio, Corso, *Commento alla legge di pubblica sicurezza: Testi di legge-dottrina-giurisprudenza* (Naples: Eugenio Jovene, 1936).

Codice penale, eds. Ruffo Mangini, Francesco Gabrieli, and Ubaldo Cosentino (Rome: C. Colombo, 1930).

Colajanni, Napoleone, *Democrazia e socialismo in Italia: Carteggi di Napoleone Colajanni, 1878–1898*, ed. Salvatore Massimo Ganci (Milan: Feltrinelli, 1959).

Colajanni, Napoleone, *La sociologia criminale* (Catania: Tropea, 1889).

Colajanni, Napoleone, *Latini e anglo-sassoni (Razze inferiori e razze superiori)* (Rome-Naples: Rivista popolare, 1906) 2nd ed.

Colajanni, Napoleone, *Socialismo* (Catania: Tropea, 1884).

Comtes-Rendus du VI Congrès international d'antropologie criminelle (Turin, 28 Avril–3 Mai 1906) (Turin: Bocca, 1908).

Conrad, Joseph, *The Secret Agent* (New York: Penguin, 1984; orig. published 1907).

Corsi, Pietro, *The Protection of Mothers and Children in Italy* (Rome: Società Editrice di Noveissima, 1938).

De Blasio, Abele, *Nel paese della Camorra* (Naples: Luigi Pierro, 1901).

Diana, F. P., *Femminismo e anti-femminismo: Conferenza tenuta nel Circolo degli Impiegati il 6 Maggio 1905* (Agrigento: Montes, 1905).

Di Tullio, Benigno, "L'organizzazione della profilassi criminale in Italia," *Atti del 1. Congresso internazionale di criminologia* (Rome: Mantellate, 1938), pp. 63–95.

Di Tullio, Benigno, *Manuale di antropologia e psicologia criminale applicata alla pedagogia emendativa, alla polizia ed al diritto penale e penitenziario* (Rome: Anonima Romana Editoriale, 1931).

Ellero, Pietro, "Della minore responsabilità penale delle donne," *Opuscoli criminali* (Bologna: Fava e Garegnani, 1874).

Ellis, Havelock, *The Criminal* (New York: Scribner & Welford, 1890).

Enciclopedia italiana di scienze, lettere ed arti (Rome: Istituto Giovanni Treccani, 1929–39), 36 vols.

Enrico Ferri: Maestro della scienza criminologica (Milan: Bocca, 1941).

Eugenio Florian: Maestro del positivismo penale (Milan: Bocca, 1940).

Falco, Giuseppe, *"Identità": Metodo scientifico di segnalamento e identificazione* (Rome: P. Maglione & C. Strin, 1922).

Falco, Giuseppe, "La profilassi criminale nell'attività della polizia italiana," *Atti del 1. Congresso internazionale di criminologia* (Rome: Mantellate, 1938), pp. 117–38.

Ferraro, Augusto, *Delinquenti abituali e le colonie penali* (Naples: Veraldi, 1910).

Ferrero, Guglielmo, Bianchi, Augusto G., and Sighele, Scipio, *Il mondo criminale italiano* (Milan: Omodei Zorini, 1893 [v. 1], 1894 [v. 2]).

Ferrero, Guglielmo, "The Problem of Woman. From a Bio-sociological Point of View," *The Monist*, v. 4 (1894), pp. 261–74.

Ferri, Enrico, "L'antisemitismo," *Studi sulla criminalità* (Turin: Bocca, 1901), pp. 533–42.

Ferri, Enrico, *Criminal Sociology* (Boston: Little, Brown, 1917).

Ferri, Enrico, *Difese penali, studi di giurisprudenza, arringhe civili* (Turin: UTET, 1923), 2nd ed., 2 vols.

Ferri, Enrico, "I delitti della donna," *Difese penali*, vol. 2, pp. 680–90.

Ferri, Enrico, *L'omicidio nell'antropologia criminale* (Turin: Bocca, 1895).

Ferri, Enrico, *Socialism and Modern Science (Darwin-Spencer-Marx)* (New York: International Library, 1900).

Ferri, Enrico, *Socialismo e criminalità: Appunti* (Turin: Bocca, 1883).

Ferri, Enrico, *Sociologia criminale* (Turin: UTET, 1929), 5th ed.

Ferri, Enrico, *The Positivist School of Criminology: Three Lectures* (Chicago: Charles H. Kerr, 1913).

Ferriani, Lino, *Minorenni delinquenti* (Milan: Kantorowicz, 1895).

Florian, Eugenio, Niceforo, Alfredo, and Pende, Nicola, eds., *Dizionario di criminologia* (Milan: Francesco Vallardi, 1943), 2 vols.

Forni, Eugenio, *Dei criteri d'investigazione nei segreti dei reati* (Naples: Antonio Morano, 1877).

Fosdick, Raymond, *European Police Systems* (New York: Century, 1916).

Frassetto, Fabio, *Lezioni di antropologia* (Milan: Hoepli, 1918) 2nd ed.

Gambarotta, Guglielmo, *Inchiesta sulla donna* (Turin: Bocca, 1899).

Garofalo, Raffaele, *Criminology* (Montclair, N.J.: Patterson Smith, 1968; orig. published in English, 1914).

Garofalo, Raffaele, *La superstizione socialista* (Turin-Rome: Roux, Frassati, 1895).

Gemelli, Agostino, *Le dottrine moderne della delinquenza: Critica delle dottrine criminali positiviste* (Florence: Lib. Ed. Fiorentina, 1908).

Glueck, Sheldon, *Continental Police Practice* (Springfield, Ill.: Charles C. Thomas, 1974; orig. published 1926).

Grande, Dino, *Bonifica umana* (Rome: Mantellate, 1941) 2 vols.

Guarnieri-Ventimiglia, Antonio, *La delinquenza e la correzione dei minorenni* (Rome: Nazionale, 1906).

Guarnieri-Ventimiglia, Antonio, "La difesa ed il giudice dei minorenni," *Congresso giuridico nazionale (VII): Relazioni* (Rome: Gianandrea, 1911), pp. 1–43.

Kurella, Hans, *Cesare Lombroso: A Modern Man of Science* (London: Rebman, 1911).

Labriola, Teresa, *Per voto alla donna: Conferenza (24 marzo 1906)* (Rome: E. Loescher, 1906).

Lombroso, Cesare, and Ferrero, Guglielmo, *The Female Offender* (Littleton, Col.: Fred B. Rothman, 1980; orig. published in English 1895).

Lombroso, Cesare, and Ferrero, Guglielmo, *La donna delinquente, la prostituta e la donna normale* (Turin: Roux, 1893).

Lombroso, Cesare, "Criminal Anthropology: Its Origin and Application," *Forum*, v. 20 (1895–96), pp. 33–49.

Lombroso, Cesare, *Criminal Man summarised by G. Lombroso Ferrero* (New York: Putnam's, 1911).

Lombroso, Cesare, *Crime: Its Causes and Remedies* (Boston: Little, Brown, 1912).

Lombroso, Cesare, *Delitto, genio, follia: Scritti scelti*, eds. Delia Frigessi, Ferruccio Giacanelli, and Luisa Mangoni (Turin: Bollati Boringhieri, 1995).

Lombroso, Cesare, *Il momento attuale* (Milan: Moderna, 1903).

Lombroso, Cesare, *In Calabria (1862–1897)* (Catania: Niccolò Giannotta, 1898).

Lombroso, Cesare, *L'antisemitismo e le scienze moderne* (Turin: Roux, 1894).

Lombroso, Cesare, *L'uomo bianco e l'uomo di colore: Letture sull'origine e le varietà delle razze umane* (Padua: F. Sacchetto, 1871).

Lombroso, Cesare, *L'uomo delinquente* (Milan: Hoepli, 1876), 1st ed. (Turin: Bocca, 1878), 2nd ed. (Turin: Bocca, 1884), 3rd ed. (Turin: Bocca, 1889), 4th ed., 2 vols. (Turin: Bocca, 1896–97), 5th ed., 4 vols.

Lombroso, Cesare, *Sull'incremento del delitto in Italia* (Turin: Bocca, 1879).

Lombroso, Gina, *Cesare Lombroso: Storia della vita e delle opere narrata dalla figlia* (Turin: Bocca, 1915).

L'opera di Cesare Lombroso nella scienza e nelle sue applicazioni (Turin: Bocca, 1908).

Lucchini, Luigi, *I semplicisti del diritto penale* (Turin: UTET, 1886).

Lucchini, Luigi, *La criminalità in Italia* (Venice: M. Fontana, 1884).

Majno, Edoardo, "La difesa ed il giudice dei minorenni," *Congresso giuridico nazionale (VII): Relazioni* (Rome: Gianandrea, 1911), np.

Mantagazza, Paolo, *Physiognomy and Expression* (London: Walter Scott, n.d.).

Mantegazza, Umberto, and Ciuffo, Giuseppe, *La prostituzione studiata specialmente in Toscana e Sardegna* (Cagliari-Sassari: G. Dessi, 1904).

Marro, Antonio, *I caratteri dei delinquenti: Studio antropologico-sociologico* (Turin: Bocca, 1887).

Marselli-Valli, Maria, *Donne e femminismo* (Florence: Rassegna Nazionale, 1908).

Michelangeli, Ernesta, *La vera missione della donna* (Bologna: Zanichelli, 1901).

Mortara, Giorgio, *La salute pubblica in Italia durante e dopo la guerra* (New Haven: Yale University, 1925).

Niceforo, Alfredo, *L'Italia barbara contemporanea* (Milan: Sandron, 1893).

Niceforo, Alfredo, *La delinquenza in Sardegna* (Palermo: Sandron, 1897).

Niceforo, Alfredo, *Les Germains: Histoire d'un idée ed d'une race* (Paris: Bossard, 1919), 2nd ed.

Ottolenghi, Salvatore, *L'insegnamento della polizia scientifica* (Rome: Mantellate, 1914).

Ottolenghi, Salvatore, "L'opera di Cesare Lombroso e la polizia scientifica," in *L'opera di Cesare Lombroso*, pp. 220–37.

Ottolenghi, Salvatore, *La sensibilità della donna* (Turin: Bocca, 1896).

Ottolenghi, Salvatore, *Polizia Scientifica: Quadri sinettici delle lezioni tenute nella Scuola di Polizia* (Rome: Società Poligrafia, 1907).

Ottolenghi, Salvatore, *Trattato di polizia scientifica* (Milan: Società Editrice Libraria, 1910 [v. 1], 1931 [v. 2]).

Patrizi, Mariano L., *Dopo Lombroso: Nuove correnti nello studio della genialità e del delitto* (Milan: Società Editrice Libraria, 1916).

Pereira de Azevedo Neves, João Alberto, *Médecine légale et police criminelle (France, Belgique, Allemagne, Autriche et Italie)* (Lisbon: Imprimerie Nationale, 1931).

Pessina, Enrico, "Il diritto penale in Italia da Cesare Beccaria sino alla promulgazione del codice penale vigente" in Pessina, ed., *Enciclopedia del diritto penale italiano* (Milan: Società Editrice Libraria, 1906), vol. 2, pp. 539–768.

Pessina, Enrico, *Il nuovo Codice Penale Italiano con brevi note dilucidative* (Milan: Hoepli, 1890).

Saracini, Emilio, *I crespuscoli della polizia: Compendio storico della genesi e delle vicende dell'amministrazione di pubblica sicurezza* (Naples: SIEM, 1922).

Saracini, Emilio, *Nuova pratica di polizia amministrativa* (Naples: Elpis, 1929).

Sergi, Giuseppe, *Arii e italici* (Turin: Bocca, 1898).

Sighele, Scipio, *Eva moderna* (Milan: Treves, 1910).

Sighele, Scipio, *Idee e problemi d'un positivista* (Milan-Palermo-Naples: Sandron, 1907).

Società Anonima Editrice, *Avanti! Catalogo della Libreria* (Milan: Avanti!, 1914).

Spallanzi, Alfredo, *Sull'omicidio in Italia dal 1881 al 1911* (Rome: Ludovico Cecchini, 1916).

Spirito, Ugo, *Storia del diritto penale italiano da Cesare Beccaria al nostri giorni* (Florence: Sansoni, 1974; orig. published 1924).

Tolstoy, Leo, *Resurrection* (New York: Washington Square Press, 1963).

Tomellini, Luigi, *Manuale di polizia giudiziaria* (Milan: Hoepli, 1912).

Tringali, Sebastiano, *Dizionario legale* (Milan: Hoepli, 1914).

Turati, Filippo, "Il delitto e la questione sociale," reprinted in Luigi Cortesi, ed., *Turati giovane: Scapigliatura, positivismo, marxismo* (Milan: Ed. Avanti!, 1962), pp. 138–213.

Vidoni, Giuseppe, *Prostitute e prostituzione* (Turin: S. Lattes, 1921).

Vidoni, Giuseppe, *Valore e limiti dell'endocrinologia nell' Antropologia criminale* (Turin: Bocca, 1923).

Zingali, Gaetano, *La statistica della criminalità: Studio teorico* (Bologna: Il Seminario Giuridico, 1916).

SECONDARY SOURCES

Akers, Ronald L., ed., *Criminological Theories: Introduction and Evaluation* (Los Angeles: Roxbury, 1997).

Allen, Francis A., "Raffaele Garofalo, 1852–1934," in Mannheim, ed., *Pioneers in Criminology*, pp. 254–75.

Andreucci, Franco, and Detti, Tommaso, eds., *Il movimento operaio italiano: Dizionario biografico (1853–1943)* (Rome: Riuniti, 1978) 5 vols.

Angioni, Giulio, *Tre saggi sull'antropologia dell'età coloniale* (Palermo: S.F. Flaccovio, 1973).

Arrù, Angiolina, "Protezione e legittimazione: Come si usa il mestiere di serva nell'800," in Lucia Ferrante, Maura Palazzi, and Gianna Pomata, eds., *Ragnatele di rapporti: Patronage e reti di relazione nella storia della donne* (Turin: Rosenberg & Sellier, 1988), pp. 381–416.

Baima Bollone, Pier Luigi, *Cesare Lombroso ovvero il principio dell'irresponsabilità* (Turin: Società Editrice Internazionale, 1992).

Beirnes, Piers, *Inventing Criminology: Essays on the Rise of "Homo Criminalis"* (Albany: State University of New York Press, 1993).

Bigaran, Maria Pia, "Per una donna nuova: Tre giornali di propaganda socialista tra le donne," *Nuova DonnaWomanFemme*, v. 21 (1982), pp. 53–72.

Boschi, Daniele, "Homicide and Knife Fighting in Rome, 1845–1914," in Pieter Spierenburg, ed., *Men and Violence* (Columbus: Ohio State University Press, 1998), pp. 128–58.

Brucker, Gene, *Giovanni and Lusanna: Love and Marriage in Renaissance Florence* (Berkeley: University of California Press, 1986).

Bulferetti, Luigi, *Cesare Lombroso* (Turin: UTET, 1975).

Burgio, Alberto, ed., *Nel nome della razza: Il razzismo nella storia d'Italia, 1870–1945* (Bologna: Il Mulino, 1999).

Buttafuoco, Annarita, *Le Mariuccine: Storia di un'istituzione laica l'Asilo Mariuccia* (Milan: Franco Angeli, 1985).

Canosa, Romano, *La polizia in Italia dal 1945 a oggi* (Bologna: Il Mulino, 1976).

Casalini, Maria, *La signora del socialismo italiano: Vita di Anna Kuliscioff* (Rome: Riuniti, 1987).

Catalano, Franco, *Filippo Turati* (Milan-Rome: Edizioni Avanti!, 1957).

Cavallo, Sandra, and Cerutti, Simona, "Female Honor and the Social Control of Reproduction in Piedmont between 1600 and 1800," in Edward Muir and Guido Ruggiero, eds., *Sex and Gender in Historical Perspective* (Baltimore: Johns Hopkins University Press, 1990), pp. 73–109.

Clark, Martin, *Modern Italy, 1871–1982* (New York: Longman, 1984).

Cohen, Sherrill, *The Evolution of Women's Asylums since 1500* (New York: Oxford University Press, 1992).

Cohen, William B., *The French Encounter with Africa: White Response to Blacks, 1530–1880* (Bloomington: Indiana University Press, 1980).

Colao, Floriana, *Il delitto politico tra Ottocento e Novecento* (Milan: A. Giuffrè, 1986).

Collin, Richard, "The Blunt Instruments: Italy and the Police," in John Roach and Jürgen Thomaneck, eds., *Police and Public Order in Europe* (Dover, N.H.: Croom Helm, 1985), pp. 185–213.

Colombo, Giorgio, *La scienza infelice: Il museo di antropologia criminale di Cesare Lombroso* (Turin: Boringhieri, 1975).

Corsi, Pietro, and Weindling, Paul J., "Darwinism in Germany, France and Italy," in David Kohn, ed., *The Darwinian Heritage* (Princeton: Princeton University Press, 1985), pp. 683–729.

Cullen, Francis T., and Agnew, Robert, eds., *Criminological Theory: Past to Present. Essential Readings* (Los Angeles: Roxbury, 1999).

Davis, John, *Conflict and Control: Law and Order in Nineteenth-Century Italy* (Atlantic Highlands, N.J.: Humanities Press, 1988).

Debuyst, Christian; Digneffe, Françoise; Labadie, Jean-Michel; and Pires, Alvaro P., *Histoire des savoirs sur le crime et la peine* [Vol. 1: *Des savoirs diffus à la notion de criminel-né*] (Brussels: DeBoeck Université, 1995)

De Grazia, Victoria, *How Fascism Ruled Women: Italy, 1922–1945* (Berkeley: University of California Press, 1992).

De Leo, Gaetano, *La giustizia dei minori* (Turin: Einaudi, 1981).

De Longis, Rosanna, " 'In difesa della donna e della razza,' " *Nuova Donnawomanfemme*, n. 19–20 (Winter-Spring, 1982), 149–77.

De Longis, Rosanna, "Scienza come politica: Vita femminile (1895–1897)," *Nuova DonnaWomanFemme* 21 (1982), pp. 35–51.

Destragiache, Denise, "Un aspect de la politique démographique de l'Italie fasciste: La répression de l'avortement," *Mélanges de l'École francaise de Rome*, v. 92, pt. 2 (1980), pp. 691–735.

Di Cori, Paola, "The Double Gaze: Visibility of Sexual Difference in Photographic Representation (1908–1918)," in Mirna Cicioni and Nicole Prunster, eds., *Visions and Revisions: Women in Italian Culture* (Providence, R.I.: Berg, 1993), pp. 89–116.

Di Scala, Spencer M., *Italy: From Revolution to Republic, 1700 to the Present* (Boulder, Col.: Westview, 1995).

Dolza, Delfina, *Essere figlie di Lombroso: Due donne intellettuali tra '800 e '900* (Milan: Franco Angeli, 1990).

Dunnage, Jonathan, *The Italian Police and the Rise of Fascism: A Case Study of the Province of Bologna, 1897–1925* (Westport, Conn.: Praeger, 1997).

Farolfali, Bernardino, "Antropometria militare e antropologia della devianza, 1876–1908," *Storia d'Italia, Annali*, v. 7 [*Malattia e medicina*, ed. Franco della Peruta] (Turin: Einaudi, 1984), pp. 1179–1219.

Ferrante, Lucia, "L'onore ritrovato: Donne nella Casa del Soccorso di San Paolo a Bologna (sec. XVI–XVII)," *Quaderni Storici*, v. 53 (Aug., 1983), pp. 499–527.

Figurelli, Michela, "L'alcool e la classe: Cenni per una storia dell'alcoolismo in Italia," *Classe*, n. 15 (June, 1978), pp. 93–135.

Fink, Arthur E., *Causes of Crime: Biological Theories in the United States, 1800–1915* (Philadelphia: University of Pennsylvania Press, 1938).

Fishbein, Diana H., "Biological Perspectives in Criminology," *Criminology*, v. 28, n. 1 (Feb., 1990), pp. 27–72.

Franzina, Emilio, *Casini di guerra: Il tempo libero dalla trincea e i postriboli militari nel primo conflitto mondiale* (Udine: P. Gaspari, 1999).

Frigessi, Delia, "Cattaneo, Lombroso e la questione ebraica," in Alberto Burgio, ed., *Nel nome della razza*, pp. 247–77.

Gadebusch Bondio, Maria Carla, "La tipologizzazione della donna deviante nella seconda metà dell'ottocento: La prostituta, la criminale e la pazza," *Per una storia critica della scienza* (Milan: Cisalpino, 1996), pp. 283–314.

Ganci, Massimo, "La formazione positivistica di Filippo Turati," *Rivista storica del socialismo* (Jan.–June, 1958), pp. 56–68.

Garin, Eugenio, "Il positivismo italiano alla fine del secolo XIX fra metodo e concezione del mondo," *Giornale critica della filosofia italiana*, Series 5, v. 1 (Jan.–Dec., 1980), pp. 1–27.

Garland, David, "British Criminology Before 1935," The British Journal of Criminology, v. 28, n. 2 (Spring, 1988), pp. 1–17.

Gattei, Giorgio, "La sifilide: Medici e poliziotti intorno alla 'Venere politica,'" Storia d'Italia, Annali, v. 7 [Malattia e medicina, ed. Franco della Peruta] (Turin: Einaudi, 1984), pp. 741–98.

Ghezzi, Morris L., "La questione penale nella Critica Sociale" in Emilio R. Papa, ed., Il positivismo e la cultura italiana (Milan: Franco Angeli, 1985), pp. 405–13.

Gibson, Mary, Prostitution and the State in Italy, 1860–1915 (New Brunswick, N.J.: Rutgers University Press, 1986).

Gould, Stephen Jay, The Mismeasure of Man (New York: W.W. Norton, 1981).

Groppi, Angela, I conservatori della virtù: Donne recluse nella Roma dei Papi (Roma-Bari: Laterza, 1994).

Guarnieri, Luigi, L'Atlante criminale: Una scriteriata di Cesare Lombroso (Milan: Mondadori, 2000).

Gunzberg, Lynn M., Strangers at Home: Jews in the Italian Literary Imagination (Berkeley: University of California Press, 1992).

Horn, David, Social Bodies: Science, Reproduction and Italian Modernity (Princeton, N.J.: Princeton University Press, 1994).

Hughes, Steven C., Crime, Disorder and the Risorgimento: The Politics of Policing in Bologna (New York: Cambridge University Press, 1994).

Hughes, Steven C., "The Theory and Practice of Ozio in Italian Policing: Bologna and Beyond," Criminal Justice History, v. 7 (1986), pp. 89–103.

Ipsen, Carl, Dictating Demography: The Problem of Population in Fascist Italy (New York: Cambridge University Press, 1996).

Izzo, Domenico, "Il trattamento dei minorenni delinquenti dalla circolare Orlando al progetto Ferri (1908–1921)," Rassegna di studi penitenziari, v. 8 (March–April 1957), pp. 146–94.

Jacoby, Joseph E., ed., Classics of Criminology (Prospect Heights, Ill.: Waveland, 1994), 2nd ed.

Jeffrey, C. Ray, "Genetics, Crime and the Cancelled Conference," The Criminologist, v. 18, n. 1 (Jan./Feb., 1993), p. 1.

Jensen, Richard Bach, "Italy's Peculiar Institution: Internal Police Exile, 1861–1914," in June K. Burton, ed., Essays in European History (Lanham, Md.: University Press of America, 1989), pp. 99–114.

Jensen, Richard Bach, Liberty and Order: The Theory and Practice of Italian Public Security Policy, 1848 to the Crisis of the 1890s (New York: Garland, 1991).

Jensen, Richard Bach, "Police Reform and Social Reform: Italy from the Crisis of the 1890s to the Giolittian Era," Criminal Justice History, v. 10 (1989), pp. 179–200.

Kertzer, David, and Hogan, Dennis, "Reflections on the European Marriage Pattern: Sharecropping and Proletarianization in Casalecchio, Italy, 1861–1921," Journal of Family History, v. 16 (1991), pp. 31–45.

Kertzer, David, Sacrificed for Honor: Italian Infant Abandonment and the Politics of Reproductive Control (Boston: Beacon, 1993).

Klein, Dorie, "The Etiology of Female Crime: A Review of the Literature," Issues in Criminology, v. 8, n. 2 (1973), pp. 3–30.

Landucci, Giovanni, Darwinismo a Firenze: Tra scienza e ideologia (1860–1900) (Florence: Leo S. Olschki, 1977).

La Vigna, Clare, "The Marxist Ambivalence Toward Women: Between Socialism and Feminism in the Italian Socialist Party," in Marilyn J. Boxer and Jean H. Quataert, eds., *Socialist Women: European Socialist Feminism in the Nineteenth and Early Twentieth Centuries* (New York: Elsevier, 1978), pp. 146–81.

Levra, Umberto, ed., *La scienza e la colpa. Crimini, criminali, criminologi: Un volto dell'Ottocento* (Milan: Electa, 1985).

Lindesmith, Alfred and Levin, Yale, "The Lombrosian Myth in Criminology," *American Journal of Sociology*, v. 42, n. 5 (March, 1937), pp. 653–71.

Lumley, Robert, and Morris, Jonathan, eds., *The New History of the Italian South: The Mezzogiorno Revisited* (Exeter, Devon, UK: University of Exeter Press, 1977).

Macrelli, Rina, *L'indegna schiavitù: Anna Maria Mozzoni e la lotta contro la prostituzione di Stato* (Rome: Riuniti, 1981).

Maestro, Marcello, *Cesare Beccaria and the Origins of Penal Reform* (Philadelphia: Temple University Press, 1973).

Maiocchi, Roberto, *Scienza italiana e razzismo fascista* (Florence: La Nuova Italia, 1999).

Mannheim, Hermann, ed., *Pioneers in Criminology* (Montclair, N.J.: Patterson Smith, 1972; orig. published 1961), 2nd ed.

Manoukian, Agopik, "La rappresentazione statistica dei vincoli familiari," in Manoukian, *I vincoli familiari in Italia: Dal secolo XI al secolo XX* (Bologna: Il Mulino, 1983), pp. 437–47.

Melossi, Dario, "Andamento economico, incarcerazione, omicidi e allarme sociale in Italia: 1863–1994," in *Storia D'Italia, Annali*, n. 12 [*La criminalità*, ed. Luciano Violante] (Turin: Einaudi, 1997), pp. 35–62.

Melossi, Dario, "Omicidi, economia, e tassi di incarcerazione in Italia dall'Unità ad oggi," *Polis*, v. 12 (Dec. 1998), pp. 415–35.

Moe, Nelson, "The Emergence of the Southern Question in Villari, Franchetti, and Sonnino," in Schneider, ed., *Italy's "Southern Question,"* pp. 51–76.

Molinari, Augusta, "Alcool e alcoolisti a Genova tra Ottocento e Novecento: Una prima ricognizione," *Movimento operaio e socialista*, v. 11 (New series), n. 2 (May–Aug., 1988), pp. 271–91.

Monachesi, Elio D., "Cesare Beccaria and the Origins of Penal Reform," in Mannheim, ed., *Pioneers in Criminology*, pp. 36–49.

Monachesi, Elio D., "Trends in Criminological Research in Italy," *American Sociological Review*, v. 1, n. 3 (June, 1936), pp. 396–406.

Montalenti, Giuseppe, "Comment a été accueillie en Italie la révolution darwinienne," in Yvette Conroy, ed., *De darwin au darwinisme: Science et idéologie* (Paris: J. Vrin, 1983), pp. 17–31.

Mucchielli, Laurent, "Hérédité et 'Milieu social': Le faux antagonisme franco-italien [et] la place de l'École de Lacassagne dans l'histoire de la criminologie," in Mucchielli, ed., *Histoire de la criminologie francaise*, pp. 189–214.

Mucchielli, Laurent, ed., *Histoire de la criminologie française* (Paris: L'Harmattan, 1994).

Murray, Charles A. and Hernnstein, Richard J., *The Bell Curve: Intelligence and Class Structure in American Life* (New York: Free Press, 1994).

Newman, Graeme, and Marongiu, Pietro, "Penological Reform and the Myth of Beccaria," *Criminology*, v. 28, n. 2 (May 1990), pp. 325–46.

Nye, Robert A., "Heredity or Milieu: The Foundations of Modern European Criminological Theory," *ISIS*, v. 67, n. 238 (Sept., 1976), pp. 335–55.

Nye, Robert. A., *Crime, Madness, and Politics in Modern France: The Medical Concept of National Decline* (Princeton, N.J.: Princeton University Press, 1984).

Passerini, Luisa, "Donne operaie e aborto nella Torino fascista," *Italia contemporanea*, v. 151–52 (Sept., 1983), pp. 83–109.

Patriarca, Silvana, "How Many Italies? Representing the South in Official Statistics," in Schneider, ed., *Italy's "Southern Question,"* pp. 77–97.

Patriarca, Silvana, *Numbers and Nationhood: Writing Statistics in Nineteenth-Century Italy* (N.Y.: Cambridge University Press, 1996).

Pelaja, Margherita, *Matrimonio e sessualità a Roma nell'Ottocento* (Roma-Bari: Laterza, 1994).

Petraccone, Claudia, *Le due civiltà: Settentrionali e meridionali nella storia d'Italia* (Rome-Bari: Laterza, 2000).

Petrusewicz, Marta, "Before the Southern Question: 'Native' Ideas on Backwardness and Remedies in the Kingdom of the Two Sicilies, 1815–1849," in Schneider, ed., *Italy's "Southern Question,"* pp. 27–49.

Petrusewicz, Marta, *Come il Meridione divenne una Questione* (Soveria Mannelli: Rubbettino, 1998).

Pick, Daniel, *Faces of Degeneration* (Cambridge: Cambridge University Press, 1989).

Pogliano, Claudio, "Scienza e stirpe: Eugenica in Italia (1912–1939)," *Passato e presente*, v. 5 (Jan.–June, 1984), pp. 61–97.

Pogliano, Claudio, "Eugenisti, ma con giudizio" in Burgio, ed., *Nel nome della razza*, pp. 423–54.

Preti, Luigi, *Impero fascista, africani ed ebrei* (Milan: Mursia, 1968).

Pucci, Idanna, *The Trials of Maria Barbella* (New York: Vintage Books, 1997).

Puccini, Sandra, and Squillacciotti, Massimo, "Per una prima ricostruzione critico-bibliografica degli studi demo-etno-antropologici italiani nel periodo tra le due guerre," in Pietro Angelini, *et al.*, *Studi antropologici italiani e rapporti di classe* (Milan: Franco Angeli, 1980), pp. 67–94.

Rafter, Nicole Hahn, *Creating Born Criminals* (Urbana: University of Illinois Press, 1997).

Ravera, Camilla, *La donna italiana del primo al secondo Risorgimento* (Rome: Edizioni di cultura sociale, 1951).

Renneville, Marc, "La réception de Lombroso en France (1880–1900)," in Mucchielli, ed., *Histoire de la criminologie française*, pp. 107–35.

Ruggiero, Guido, *Binding Passions: Tales of Magic, Marriage, and Power at the End of the Renaissance* (New York: Oxford University Press, 1993).

Salvatore, Ricardo D., and Aguirre, Carlos, eds., *The Birth of the Penitentiary in Latin America: Essays on Criminology, Prison Reform, and Social Control, 1830–1940* (Austin: University of Texas Press, 1996).

Saunders, George, "Contemporary Italian Cultural Anthropology," *Annual Review of Anthropology*, v. 13 (1984), pp. 447–66.

Sbriccoli, Mario, "La penalistica civile: Teorie e ideologie del diritto penale nell'Italia unita," in Aldo Schiavone, ed., *Stato e cultura giuridica in Italia dall'unità alla repubblica* (Rome-Bari: Laterza, 1990), pp. 147–232.

Schneider, Jane, ed., *Italy's "Southern Question": Orientalism in One Country* (New York: Berg, 1998).

Sellin, Thorsten, "Enrico Ferri, 1856–1929," in Mannheim, ed., *Pioneers in Criminology*, pp. 277–300.

Sellin, Thorsten, "A New Phase of Criminal Anthropology in Italy," *The Annals of the American Academy of Political and Social Science*, v. 125 (May, 1926), pp. 233–42.

Smart, Carol, *Women, Crime and Criminology: A Feminist Critique* (Boston: Routledge and Kegan Paul, 1976).

Smith, Denis Mack, *Italy: A Modern History* (Ann Arbor: University of Michigan Press, 1959).

Springer, Beverly Tanner, "Anna Kuliscioff: Russian Revolutionist, Italian Feminist," in Jane Slaughter and Robert Kern, eds., *European Women on the Left* (Westport, Conn.: Greenwood, 1981), pp. 13–27.

Stepan, Nancy, *The Idea of Race in Science: Great Britain, 1800–1960* (Hamden, Conn.: Archon, 1982).

Tilly, Louise, "The Working Class of Milan, 1881–1911," (Ph.D. dissertation: University of Toronto, 1973).

Tilly, Louise, "Urban Growth, Industrialization, and Women's Employment in Milan, Italy, 1881–1911," *Journal of Urban History*, v. 3 (1977), pp. 467–84.

Tosatti, Giovanna, "Il Ministero degli interni: Le origini del Casellario politico centrale," in ISAP, *Le riforme crispine* (Milan: Giuffrè, 1990), pp. 447–85.

Tosatti, Giovanna, "La repressione del dissenso politico tra l'età liberale e il fascismo: L'organizzazione della polizia," *Studi storici*, v. 38 (Jan.–March, 1997), pp. 217–55.

Ulivieri, Simonetta, "La donna nella scuola dall'unità d'Italia a oggi," *Donnawomanfemme*, v. 2 (Jan.–March, 1977), pp. 20–47.

Villa, Renzo, *Il deviante e i suoi segni: Lombroso e la nascita dell'antropologia criminale* (Milan: Franco Angeli, 1985).

Vold, George B., Bernard, Thomas J., and Snipes, Jeffrey B., eds., *Theoretical Criminology* (New York: Oxford University Press, 1998).

Volpi, Roberto, *Storia della popolazione italiana dall'Unità a oggi* (Florence: La Nuova Italia, 1989).

Wanrooij, Bruno, *Storia del pudore: La questione sessuale in Italia* (Venice: Marsilio, 1990).

Wetzell, Richard F., *Inventing the Criminal: A History of German Criminology, 1880–1945* (Chapel Hill: University of North Carolina Press, 2000).

Wiener, Martin J., *Reconstructing the Criminal: Culture, Law, and Policy in England, 1830–1914* (New York: Cambridge University Press 1990).

Wilson, Edward O., *Sociobiology* (Cambridge, Mass.: Harvard University Press, 1980).

Wolfgang, Marvin E., "Cesare Lombroso, 1835–1909," in Mannheim, ed., *Pioneers in Criminology*, pp. 232–91.

Zedner, Lucia, *Women, Crime, and Custody in Victorian England* (Oxford: Oxford University Press, 1991).

Index

About the Author

MARY GIBSON is Professor of History at John Jay College of Criminal Justice and the Graduate School, City University of New York.